Foundations of Economics

Foundations of Economics has been specially designed to complement the conventional introductory level economics textbook so that students are relieved of the monotony and austerity which is commonly associated with economics courses. All the main concepts in introductory level economics are covered, but instead of the usual presentation of model/diagram/theory, *Foundations of Economics* introduces each concept in three steps:

1   A review of the standard material students are exposed to in conventional texts.
2   An explanation of the history and evolution of these theories/ideas.
3   These theories/concepts are put on trial and the question asked: 'Should we really believe in all this?'

In this way, students are encouraged to question what they are learning and to challenge the distant assumptions and often dry theories of their teachers. This approach makes assumptions interesting by explaining what major political and philosophical prejudices they reflect. The final section in the book looks directly at anxieties which economics students often feel but might not dare to ask, such as 'Does economic theory really matter?' or 'Should I be studying economics? Is it good for me?' and answers them honestly, though perhaps unpredictably.

Proving that passion in economics can be an essential part of the learning process, this book will be the friend that students will turn to when in need of inspiration, when they feel their course has lost all meaning, or when they are just plain stuck. It will also be of interest to the general reader who would like to know more about economics but without the pain.

Yanis Varoufakis is Senior Lecturer in Economics at Sydney University. He is the co-author with Shaun Hargreaves Heap, of *Game Theory: A Critical Introduction*, also published by Routledge.

Foundations of Economics

A Beginner's Companion

Yanis Varoufakis

LONDON AND NEW YORK

First published 1998 by Routledge
11 New Fetter Lane, London EC4P 4EE

Simultaneously published in the USA and
Canada by Routledge
29 West 35th Street, New York, NY
10001

©1998 Yanis Varoufakis

Typeset in Baskerville by Florencetype Ltd,
Stoodleigh, Devon

Printed and bound in Great Britain by
TJ International Ltd., Padstow, Cornwall

*British Library Cataloguing in Publication
Data*
A catalogue record for this book is
available from the British Library

*Library of Congress Cataloging in Publication
Data*
A catalog record for this book has been
requested

ISBN 0–415–17891–6 (hbk)
ISBN 0–415–17892–4 (pbk)

Για τον Γιώργο και για την Ελένη Βαρουφάκη

Preface

This book is written with the conviction that the economics textbook, contrary to all evidence, contains delightful mind-teasers, philosophically exciting questions and lots of intriguing politics. It is also written in the conviction that beginners, who are usually dismissed as insufficiently sophisticated to get involved with these higher order issues, are perfectly up to the detective work necessary to bring these delights on to the surface. Additionally, I embarked on this book with the certainty that pursuing these discoveries promises not only to enliven an otherwise dull course but also to help students do well in it. Who knows – it may even inspire *us*, the teachers of this all-conquering but prosaic discipline, to lift our game.

And lift it we must! Open any economics textbook. These days you will find excellent graphics, numerous examples, helpful appendices, computer disks with moving curves and, naturally, sets of solved problems to help you get a handle on how economists answer the questions they pose. Indeed, today's textbook is incredibly competent at providing answers to set questions. Already publishers of economics textbooks offer web pages on the Internet which contain numerous links to material relating to the topics in each chapter; students who have bought their book are even given passwords allowing them to submit their answers to set problems electronically. Indeed the textbook has become only an entry point into a multimedia package which provides answers to given questions with astonishing competence. But here is the rub: none of this technological wizardry provides a guide as to where the questions come from, of why different questions are not being asked, of who does the asking. It works like a do-it-yourself manual taking you by the hand and illustrating the method for doing things.

Now we all know how boring manuals are. No wonder students find economics a touch too dry. However, it might be argued that if one wants to learn to do things one has to plough through the manual. That, as in physics, beginners must conquer the boring stuff first (e.g. classical mechanics) before they can discuss black holes sensibly. I do not think this is a good analogy with economics. Let me explain why.

All physicists agree on the method of mechanics. You will not, for example, find them arguing fiercely on the value of differential equations for describing the motion of fluids. Yet economists seem unable to agree on the same scale. Effectively there is no commonly agreed borderline between (1) a set of topics within which all practitioners agree (such as there is in natural science, e.g. mechanics) and (2) another set of topics (including black holes and the origin of the universe) in which they do not. In economics the set of disagreement encompasses almost all of economic life. For instance a Keynesian and a neoclassical economist do not even agree on the meaning of probability in a social setting!

The point here is that if those who teach economics find it hard to agree with one another on basic things, is it not a trifle hypocritical to use textbooks which pretend that there is a set of answers and questions which students must learn to recite? Or, equivalently, that economics students can be trained in the same way that students of chemistry can? I think it is and this book is written with a sense of shame for such hypocrisy. It is also written with passion, though I hope without rashness.

Of course there are those who think that passion gets in the way of sound reasoning; they would prefer the detached style of conventional texts. For my part I feel that taking emotion and controversy out of economics is responsible for losing a great deal of analytical power. The greatest thinkers to have tackled economics were motivated by debates so passionate that their emotions were stirred until new ways of understanding economic relations emerged. The danger is that the way we teach economics today has become so banal that the brightest are bored and leave the discipline early for greener pastures. The future generation of economics graduates runs the risk of leaving university with a large box of tools and the motivation of a gravedigger. Perhaps the time has come to give these old emotions another stir.

The challenge for this book is to be stirring while respecting pedagogical constraints. One reviewer of an early sketch of my intentions for this book warned against the danger that my approach may resemble 'insisting that small children taking their first steps in learning to walk should be taught the subtleties of body language at the same time'. Although I recognise that principles must be well understood before being criticised (indeed there is nothing more pointless than uninformed criticism), I take a different line: learning social science is (or at least ought to be) radically different from learning how to walk. Whereas walking is best learnt mechanically, social theory is best imparted by critical thinking (accompanied of course with large doses of rigorous training). In social theory the two are parasitic on each other; rigour without critical thinking leads to bad theory while critical thinking without rigour reduces to blind moralism. The trick is to find a decent balance between the two.

This book is the result of two related personal experiences. First came the experience of learning economics as a first year student at the University of Essex back in 1978. By golly it was boring! So disheartening that I changed my degree and concentrated on mathematics. (Only by a historical accident did I return to economics much later.) The second experience was that of trying to teach first year students. How could I not inflict on them what was inflicted on me in 1978? With textbooks treating students as seals in need of training (as opposed to humans in need of an education), and with all the interesting debates involving a terminology inaccessible to first year students, one is tempted to take the easy option: follow the Text. My rebellion took the form of notes on the philosophical aspects of the various models in the Text. The idea was to animate economics; to give students a glimpse of it as a contested terrain on which armies of ideas clash mercilessly in order to win the argument. As the years went by, these notes grew. Eventually they insisted on being transformed into something bigger. You are holding the result.

How to use this book

All terms and concepts are introduced from first principles. This book has been designed as a companion to those who are just beginning to tackle economics and who find that conventional textbooks make them feel intellectually uncomfortable. It can be read by itself as an introduction to economic thinking. Or it can be utilised by university students who have chosen (or who, as is increasingly common with some degrees, have been forced) to take an introductory course in economics. The hope is that this book will be the place where you turn for inspiration, or for some hope that all your efforts to get on top of tutorials and assignments are not without meaning. A kind of friend you approach when the course gets you down and you need to pick yourself up again. A source of insights when you write essays. A companion who helps you see the forest when your face is pushed firmly into some tree.

The book's structure

As you will notice in the Table of Contents which follows, there are two segments in this book: Book 1 and Book 2. The former is the main segment and is devoted to the *Foundations* of economics. Book 2 is tiny, by comparison, but tries to reach parts of the beginner's psyche that other books are not interested in: *Anxieties* resulting from having been exposed to economic debates. Have you been wasting your time thinking critically about economic ideas? Do they matter at all in the end? Has your mind been contaminated by a perverted way of thinking about the world?

Book 1 begins with an Introduction (Chapter 1) which offers an historical account of the rise of economics as well as a simple explanation of why economics textbooks look the way they do. The rest of Book 1 is divided into three parts. There is Part 1 on the theory of how people choose between the different options available to them. The immediate repercussion of that theory is a model of consumer behaviour. Part 2 extends the theory to decisions taken by firms whose fortunes are determined in the jungle of the market. Finally Part 3 takes a broader look at how well a capitalist economy functions and at its effects on distribution of well-being amongst people.

A brief plan of the book

Book 1 FOUNDATIONS

Chapter 1 Introduction

		Chapters
Part 1	Consumption Choices	2, 3 and 4
Part 2	Production and Markets	5, 6 and 7
Part 3	Markets, the State and the Good Society	8, 9 and 10

Order of each part in Book 1

First chapter (Chapters 2, 5, 8)	Review of textbook material
Second chapter (Chapters 3, 6, 9)	The history of these ideas as found in today's textbooks
Third chapter (Chapters 4, 7, 10)	A radical assessment of these ideas

---

Conclusion to Book 1

Book 2 ANXIETIES

Two chapters (Chapters 11 and 12) addressing two central anxieties that all students of economics develop (at some stage): does all this economic theory really matter to anyone (other than to our teachers)? Is this how the world works? What effect will this exposure to economics have on me as a person? Should I be bothering with economics at all? Should I choose another course while there is still time?

From the outline above, you can see that each of the three Parts in Book 1 is identically structured and contains three chapters whose purpose is to offer a review of the material in conventional textbooks, an explanation of where these ideas came from and a radical assessment of them (faithful to the belief that understanding is achieved best through criticism) respectively.

More precisely, Chapters 2, 5 and 8 (the first chapters in Parts 1, 2 and 3 respectively) offer a review of what the conventional textbook says on the respective segment. To avoid repetition, the discussion bypasses details in preference for the juicy ideas.

Chapters 3, 6 and 9 are the 'archaeological' chapters, which aim to explain the origin of the ideas in the preceding chapter of each part. Your usual textbook does not attempt this. Instead it gives the impression that these ideas have always been around – like the laws of nature. Well, as you can imagine this is not so. By excavating the history of these concepts we can succeed in demystifying them. And there is nothing like demystification to give one sufficient confidence when one tries to learn.

Chapters 4, 7 and 10: here you have arrived at the subversive bit. These are chapters which challenge the concepts in the textbook. Unlike the latter, which tries to avoid controversy like the plague, here we question everything. Why should we assume what the textbook asks us to assume so slavishly? What is the meaning of those assumptions? If people behaved in the way that the economists' assumptions demand, what would our society look like? Could the free market – capitalism – be deeply flawed? Or is it the system of organising economic life most compatible with human nature?

The questions in the critical chapters (4, 7 and 10) are questions that according to many of my colleagues are better left to more 'mature' students. I hope, however, that these chapters demonstrate the potential for engaging beginners in serious debate without reaping confusion. My point is simple: in a fast moving world, with students eager to get courses out of the way, we cannot afford to put these controversies to one side 'until later' for three reasons.

1   It is never a good idea to treat students as immature children.
2   If we leave these controversies aside 'for a while', there is a danger we will never come back to them, either because we will have forgotten them, or because the more thoughtful students who detest being treated like children may abandon us and our discipline too early.
3   Because by asking the impertinent questions in Chapters 4, 7 and 10 one gets a much better idea of what the concepts under scrutiny are: a little passion goes a long way in motivating analytical thinking; a

motto which, as economists, we seem to have forgotten. So, if at the end of all this you find the economists' theories convincing, you will know why. And if you remain unconvinced, then no one will have fooled you. In a sense Chapters 4, 7 and 10 are motivated by that other motto which brought us the Enlightenment: 'On no one's word'.

In summary, the contents of Book 1 follow closely that of any textbook's main segments. While tackling the theory of demand (or consumer theory), read Part 1. Once you have moved to the theory of supply (or of the firm, production and markets) turn to Part 2. When the course takes you into the territory of welfare economics (or market failure, public choice, government policy, etc.), Part 3 will become timely.

Finally, there is Book 2 to turn to, not because it contains material that you are likely to encounter in your course, but for personal gratification! Indeed Book 2 does not correspond to anything in your textbook. Its role is to pose questions that you are likely to wonder about but never dare (or bother) ask your teachers (perhaps for fear of sounding unschooled, or uncommitted to your course). Chapter 11 asks: *does economic theory matter?* How many students of economics (compare say with engineering students) respect their chosen field of study today? In the 1950s and 1960s students used to believe that by learning about economics they are learning about society. How many still think so today? Depressingly few. Are they wrong to be so cynical? Or is there indeed a very loose connection between economics and the economy? And why do we economists insist on disagreeing so much? Why can we not (like 'real scientists' do) put our different theories to the test and find out which works better? Why does this book have to waste so much ink and paper on debates and philosophical-cum-political criticism? These are the questions that almost all economics students I have known wanted answers to. Chapter 11 presents my answers.

Lastly Chapter 12 cuts closer to the bone by adopting a more personal and less abstract perspective: what effect does an economic education have on the personal development of those who acquire it? Put bluntly, is an education in economics good for you? And why is it that economics is increasingly developing an image problem with hoards of bright students abandoning economics degrees and courses midstream, visibly fed up with the coldness and arrogance of a discipline which, once upon a time, was considered essential by those passionate enough to want to make the world a better place? Perhaps surprisingly, given the general tone of this book, Chapter 12 ends with a plea to all those ready to jump ship: don't do it! An understanding of economics remains crucial.

A note for the general reader

Although I wrote this book with the undergraduate student in mind, this is by no means a book inaccessible to the reader with a general interest in (yet no great commitment to) the subject. When you come across a diagram that the undergraduate has already endured in class, feel free to do one of two things: either attempt to understand it (there should be enough in this book to allow you to grasp all the technicalities used) or, alternatively, skip it. In the latter case the loss of continuity will be insufficient to prevent you from enjoying the main debates on which the book turns. I hope you have fun!

Acknowledgements

If it was not for seven generations of first year students at the University of Sydney (1989 to 1995), I would not have had cause to think about a book such as this. They acted as guinea-pigs for my quasi-philosophical lectures and were subjected to reading notes on introductory economics which later grew into this book. One of those students, John Michael Howe, conscientiously scanned an earlier draft, spotted mistakes and suggested improvements. I also wish to thank my colleagues at Sydney for being so tolerant to someone who insisted on teaching weird things in the context of an otherwise perfectly respectable course. In particular I am grateful to Warren Hogan for recklessly assigning me to the introductory segment of the course. Tony Aspromourgos (who also read the first draft and diligently marked it with helpful comments), John Carson, Peter Docherty, Flora Gill, Bruce Ross, Graham White, Don Wright and Steffen Ziss were the other members of the team who, over the years, tried against all the odds to make Economics 1 a decent educational experience for students. I am grateful to them for the warm atmosphere they helped create and for the many ideas they gave me, some of which are now lost somewhere in this book. I am also grateful to the University of Sydney's management who, in early 1997, with a stroke of brilliance destroyed the atmosphere of collegiality and public spiritedness which characterised this course hitherto. I thank them for releasing me from any moral imperatives, namely teaching introductory economics passionately, and thus for turning this book into a kind of testimonial.

There are of course many more people who contributed ideas which I have taken on board and whom I cannot properly acknowledge. Alison Kirk offered valuable editorial assistance and organised anonymous reviews which proved helpful and thought-provoking. Of my eponymous colleagues I must mention two from a previous life: Shaun Hargreaves Heap, with whom we have been sharing other projects, and Martin Hollis, whose writings I have plundered before. I do it again in this book excusing myself with the thought that Martin's ideas for impressing certain points on students' minds cannot be improved upon.

Finally, it is to the fine city of Glasgow (where I completed the book's first draft) and to Margarita that I must direct the last 'thank you'.

Contents

BOOK 1

FOUNDATIONS

Part three   MARKETS, THE STATE AND THE GOOD SOCIETY

8 Review: textbooks on markets and social well-being   205

BOOK 2

ANXIETIES

Figures

Tables

Book 1

Foundations

Introduction

The textbook definition of economics

Economics studies the allocation of scarce productive resources (e.g. workers, machines, land) to different productive activities (e.g. factories, offices, farms, labour, machinery) whose purpose is to generate commodities that will satisfy consumers' needs. In the economists' own jargon, economics examines how scarce, or limited, 'factors of production' (usually defined as land, labour and capital) can be used wisely when there are many competing uses. In brief, economics is hailed as the *science of rational choice under conditions of scarcity*.

Yet, not everyone agrees . . .

Economics has been defined as the logic of choice . . . Economists have said that their subject is about reason . . . But almost none of them have said that their subject is concerned with imagination.
George Shackle, *The Nature of Economic Thought*, 1966

1.1 A world without economics

Let's face it. Beginning a lecture with the textbook definition of economics (see box) is not the kind of opening line that is likely to send ripples of excitement through an audience. So allow me a different introduction: why are *you* interested in economics? If you are a university student, why have you not chosen to study something else? Your university offers a multitude of courses from astronomy to zoology. Why economics?

Ignoring the usual answer of the sort 'er ... because my friends/ parents suggested it' or 'because I want a job and economics is compulsory for a business degree', the usual response to this question more often than not involves some general statement on the importance of the economy in social life. But then the question becomes: was economic life not important in the past, e.g. in the seventeenth century? Why were there no people thinking of themselves as students of *economics*? (Even Adam Smith, the founder of modern economics who wrote during the second half of the eighteenth century, was a moral philosopher.) And why did it take so long (i.e. not before the 1890s) for universities to offer degrees dedicated to economics?

Ancient economics

Economic questions have, of course, featured in the minds of intellectuals since the dawn of civilisation. The ancient Greeks, for example Aristotle, have written on matters which, today, we can identify as economic. Yet, unlike the first western economists (e.g. Adam Smith), none of those ancient writings were part of an overarching economic thesis (that is, an economic theory) on how society as a whole worked.

One may be tempted to think that our ancestors were less sophisticated and developed than we are in all the intellectual pursuits and economics, just like the other disciplines that make up today's university curricula, took its time to evolve. To some extent this is true. The oldest European universities, dating back to the twelfth century, taught almost exclusively the classics, law and theology. The natural sciences – physics, astronomy, chemistry (all known as natural philosophy back then) – were introduced only gradually after the sixteenth century. But why did economics take two or three centuries longer? Moreover it is not true at all that our ancestors were intellectual slouches. The ancient Chinese, Egyptians and Greeks were responsible for admirable technological advances and built incredible monuments to them. The depth of their philosophical thinking still tortures and shapes the mind of our best thinkers today. As for the modern, post-Dark Ages era, at least since the fourteenth century physics, chemistry, botany and mathematics have been flourishing. Yet genuine economic thinking had barely taken off the ground four centuries later. Why?

I suggest that contemplating this question is the best introduction to economics. It helps us to realise that the current collection of economic concepts is puzzlingly recent. That it is not as if the contents of the textbook have always been there waiting for you to come along and digest them. No, economic models are recent concoctions which are impossible to understand properly without understanding how they came into being. Back to the question then: why was there no *discipline* of economics until so recently? Did the Romans not care about their economy? Were Elizabethans unaware of the importance of economic might? Was the aristocracy of the French so-called *ancient régime* (i.e. the pre-Revolution establishment) uninterested in matters economic? Surely they must have wanted more power and wealth. So, why did they not develop a systematic *economic* approach? My answer (and I say 'my' because not everyone agrees with it) is that earlier societies had no use for economics; that they could understand social power and wealth without a *specifically* economic analysis. By contrast, in our days it is unthinkable that we can say something sensible about the state of a society (e.g. the distribution of income, of opportunities and of power) without engaging with ideas which are specifically economic.

How come there was no such need in past societies? Consider one example. In medieval times the success of the Spanish merchants in Latin American markets could be explained adequately by pointing out the military presence and power of the Spanish *conquistadores* on that continent. Similarly the success of English and Dutch traders made sense in terms of the domination of important sea routes by the English and Dutch navies. Contrast this type of extra-economic explanation to what is needed today in order to explain why it is that Japanese firms are successful at selling cars in the USA. Unlike medieval successes, modern commercial triumphs or disasters have to be narrated in terms of purely *economic* concepts such as price competitiveness, costs of production, quality control in factories, innovation, etc.

Let me now make an even more controversial claim: not only was there no use for economics in earlier societies but, in addition, those societies could not possibly develop the kind of economics that you will find in any modern textbook. To see this point, consider the textbook definition of economics in the box on p. 3: the economics textbook tells a story about the creation of goods for the purpose of selling or exchanging them. Such goods are called *commodities*. And what are those commodities made of? The ingredients necessary to produce them are known as *factors of production* and they fall under three main categories: *Land, Labour* and *Capital* (by the way, the latter refers not to money as such but to the tools and machinery necessary in the production process; that is, 'means of production', which were produced earlier – I shall be returning to this shortly). To produce commodities, the modern textbook continues, a firm needs to mix some land (and the minerals, oil, etc. found under its surface) with some human labour and, preferably, with some machinery other humans produced earlier (i.e. capital). But where does the firm get these factors from? In later chapters the standard economics textbook explains: it gets them at the same place that one buys all things, the market-place. Indeed this makes much sense today given our experience of such markets, e.g. estate agents selling or renting land, the local employment bureau (or the newspaper's job pages) in which labour is traded and the well-developed market for machinery, computers, etc. (that is, the market for so-called capital goods).

So, production generates commodities required by consumers by utilising other commodities which are needed by the firms (that is, the factors of production). Both the output (i.e. goods and services) of and the input (i.e. factors of production) to the process of production are commodities which are traded in various markets (e.g. the market for bananas, the market for land, the market for labour, etc.). Then economics is defined as the science of how markets, as a result of competition between many buyers and sellers, allocate rationally *all* these commodities in a society which always wants more of them. In short, economics is defined by the textbook as the science of how commodities are distributed under conditions of *scarcity*.

What we call today the discipline of economics (as opposed to some disconnected thoughts about prices, etc.) tries to disentangle the above process; to explain the workings of societies in which both its material products and the raw materials (human and non-human) used to produce them are commodities; that is, goods freely traded in markets. *This is precisely why it was irrelevant a few centuries ago!* If this conclusion seems too sudden, consider this. The description so far of what economics tries to achieve would have been out of place in ancient Greece, imperial Rome or feudal France. Granted that production and exchange are as old as *Homo sapiens*, it is easy to forget how different pre-industrial societies were from ours. Take the three factors of production mentioned in the previous paragraph: land, labour and capital. They always existed. Yet not in the way they do today, not as fully-fledged *commodities*.

Start with *land*. Of course there was land. Recalling that a commodity exists only to the extent that its very function is to be traded, a commodity called land has not always existed. That is, until a few centuries ago there was no established market for land deciding who owned which plot of land and how much someone had to pay to get it. In ancient times when the powerful wanted more land, they did not contact an estate agent; instead they formed an army made up of hapless subjects, often slaves, and started a war of conquest. Under those circumstances no one had an urgent need for an economic analysis of land-ownership. Things changed under feudalism. In the feudal era, the lords owned whole estates (including the peasants living in them) and usually considered the sale of inherited land shameful. Indeed property rights to land were passed on to the lords by kings and queens as reward for political services and even though land prices were quoted extensively in medieval archives, their function was not what it is today (that is, to regulate the demand for and supply of real estate). Instead they played the role of reflecting the power and political status of the landlords. In short, land was not a commodity with a price determined by the level of demand by prospective owners whose eagerness to buy the land was, in turn, its capacity to generate profit in some market (e.g.

the market for agricultural commodities or indeed in the market for land). A handle on war history and political machination would have proved much more useful than economics in explaining land transfers and prices.

A glimpse of the pre-industrial world

AD 1305 Europe

The total amount of goods which came into France in a year over the Saint Gothard pass (on the first suspension bridge in history) would not fill a modern freight train; the total amount of merchandise carried in the great Venetian fleet would not fill a modern steel freighter.

Sixteenth century

German traders had to stop every 10 km to pay customs tolls which were decided after intense bargaining. Most villages had their own currencies and in an area the size of London there were 112 different measures of length. Moreover, from France to Russia, from the Ottoman Empire to Scotland, there was nothing that we would recognise today as markets for labour or for land.

Historical points borrowed from Robert Heilbroner, *The Worldly Philosophers*, 1953

The same applies to factor of production *labour*. Of course there was labour and plenty of it. The pyramids could not have been built without the rivers of sweat and blood of countless Egyptian workers. And while Plato was leisurely exploring the distinction between a perceived and an ideal reality, surrounded by adoring disciples and intellectual antagonists in his *Academe*, slaves and Athenian women were doing all the work. Under feudalism, and excepting the idle classes, the European peasants worked much harder than any of us will ever do. Nevertheless the immense toil of slaves, peasants and women was not a *commodity*. Its product was, of course, greatly enjoyed by those who benefited from it (e.g. the philosophers, the rulers, the men). Yet all this effort was not something that was bought by some employer at a price (i.e. a wage) determined in accordance to its productivity and to the demand for its output. In feudal Europe, for example, those unfortunate enough to have been born peasants did a lot of work in the footsteps of their mothers and fathers. They cultivated the same land generation after generation producing harvests in the hope that the landlord would allow them to keep a portion which would see them through the next winter. To understand how much of their harvest they were allowed to keep, modern economic thinking would have been irrelevant. Why?

Because the distribution of the harvest between lord and peasant was a political matter depending on the lord's cruelty as well as on his fear of a peasant revolt, the role of the sheriff, the degree of solidarity between landlords (and between peasants), the relations between the political centre (i.e. the king or queen) and the regional powers (i.e. the estates and the lords and even the bishops), the threat of invasion by foreign armies and so on. By contrast, if we want to explain today the wages of farm labour in the United States, Germany or Indonesia we cannot rely on purely political notions. Instead we need to ask questions about the market value of agricultural products, the productivity of the farm labourers, their alternative employment prospects, etc. In brief, we need an economic approach that would have been impossible to conceive in a feudal world in which the lord simply collected a portion of the harvest from the peasantry.

Two definitions of capital: a means of production or a property right

Students of economics may be confused by the fact that the term 'capital' is used by economists in two seemingly very different ways: (1) machines, tools or any produced means of production; (2) a right to own the revenue that is left after land (i.e. rent) and labour (i.e. wages) have been paid for. The two definitions are brought closer together if it is assumed that those who own the 'tools' also own the right to appropriate the surplus (i.e. revenue minus cost) that they produce.

The third factor of production mentioned in economics textbooks, *capital*, was in its infancy. First, a reminder of the fact that, unlike accountants, when economists speak of capital, they do not mean money (see box). Instead they are referring to a commodity (e.g. a tractor) that was produced at an earlier stage in order to be used in some productive process (e.g. in ploughing a field). With this definition out of the way, let us agree that, just like land and labour, capital also existed since palaeolithic times in the form of tools, ploughs, etc., even if its presence in production was minuscule by comparison to how crucial it is today (think of industrial robots, computers, production lines, etc.). However, what is crucial is that capital did not really exist as a commodity. In ancient times it was produced mostly by slaves for their masters. In feudal estates tools were produced locally, often at the estates themselves, by artisans who found a niche in between the aristocracy and the peasantry. Even when they were sold at the town's market, it was never under competitive conditions as competition was ruled out either by the fact that there was a single producer in each municipality or because, when there were more than one, they were part of a guild which expressly banned competition amongst them. Thus, it is impossible to think of the utilisation of capital in a modern economist's terms: that is, as a scarce *commodity* which the competitive market was allocating to its best possible use. Again we find that the economics textbook's conception of capital would have been irrelevant back then.

Lastly, markets and trade were not what they are now. When merchants arrived in a medieval town, they brought with them some spices, some fancy clothing, a few luxury items. Their volume was microscopic as a proportion of all the goods consumed in the area. (Let us not forget that, back then, when the peasants and villagers wanted something they did not shoot off to the shops to get it; they made it themselves instead.) Moreover there was no competition since it was unlikely that there would be more than one merchant selling the same type of good in the same village. And when they were, the authorities (including the priest and the local lord) ensured that there would be no price competition between them. In larger towns, the artisans and the merchants would belong to guilds whose function was, partly, to prevent competition whenever price cutting reared its ugly head. You see back then, in startling contrast to today, profit-driven competition had a bad name; it was thought of as a disorganiser of trade!

External, long-haul trade was not much different. Commercial success depended on the capacity to carry goods from one part of the world to another; on extra-economic factors such as navigation skills, naval strength, control of important routes and so on. And just as within European villages and towns, there was negligible *economic* competition between sea-faring merchants. When merchants did clash against one another the matter was not resolved (as it is today in globalised markets) in favour of the one whose merchandise had been produced more cost-effectively; indeed clashes were resolved by political or military means.

In conclusion, with limited trade in mostly luxury goods (a tiny proportion of overall production), with precious little economic competition, with uncommodified land, labour or capital, these societies could be adequately understood without any economics. Yes, they did feature markets. But they were not market societies. Pure economic relations were embedded in social and political relations and were thus insufficiently visible to enable thinkers of the time to reason in the terms of contemporary economists. Thus it is not because the thinkers of the past were unsophisticated that coherent economic thinking took so long to flourish; it arrived late because in pre-industrial social structures there was little room for it. We had to wait until those structures were swept away by the capitalist industrial revolution before economics became possible.

1.2 The birth of economics

1.2.1 The coming of industrial revolution

If the era of economics was made possible only by the industrial revolution, what was it that gave rise to that revolution? This is a big question on which generations of historians have been feasting. Any short, decisive answer is therefore bound to be oversimplified and anathema to historians. Nevertheless without the rudiments of an answer, it would be impossible to begin to understand the gradual emergence of a demand for economic explanations.

What was it that shattered the tranquillity of pre-industrial Europe? What caused societies with markets to be transformed into market societies? A prominent historical answer is known as the *commercialisation thesis*. According to this account, the seeds of the upheaval which brought feudalism down and occasioned the rise of capitalism were planted by the growth of international trading networks due to improvements of navigation and shipbuilding. As the Spanish, Dutch, British and Portuguese traders began to exchange wool for Chinese silk, silk for Japanese swords, swords for spices and spices for much more wool than they started with, certain commodities established themselves as international currencies. Those who traded in them prospered. Their increasing fortunes were a totally different species of wealth from the riches of the traditional European aristocrats who had the hard work of their own people to thank for their well-being. The emerging class of merchants benefited not from appropriating the produce of the peasantry but from taking commodities undervalued in one market and selling them in some other market where they were highly valued: a case of what economists call *arbitrage*.

In contrast to the landed gentry whose only claim on wealth was that they were born with a silver spoon in their mouth, the merchants' claim was based on shrewd and risky deals some times involving the perils of selling precious goods (at huge prices of course) to countries under military siege or smuggling under the noses of belligerent colonial rulers in India and South East Asia. At the end of the day, they would return home (or should I say *if* they returned home?) with economic power not derived in the conventional way, that is by virtue of having been born into a land-owning family.

The trade in commodities was tragically not the only kind of trade that burgeoned. As the newly established internationally traded commodities gained prominence (quite simply by creating wealth for those who traded in them), it was inevitable that a new horrific trade would surface: the trade in people; a trade in the productive power to produce such commodities. Lands that were expropriated through western organised violence against the native populations (e.g. Jamaica and elsewhere in the 'New World') were combined with slave labour imported mainly from Africa to produce these commodities which then entered into the international trading circuit. Along the way more wealth was created for the entrepreneurs who participated in it.

At some stage landowners in Britain realised that their location at the top of the social power hierarchy was being threatened. They had to reassert themselves; and since they could not stop the merchants, their only option was to join them. How did they do this? For example, one of the commodities that was all the rage was wool. The lord of the manor would look out of his window and see peasants who for generations would be toiling the land producing a bit of wheat, some potatoes, a little corn. Useless stuff in other words that he could not sell to any self-respecting international merchant. What if he got rid of these peasants who were occupying so much space and substitute them with nice fat sheep? That way he could produce lots and lots of shiny wool which would find many willing customers. That was exactly what he and hundreds of other lords in England and Scotland did. In the mean time, the value of their land became intimately connected with the value of the wool that 'grew' on it. Land slowly became more than an inheritance; it became an economic asset whose value fluctuated with the price of the commodity (i.e. wool) it produced.

This historic turn of events simultaneously transformed not only land but also labour into a commodity. In a relatively short space of time, thousands of unsuspecting peasants found themselves in the muddy streets. They had no idea what hit them. After generations on what they considered to be *their* land (by tradition though not by ownership) they now had nowhere to go. Their destitution gave rise to a phenomenon that is still with us: urbanisation. Question: where do you go after you have been thrown out of the farm? Answer: To the nearest village to beg. Thus the villages of Britain became towns and the towns grew into cities. Whereas during the early phase of feudalism the peasants' labour was simply work which produced a harvest a part of which they kept (but not a commodity which they traded), now that they found themselves without access to land they were forced for the first time to try and sell their labour. Visualise the scene where an evicted peasant knocked on some door and said: 'Give me some food – I will do any job you ask of me' – an attempt to sell labour as a commodity. Meanwhile the peasants who remained on the land were increasingly forced to enter the newly formed market for land. How? By being asked to pay rent to the lord. Their market relation with the lord led them instantly to dependence on another market: the market for agricultural commodities, in which they had to get a good price for their wares in order to pay the rent. In one stroke, agricultural products, the land on which it was produced *and* the peasants who used to produce them (both those roaming the streets and the ones who were allowed to stay on the land) all became *commodities*.

Recapping, so far the *commercialisation thesis* has highlighted three related developments: an influx of merchant wealth from the new worlds, the transformation of peasants into producers of commodities (as opposed to just goods), and the formation of a group of wretched ex-peasants who found themselves, for the first time, without access to land or tools (i.e. without a capacity to produce a living) and who, therefore, were forced to sell a brand new *commodity* called 'labour'. Focusing on the first and the last links of the explanatory chain offered by the *commercialisation thesis*, intensified external commerce gave rise to the transformation of peasant labour into a commodified factor. On the one hand we have accumulating funds in the City of London (mainly the product of trade in international markets and slave production in the colonies) while on the other we have heavy concentrations in small areas in England and Scotland of a group of people desperate to sell their labour. Add to this brew a steam engine and what do you get? A factory.

The last sentence implies the following large claim: if James Watt, the Scottish inventor of the steam engine, had lived centuries before he did and still managed to build an engine, his invention could very well have gone unnoticed; it would have probably ended up as a curiosity in the palace of some royal person who would be using it to entertain guests. Thrust though into the scene described in the previous paragraph, the steam engine had a hand in changing history. It, more than any other single physical development, symbolises the momentous changes that wrecked the tranquillity of the Middle Ages and shattered once and for all the feudal social relations.

Although most historians accept many aspects of this *commercialisation thesis*, there are those who think that the unravelling of feudalism cannot be explained simply by pointing to the intensification of international trade. For them, it is unsatisfactory to place the entire burden of explanation of feudalism's collapse on external factors; on things that happened outside feudal Europe. Instead they believe that the primary mover was to be found in the social relations within Europe in general and Britain in particular. The development of reliable forms of money (and financial institutions) and, more importantly, the maturation of trade in market towns were of equal significance as the increase in international trade. In this account, market societies came into being as local trade in unglamorous commodities was steadily liberated from the fetters of feudal regulation.

Yet other historians object to both the *commercialisation thesis* and the above view of the industrial revolution as the outcome of the 'liberation' of local markets. They claim that both of these views assume what they are trying to explain; that they presuppose that capitalism was always there, at least in embryonic form, waiting to be 'released' or 'liberated' by some external or internal influence. It is as if the economic logic which became so dominant with the emergence of market societies was always there, even before market societies were established, waiting to be shaken loose. They argue that if this was indeed so, we should be trying to explain what took capitalism so long to emerge (rather than why feudalism collapsed). Additionally they point out that neither of the accounts of the emergence of market societies above can explain why it happened in Britain and spread quickly to the rest of Europe rather than in the equally commercialised East.

One explanation of the birth of market societies which does not involve the presupposition that their logic existed always in embryonic form, and also accounts for the fact that it was British feudalism which collapsed first, begins by focusing on the evolution of land-ownership in Britain. Compared to most other parts of the world, land-ownership in England and Scotland was highly concentrated (i.e. a few lords owned huge chunks of the British Isles). With such huge estates to plunder they found it cumbersome to collect a portion of the peasants' different harvests (as for instance their French counterparts did) and resorted increasingly to charging peasants rent (i.e. a charge independent of the size of the actual harvest). In so doing they turned peasants into 'tenants' who had an urgent incentive to increase production, reduce cost and sell their produce for a good price at the local market so as to be able to pay the rent. With one stroke, as already explained, the peasants were *forced* to enter the market in search of consumers while, at the same time, land became a commodity whose value was linked effectively to the rent paid by the tenants (which in turn was linked to the price of the harvest). This was one reason why the first market society emerged in Britain. The second reason is political: British landlords were demilitarised before any other aristocracy. Moreover the English state was uniquely centralised and wary of the power of the local gentry. Thus the ruling class of the British Isles was becoming increasingly dependent on charging rent, as a means of enrichment, rather than on physical coercion. They used as a weapon not their henchmen's armour but purely *economic* instruments. And as the rent rose, fewer peasants could afford to pay it. Those who were not chucked out of the estates in order to make way for sheep, were turned into wage labourers employed by the tenants. A whole new economic chain was thus created: the lords' higher rent pressurised the tenants (1) to cut costs and enter the local markets in pursuit of customers, and (2) to increase the productivity and reduce the wages of the wage labourers. By the time the landless peasants who had moved to the towns had been metamorphosised into an army of industrial workers operating the factories, the increases in agricultural workers' productivity made it possible to sustain a large and increasing non-agricultural population.

In summary the above theory suggests that the heavy concentration of British agricultural land, as well as the centralisation of political power in London, created a pattern where both lords and their tenants became highly dependent on market success for their preservation. In France where rents were nominal and the lords continued to rely on the forced expropriation of the peasants' harvest, no such reliance on markets existed. Add to this account the effects of the British domination of the major sea routes and of the rivers of wealth produced by the African slaves in the Caribbean, and a plausible explanation of Britain as the birthplace of the first truly market society emerges. Is it then any wonder why it was in Britain that economics, as a distinct discipline, took roots?

Such were the historical surges that led to the building of the smoke-infested industrial cities of Manchester and Birmingham in England and Glasgow in Scotland. Of course history is far messier and uneven than any narrative as simplistic as this. The transition from feudalism to capitalism was nowhere near as seamless as the preceding explanation makes it sound. For a start, the factories which absorbed the evicted peasants were erected up to a century after their eviction. What did happen to these people in between? They starved, they begged, many of them died of unnatural causes (unless famine counts as natural). Nevertheless the factories did come and slowly, yet never fully, the newly created working class was let through the gates. Wages and conditions were worse than any horror movie can conjure up; yet the industrial society had emerged.

Business ethics

Robert Heilbroner quotes in his book *The Worldly Philosophers* an article in *The Lion* circa 1828. The article was about Robert Blincoe, one of eighty pauper children sent off to a factory in Lowdham. Productivity was kept up by continually whipping, day and night, 10-year-old boys and girls. At another factory where they were taken later, they had to wrestle with pigs over scarce food. Sexual abuse and physical violence was also part of the menu. Robert Blincoe would spend the winters almost naked and had his teeth filed down. Although this was the exception rather than the rule, a fourteen hour day for 8 to 10 year olds was standard.

With its emergence, a fundamental shift of power occurred. The centre of gravity of economic power started shifting away from those who had political power – the aristocracy, the landlords, the bishops. Whereas once upon a time all power was simultaneously political and economic (as it emanated exclusively from land-ownership), capitalism changed all that. Economic power gradually visited the merchants, and later those who ran factories; people of a relatively low social status who hitherto enjoyed little, if any, political power. People whom the king and his lords looked down upon with disgust seeing in them 'men without breeding' getting wealthy through the indulgence in the unworthy pursuits of competition and profit making. Perhaps what fuelled the aristocrats' ire most was the fact that these unworthy profiteers were making a great deal of money. And since money could buy power, the aristocracy's political power was being usurped by the independent rise of economic, capitalist, power.

The rise of economic power as a force separate from political power had a profound effect not only on the aristocracy and the common folk but on the intellectuals who felt the pinch as well. For the first time, their traditional analysis of social phenomena (based on treatises about political power, e.g. of what the king's men were doing or trying to do) was useless. They had not a clue why the tranquillity of rural life had been interrupted so abruptly, why whole communities had been destroyed, where the factory and its discontents had come from. The reason why they could not understand any of this was because it was due to a new kind of gale, sweeping everything in its wake, never encountered before in the history of humanity. Yet the need to explain it was extremely urgent: society was undergoing a series of violent spasms. People demanded to know why. They wanted to grasp why countless former peasants were starving through no fault of their own, why factory workers were being worked into the ground, why people with nowhere to turn to for help desperately tried to sell everything ranging from sexual favours to their labour power. They wanted to understand just in case they could come up with a cure. Bishops, princes and well-meaning philanthropists despaired. The first two because they had lost their influence, the latter because of their helplessness in the face of the spiralling human misery.

Perhaps the most intriguing aspect of these developments to those who were trying to understand them was that no one could be blamed seriously. A hypothetical opinion poll during the eighteenth century would most certainly return the people's verdict: 'We do not want change. We do not want the industrial revolution.' It was not even as if the king or some other person had decided on changes that led to vast dislocation and suffering. Indeed the king was as surprised and horrified by the changes as the next man or woman. The change in the distribution of economic power meant that some low 'caste' people could now afford to raise an army against those, like the royals, holding political power. (And some did with the result that quite a few royal heads were separated from royal shoulders!) No one could point the finger at anyone. History moved in unpredictable ways impervious to the wishes of rulers and subjects alike. It was as if there were hidden, dark forces behind people's backs changing life as it was hitherto known. Some other explanation became painfully necessary: economic theory.

1.2.2 The moral philosopher: Adam Smith

Examples of unintended consequences

Negative consequences: you are at a concert. Everyone wants to have a better view of the stage. So everyone stands up. The result is that each has the same view as before only they are less comfortable.

Positive consequences: the heads of the Mafia vie for control of the organisation, each wanting to gain full control. However, a likely (and certainly unintended) result of these intentions is that the aspiring Godfathers wipe each other out.

Adam Smith hoped that capitalism (and the free market) would foster a variety of positive social effects which, nevertheless, would be unintended by capitalists.

Adam Smith (1723–90) was the first to satisfy this need at a grand scale. A Professor of Moral Philosophy at the University of Glasgow, Smith looked outside his window and instead of seeing the gloom, wickedness, misery and smoke from the factory chimneys that everyone else could see, he saw the makings of a brave new world. Being a philosopher, he was aware of an interesting tension between people's intentions and the result of these intentions when people are allowed to act on them. To offer a silly, yet useful, example, suppose a group of lazy farmers are told that there is a pot of gold somewhere in the valley on which their land lies. Overcome by gold fever they maniacally, day and night, dig the land. Of course they find nothing since the rumour was untrue. But at the end of the day, because all the soil has been dug up and thus revitalised, the productivity of their farms increased dramatically and they all become much better off than before. This is an example of *unintended consequences*, of the tension between what people intend and what happens as a result of these intentions.

How is this example related to Adam Smith's optimistic vision of a brave new world? We have to start from the worries that were dominating public debate at the time. Following the breakdown of central authority and the demise of the unity of political and economic power, people were asking: given that the king's government and his lords have lost control, who is in charge? The following two questions sum up their anxiety:

1   With no central control, how can we be sure that society will be in a position to produce the commodities that it needs rather than over-producing unnecessary things and under-producing essential stuff?

2   With no political control of the economy, how can we know that misery will not grow to such an extent that society will disintegrate and be reduced to skirmishes between different interest groups fighting each other for supremacy?

Smith's answers to both questions are based on two ideas: the first was that the logic of the shopkeeper had become widespread amongst entrepreneurs. The second was the idea of unintended consequences above. Consider some useful good such as shoes and imagine that there are many shoemakers and countless buyers. How will it be possible, without anyone instructing the producers as to how many pairs of shoes to make, that the quantity of shoes produced (i.e. supply) will equal the number of pairs that consumers want to buy (i.e. demand)? Surely only by a fluke will the two quantities coincide. Not so, argued Smith. Even if no one does the coordination, provided we let consumers and producers act on their intentions, the two quantities will automatically become equal.

Adam Smith on trade and virtue

Man has almost constant occasion for the help of his brethren, and it is in vain for him to expect it from their benevolence only. He will be more likely to prevail if he can interest their self-love in his favour, and shew them that it is for their own advantage to do for him what he requires of them.

On the merchant

By pursuing his own interest he frequently promotes that of the society more effectually when he really intends to promote it. I have never known much good done by those who affected to trade for the public good.

Adam Smith, The Wealth of Nations, 1776

What are the consumers' intentions? To buy a certain quantity of shoes at the lowest possible price. And of producers? To sell a certain quantity at the maximum price. That's all. Neither side is interested in the least in whether supply and demand will be coordinated nicely. Yet, Smith contented, if we let them act on their intentions coordination will be automatic. How? If more shoes are produced than are needed, there will be many unsold pairs. How can the sellers get rid of them? Simply by reducing the price. And if fewer shoes are produced than are needed, there will be empty shelves and customers will be out-bidding each other for the few available pairs. Thus the price of shoes will rise. It is the fluctuations of price that will do the job of *coordination*. Provided that consumers limit their purchases and producers increase their output when prices rise, the price of shoes will fluctuate automatically until the number of pairs produced exactly equals the number of pairs customers want to purchase. In the end price will find a level at which supply will equal demand. Thus question (1) has been answered.

The gist of this answer is that even though no one tried to coordinate the demand and the supply of shoes, or indeed of other commodities, the market will act to ensure that the exact quantity of each good produced will equal the quantity required by consumers. The beauty of this result is that no one intends it! Just like the farmers in the silly example above, none of whom *intended* to increase the productivity of the soil when they dug it up (even though they all benefited from it in the end), no consumer or producer ever *intended* to help the market equilibrate demand and supply. It just happened once they were allowed to follow their intentions and, in spite of their intentions, they all benefit since there is neither a shortage nor a glut of shoes.

The answer to question (2) is even more of a gem. Smith recognised that the prerequisite for a successful industrial society is the proliferation of commodities. When he looked around him and saw great poverty, he resisted a moralist's stance (i.e. to pray for the redemption of the soul of the poor, wishing them luck in the next life) and adopted instead a practical perspective. These people needed more commodities: more food, clothes and shelter. And if society is to be harmonious it must provide more of these to the masses. A pretty level-headed moral philosopher!

His notion of unintended consequences was utilised once more. To those who pointed out that the nouveau riche, the merchant and capitalist class, did not give a damn about the good of society, Smith's attitude was that of a pragmatist: granted that they are not the kind of person I would want my children to befriend, these entrepreneurs, guided as they are by greed, will end up making a contribution totally at odds with their intentions. They intend to knife each other in the back for private gain but in the end, and totally against their intentions, they will end up contributing to the public good; just like the farmers who, in the selfish pursuit of the pot of gold, ended up helping the whole community by, unintentionally, fertilising the land.

Of course Smith could not support his view that competition and profiteering was the best way of serving the Common Interest without redefining it. Thus while others were speaking of the importance of solidarity, of bonds between people and families, of tranquillity and stability (all shattered by the coming of the industrial age), for Smith the public good meant only one thing: more commodities at lower prices (so that the masses could eventually afford them). This explains why, in his eyes, the contribution of the individually untrustworthy entrepreneurs was pivotal: they were the new

Adam Smith's audacious idea

Smith's central idea that we shall all benefit by competing against each other without any concern about our neighbour (except for what we can get from them and how we can appeal to their 'self-love' in order to gain personally), was and remains controversial (it was described by American philosopher Richard Rorty as 'strange' and 'dangerous'). Yet it is a measure of this idea's power that it has become a dominant ideological creed from Anglo-America to Japan and, more recently, from Budapest to Vladivostock.

messiahs because of their role in *mechanising* society; of introducing more and more machinery (i.e. capital) in the production process so that we can collectively, as a community, produce more for less. Why on earth would the entrepreneurs do this? The point is, again, that they would not be aiming to do it. Instead all they would be looking after is their own hip pocket – their profit. However, the prerequisite for this unintentional convergence of the capitalists' and merchants' interest and the good of society is that there are many of them and that they are at each other's throats; that is, what we euphemistically call *competition*.

Trade keeps prices low and even: an example from a POW camp

While in captivity during the Second World War, R. A. Radford studied the economic activities of his fellow prisoners. In an article published by *Economica* in 1945, he explains how prisoners exchanged the various articles sent to them by the Red Cross. Initially each section established its own prices expressed in cigarettes. However, some prisoners recognised the possibility of improving their material situation in the camp by buying in one section and selling in the other. For example, the price of tea in the English section was at first higher than that of coffee (reflecting the preferences of the prisoners). However, after some entrepreneurial Englishmen discovered that they could buy tea cheaply in the French section and then resell it in the English section, prices in the two sections eventually equalised. Moreover, with quite a few prisoners acting as merchants, in the end there was no significant profit to be made from trading: competition had pushed prices to the lowest possible level.

The virtue of competition according to Smith is that, as the Australians like to say, 'it keeps the bastards honest'. In effect it ensures that no one can sell anything for more than it is truly worth. If one tries to, then there will be countless others prepared to undercut the asked price. Eventually prices will tend to hover just above costs and as a result no one will be able to make a profit just by trading. This should, according to Smith's logic, help capitalists focus their mind on how to create profit. The first thing they will think of is how to squeeze more for less out of their workers. Well, provided they all squeeze more or less the same, no one will be in a position to make money just by pushing hourly wages down to its lowest level. Smith presumed that the wages have a lower limit and if employers try to push them further down, workers will simply quit (or starve to death) – the so-called *subsistence wage*.

Once they realise that they must be more ingenious than that if they are to profit significantly, they will see that the best way of undercutting their competitors without losing money is if they can automate the production process so as to need fewer labour hours per unit of output. That is, if they mechanise or, equivalently, if they introduce more capital in their operation. Suppose they are successful. Immediately they will wrestle market share from the competition (since they will be able to charge less than the others) and profit greatly. However, before long others will follow their lead and also invest in more machines. In the end, all firms (at least those that survive) will use more machines and no one will have an advantage. Indeed competition between them will see prices drop further. In the end no one will be making any significant profit and the only beneficiary is society at large since more commodities will be produced (due to the greater automation of production) and prices will have fallen. To use a popular phrase, private vices (i.e. the profit motive of capitalists) will have given rise to public virtue (i.e. the proliferation of cheaper commodities which are essential for combating need).

In conclusion, the optimism of Smith about the emerging industrial capitalism of his time boils down to his view of competition as the lever by which society harnesses the selfishness of industrial and merchant capital and transforms it, against the intentions of the capitalists, into economic growth and prosperity for the many. The engine which is to pull society forward and away from misery and need is the urge to accumulate capital (or mechanisation/automation). When a firm orders a new piece of machinery from another firm, it passes on to the latter a part of its previous profits. That money is used to hire previously unemployed workers to produce this piece of capital equipment. In the meantime, they receive a wage which they spend on other commodities. So the profits of the first firm, instead of being spent on a holiday by the entrepreneur, is channelled into the economy. Not only does it help buy a piece of machinery that will help mechanise society and thus boost its capacity to produce needed commodities, but also it ends up in the pockets of workers who then pass it on (e.g. at the supermarket) to other producers. It is like an endless chain reaction that keeps the home fires burning.

No wonder Smith was optimistic about capitalism. For if the above vision was correct, then society would resemble an escalator which constantly moves upwards. Some social classes will be higher up but all will be moving in the right direction. The motor of the escalator being capital accumulation (or, in everyday parlance, investment in machines), it is clearly essential that it is kept going. And the motor power which can alone keep it going is competition. Any slackening in the war between capitalists and the urge to amass capital (i.e. to invest) will be dampened with horrific consequences: the escalator will stall and may well start going backwards.

But as long as it keeps going, society can look forward to prosperity and, one hopes, harmony. The last point depends on the thought that as capital accumulation and economic growth gather pace, the inequalities between the classes will shrink; people from different backgrounds will start moving closer together on the ever rising escalator. The reason why this may happen is that whereas purchasing power will be improving (recall the proliferation of commodities at ever decreasing prices), the profit of capitalists will always remain minuscule due to competition. Consequently the scissors between employers and employees will be closing steadily. In the long run capitalists would never make much money in spite of their great interest in doing so; a desire that is most successful in promoting the public good provided it remains unfulfilled.

Those who heard Smith's theories and read his 1776 book, the celebrated *An Inquiry into the Nature and Causes of the Wealth of Nations*, must have been reassured. There was some order to be discerned in the chaos around them. And it was not so bad that the new holders of economic power (i.e. the capitalists and merchants) may have seemed too crass and greedy. If their greed is self-defeating and in the end contributes to the good of society, so be it. The whole vision seemed like a product of divine providence. Here is a bunch of selfish people who act on their own interest and yet forces behind their backs contrive the best and most noble of all possible social worlds. It is as if an *invisible hand* forces on those who act shamelessly a collective outcome fit for saints. Not surprisingly, Adam Smith became a celebrity in his time. He had offered, in true twentieth-century Hollywood style, a nice story with a great twist and a happy ending. It was popular.

1.2.3 The stockbroker: David Ricardo

The problem with feel-good theories is that when the good feeling gives its place to discontent some impertinent soul will emerge with a repudiation of the theory, or even worse with an *alternative* theory. No theory can defy history. In the case of British capitalism economic growth nose-dived soon after Smith's death when Britain got involved in continental conflict leading to the Napoleonic Wars. One of the immediate repercussions of these wars was the slowing of trade owing to the naval stand-off between the combatants. In particular the discontinuation of corn imports into Britain inflated food prices and gave rise to more rather than less hunger. Smith's escalator initially stalled and then started going into reverse wrecking the prospects of harmony promised by Smith. As working-class families were forced to pay more for less food, a vociferous minority of landowners insisted that no corn should be imported after the war's end for the simple reason that their wealth increased in direct proportion to the misery of the majority (in short, the shortages of corn inflated its price and, subsequently, their bank accounts).

Excited by all this, David Ricardo (1772–1823) sat down and tried to re-examine Adam Smith's narrative. His answer came in the form of a best-selling book, published in 1817, entitled *Principles of Political Economy*. Was Smith justified to place so much trust in the power of competition? Would capital accumulation do the trick? Ricardo concluded that, though Smith was right that long-run capital accumulation (i.e. mechanisation/automation) was society's only hope, competition would not necessarily bring it about. The reason is that there are some factos of production (or resources) which are limited in volume (e.g. fertile land). As production and income rises, demand for these scarce resources escalates but, unlike other commodities (e.g. bread or guns), their supply does not respond to this increase in demand. Those who happen, by some historical accident, to own them will receive more and more money with every increase in the demand for commodities requiring the employment of that resource. This gave rise to Ricardo's idea of *economic rent*.

Economic rent

A farmer is willing to produce wheat at $10 per ton. If the market price is less than $10, she would switch to some other productive activity (e.g. would grow strawberries or turn the farm into a theme park). Suppose now that demand is high and the price of wheat rises to $15. For every ton produced she is receiving $5 *more than is necessary to keep her in wheat production*. This difference was termed by Ricardo *economic rent*.

For Ricardo, rent was a payment to some supplier *over and above* what is necessary to keep the supplies coming. From the point of view of a society which needs to invest every spare penny into more machines (recall Smith's

Economic rent as a brake to growth

According to Adam Smith, competition ensures that most profits are invested into better machinery (and thus future productivity). However, Ricardo pointed out that competition does not help convert economic rents into more investment in machinery. The reason is that, unlike industrial profit, economic rents are not a reward for entrepreneurship and greater productivity. Instead they are a payment to those people who, as a result of good fortune, happened to have inherited owner-ship of productive resources (e.g. land) in short supply. These people can enjoy their rents without ever having to invest (unlike capitalists fearful of competition). Thus a society in which economic rent is a large portion of overall income is one which will grow slower and therefore be more prone to stagnation.

point about the escalator running on capital accumulation), such payments, or rents, were a waste. Smith and Ricardo agreed on that. However, whereas Smith was confident that competition will make rents vanish (as sellers would cut prices to the bare minimum in order to compete with each other), Ricardo feared that the opposite is true. His experience with landowners trying to ban corn imports in order to boost their rents (at the expense of capitalists, workers and economic growth) taught him that it was unwise to assume that rents would simply wither away as a result of competition. His reason for thinking this was that landlords did not compete against anyone. Take for example the owner of an office block in central London. Who is the owner competing against when the demand for office space is high during an economic boom (e.g. the late 1980s)? As space in central London is more or less fixed, an economic boom is guaranteed to boost the landowner's income by virtue of the location of the building. Ricardo consid-ered this and saw a chink in Smith's theoretical armour: here is a great pool of income (i.e. rent) which is neither a reward for mechanising society nor for anything else which is likely to enhance society's capacity to produce and, additionally, which is bound to increase (as opposed to decline) when the economy grows and competition amongst all other (capitalist) producers hots up.

This last point worried Ricardo immensely. Unlike industrialists who must invest whatever profit they make back into capital equipment (if they are to survive the competitive jungle), these rentiers (i.e. the recipients of rents) do not have to invest at all; after all they own the limited supply of this increasingly valuable resource and they do not have to compete with anyone (since no one else can produce more of that resource). Thus they can spend their rent on holidays or simply put it in a vault and, in this way, stay well out of what Smith considered to be the miracle of capital accumulation which is driven by competition and reinvestment. For Ricardo, the money that rentiers 'smuggled' out of the cycle of 'production → profit → reinvestment → greater-production → . . .' resembled lost socio-economic energy; energy that was drained out of the economic system and retarded capital accumulation. It is as if some people on Smith's escalator had found a way to drain its motor of energy in order to propel themselves further up. The only problem was that, if they were successful in doing this, they would cause the escalator to stall.

Intellectual integrity and economic theory

Although (I still insist) history and ideology are the twin masters of economics (and therefore of economists), this does not mean that economic theory has always reflected the self interest of those who devised it. For instance, David Ricardo was a major landowner and stood to benefit a great deal from the policies that he fought against in the House of Commons (a seat that he actually purchased!). His friend and theoretical adversary, Thomas Malthus (1766–1834), wrote the following on this subject:

> It is somewhat singular that Mr. Ricardo, a considerable receiver of rents, should have so much underrated their national importance; while I, who have never received, nor expect to receive any, shall probably be accused of overrating their importance. Our different situations and opinions may serve at least to shew our mutual sincerity, and afford a strong presumption, that to whatever bias our minds may have been subjected in the doctrines we have laid down, it has not been that, against which perhaps it is most difficult to guard, the insensible bias of situation and interest.
> Quoted in Robert Heilbroner, The Worldly Philosophers, 1953

Another thinker belonging to this category is Friedrich Engels (1820–95), Karl Marx's life-long friend and collaborator. Although born into a capital-owning family (he was himself the owner of a factory in Manchester), he spent most of his life championing the right, and obligation, of workers to acquire the ownership of factories by force.

In summary, it is not difficult to see how historical events at the beginning of the nineteenth century produced a fledgling theory of economic recessions. Ricardo's dislike for the stance of landowners, and their demand that food imports are banned so that they can profit, caused him to re-think the dominant economic theory at the time. Startlingly Ricardo was himself the owner of much land and the recipient of significant rents (see box on p. 24). Nevertheless intellectually, ideologically and politically he identified with industrialists whom he, just like Smith, saw as the usherers of progress. He detested the flow from higher rents for land to increased food prices to higher wages (so that workers could buy enough food to avoid collapsing of malnutrition on the job), on to lower profits and thus lower capital accumulation. Therefore his theoretical intervention can be understood in terms of his assessment of new historical data and his ideological position (i.e. pro-industrial capital).

1.2.4 The revolutionary: Karl Marx

Marx on the centrality of wage labour under capitalism

Labour not only produces commodities. It also produces itself and the worker as a *commodity*, and indeed in the same proportion as it produces commodities in general.

Karl Marx, *Economic and Philosophical Manuscripts*, 1844

Perhaps it is not unreasonable to generalise that all major economic insights where produced in the same way: based on a combination of history and ideology. We just saw how the Napoleonic Wars and an ideological commitment to capitalism influenced Ricardo to turn against his social class and to compose theories which dispute Adam Smith's optimism about capitalism. Another example can be seen in the economic works of Karl Marx (1818–83). Like Ricardo, he did not think that competition guaranteed a growing economy. Moreover, and again like Ricardo, he felt that inequality would deepen and social conflict would intensify. But unlike the political environment in which Ricardo had developed his ideas, when Marx was shaping his economic theory the conflict between landlords' rents and capitalists' profit had dissipated substantially (indeed rent, as a proportion of total income, had ceased to grow). In Marx's case another conflict and another sympathy marked his thinking. It was the clash between capital and labour (culminating in the Europe-wide revolutions of 1848) and Marx's identification with the lowest of the low: the workers for whom Ricardo had little interest focused as he was on the conflict between landlords and capitalists. Writing at a time of wild fluctuations in the fortunes of capitalism,

Marx on the employer–employee relation

> The possessor of money has paid for a day's worth of labour; hence the use of a whole day's labour belongs to him during that day. The circumstance that it costs only a half day's labour to get a day's labour power . . . that therefore the value created by its use during one day is twice as much as its own value of that day – this is a piece of luck for the buyer, but no injustice at all to the seller.
>
> Karl Marx, *Capital, volume 1*, 1867

Thus, contrary to popular opinion, Marx did not blame the capitalists for the ills of capitalism. His critique focused on the 'internal contradictions', or, as we would say today, the irrationality of a system in which the workers' labour is not rewarded as such but instead workers are paid a wage in return for their labour time.

and in an attempt to explain these fluctuations (as well as the ensuing social conflict between workers and capital), Marx asked a simple question: what is it that gives value to commodities?

His answer, influenced crucially by Smith and Ricardo, was that *the value of a commodity reflects the amount of human labour that is needed for its production.* (Note how his ideological commitment to the workers caused him to be extremely receptive to this theory linking economic value to human labour.) So automation (i.e. capital accumulation) reduces a commodity's value because it reduces the amount of human labour (both current and previous) that has been 'crystallised' in the commodity. Then he asked: where do profits come from? He agreed with Smith that they cannot come simply from buying cheaply and selling expensively since competition would force all prices down to a minimum level that would reflect the commoditity's value. And if no one can sell anything above its value, no one can profit from just buying and selling. Marx's answer was that profits were made not at the point of selling but at the point of production. More precisely, they were due to the difference between the value of labour as a commodity and the value that workers put inside commodities. Let us define these two different values carefully: (1) the value of a worker's labour as a commodity; that is, the *value of labour time (or power)* and (2) the value of the commodity that the worker's labour has produced; that is the *value of labour.*

1   *The value of labour time (or power)*
     Labour time (or labour power) is traded as a commodity between employers and workers in the so-called labour market and fetches a

price (i.e. the wage) reflecting the demand for and supply of workers' time. Thus the wage corresponds to the value of labour time. But what is this value? Take for example an industrial worker, say Bill. What is the (economic) value of Bill's time? Recall Marx's definition of the value of any commodity: it equals the labour that has gone into its production. What has gone into the production of Bill's 'labour time'? All the commodities which are necessary for the continuation of Bill's life (i.e. food, shelter, etc.), answers Marx. The ones that are necessary so that he can report to work every morning ready for a full day's work. The total value of these commodities (equal to the human labour expended, by other workers, to produce them) determines the value of Bill's labour time.

2   *The value of labour*
During the process of production Bill puts his own work into commodities (so to speak) and thus lends them value (recall Marx's definition of a commodity's value as being proportional to the work effort expended in its production). Thus the value of Bill's labour corresponds to the value of the commodities he produces.

Marx pointed out that (1) and (2) above are different; that there is no reason at all why the total amount of work other workers have done in order to 're-produce' Bill as *a worker* (by creating the commodities which are necessary for Bill's re-production) must be the same as the total amount of Bill's work in the factory. Indeed Bill's employer would have no reason to employ him unless the work Bill put in was greater than the work other workers have put into 'keeping' Bill (which Bill 'purchases' with the wage his employer pays him). And this is the rub: The difference between (2) and (1) above is retained by the employer and is the source of the employer's profit. Marx calls this difference *surplus value*. From this surplus value, the capitalist pays rent to the landlord, interest to the bank and keeps the rest as profit.

How can this explain the fluctuations in the fortunes of capitalism? Suppose, says Marx, that we start with circumstances which would warm Adam Smith's heart; that is, a period of growth spearheaded by capital accumulation; that is, by capitalists eagerly reinvesting their profit into more and better machinery. Is it sustainable? Marx looked at this rosy picture of a growing capitalist economy and saw the seeds of an imminent economic crisis. As production becomes mechanised, each unit of output encompasses less and less human labour. And since it is the latter that determines the values of commodities, it is a matter of time before values are reduced, prices decline and thus profit plummets. Some firms, the more vulnerable ones, will go under causing a negative chain reaction: the first workers who lose their jobs will cut down on their purchases and this will reduce the profit of some other firms further which will then fire more workers and so on until the economy stagnates and huge queues of unemployed workers gather outside the gates of under-utilised (or, even worse, closed) factories desperately seeking jobs.

At some point, the recession will be so deep that those firms which have survived will start doing rather well. The reason is that, with many of their competitors out of the market, they will be enjoying a much bigger share of the market. Even if the pie has shrunk there will be far fewer firms competing for pieces of it and therefore those still left in the game will get their hands on a larger piece of the (albeit shrinking) pie. Additionally, a recession reduces firms' cost by creating a large pool of idle capital and labour whose prices drop below its values. In plain language, during a recession surviving firms can purchase raw materials, computer equipment, machinery, etc. for a song. As for workers, desperate as they are for work they will labour for lower wages and, even if they receive the same wage as before, they will be working twice as hard fearing that, at the employer's whim, they may join the scrapheap of wasted humans who are knocking pathetically on the factory's gates. It is not at all surprising, in this theoretical context, that in Marx's eyes economic recessions are to capitalism what hell is to Christianty: indispensable.

However, unlike hell, an economic recession is not permanent. In an attempt to shore up their market dominance, surviving firms start expanding in the middle of the recession. As they expand (e.g. by employing more workers) they start another chain reaction, this time a positive one, which boosts output, employment and eventually capital accumulation. The economy thus exits the recession and enters a period of growth. But as before, this upturn contains the seeds of the next recession. And so on.

Marx went on to predict that every recession revitalises capitalism as it plays a culling role which helps the fitter companies survive at the expense of the fragile; a process that, many years after Marx, the Austrian economist Joseph Schumpeter (see p. 190) described as the process of 'creative destruction'. However, Marx believed that with every recession that passes the poverty and inequality left behind would worsen. And every new period of growth will be less likely to undo the social and economic damage caused by the previous recession. In time, capitalism will exhaust its capacity to innovate and to utilise resources (especially human resources) with any semblance of efficiency. The answer to this senseless cycle, Marx argues, is to devise a more rational economic system than capitalism: socialism. For this revolutionary thinker, capitalism is not 'wrong' because it is unfair; it is unfair because it is irrational and fundamentally wasteful.

1.2.5 The twin masters of economics: history and ideology

This is not a book on the history of economic thought. The point in skimming through the surface of the simultaneous development of capitalism and of economic ideas about capitalism is to give the reader a feeling for the precariousness of economic theory. Unlike physics, it is not simply a response to the need to know how an objective reality 'out there' works. Unlike nature which conveniently stays at an arm's length from our theories, society is less accommodating: our theories about society are so bound up with society itself that it is radically harder for a social scientist to create enough distance between her and the object of her study than it is for a natural scientist. The result is that economics is partly science and partly ideology. Which part is greater is also a source of contention amongst economists!

Can economics be a science?

Most economists answer with a resounding 'Yes'. They distinguish between two types of economics: *positive* and *normative*. Positive economics is proclaimed as the scientific study of how things are, of how particular economic systems work. Normative economics is about how we would like things to be, of which type of system we favour. (Textbooks make this distinction and then concentrate on positive economics. Indeed a famous textbook by Richard Lipsey is entitled *Positive Economics*.) The idea is that we keep positive economics free of ideology, ethical judgments, political passions, etc. and, once we have a clear picture of what is feasible, we can then let the passions in to decide what is desirable (that is, move on to normative economics).

Others (including me) disagree. They point out that the positive–normative distinction is impossible to hold on to. For example, they suggest that behind every piece of 'positive economic thinking' lies an ideological position. Even worse, and unlike in physics or chemistry, there can be no ideology-free economic facts. Take inflation, that is, the rate of increase in prices: which prices do we measure? Do we look at the price of a Rolls-Royce, of a bus ticket or a combination of the two? And if we choose the latter, how much emphasis should be given to the price of the Rolls relatively to bus fares when calculating the average change in the cost of transport? In other words, *every* measure of inflation hides a *political* decision as to which group of people matter more (e.g. the rich or the poor). And to try to pretend that economics is an objective study of the possible (as opposed to the desirable) is a political attempt to present certain politically loaded views as objective and thus superior.

Regardless of all this, economic textbooks seem strictly un-ideological. Yet every economic theory is based on some ideological or political prejudice. We saw how Adam Smith created a theory consistent with his commitment to free trade and the historical events of the eighteenth century which were marked by the rise of market societies out of feudal societies with markets. Smith takes the logic of the 1770s tenant (who rents land from the lord and hires wage labour), of the merchant, of the butcher and assumes that theirs is the logic of rational men (note that the rationality of women was hotly disputed on sexist philosophical grounds during that time) at all times and in all places. He forgets that this logic is also a product of history; that it did not exist until the tenant, the smith, the butcher and the worker were all forced by historical change to enter the competitive market and to develop a specifically market-oriented mentality. Adam Smith's *ideological* identification with this mentality spawned a particular view of human nature and of the type of social organisation (i.e. free market capitalism) which can serve it best. However impressed one is by Smith's vision, it is unwise to interpret it as an objective, scientific, unideological model of the social world.

David Ricardo's theory was also a product of his ideology and of the period during which he thought and wrote. It was utterly in tune not only with Ricardo's dislike for rentiers (i.e. landowners, like himself, who creamed off the benefits from capital accumulation without contributing anything to it) but also with the historical developments of his time (i.e. the Napoleonic Wars and the subsequent political tussle against protectionist landowners). Finally, Karl Marx's model of capitalism reflected not only his solidarity with the working class against its exploiters but also the history of recessions and revolutions during the period when he was writing.

Since then ideology and history have continued to spawn contradictory economic perspectives like those (to mention a few who probably mean nothing to you at the moment) of Rosa Luxemburg, Joseph Schumpeter, John Maynard Keynes, Friedrich von Hayek, Paul Sweezy, John Kenneth Galbraith, Joan Robinson, Milton Friedman and Robert Lucas. The reason why they disagree violently amongst them is not that some are more intelligent than others. Rather it is because their starting ideological position was different and because they did not have a shared history.

1.3 Modern textbook economics (or neoclassical economics)

1.3.1 The transition from classical to neoclassical economics

Imagine that you are the first ever Professor of Economics in some prestigious European university towards the end of the nineteenth century. After your first lecture you enter the Common Room where all the professors meet at tea-time. You sit around the table unobtrusively listening to the various conversations. The Professor of Physics is going on about the latest advances in thermodynamics and the exciting possibility of understanding the universe in a non-Newtonian manner. The Professor of Biology predicts that Darwinian theories will eventually focus on the evolution not of whole animals but of genes and perhaps of smaller entities which make up genes. Meanwhile the Professors of Philosophy, Law and Linguistics are immersed in witty exchanges on the nature of language. At some point, they notice your presence and interrupt their discussions. One of them shatters the awkward silence by asking: 'Tell us old boy, what is this economics science of yours? Is it worth the candle?'

What do you say? Do you give them a spiel on how when the demand for shoes exceeds the supply of shoes, shoes will appreciate in price? Or do you tell them about Adam Smith's escalator? Or David Ricardo's dislike of landowners? It is embarrassing, isn't it? I suspect that in that position you would have a great urge to convince these snobs that your discipline is as scientific and respectable as theirs. Regardless of whether the first academic economists actually felt that way, their theoretical endeavours are not incompatible with such feelings of embarrassment at what is now called classical political economy, or classical economics (i.e. the work of Adam Smith, David Ricardo, Karl Marx and others).

Although they recognised the gravity of the main economic ideas in the classical texts, they thought of them as too bound up with politics, ideology and guesswork; features which precluded the development of a discipline as well behaved and professional as, say, physics. In a short space of time, academic economists like Alfred Marshall (1842–1924) and Léon Walras (1834–1910) (see box on p. 32) recalibrated economic theory to fit into the mould of natural science. By the turn of the century economics' main new feature was the extensive use of mathematics and the explicit attempt to rid economics of the politics, the passion and the philosophical wanderings which people like Smith, Ricardo and Marx had woven into it. Today we refer to the product of their labours as neoclassical economics. Modern textbooks attempt to convey competently a synopsis of those *neoclassical* efforts from the end of the nineteenth century to date.

Imagine now that it was you who had the job of reworking economic theory so that it comes to resemble physics rather than politics and philosophy. How would you go about doing it? Borrowing ideas from physics on how to construct a distinctly 'scientific' approach would be a good start. At that time the dominant physics' model was that of classical mechanics as conceived by Isaac Newton (1642–1727). To cut a long and glorious story very short, Newtonian classical mechanics comprised four steps. Starting with a decision on what the focus of study ought to be (i.e. objects with certain physical characteristics like mass, location, velocity and so on), physics founded its great theoretical breakthrough on certain assumptions concerning the way nature worked (i.e. the Laws of Nature).

A founder of neoclassical economics speaks out

As for those economists who do not know any mathematics . . . and yet have taken the stand that mathematics cannot possibly serve to elucidate economic principles, let them go their way repeating that 'human liberty will *never* allow itself to be cast into equations' or that 'mathematics ignores frictions which are *every-where* in social science' and other equally forceful and flowery phrases. They can never prevent the theory of the determination of prices under free competition from becoming a mathematical theory. Hence, they will always have to face the alternative either of steering clear of this discipline and consequently elaborating a theory of applied economics without recourse to a theory of pure economics or of tackling the problems of pure economics without the necessary equipment, thus producing not only very bad pure economics but also very bad mathematics.

Leon Walras, unpublished correspondence, 1900

And the first Professor of Economics at Cambridge offers a word of caution

Most economic phenomena 'do not lend themselves easily to math-ematical expression'. Economists must therefore guard against 'assigning wrong proportions to economic forces; those elements being most emphasised which lend themselves most easily to ana-lytical methods'.

Alfred Marshall, *Principles of Economics*, 1891

One of these assumptions is the *Principle of Energy Conservation* which, stated simply, suggests that energy is never born out of nothing and equally it never vanishes (this is why when a car crashes it explodes: kinetic energy does not evaporate but transforms itself into thermal energy). Notice how, at first, this is a theoretical proposition, an assumption. For all we know, it could be wrong. To find out more, physicists traced the repercussions of this assump-tion on the behaviour of the things it chose to study – of objects. They worked out mathematically what type of behaviour is compatible with the initial assumptions. For example they showed that for energy to be conserved the acceleration of an object subjected to some force must be a particular function of its mass and of the magnitude of that force. Finally, the time came where this whole model can be put to the test. If objects behaved in the laboratory according to the mathematical rules just derived, then the theory was to be accepted as true. Otherwise back to the drawing board. The question then becomes: how could we build an economic theory along these lines?

The structure of explanation in classical mechanics

Step 1   *Identify the focus of study*
Objects (e.g. atoms, molecules, electrons, a pendulum, etc.)
Step 2   *Articulate a grand theoretical assumption*
The *Principle of Energy Conservation* (i.e. energy neither vanishes into nothing nor is it born from nothing)
Step 3   *Describe mathematically the behaviour of our focus of study consistent with Step 2*
Mass = force times acceleration
(i.e. if a force is applied on some object, its acceleration will equal the ratio of its mass and the magnitude of the force)
Step 4   *Observe in the laboratory if actual objects behave according to Step 3*
If yes, accept the assumption in Step 2 and the theory in Step 3.

The structure of explanation in neoclassical economics

Step 1   *Identify the focus of study*
Decision makers (e.g. individuals, firms, organisations, governments, etc.)
Step 2   *Articulate a grand theoretical assumption*
The *Principle of Utility Maximisation* (i.e. decision makers strive to satisfy their preferences)
Step 3   *Describe mathematically the behaviour of our focus of study consistent with Step 2*
Marginal benefits = Marginal losses
(i.e. agents will do X until the last smidgen of X produces the same benefits as it does losses)
Step 4   *Use statistical methods (i.e. econometrics) to find out if Step 3 is correct*
If yes, accept the assumption in Step 2 and the theory in Step 3.

1.3.2 The rise of neoclassical economics: utility and the Equi-marginal Principle

If we were to follow in the footsteps of the physics method above, it is easy to see what the focus of study would be: just as natural science focuses on atoms, molecules and objects, the behaviour we will want to explain is that of individuals, firms and institutions (e.g. universities or government departments). That was easy. But then comes the difficult step. What assumption can we make that will be as all-encompassing in economics as Newton's Principle of Energy Conservation proved to be in physics?

Jeremy Bentham on the Utility Principle

Nature has placed mankind under the governance of two masters, pain and pleasure. It is for them alone to point out what we ought to do, as well as to determine what we shall do.

Jeremy Bentham, *An Introduction to the Principles of Morals and Legislation*, 1789

Imagine that while searching for an appropriate unifying principle for our new 'social physics', you stumbled on the quotation in the box. Notice how human motivation is reduced to a single dimension: positive energy (i.e. pleasure) or negative energy (i.e. pain = negative pleasure) with the former attracting and the latter repelling – pretty much like electricity. Well, is this not the basis for an ultra-simple, let us call it, Principle of Human Choice? Something like this: 'Do what gives you pleasure and avoid painful experiences.' If *all* experiences can be reduced to this uni-dimensional common currency by which all sorts of different experiences can be measured, then we can just argue that people always strive for more of this currency. Borrowing the term 'utility' from Jeremy Bentham you could then, at last, announce to the world your assumption: the *Principle of Utility Maximisation*.

What does this principle say? It states that people do what makes them happy and avoid doing unpleasant things; nothing spectacular but a start nevertheless. How can we take this further? Recalling that physicists moved from their assumption to a mathematical proposition on how nature works, our task is clear: we need a mathematical formulation of how human nature works in economic settings. A good strategy for making theoretical progress is through the resolution of paradoxes. Consider this paradox: if we value experiences or things, commodities, etc. because they give us pleasure, then why is it that, in contradistinction to all the rubbish we spend our money on usually, we are not prepared to pay a penny for the one 'thing' which gives us most pleasure: the air we breathe? Surely without it we are dead and one presumes that death will lose us many units of 'utility'.

Here is our first opportunity to create a logical/mathematical proposition stemming out of our *Principle of Utility Maximisation*: suppose we were to conclude that our propensity to pay for X depends not on the total amount of utility from having a quantity of X but, instead, on the increase in our utility following the acquisition of a little more X. This is simpler than it sounds. It states that even though the utility (or pleasure) we get from the surrounding air is enormous, if someone were to offer us a bit more air (in, say, some cylinder) we would have no use for it. Thus because the addition to our utility from a bit more air is zero (i.e. we have enough air as it is), we are not prepared to pay anything for this extra quantity of air. Perhaps unwittingly we have hit on our first mathematical principle: the economic value of X depends on the rate of change in our utility from X (and not from the total utility we enjoy).

To enhance the generality of this principle, suppose the question is: when should we stop 'acting' (e.g. jogging, drinking, consuming, producing, singing or whatever it is we do)? The answer is, *When the last thing we did* (e.g. the last step we took, the last house we viewed while house-hunting or the last banana we ate) *gave us as much utility as the utility that it cost us* (e.g. the pain from the last step, the cost of viewing that last house in terms of both money and extra fatigue, the cost of that banana). In the language of rates of change, *We should stop 'acting' when the rate of change in utility equals the rate of change in dis-utility* (or losses/cost). If we replace the unwieldy 'rate of change' with the term 'marginal', our grand theory can be expressed simply by the following dictum: Stop 'acting' when your marginal benefits from the 'activity' equals your marginal costs. From now on this will be known as the *Equi-marginal Principle*; a principle at the heart of neoclassical economics – which is also known, for obvious reasons, as *marginalist* economics.

To sum up, Step 2 of the new social physics (see box on p. 33) comprises the *Principle of Utility Maximisation* which yields a simple mathematical relation in Step 3 – the *Equi-marginal Principle*. Finally Step 4 involves the conjuring of statistical tests whose purpose is to emulate the physicist's laboratory and provide empirical proof of the theory's validity.

Alfred Marshall tries to steer a course between physics and history by turning to biology

Although the commitment of the first professional academic economists to a kind of social physics is indisputable, the first economics professor at Cambridge, Alfred Marshall, had his doubts about the wisdom of trying to model economics on physics. He thought that economics should aim at explanations somewhere in between, on the one hand, objective physics and, on the other, subjective historical studies. Indeed he thought that biology offers a good model for economics since economists, like biologists, try to understand the growth and development of 'organisations' (e.g. markets and companies seen as complex organisms). What impressed him most about biology was its view of the evolution of the individual and the group (or species) in response to changing conditions.

1.3.3 The imperialism of neoclassical (or marginalist) economics

Section 1.3.2 described how the *Equi-marginal Principle* purports to have the answer to all sorts of decisions economic and non-economic alike. It is easy to see why economists were overwhelmed by this approach. Not only did it promise to explain everything (i.e. all types of behaviour) but it did so in a fashion compatible with the scientific principles of Newtonian physics. At long last, a chance to be recognised as 'scientists' rather than as story-tellers. Once economics came under the spell of this approach (some time towards the end of the nineteenth century), it developed two tendencies. The first was to kill off the approach developed by the classical economists (e.g. Smith, Ricardo and Marx). The second was to start spreading into the other social sciences.

The first tendency (its disdain of classical economics) was responsible for a dramatic change of focus. Whereas the classics, starting with Adam Smith, were concerned with the big issues like capital accumulation, income distribution among the various social classes (i.e. capitalists, landowners, workers), the dynamics of capitalism (e.g. the succession of recessions and upturns), neoclassical economics changed all this. The reason is evident: with an exclusive focus on individuals, social classes ceased to exist in the eye of the theorist. People were simply distinguished along the lines of how much utility they ended up with and, thus, the concept of a capitalist or a worker was lost: everyone became an entrepreneur, a seller, a consumer. Each maximised utility the best they could. The only difference concerned what they sold (i.e. commodities or labour); a difference which is not significant enough to justify preserving social class as an analytical category.

Similarly, capital (whose accumulation was so central to the classical economists theories) also vanished from view. Whereas capital to the classics meant machines capable of physical production, in neoclassical theory the only thing that mattered was the production of utility. As long as utility was produced, it did not matter *how* it was produced: by a commodity manufactured in a factory brimming with technology or by a comedian who makes people laugh. In other words, the special place that machines had in Adam Smith's (but also Ricardo's and Marx's) theory is nowhere to be seen in neoclassical economics.

To summarise the first tendency of neoclassical (or marginalist) economics, its effect was to blur the concepts used by classical economists; to change the focus away from the big issues such as capital accumulation, income distribution, cycles and recessions etc. and redirect it to preference-driven individual behaviour. The result of this tendency was to turn economics from a grand, albeit speculative, narrative on the march of capitalism, to a professionalised attempt at creating a universal behavioural science (or social physics). Whereas the classical economists talked of growth and recession, income inequality and the economic role of the social classes, the neoclassical economist seemed happier to spend hours scrutinising small-scale phenomena (e.g. the fluctuations in the price of tea) and was, in general, content to trust that the market would take care of the big issues (e.g. growth and unemployment).

Economic expansionism

Gary Becker (b. 1930), a Nobel Prize winner in economics, wrote in his 1976 book *The Economic Approach to Human Behavior*: 'I have come to the position that the economic approach is a comprehensive one that is applicable to all human behavior, be it behavior involving prices or imputed shadow prices.' He reports that he 'applied the economic approach to fertility, education, the uses of time, crime, marriage, social interaction'. His critics acknowledge that such an application is straightforward. What they do doubt is whether it is interesting, let alone desirable.

Turning to its second tendency, neoclassical economics expanded its territory into the rest of the social sciences. It was inevitable. Since the *Equimarginal Principle* is meant as a general theory of rational behaviour, it was only a matter of time before some economist would claim that this economic approach has the key to all sorts of problems: from why political parties change their policy positions (they keep changing it as long as their marginal gains measured in votes equal their marginal losses) to why people marry (because the cost of considering *another* potential partner exceeds the expected benefits from doing so), it now seems that there is a single, simple principle which answers all questions concerning human behaviour. What a grand (or should I say grandiose?) claim!

Finally, history itself was not immune to the attentions of economists equipped with the *Equi-marginal Principle*. For if the latter was the kernel of all social truth, then why not use it to rethink history (e.g. reassess the historical ground covered earlier in Section 1.2.1). Indeed some influential economic historians rewrote the history of slavery, of feudalism and of the transition to capitalism utilising the method of neoclassical economics. For them, my claim at the outset of this chapter (namely that economics was useless prior to the emergence of market societies) must be false. Their point would be that if neoclassical economics can explain how past (pre-market) societies functioned and even changed (by utilising the *Equi-marginal Principle*) then it must have been quite useful (if not utterly desirable and, therefore, imaginably possible) back then. Are they right? Decide for yourself. Make sure however that you note one pivotal aspect of this argument: it presupposes that people behave according to *exactly* the same principles whether they live in a market society like today's or in a society which gives them no access to markets whatsoever (e.g. the slaves of ancient Egypt) or in largely non-market societies which do feature some marginal, epidermic market transactions. In a sense it assumes that there is no profound difference between societies with markets and market societies, thus making it possible to apply the same analysis to all types of societies at all times. This assumption, regardless of whether right or wrong, is quite revealing of what can be, not unfairly, termed the imperialism of neoclassical economics.

1.3.4 Economics and textbooks

The standard economics textbook is decidedly neoclassical (or marginalist). It explains the behaviour of consumers and firms, governments and trade unions, central banks and lazy bums by applying the same *Equi-marginal Principle*. This does not mean that all economists agree with the neoclassical turn. Indeed a large number do not. Some of the dissenters rely on the method of the classical economists, others espouse different perspectives (e.g. the so-called institutionalists who place a great deal of emphasis on the evolution of institutions in society). Since the emergence of neoclassical theory, its popularity has fluctuated depending on the two masters of economics: history and ideology. Given its natural tendency to look at the small picture while implicitly trusting the market to sort out the larger picture (or the macro-economy as it is called), neoclassical economics gains brownie points in periods of low unemployment and relative stability. But in periods when the market clearly fails to deliver the goods at a large scale (e.g. the late 1920s, 1930s and, increasingly, in the 1990s – at least in Europe, Canada and Australia), it becomes more vulnerable to alternative approaches. It was precisely during one of these periods (the 1930s) that economists like John Maynard Keynes removed economics from the neoclassical terrain and reinstated concepts and techniques dating back to classical economics; e.g. an interest in what happens when the economy is out of balance, a conviction that economies can remain imbalanced for long periods of time, the concept of an aggregate (or economy-wide) demand for commodities, involuntary unemployment, the emphasis on capital accumulation and the distribution of income in society.

In short, the fate of the neoclassical approach varies both with historical transformations and with the current ideological climate: the better disposed the world is towards free-market ideology the more revered the neoclassical approach. Nevertheless the profession as a whole, for better or for worse, has accepted that the first two years of undergraduate courses must be primarily neoclassical in content. The only difference between universities is the degree of enthusiasm or reluctance with which this is accepted. So, here you are: at the beginning of a perilous journey through the maze of economic models in your textbook. What can this little book do for you?

Two things, I hope. First, it reviews and highlights the central (neoclassical) economic concepts in economics textbooks. Without going over everything in detail, it focuses on those ideas which, if you understand well, will help you sail through the rest. Second, it returns some *control* back to the student of introductory economics. The point here is that your textbook looks very impressive and authoritative. Its glossy pages triumphantly announce the scientific answers to all sorts of economic problems. Indeed you will be excused if you feel overawed by this display of intellectual power. Economics will seem much bigger than you! However, on every glossy page, behind each pristine diagram, lies some fragile, and often dark, idea which is kept well hidden from the beginner's eye. Some of my colleagues think that you are not sophisticated enough to handle its fragility or darkness. I

Why should people study economics?

One popular answer is that it helps graduates get a job. Another is that it promises to help understand how society works. However, the best reason for studying economics which I can think of was given by Joan Robinson (Professor of Economics at Cambridge University in the 1960s and 1970s), 'The purpose of studying economics is to learn how not to be deceived by economists' (Basel Lecture, 1969).

think they are wrong. For if you are allowed to discover the dark and problematic stuff which lie behind the colourful curves, you will perhaps experience a sense of victory over the beast; feel like a kind of David who has the measure of this Goliath. This, I trust, will help you regain the *control* mentioned above. Who knows? You may even become fascinated with the subtext of economics. I suggest there is no better way of doing well in a subject than by becoming fascinated with it.

Summarising the main objective of the following chapters, economic ideas are playthings of history and ideology. Economic textbooks try to protect you from all this by filtering out all the ideology and by concentrating on the techniques. The price of this is that only a single version of the truth comes through. You are then asked to learn it. This book aims at putting you back in the driving seat from where *you* will choose which is the truth about the various economic concepts. To help you separate knowledge from ignorance for yourself, there is an urgent need to keep into perspective the ideology and history underpinning every economic theory. Part 1 begins with the economic theory of rational choices which lies at the heart of the economists' theory of behaviour. Like all the three parts that follow, its first chapter dispassionately reviews the material that you will find in any decent neoclassical textbook, its second chapter explains where the textbook's ideas came from (something that textbooks avoid doing) and the third chapter subjects these ideas to passionate criticism.

Consumption

choices

Review: textbooks on consumer and choice theory

2.1 The model of rational decisions

2.1.1 Instrumental rationality and the concept of equilibrium

Crazy people are a problem for the economist because their choices are mostly unpredictable. The same applies to unintelligent as well as to forgetful people. They often make choices which they regret and, therefore, choices they would happily reverse later given the chance. Thus they could act differently under precisely the same circumstances; a nightmare for someone (an economist?) who tries to devise a theory of choice.

It is therefore understandable why economists concentrate on what they call rational behaviour. Unlike psychologists who relish irrationality, inconsistency, phobias and other such manifestations of the complexity of the human condition, economists are eager to develop a model of rational women and men who act in their own best interest consistently. Not only does this dispense with the impossible task of building a rational theory of silly or mad choices (an obvious contradiction!) but also it precludes paternalistic conclusions (e.g. the theorist telling the individual: 'You wanted X when you should have wanted Y').

Of course economists recognise that people can and often do make mistakes which they regret later. Yet they would claim that, as a working assumption, it makes good sense to assume that people are the best judges of what is good for them and that, as a large group of people, society is best modelled in terms of a collection of individuals who act rationally (that is, their mistakes cancel out in the long run).

Economics and the logic of shopkeeping

People who live and work outside a market understand the meaning of the word 'reasonable' differently to those whose survival depends on succeeding in some market. The latter identify 'reasonable' or 'rational' with 'profitable' or 'effective'. The former (e.g. volunteers helping in a famine situation in Africa, school teachers, jobless single mothers, etc.) would probably come up with other synonyms to 'reasonable' or 'rational'; for example, with 'responsible', 'appropriate', 'intelligent', 'sympathetic', etc. Ever since most people (peasants, workers and bosses) were forced to enter some market (recall Chapter 1), the logic of the market has dominated all other types of logic. Economics, itself a product of the emergence of market society, assumes all people in all places and at all times to be 'reasonable' in the manner of Adam Smith's brewer, baker and butcher. The logic of *Homo economicus* is the logic of the shopkeeper.

Instrumental rationality defined

A person is instrumentally rational if she applies her resources efficiently in order to satisfy her preferences.

This assumption translates into a very simple notion of rationality: to be rational is to know how to use one's means in order to achieve one's ends. In other words, your *rationality* is an *instrument* which you apply in order to get what you want. And you are as rational as you are skilful in getting what you want by using whatever means at your disposal. In this sense the rational consumer is the one who gets the most satisfaction out of a given budget. On the other hand, you are deemed as less than rational if you have wasted opportunities to extract as much satisfaction as possible given your budget and the prices you have to pay. For example, if at the supermarket you can get more satisfaction at the end of the day not by spending more money but rather only by a mere rethink of what you put in the shopping trolley, then you are judged to be rational if you end up choosing the best possible combination of goodies.

Of course there is a catch. Even though it is true that simple solutions have a natural elegance about them, the economist's commitment to a simple theory in which the consumer always knows best (what is good for her) comes with a price: if for instance I start bashing my head against the wall maniacally, while simultaneously maintaining that this is what is good for me, you have no grounds for disputing this. Since rationality is defined here to be a mere instrument for satisfying the preferences, it cannot be used in order to assess them.

Nevertheless instrumental rationality is a founding assumption of mainstream (i.e. neoclassical) economics. Its central merit is that, in the hands of skilful economists, it can become the core of a complete theory of *equilibrium* in society. What is an equilibrium? A natural state of rest towards which a 'body' or 'system' tends. For instance, a rock tumbling down a hill is tending towards an equilibrium state. It will get to that equilibrium when it reaches a plain and comes to a standstill. This metaphor has always excited economists from Adam Smith onwards: the idea of an economic situation (or state) from which society does not have an incentive to move until disturbed. Just like the physicist who can describe fully the movement of the falling rock by reference to its tending toward a position of rest (that is, an *equilibrium*), economists became excited by the idea of describing changing prices, production, etc. in terms of a theory of how society is tending towards some economic equilibrium.

To see how *instrumental rationality* can help them forge that idea of an *economic equilibrium*, consider the following game that you may play with a group of friends: ask them to guess one number between 1 and 100. The one who is closest to one-half of the largest number chosen by anyone in the group wins a prize. So, if your six friends have chosen 50, 80, 40, 60, 30 and 100 respectively, then the one who chose 50 wins since the maximum is 100 and half of it is 50. Which number would you choose if you were asked to play this game and the prize were substantial, say $1000? The answer is that it depends on what you think the largest number chosen in the group will be. But then again, that (largest) number is also chosen by someone who is trying to guess the largest number exactly as you are. This is where *instrumental rationality* comes in and helps economists create an *equilibrium* theory of what will happen.

Clearly, everyone in your group will want to win the $1000 prize – this objective is given. If they are all instrumentally rational, each will try to imagine what the largest choice of someone else will be and will then select half that number (thus if you think the largest choice will be 80, you will choose 40). But if everyone is thinking like this (and is aware that this is how everyone else thinks), each will be constantly revising down their estimates of the largest number. Thus, eventually, people will select zero. This is the *equilibrium* of this game: each player selects zero which is equivalent to the rock coming to a stop when it reaches the plains and runs out of momentum.

Of course for this *equilibrium* to be reached not only must each player be *instrumentally rational* but also everyone must know that everyone else is thinking in the same way. You could be, for instance, fully instrumentally rational but not trust that everyone else is. Indeed you may think that some fool in your group will, without thinking of the rules of the game, select 100 simply because it is a round, big number. Then your best selection is 50, not zero. This is why economists have a more difficult job than physicists; unlike falling rocks and magnetic fields which have no thoughts to influence their behaviour, people's actions are determined totally by mental processes.

However, economists hope that experience irons these problems out and the theoretical equilibrium triumphs in the end. For example if our game is repeated, the person who chose 100 will immediately realise that it was a mistake to choose such a high number since no selection above 50 makes sense (recall that the prize is won by the person who selected a number half the magnitude of the largest; and since the largest possible number is 100, why choose a number above 50?). Thus the next time she plays this game, she will choose 50 at most. But then if 50 is the largest number chosen, she will again not win because the prize will go to the one who chose 25 (half the maximum) or some number close to 25. So, the third time someone plays this game, she will choose at most 25. And so on until, after a few rounds, all choices will *tend* to zero: the *equilibrium* choice to which *instrumentally rational* people will tend (even if they actually never reach it exactly).

This simple example illustrates the manner in which economists use the assumption that people are efficient (or learn to become efficient) in pursuing their objectives (that is, they are, or become, instrumentally rational) in order to create a theory of how groups of people behave and how that aggregate behaviour of groups can be understood in terms of some *equilibrium* towards which they are tending. In our little game your friends, motivated by the desire to win the prize, and assisted by their capacity to reason, will select increasingly smaller numbers. It is as if they are drawn to the equilibrium choice (zero). Similarly in markets: sellers and buyers alter their behaviour (e.g. produce more, buy less, etc.) in pursuit of greater utility or, equivalently, profit, and in so doing the prices and quantities of goods tend towards a market equilibrium. When the market arrives at that equilibrium, just like the tumbling rock at its position of rest, prices and quantities will stop changing and the market will stabilise.

In conclusion, economists believe that, unlike the natural world in which it is gravity and other laws of nature that cause equilibrium, in society it is the individuals' rationality that does the same trick. Neoclassical economists define rationality instrumentally (i.e. your rationality as an instrument for satisfying given objectives) and model the human decision maker as a creature who maximises utility.

2.1.2 Utility and the *Equi-marginal Principle*

Granted that rational people strive to satisfy their preferences the best way they can, how can we develop a precise theory of their behaviour? The answer was foreshadowed in Section 1.3.2: if you act in order to satisfy your preferences, each time you succeed in doing so, it is as if your well-being improves. Alternatively we could say that you got more satisfaction or, equivalently, that you derived more 'utility'.

Now, what is this 'utility'? One way of conceptualising it is to think that different experiences (e.g. consumption of commodities, enjoyment of a service, a piece of music, or even a toothache) give us different degrees of satisfaction, or utility. If utility is something we experience more of when our preferences are satisfied (and less of when they are thwarted), then suddenly we have a mathematical representation of instrumental rationality: to be instrumentally rational is to maximise one's utility.

However, economists these days are not too keen on this idea of utility as some inner psychological glow which we wish to get more of. They think that it trivialises their model of human nature and opens them up to many unnecessary criticisms (e.g. the criticism that they assume individuals as hedonic creatures incapable of appreciating the higher things in life). So instead of conceptualising utility as micro-joules of inner radiance, they ask us to think of it in terms of a catalogue of experiences or things we want, listed in order of preference with the most desirable outcome at the top and the most loathed one at the bottom. In this context, humans are assumed to want to move as high up towards the top of the list as they can. The higher they are on that list, the larger their utility (or satisfaction) index (notice that according to this interpretation nothing is said about warm feelings in the person's soul). Instrumental rationality then means that each will try to climb as high up, to achieve the greatest utility index; it becomes synonymous with *utility maximisation*.

Nevertheless and regardless of whether we think of utility as inner radiance or as an index of preference satisfaction, the calculus of choice remains the same: as explained briefly in Section 1.3.2, the concept of utility leads to a single unshakeable conclusion: those who always prefer more to less utility shall stop acting when the rate of change in utility equals the rate of change in dis-utility (i.e. the rate of utility losses). To demonstrate this, consider the following example.

Imagine you have to choose between different quantities of some 'experience'. The more you choose the more the utility that you derive. Unfortunately, each unit of this 'experience' comes at a cost. Assume that the data in Table 2.1a describe your situation accurately. How much is enough?

To motivate the question better, suppose that the 'experience' in question is jogging. Then the problem reduces to how many kilometres between 1 and 7 you want to run. The 'price' in this example is, not surprisingly, fatigue or pure muscular pain. You enjoy running in the park (witness the increasing utility from running) but the more you run the greater the accumulation of fatigue. Provided of course that the units of dis-utility (i.e. fatigue)

Table 2.1a Utility and dis-utility

Quantity chosen	Utility (e.g. pleasure)	Dis-utility (e.g. pain/cost)
1	10	2
2	18	4
3	22	6
4	25	8
5	25.5	10
6	24.5	12
7	21.5	14

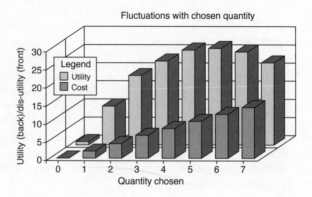

Figure 2.1a   Utility and dis-utility

are the same as the units of utility (i.e. pleasure), it is natural to presume that you will choose a distance that will maximise your overall pleasure (that is, pleasure minus pain).

Before moving on, it is helpful to ponder the shape of the utility function in Figure 2.1a: why does utility start falling after a while? The only explanation in this context is that after the fifth kilometre you are starting to get bored. In other words, even if you were experiencing no fatigue at all, you would still stop after the first five kilometres. In general, economists seem to believe that the utility from an 'experience' rises more slowly the more of it we have already had (e.g. the first glass of water when you are thirsty is always more enjoyable than the second even if you are thirsty enough to want a second glass.) Eventually we do not want more of that experience (e.g. we had enough of water) and then we stop. To demonstrate

Table 2.1b The calculus of pleasure

Quantity	Marginal utility	Marginal dis-utility	Net utility
1	10	2	8
2	8	2	14
3	4	2	16
4	3	2	17
5	0.5	2	15.5
6	−1	2	12.5
7	−3	2	7.5

very close to each other [handwritten annotation]

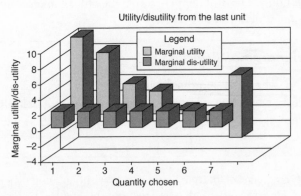

Figure 2.1b   The calculus of pleasure

this thought better, it helps to derive from Table 2.1a another table (Table 2.1b) depicting the *changes in utility* and *dis-utility*. We call the change in utility *marginal utility*; that is, utility at the margin.

In general, economists refer to the change in X as the marginal X – whatever X may be (i.e. utility, cost, revenue, etc.) Thus the change in utility due to the *last* unit of our 'experience' is called marginal utility. For example, the second kilometre you ran would increase your utility by 8 units from 10 to 18. However the sixth kilometre would reduce your utility (through boredom) by 1 unit and the seventh by an extra 3; we say that the marginal utility from the second, sixth and seventh kilometres is 8, −1 and −3 respectively.

Immediately we see that people who prefer more rather than less utility will certainly stop doing something (e.g. running, eating, resting, working) when the marginal utility becomes zero or, worse, when it becomes negative. Of course they may stop earlier if utility comes at a price. In the case of our jogging example, this 'price' is fatigue: every kilometre you run adds two units of tiredness to your overall level of fatigue. Which is the same as saying that your marginal dis-utility is 2 units regardless of how much you have run already. (Perhaps it would have been more realistic if the marginal dis–utility was also variable: e.g. the more you have run already, the greater the pain from that extra kilometre.)

Assuming that you want to maximise net utility (that is, utility minus fatigue), when do you stop? Do you stop after 1 km? Looking at Table 2.1b, we see that the second kilometre would contribute more to your utility (an extra 10 units) than to your fatigue/dis-utility (an extra 2 units). Thus you should run for at least 2 km. Should you run the third kilometre? Even though the extra utility you get from the third kilometre (8 units) is less than the utility from the second (which was 10), it is still more than the extra fatigue (2 units). Again you should go ahead. When should you stop? Clearly, when there is a danger that the extra kilometre will add more to your fatigue than to your utility. This will happen during the fifth kilometre which, clearly, you should not embark on.

The *Equi-marginal Principle*

Stop acting when the marginal utility (i.e. the contribution to utility from the last unit of activity) comes as close to (without being less than) the marginal dis-utility (i.e. the losses of utility following that last unit of activity).

In the language of marginal utilities, you should stop when marginal utility from the next kilometre that you will run threatens to be lower than the equivalent marginal dis-utility. Or, put simply, stop at about the quantity which equalises marginal utility to marginal dis-utility: the *Equi-marginal Principle*. (In our example, this principle advises you to stop jogging after 4 km.)

From *Instrumental Rationality* to the *Equi-marginal Principle*

According to instrumental rationality, the rational person chooses the quantity which best satisfies her preferences *all things considered* (e.g. cost, fatigue, etc). If preferences are translated into utility, to be instrumentally rational is to maximise utility subject to various constraints (e.g. fatigue, cost, etc.). And since utility is maximised when the Equi-marginal Principle is satisfied, the instrumentally rational person must always respect this principle.

Notice how the *Equi-marginal Principle* is no more than a truth of geometry: net utility is indeed maximised when marginal utility and marginal dis–utility are as close as possible. In Table 2.1b net utility reaches its maximum (17 units) at a distance of 4 kilometres at which marginal utility (3 units) is nearest to marginal dis–utility (2 units).

Of course this is not just a model of how to choose your optimal jogging distance. It applies generally to any situation in which you have to choose between different quantities of a single 'experience'. For instance, imagine that in order to quell your hunger you are picking berries while walking in the fields. At first you are really hungry and thus the first couple of berries prove highly satisfactory (Table 2.1a could apply here just as well). However, the more berries you pick the less 'utility' you get from the next one. Assuming that there is some fatigue involved in picking berries (let us say that it is fixed – as marginal dis-utility is in Table 2.1b), at some point you will come across a berry that will not be worth picking (in the context of Table 2.1a this will be the fifth berry).

Silly as it may sound, this is an economic proto–theory: a joint theory of production (picking berries) and consumption (eating them). Moving from this simplistic level to a more complex theory which involves money and other people is, for neoclassical economists, straightforward. To see how this transition to the market is accomplished, imagine for a moment that you are desperately thirsty and you are choosing how many glasses of orange juice you want to buy. Then the utility column could signify the amount of money you would be prepared to pay for the different quantities of juice. The fact that marginal utility is high for a single glass means that at the outset you are so thirsty that you would be prepared to pay up to $10 for the first glass (consult the marginal utility column of Table 2.1b).

However, once you have drunk the first glass, the second glass is worth less to you (i.e. $8 as you are less thirsty than before) and the third glass is worth even less ($4). Indeed after the fifth glass you are fed up with orange juice – you would not want to touch it even if it were free! (Actually the fact that marginal utility is negative means that you would need to be paid before you agreed to drink an extra glass.)

So, we see that if orange juice were free you would drink five glasses and then stop. But what if it cost $2 per glass? Then you would consume only four glasses. The reason is simple: how much money would you be prepared to pay for the fifth glass? Answer from Table 2.1b: 50 cents. Well, would it not be silly to then pay the $2 price? By contrast the fourth glass was a bargain (so to speak): you were willing to pay up to $3 for it when it sells for $2. Of course your best choice (of four glasses) does not exactly equalise marginal benefits and marginal losses (or marginal utility and marginal dis-utility). The reason is that you are not allowed to buy fractions of glasses. If you were allowed to pay by the gulp, then you would keep drinking until the last gulp made you as happy as it detracted from your happiness (due to its cost). Similarly in the jogging example, if you could choose to stop your run anywhere you wanted, you would choose to run

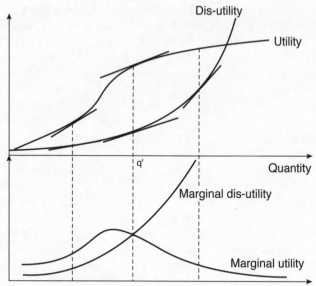

Figure 2.2   The geometry of the *Equi-marginal Principle*

more than 4 km but less than 5 km. Then the marginal utility would be *exactly* equal to marginal dis-utility.

Figure 2.2 offers a diagrammatic illustration of the *Equi-marginal Principle* in cases where you are allowed to choose fractions of units (i.e. you are not constrained to choose discrete quantities). Additionally it offers a general example by dropping the assumption of constant marginal dis-utility (notice how dis-utility rises faster the greater the quantity already experienced). Marginal utility (or dis-utility) being the rate of change in utility (or dis-utility) at different quantities, it can be defined geometrically as the slope of the utility (or dis-utility) curve. The second diagram traces the levels of marginal utility and dis-utility for different quantities.

It is easy to see that for quantities less than q', it makes sense to choose a greater quantity as utility rises faster than dis-utility (that is, marginal utility exceeds marginal dis-utility or, equivalently, the slope of the utility curve exceeds the slope of the dis-utility curve). Similarly, any quantity above q' represents a bad decision: notice that at q > q' utility increases more slowly than dis-utility and thus the last unit chosen must have added more to pain than to pleasure (i.e. it would not have been chosen by a rational person).

Lastly, observe the best choice which, quite naturally, corresponds to the *Equi-marginal Principle*: it is none other than quantity q' at which the distance between the two curves (utility and dis-utility) is maximum – that is, net utility is maximum. Notice also that at that point the slope of the two curves is the same. This is no accident: the vertical distance between two curves is greatest when their slope is equalised. Alternatively expressed, this means that at q' marginal utility (the slope, or rate of change, of utility) equals marginal dis-utility (the slope, or rate of change, of dis-utility). This is no more than a diagrammatic restatement of the *Equi-marginal Principle* demonstrating once more that net utility is maximised when marginal benefits equal marginal losses.

Question: Why do economics like to assume diminishing marginal utility?

Answer: The reason is that otherwise instrumentally rational people may start looking rather foolish!

Example: Suppose that the quantity in question is not glasses of orange juice but shots of whisky. Then it is possible to envision increasing marginal utility; that is, the more shots you already had, the happier the next shot will make you. In this case (as in all cases of increasing marginal utility), check for yourself that the Equi-marginal Principle recommends that you never stop drinking! In the end, either you run out of money or you will collapse – hardly an intelligent choice.

2.1.3 Consistent preferences as rationality

The *Equi-marginal Principle* can be extended to the case where a person has to choose among many different experiences (e.g. commodities at a super-market, types of music, running as opposed to playing tennis). Choosing one combination rather than another can be modelled in much the same way as above. Again the assumption is that an instrumentally rational person will always choose the combination of experiences which satisfies her preferences best (i.e. that maximises her net utility).

However, this time things are a bit more complex. Whereas in the case of a single experience (or commodity) it was easy to compare one option with another (e.g. it was not too demanding to ask whether you prefer one or two glasses of juice), with more than one experience things become trickier. Consider the case of someone who tells you that, in general, she prefers Mozart to Beethoven. Later on she lets it be known that if she had a choice between Beethoven's Fifth Symphony and a track by the grunge band Nirvana, she would much rather listen to Beethoven. Yet she confesses that when she looks at her Mozart collection and then glances at her Nirvana album, she ends up in a strange mood and plays the Nirvana CD. The question then is: assuming that you want to respect *her* preferences, what type of CD should you give her on her birthday?

The problem with your friend's preferences is that they are inconsistent: she prefers Mozart to Beethoven, Beethoven to Nirvana and Nirvana to Mozart. Do you buy Mozart (since she prefers him to Beethoven)? No, better buy her a Nirvana record. But does she not prefer Beethoven to Nirvana? Yet if you settle on Beethoven, why not buy her some Mozart? It turns out that if you try hard to satisfy the preferences (or maximise the utility) of a person with preferences of this sort, you will end up like a cat chasing its own tail. From a theoretical point of view this means that such preferences cannot produce any clearcut predictions about action (as in our example where it is impossible to know which particular record this person will buy given the opportunity to buy only one). Understandably therefore economists assume that rational people have consistent preferences: that when they prefer A to B and B to C that they will always also prefer A to C (we call these preferences *transitive*; notice that transitivity precludes the cyclical preferences of our example above).

The above paragraph helps to augment and clarify the definition of instrumental rationality. Accordingly a rational person satisfies her preferences efficiently; but in order for us to be able to know how she will act, her preferences must be consistent: if she prefers A to B she must *always* prefer A to B. And, as mentioned above, if she also prefers B to C, she cannot at the same time prefer C to A. Finally, if her preferences are to guide her choice in all cases, she must always have one: That is, given two alternative options A and B she must know whether she prefers A to B, B to A or whether she is indifferent between the two – put bluntly, she is not allowed to say: 'I am not sure what I want.' (Notice that the latter is not the same as saying: 'I am indifferent between the two.')

Now, it is obvious why economists make such demands of people's preferences: the simple reason is that otherwise their model of choice does not work! Thus it is advisable to lighten up about these requirements. If there are times when you are at a loss deciding whether you want to go to the theatre as opposed to going out to a restaurant, it does not mean that there is something wrong with you. Similarly, if your musical preferences turn out to be intransitive (i.e. cyclical as in the earlier example with Mozart, Beethoven and Nirvana), again this may be what makes you an interesting person. The only problem is that such interesting inconsistencies make the job of the economist who is trying to predict what you will *do* very difficult. But then again this is the economist's problem – not yours.

Nevertheless, there are many cases in which consistency matters. The box gives one example where a rational choice on which matters of life and death depend must be consistent. Economists make the assumption that all rational choices must be consistent. Even though, as we have seen, they make this assumption only because it suits their purposes, it is an appealing assumption at least for the purposes of building a theory of *rational* choices. They would argue that if a degree of inconsistency makes a person more

Instrumental rationality and consistency

Instrumental rationality demands that our choices are consistent with our preferences. Thus the same preferences must produce the same actions given the same information. In a study published in 1982 in the New England Journal of Medicine 247 people were asked the following hypothetical question: 'Which lung cancer treatment would you prefer, surgery or radiation, given the following data?'

- *Surgery*: Of 100 people having surgery, 90 live through the post-operative period, 68 are alive at the end of the first year and 34 are alive at the end of five years.
- *Radiation therapy*: Of 100 people having radiation therapy, all live through the treatment, 77 are alive at the end of one year and 22 are alive at the end of five years.

Of the 247 respondents only 18 per cent preferred radiation therapy. Then the researchers asked 336 people the same question only this time the data were presented as follows.

- *Surgery*: Of 100 people having surgery, 10 die during the post-operative period, 32 die by the end of the first year and 66 die by the end of five years.
- *Radiation therapy*: Of 100 people having radiation therapy, none dies during treatment, 23 die by the end of one year and 78 die by the end of five years.

This time 44 per cent chose radiation therapy. Since the data are identical, it seems that the way the data are framed (i.e. in terms of the survival or the death rate) makes a significant difference. Instrumental rationality insists (reasonably) that these differences are irrational and that a rational person should see through mere presentational differences. Preferences should be consistent regardless of presentation.

interesting, that is fine but not relevant to what they are attempting: they are trying to put together a model of how rational people act (not of what makes a person interesting). Let us follow them down this path.

How do we extend the *Equi-marginal Principle* (that is, the principle which guides instrumentally rational people) to decisions involving more than

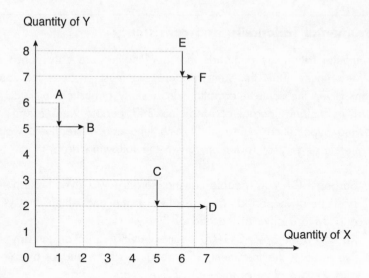

Figure 2.3   Trade-offs

one 'experience' (or commodity)? First we must capture the person's preferences in a manner similar to the single-'experience' case of Figures 2.1 and 2.2. Figure 2.3 does this in the case of two 'experiences': X and Y. Each point in Figure 2.3 corresponds to some combination of quantities of X and Y at your disposal. Let us begin with combination A which gives you 1 unit of X and 6 of Y.

Suppose now that you are about to lose 1 unit of Y – I am about to take it away from you (this would take you in the direction of the downward arrow). How would you respond if I were to tell you: 'OK, I know I upset you by reducing your Y from 6 to 5. I am willing to make amends. How much more of X would you want in order to be compensated for that loss of the 1 unit of Y?' You think about it and you reply: 'Give me an extra unit of X and we will call it quits.'

From this I surmise that you are indifferent between combinations A and B. Indeed if you feel compensated (yet not better off) after exchanging 1 unit of Y for 1 unit of X, then A and B must give you the same amount of utility. Now take my word that starting with combinations A, E and C I have drawn the arrows leaving these points such that the downward arrow always represents a loss of 1 unit of Y whereas the rightward arrow represents the amount of extra X necessary in order to compensate you in each of these three cases.

Hence if you are at A, as we have seen already, the loss of 1 unit of Y requires 1 extra unit of X if you are to be compensated. But when you begin with combination C, you grieve the loss of that 1 unit of Y more and thus you need 2 extra units of X to feel as happy as you did at C. (One plausible reason for this is that at C you started with less of Y than at A and therefore you missed that 1 unit more. See if you can link this to the notion of *diminishing marginal utility* in Section 2.2.) Finally, when at combination E, it seems you have quite a lot of Y to begin with (8 units to be precise) and therefore the loss of 1 unit of Y can be compensated with less than 1 extra unit of X (diminishing marginal utility again).

So far we know that you are *indifferent* between A and B, C and D and E and F. What we do not know is how you rate combinations A, C and E relative to each other. If you have told me that X and Y are 'experiences' (or, of course, commodities) which you actually like (and, consequently, which you prefer to have more of), it is clear that you must prefer E to A since combination E contains more of both X and Y than combination A. So far so good: we have established that you prefer either E or F to either A or B (since you are indifferent between A and B as well as between E and F).

Finally, suppose that you tell me the following: 'Come to think of it, I really do not care whether I have 2 units of X and 7 of Y or 6 units of X and 1 of Y. These two combinations would make me equally happy.' Well, now you are telling me a great deal. For it means that you are indifferent between combinations A and D. But I already know that you are indifferent between A and B as well as C and D. Clearly, if your preferences are consistent, you ought not to care as to whether you have access to combinations A, B, C or D! It is as if they are members of a set of combinations each capable of making you equally happy; that is, of giving you the same amount of utility. In Figure 2.4 this set is captured by the downward sloping line to which points A, B, C and D belong: we call this an *indifference curve* and it is defined as the collection of all combinations that generate exactly the same amount of preference-satisfaction or utility.

To summarise, combinations on a single indifference curve are equally desirable (e.g. you have already admitted that A, B, C and D appeal equally to you. And so do E and F). On the other hand, any combination lying above and to the right of an indifference curve must be more valuable to the person than any of the combinations of the indifference curve in question. So, for example, you must prefer E to A, B, C or D since E lies above and to the right of the indifference curve joining points A, B, C, and D. Let us now see how Figure 2.4 can help us extend the *Equi-marginal Principle* to the case of more than two experiences/commodities.

2.1.4 Extending the *Equi-marginal Principle*

Suppose you are at combination A. We have established that you would not mind exchanging 1 unit of Y for 1 of X. Suppose that Y is twice as

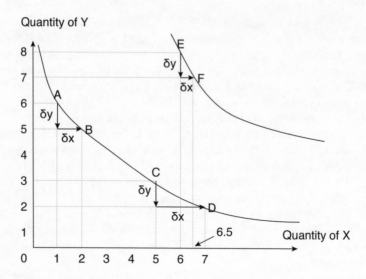

Figure 2.4   Indifference curves

dear as X; that is, the cost per unit (or price) of X relative to that of Y is 0.5. To be more precise, let me define the relative price of X and Y as the ratio between the price of X, p_x, and the price of Y, p_y. Thus the relative price $= p_x/p_y$. The question then becomes: *Is it instrumentally rational for you to purchase combination A?* The answer is negative. The reason, as we shall see below, is that if you spend your money on combination A, then you are not satisfying your preferences as well as you could have.

Consider this: suppose that after having bought 1 unit of X and 6 units of Y, you were to swap the sixth unit of Y for one unit of X. Would you mind doing so? Of course not, since effectively you would be going from point A to point B in Figure 2.4 – that is, you would get the same amount of satisfaction as before the swap (recall that A and B are on the same indifference curve). However, this swap would save you money since the unit of X you just acquired costs half the price of the unit of Y you gave up. Thus starting from A you can move to B and, while enjoying the same level of utility, save money. There is only one conclusion: combination A is not a terribly sensible choice since combination B is equally satisfying but costs less.

In general, notice that the rate at which substituting one unit of Y for extra units of X leaves you indifferent is given by the ratio $\delta y/\delta x$ which equals the change in Y divided by the small change in X which brought it about, e.g. at A this ratio is $1/1$; at C it is $1/2$; at E it is $(1/0.5) = 2$. We call this the *marginal rate of substitution*. When this rate is different from the ratio of prices, this disparity indicates that you have not made the best possible choice. In the case of point A, a relative price of 0.5 means that you can do better for yourself by moving to point B. Similarly, combination E is not a good idea if the relative price p_x/p_y equals 0.5: observe that starting at E, you would not mind swapping 1 unit of Y for half a unit of X (i.e. moving up to E). And since X is cheaper than Y, that extra 0.5 unit of X can be purchased for less than the one unit of Y you are giving up thus saving your money for the same utility; clearly you ought to abandon E. The question then is: *When is a combination a sensible choice?* And the answer: *When the marginal rate of substitution is as close as possible (ideally equal) to the relative price (or the ratio of prices).*

Opportunity cost and the marginal rate of substitution

Economists measure the cost of doing X not in terms of just how much money X costs but in terms of what you had to give up (other than money) in order to do X. Thus the opportunity cost of reading this book includes two things: (1) having to do without the item that you would have bought had you *not* purchased this book; (2) the benefit from doing something *other* than reading this book now. So, even of you borrowed this book from the library at no monetary cost, reading it involved an opportunity cost. This explains one of the most over-rated economic sayings: there is no such thing as a free lunch.

Notice how the marginal rate of substitution measures the opportunity cost of small amounts of 'experience'/commodity Y: it measures how much you value the loss of a small amount of Y in terms of extra quantities of X, that is the opportunity cost of that one unit of Y.

To see why this is so, consider combination C when the relative price p_x/p_y is 0.5. Again Y is twice as dear as X. Yet in this case, you would only be happy to give up 1 unit of Y if you were compensated by 2 extra units of X (i.e. going from C to D). However, notice that this would not constitute a saving: indeed moving from C to D does not make much sense since these combinations cost the same *and* are equally satisfying. You might as well stay with C. Geometrically speaking this is so because the relative price (i.e. the ratio of prices) is the same as the *marginal rate of substitution*.

Figures 2.5a, 2.5b and 2.5c illustrate geometrically. Each of the three cases examines if it makes sense to purchase combination A or not when the relative price of the two commodities is given by the slope of the straight line going through points A and D. To see why this line represents the relative price, if we start at point A it tells us that we can afford to give up AB units of Y (i.e. the commodity on the vertical axis) for BD extra units of X (the

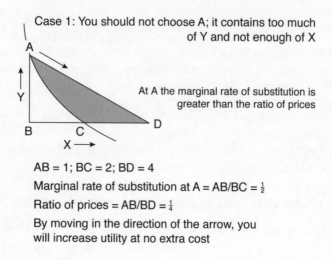

Case 1: You should not choose A; it contains too much
of Y and not enough of X

At A the marginal rate of substitution is
greater than the ratio of prices

AB = 1; BC = 2; BD = 4

Marginal rate of substitution at A = AB/BC = $\frac{1}{2}$

Ratio of prices = AB/BD = $\frac{1}{4}$

By moving in the direction of the arrow, you
will increase utility at no extra cost

Figure 2.5a   Not enough X

commodity on the horizontal axis). This is the same as saying that the price of X relative to the price of Y is AB/BD. The question then is: given that we *can*, would we *want* to give up AB units of Y for BD extra units of X?

In Case 1 (Figure 2.5a) you would not mind exchanging AB units of Y for BC units of X since points A and C lie on the same indifference curve. But we know that, were you to purchase AB less of Y, you could afford to get your hands on BD extra units of X – which gives you CD units of X more than the extra X you needed as compensation for the loss of the AB units of Y. Thus by making the move from point A to point D, you will be spending the same money for more utility than at A. Combination A cannot be such a good idea then.

Let us turn to Case 2 in Figure 2.5b. Would you want to be at combination A? No, because if you can afford point A you can also afford point D which corresponds to greater utility. To see this, notice that moving from A to D means forfeiting BA units of X in exchange for DB units of Y. However, the indifference curve tells us that the loss of BA units of X can be compensated fully by an extra CB units of Y. But at D you get, not only these CB extra units of Y, but also an additional CD units of Y; therefore you are *over*-compensated for the loss of BA units of A. In summary, you are better off making the move from A to D.

Finally, we have Case 3 in Figure 2.5c which illustrates an equilibrium choice; that is, a situation in which you have no reason to move away from point A. At last we have found one combination of quantities of X and Y which is OK! What makes it OK? Geometrically speaking, it is the fact that the indifference curve through point A does not cut across the relative price

Case 2: you should not choose A; it contains too little
of Y and too much of X

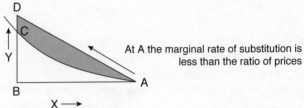

At A the marginal rate of substitution is
less than the ratio of prices

$AB = 3$; $BC = 1$; $BD = \frac{3}{2}$

Marginal rate of substitution at A = CB/BA = $\frac{1}{3}$

Ratio of prices = DB/BA = $\frac{1}{2}$

By moving in the direction of the arrow, you
will increase utility at no extra cost

Figure 2.5b   Not enough Y

Case 3: Stick to A; it is your best choice

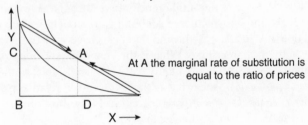

At A the marginal rate of substitution is
equal to the ratio of prices

$BC = 1$; $BD = \frac{3}{2}$

Marginal rate of substitution at A = CB/BD = $\frac{2}{3}$

Ratio of prices = CB/BD = $\frac{2}{3}$

There is no direction away from A which can increase
utility at no extra cost, i.e. along the relative price line

Figure 2.5c   Just right

line (as it did in Cases 1 and 2) but instead just touches it at point A. In
other words, the indifference curve and the relative price line share a single
point, a point of tangency, at A. This is why A cannot be improved upon
without extra expense: Whereas in Cases 1 and 2 (Figures 2.5a and 2.5b)
the indifference curve through A and the relative price line defined a
common area (see the shaded area in Figures 2.5a and 2.5b) full of points
that were cheaper than A (as they fell below the price line through A) but

also better than A (since they lay above the indifference curve through A), in Case 3 there is no such common area since A is the only common point between the two lines. This uniqueness of point A is the reason why it is the best choice.

Put differently, point A (being the point of tangency between the indifference curve and the relative price line) is characterised by an equality between the slope of the indifference curve and that of the relative price line. In economic terms this means that at point A the *marginal rate of substitution* equals *the ratio of prices*. It is when this equality holds, as it does at point A in Case 3, that the individual has reached her best choice.

The extension of the *Equi-marginal Principle* is now complete and answers the question: *when is a combination a sensible choice?* The answer is: *when the marginal rate of substitution is as close as possible (ideally equal) to the relative price (or the ratio of prices).*

To recap, we have seen how combination A is the ideal choice in Case 3. By contrast, combination A was not as appealing in Cases 1 and 2. Why? The answer we discovered was that, in Case 1, at combination A the relevant indifference curve is steeper than the relative price line. This meant that the ratio of prices was less than the marginal rate of substitution which meant that more X and less Y would engender more utility for no extra cost.

Similarly, in Case 2 the indifference curve through A was flatter than the relative price line (in which case A contains too much X and not enough Y). But at point A in Case 3 the indifference curve and the relative price line have exactly the same slope. What is the economic meaning of the slope of the indifference curve? From Figure 2.2 we know that it is the so-called *marginal rate of substitution*. And what is the slope of the relative price line? It is the *relative price (or the ratio of prices)* of course! The box on the next page summarises this extension of the *Equi-marginal Principle*.

2.1.5 From the *Equi-marginal Principle* to the theory of consumer demand

Generating a theory of consumer demand is now a procedural matter. What is the purpose of the theory of demand? It is to offer a relationship between the price of a commodity and the quantity of it that a consumer (or many consumers) will wish to buy. Let M be the total amount of money our consumer has set aside in order to purchase commodities X and Y. If their prices per unit are p_x and p_y then $M = p_x X + p_y Y$ (i.e. her expenditure on quantity X plus her expenditure on quantity Y must equal M). Rearranging, it transpires that $Y = M/p_y - (p_x/p_y)X$. (Notice how the slope of this line is, as was presumed in Figures 2.5a–c, equal to the relative price.) This equation forms the straight line AB in Figure 2.6 which contains all the combinations of X and Y that our consumer can afford: we call this line the consumer's

The *Equi-marginal Principle* extended

When a person chooses between different combinations of quantities of two experiences/commodities X and Y, the *Equi-marginal Principle* suggests that she opts for a combination such that *the ratio of the marginal utilities from Y and the marginal utility from X* equals *the ratio of the price of Y and the price of X*.

Quick proof: according to the *Equi-marginal Principle*, the best choice happens when the marginal rate of substitution equals the ratio of prices. However, the marginal rate of substitution at any combination (see Figure 2.4) is no more than the slope of the indifference curve through that point: $\delta y/\delta x$. At the best choice available to this person (e.g. point A in Figure 2.5c), $\delta y/\delta x = p_y/p_x$. However, recall that we defined marginal utility from X and Y as the rate of change in utility, say U, subject to changes in the quantities of X and Y respectively: $\delta U/\delta x$ and $\delta U/\delta y$. Dividing one by the other we get $\delta U/\delta x / \delta U/\delta y = \delta y/\delta x$. Thus the marginal rate of substitution is equal to the ratio of the marginal utilities and, hence, the *Equi-marginal Principle* can be expressed as follows:

> When there are more than one experience/commodity to choose from: choose the combination of quantities that sets the ratio of marginal utilities equal to the ratio of marginal dis-utilities (or prices).

Compare this to the situation in Section 2.1.2 in which a person chooses between different quantities of a single experience/quantity X.

> The *Equi-marginal Principle* when there is only one experience/commodity X: choose the quantity of X that sets the marginal utility from X equal to the marginal dis-utility from X (or the price of X).

It is evident that the Principle has not changed significantly when we moved from one to two experiences/commodities. Indeed it is applicable regardless of how many different quantities we have to choose.

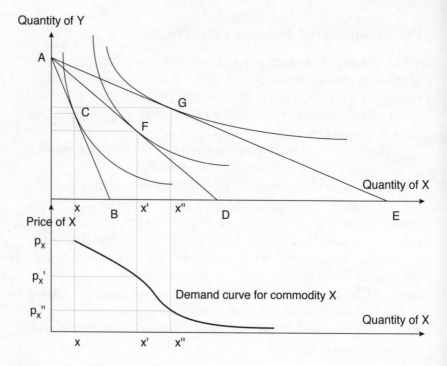

Figure 2.6   The birth of a demand curve

budget constraint. According to the *Equi-marginal Principle* developed above, the best choice on this line is point C – since it is the point of tangency between budget constraint AB and one of the indifference curves. How much of X does she want to buy given these prices and available money M? Answer: x units corresponding to point C of her budget constraint AB.

Suppose now that the price of X declines from p_x to p'_x and then to p''_x. This will reduce the slope of the constraint such that it rotates from position AB to AD and then to AE (corresponding to prices p'_x and p''_x respectively). Then the best combinations become F and G respectively and the level of demand for X increases from x to x' and then to x''. Hence, we end up with three prices and three levels of demand for X by our consumer. Putting these combinations together into one diagram (see the lower part of Figure 2.6) completes our derivation of the demand curve for X.

In conclusion the derivation of demand curves is the result of a simple application of the *Equi-marginal Principle*. Once the latter is understood, the theory of demand follows naturally. Figure 2.6 shows how the demand of one person is constructed. The next step is to add different people's demands for X to get the overall demand curve for X. If you can add horizontally two or more curves, this aggregation is straightforward.

So, what was all this fuss about? Did we need to go through all this in order to conclude that demand curves are downward sloping and reflect people's preferences (i.e. the location and the slope of indifference curves), the prices of other commodities (e.g. Y) and how much money the consumer intends to spend? True, we sort of knew all these things before. However, what we did not have prior to this analysis is a complete story of how the attempt to satisfy preferences as best as one's resources will allow culminates into *particular* decisions (e.g. the decision to purchase x units of X). Once this model (or story) is in place, all manner of extensions (some of which we could not have thought of without the above theory) become possible. The economist's justification for having put us through all this is that, with all these esoteric diagrams behind us, we can now present to the world a unifying theory of all human behaviour! (Could this be true? Read on!)

Demand curves: the economist's illusory friend

The problem with demand curves is that they are figments of the economists' imagination. In reality they are nowhere to be found! This is why: look again at Figure 2.6 in which we derived the demand for X. To do this we assumed that the only thing that changes is the price of X (this is why the budget constraint rotated). All other things must remain the same (*ceteris paribus*, i.e. other things being equal, as the Latins used to say.)

The reason for this assumption is that unless other things (like the price of Y, money available and preferences) remain the same, we will not be able to trace the demand for X the way we did. To illustrate this point, look at what happens to the demand for commodity Y as the price of X changes: it also changes even though the price of Y remains fixed. So the only way we could have traced (the way we did) the demand for X is by assuming everything, with the exception of the price of X, to remain constant.

Of course in real life, all the 'other things' have a bad habit of refusing to remain constant: prices of other goods change, people's income fluctuates and, notoriously, so do their preferences. Thus the only part of the demand curve of a certain commodity which might be observed is a single point: the current combination of price and quantity. The rest of the demand curve is in the economist's imagination.

2.2 Towards a general theory of choice: the *Equi-marginal Principle* becomes ambitious

Having manufactured an explanation of when people stop running, of how many bananas they buy, of why they may decide to skip a theatrical performance in order to go to the movies instead . . . and so on, neoclassical economists realised that a grandiose claim was in their reach: their *Equi-marginal Principle* could be the basis for explaining every human action. As with all grand theoretical statements, this one required a leap of the imagination that some were happy to make while others poured scorn over. On the one hand, such great expectations of theoretical enlightenment stemming from the *Equi-marginal Principle* helped economists cultivate an image for economics as the queen of the social sciences. On the other hand, these very claims also provided potent ammunition to those who thought of the whole affair as a farce.

Four examples are given below of how economists attempted to take the *Equi-marginal Principle* beyond the mundane (i.e. beyond a theory of how consumers select the combination of commodities in their shopping trolley). Each example is followed by brief notes on the type of criticism that such extensions of the Principle incite.

2.2.1 Gathering information

In our uncertain world of ever-changing prices, images, commodities, incomes, and even preferences, a theory which assumes that you know everything you need to know prior to making a choice seems absurd. Yet in our explorations of the *Equi-marginal Principle* so far this is precisely what we were asked to assume: that we know exactly how much utility and dis-utility (e.g. pain, cost, fatigue, prices, etc.) to anticipate from each available option. Unless economists can demonstrate that their Principle survives an attack of uncertainty, that it can still guide us when we are lashed by waves of ignorance about important aspects of our choice, they will not have convinced us about their theory's generality.

Aware of this task, neoclassical economists tried to respond. And they responded in a marvellously creative manner: they actually showed that the best strategy for dealing with uncertainty is to utilise the *Equi-marginal Principle* itself. What a master-stroke: in an attempt to convince that the Principle is not rendered useless in the presence of uncertainty, they turned the criticism on its head claiming that uncertainty is best dealt with by utilising this very Principle!

The argument runs like this: when in the clasps of uncertainty, it becomes hard to know which is the best choice. The more information you

> ## Why do people marry?
>
> According to a Nobel Prize winner in economics, Gary Becker, they do because they have found some person whom they think of as an acceptable partner. In other words, they decide to stop looking because they do not think that continuing the search is worth their while. The theoretical reason must be, our eminent economist continues, that they expect the extra utility from seeking more information (e.g. by going on yet another date) to be no larger than the dis-utility from that continuing search (e.g. the extra expense, probability of being disappointed, etc.).
>
> As the philosopher Martin Hollis has commented on this train of thought, if this is how people look for partners, good luck to them: they need it quite badly!

can gather, the higher the quality of your choice; it is as if uncertainty is like a mist engulfing you while information helps lift this mist and thus assists you in seeing more clearly the path ahead. The problem of course is that information costs. Then the question becomes: how much information should you try to gather before making a decision?

Not surprisingly, the economist's answer is: use the *Equi-marginal Principle* to find out how much information is enough (or, equivalently, to decide when to stop looking). Looking back at the original formulation of the Principle, the answer must be: stop looking when the marginal utility from looking equals the marginal dis-utility (or cost) of search.

For example, imagine you have just moved into a new area and that you are looking for a house to buy. At first you have very little information on which to base an informed choice. So, you do the obvious: you visit one estate agent after another and you inspect one house after another. When do you stop? The problem is that even if you find a house that you really like, there is always a chance that the next house you will view will be as nice (if not nicer) and will cost less. But this is recipe for exhaustion, if not for perpetual indecision. There comes a time when you must decide to stop. (Remember that a decision to act must be preceded by a decision to stop thinking about it!) When is it a good idea to stop?

The *Equi-marginal Principle* suggests that you will stop when the last house you viewed gave you information whose utility (or value) to you is equal to the dis-utility of having inspected that house (i.e. the cost of going to see another house, the inconvenience, as well as all your valuation of your time). As long as you expect that the utility from the information the next house you are about to have a look at will exceed the dis-utility from that visit, you should see the next house. Otherwise stop!

Criticism

The problem with this analysis is that it makes a highly controversial assumption: That even before viewing the next house on your list, you know *exactly* how much utility to expect *on average* from the information you will get from this visit. But how can you know this before you see the house? When do you stop gathering information whose purpose is to help you decide when you should stop searching?

Critics of this extension of the Principle point out that information is not like other commodities. With other commodities (like coffee and bananas) you have a fair idea of how satisfactory an extra quantity of them will turn out to be. With information, however, things are different. Information is more like wisdom and less like some commodity: you cannot know its value (not even have a good estimate of it) until you have it – see the box.

Wisdom and information

Myth has it that a Roman centurion named Tarquinius Superbus was offered by Sibyl of Cumae the Nine Books containing all human wisdom. Because of the high price demanded, Tarquinius declined. But then Sibyl had three of them burnt right in front of his eyes and proceeded to offer him the remaining volumes for the same price. Again he refused. She kept up her strategy: another three volumes were burnt and the remaining three were offered for sale at the original price. Tarquinius succumbed and paid for the remaining volumes what Sibyl had initially requested for all nine. Apparently it turned out to be an excellent buy.

Can you explain his decision? The *Equi-marginal Principle* cannot!

2.2.2 From demand to supply: time and the supply of savings

Another criticism of the theory which readily comes to mind is that it does not make allowances for time. Decisions so far have been instantaneous choices which affect the person immediately and which have no long-term effect. It is as if time is standing still and, in a single leap, the person jumps on to the highest level of preference-satisfaction allowed by her resources and circumstances. Of course reality is not like that. Decisions we make now affect not only our current self but also our future selves. Time waits for no one and, even more crucially for the economist's neoclassical theory of choice, it makes decisions which look straightforward in the short run look terribly complex once the long-term effects are considered. To make this point sharply, imagine how the behaviour of people around you would change if it became known that the world would end tomorrow.

Predictably neoclassical economists claim to have the measure of this problem. They ask: if one wants to satisfy contemporary preferences but also cares about future preferences, what is there to stop us from thinking of this as the larger decision problem of how best to satisfy current and future preferences? Indeed. Let us see precisely how they attack this larger problem. Suppose your grandmother gives you $1000 on your birthday. You can go to the shops and spend it all at once, or you can put it in the bank so that it accumulates interest, or you can do something in between (e.g. spend $400 now and save the rest).

But why would you ever save money? The answer consistent with our notion of instrumental rationality is that, in addition to wanting to satisfy your current preferences, you also predict that you will have preferences next year in need of satisfaction. Moreover the thought of preference-satisfaction in the future, gives you utility now. Put differently, you currently have a preference for satisfying future preferences. This preference over current and future preferences (a kind of meta-preference as philosophers would put it) is the reason why it may be instrumentally rational to save part of your granny's $1000.

Exactly how much you will save depends on two things: first, it depends on how much weight you attach to your immediate preferences relative to your future preferences. That is, on how much you care *today* about your future well-being. Naturally the greater your concern about your future self, the more you will save today. And vice versa. (Thus the claim that saving is an act of altruism towards your future self!) Second, it depends on the rate of interest: the higher the interest rate, the more money you will have in the future for each dollar that you choose *not* to spend today.

How can the *Equi-marginal Principle* help point out the right amount to save? Well, the first determinant of your choice in the last paragraph boils down to your preferences between utility today and utility next year. Recall that Figure 2.4 was constructed such that indifference curves capture your preferences over two 'experiences': X and Y. Of course in the simplest of cases, X and Y are of the form: X = experience of eating bananas; Y = experience of drinking glasses of wine. However, there is nothing stopping us from visualising X and Y in a broader sense. For example, there is no reason why we cannot set: X = experience of satisfying my current preferences; Y = experience of setting money aside in order to satisfy my preferences next year. As long as X and Y give you utility overall *now* (even if it is due to the anticipation of future utility) we can reasonably assume that you are trying to climb from a lower current to a higher current indifference curve (see Figure 2.4 and then Figure 2.7 for this reinterpretation).

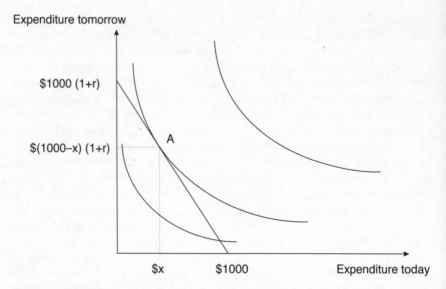

Optimal saving/expenditure: spend $x now and save $(1000–x).
Next year's expenditure = $(1000–x) (1+r) where r = interest rate

Figure 2.7   Savings as the result of current enjoyment of the anticipation of future expenditure

What does the *Equi-marginal Principle* suggest you do? It suggests that you choose a combination of X and Y (that is, of preference satisfaction now and preference satisfaction next year), such that the *marginal rate of substitution* (i.e. the slope of your indifference curves) equals the *relative price* (i.e. the ratio of prices). What is this relative price here? Can we talk meaningfully about the price of expenditure today relative to expenditure next year? Actually we can. Figure 2.7 shows how.

Let the rate of interest be r = 0.1 or 10%. This means that for every dollar that you save today (i.e. for every dollar of forgone expenditure today), you will receive $1.10 next year. Phrased differently, a 10% interest rate means that the 'price' (or opportunity cost) of spending $1 today is that you cannot spend $1.10 next year; it is what you give up next year in order to spend $1 now. In general, if the interest rate is given by r, then the price of $1 expenditure today would be exactly $(1 + r) expenditure tomorrow.

Thus the relative price of expenditure tomorrow relative to expenditure today equals $(1 + r)/$1 = $(1 + r). We have now reached the solution to our problem: today you should spend a portion of the $1000 such that the slope of the indifference curve equals the relative price (1 + r) – e.g. point A in Figure 2.7. Put differently, you choose a level of savings such that the ratio of the marginal utilities from expenditure tomorrow and expenditure today equals 1 plus the rate of interest.

Preferences across time and the marginal rate of substitution

What is the precise meaning of the marginal rate of substitution in this case where the person derives utility both from utility gained now and from the thought of future utility? It is the ratio of the additions to overall utility from a bit more of utility (or expenditure) now and the additions to overall utility from the thought of a bit more utility (or expenditure) in the future.

Criticism

In order to work as neatly as it does in Figure 2.7, the theory must assume that you know two things *in advance*. The first is the rate of interest (r) which will prevail throughout the year. However, in reality you are unlikely to have this information. The economist's response here is that, if uncertain, you will form subjective estimates in your mind concerning the average level of interest and then act on the basis of this prediction. And if you want to make a more informed choice, use the *Equi-marginal Principle* as outlined in Section 2.2.1 (of course then they will have to contend with the criticism in that section). There is, however, the second, infinitely more demanding, assumption: that you know in advance not only what preferences you will have next year but also *exactly* how to weigh current relative to future preferences. So, what's wrong with this?

   Nothing, if you happen to think that wise choices over time are all about behaving in a manner consistent with the emphasis one has placed on current satisfaction as compared with the emphasis on future benefits. By contrast, it is an unacceptable theory if you happen to be one of these people who feel that the mark of the wise person has nothing to do with a capacity to be a slave to one's current relative valuation of future happiness; for them, the genuinely intelligent person is the one that has the capacity to *ignore* the valuation of future utility as formulated by one's present self. These people, understandably, do not think much of this version of the *Equi-marginal Principle*. (If this sounds complicated, a more detailed explanation follows in Chapter 4.)

2.2.3 From demand to supply: the decision to sell one's labour

This extension in utterly undemanding. Just think of utility-generating experiences X and Y as 'income' and 'leisure' respectively. The slope of the

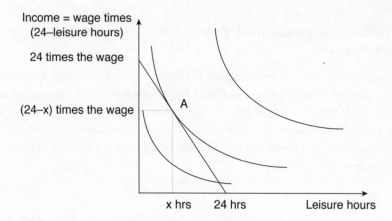

Optimal working hours = 24 minus x
Income = (24 minus x) times the wage

Figure 2.8   Choosing to labour

indifference curves in Figure 2.8 then reflect the person's preferences between having the capacity to buy things and having the opportunity to rest, or do some painting, write poetry and so on. Finally, the price of leisure relative to income is determined by the wage. If the offered wage is $10 per hour, the cost (in terms of foregone income) of 1 hour extra leisure is $10. Thus the relative price in this case *is* the hourly wage rate.

In summary, if you have a choice as to how many hours you want to work given the wage rate, the *Equi-marginal Principle* invites you to choose a number of hours (i.e. a quantity of labour supply) such that the wage (the relative price) equals the ratio of marginal utility from money (or income) and marginal utility from leisure – for example, point A in Figure 2.8.

Criticism

In real life, workers seldom have a choice as to how many hours they will work. If they are lucky (especially in regions or times of high unemployment), they are offered work at fixed working hours on a take-it-or-leave-it basis. Consequently the analysis of Figure 2.8 seems like a better description of a self-employed person's than a worker's decision problem.

A second criticism is that, behind its geometry, this model presumes that leisure generates utility and work dis-utility. Therefore the only reason people work is for the money. This ignores the fact that work is for most people more than a means of earning a living: even if money is the primary goal, work is also the source of self-esteem, social location, a chance to be creative and autonomous. The *Equi-marginal Principle*, at least in this guise, is too primitive a tool for the purposes of incorporating these thoughts within an explanation of labour supply decisions.

2.2.4 The valuation of life

It sounds ridiculous but what would you say were I to ask you: 'How much money do you want in order to let me kill you?' In other words, what is your monetary valuation of your life? You would most probably, and legitimately, instruct me to get lost. Nevertheless this is not as absurd a question as it seems. Indeed government departments confront it every day.

Imagine for instance that as the Minister for Health one of your advisers tells you that equipping hospitals with a new piece of machinery will help them save on average one life every financial year. Should you authorise the necessary funding? Well, it depends on the extent of the funding. If this machinery cost, say, $100 per hospital it would be criminally negligent of you to refuse. What if, on the other hand, it cost $1,000 million? Surely there is a cut off price beyond which you will have to say that society will not bear the cost of saving that one life. Yet finding out that cut-off point is the equivalent to answering the original question: what is the monetary value of a human life?

This is a question which is impossible to answer in cold blood. Although it is hard to imagine, neoclassical economists have suggested that we use their old workhorse, the *Equi-marginal Principle*, in order to answer the question. They point out that value is elusive when human life is concerned. For example, recall how in Section 1.3.2 the question of the economic value of air was tackled: it was answered by pointing out that, even though the total utility from air is infinite (i.e. equal to the value of human life), its economic value is zero because the marginal utility of air is zero; that is, the value of an extra small amount of air is zero. If we are now to value human life by means of the same principle, we need to value a small portion of life; to slice life up into tiny components and ask how much each one of them is valued.

Fear not however! We are not about to suggest that people should be sliced into tiny bits which are to be valued separately. Thankfully we can achieve the same end conceptually and without resorting to cruelty. Suppose that our community comprises 10 million people. Each one is asked the following question:

Imagine that for one day the probability that you will die increases from whatever level it is at by 1 chance in 10 million. Would you consent to this happening provided this tiny extra chance of dying applied for only 24 hours?

Valuing thy neighbour's life with the *Equi-marginal Principle*

The Principle shows how our economic evaluation of any commodity or experience does not depend on how happy it makes us. Instead it depends on how happy the last bit of it made us (that is, it is marginal utility which determines value, not total utility).

When assessing the economic value of a human life, the Principle works in the same way. The value of our neighbour's life is not to be measured as a whole. Rather we are encouraged to seek out the economic value of a tiny part of human life – e.g. of an extra small chance of survival or death. Given that valuation by each one of us, it is only a matter of arithmetic to sum them up into the community's valuation of our neighbour's life.

Of course the answer would be negative. However tiny an extra chance of dying, no one wants it. However, what if the government offered people money in order to accept that extra risk of dying? Would you consent in exchange of, say, $10 cash? After all it is only a tiny, a minuscule, a microscopic chance that you are taking – less risky than crossing the road to buy a newspaper. For the sake of argument, suppose that the offer is accepted universally. Then, according to neoclassical economists, we will have concluded that the community believes a human life to be worth 100 million dollars!

To see how this valuation obtained, recall that each person accepted $10 for an extra 1 in 10 million chance of death. Overall this would have cost the government $10 times 10 million people = $100 million. Seen from a slightly different perspective, the community *consented to one extra death* than would have normally occurred *in exchange of $100 million*. Why?

Because when we all agreed that the probability of death for each one of us would increase by 1 in 10 million, we effectively agreed that, on average, during this 24 hour period, one person will die in our midst (remember there are 10 million of us) as a result of our collective decision. The pieces of silver we collected in order to consent to this amounted to a total sum of $100 million. Neoclassical economists conclude that this must be the dollar value we, as a community, subconsciously think a person's life is worth. The trick that prised this valuation from us was that we were not informed in advance of which one of us will die.

Criticism

Setting aside the obvious ingenuity of this theoretical suggestion, one cannot but be frightened by the proposed procedure. Is this merely an irrational fear (similar to the well-documented aversion by lay-persons of all scientific discoveries), or is there something more to it in this case? To show that there is, think of what will happen if many of our fellow citizens develop a gambling disposition. For example, what if they were to accept the increased risk for less money; say, for $5. Then the community's valuation of life would diminish. Do we want a situation where the value of life is deemed lower the greater the proportion of gamblers in the population?

More generally, some object most strongly to any attempt at valuing life on the basis of the subjective views of the community's members. Surely, they would argue, not all views should be weighed equally. For example, my racist neighbour's views, who loudly proclaims that ethnic minorities should be exterminated, ought to be excluded from any exercise in assessing the community's value of human life.

2.3 Summary: from instrumental rationality to an economic theory of choices

Undoubtedly the greatest transition in economic thinking took place during the second part of the nineteenth century with the emergence of neoclassical (or marginalist) economics. Modern economic textbooks are the last link in the chain reaction which started back then. This chapter presented the essence of the marginalist approach. Starting at the beginning (that is, the assumption that people are instrumentally rational), it developed the central proposition of neoclassical economics: the *Equi-marginal Principle*. It then put it to work in various contexts.

Once the algebra and geometry of this principle were established, four examples were given of how one can try to explain all sorts of human choices ranging from saving to putting a money value on to human beings. However, with every extension of the theory, potential criticisms began to make their presence felt. This is hardly surprising. Humanity has been debating the essence of wisdom and the good life since time immemorial. It would be puzzling if a theory which claims to hold the key to rational human choices were to escape these ancient debates. Whereas economics textbooks try hard to avoid these controversies, the basic premise of this book is that immersing ourselves in these debates helps us understand better the capabilities as well as the limitations of economics. With this thought in mind, Chapter 3 traces the history of the neoclassical theory of choice. Finally, Chapter 4 puts it in the spotlight: do we really behave according to the *Equi-marginal Principle*? Moreover, should we?

History of textbook models

The roots of utility maximisation

3.1 Tracing the origins of utility maximisation

3.1.1 A short history of self-interest and instrumental rationality

---

Socrates and Sartre on ourselves and other people

Socrates (470–399 BC) argued that other people are the true judges of the way we live our life. Thus he thought it imperative that, before acting, we ought to envision our actions through others' eyes. Whether an action satisfies us or not is not *that* central. 'The unexamined life is not worth living,' he insisted (see Plato's *Apology*).

The French philosopher Jean Paul Sartre (1905–80) agreed that we can know ourselves only through others. He went as far as to claim that the only way of truly knowing who we are and what we *really* want is to attend our own funeral and listen to our obituary. He also thought that: 'Hell is other people.'

Utility maximisation is founded on the idea that people care ultimately about themselves. Who would disagree with that? But what does it mean to 'care about one's self'? For economists it means to be preoccupied by an unwavering pursuit of preference-satisfaction. However this notion of good living is not universal. The ancient Greek philosophers also thought that people aimed at living well but they had a slightly different perspective on what this meant. Socrates, for example, asked: how should we live?

He suggested that our goal ought to be a successful life. Nevertheless he did not think that we are capable of knowing how to do so unaided. The implication here is that living a successful existence is more complicated than satisfying our own desires. And if our current desires are not the best guide to clever action, we need to reflect, to reason, to examine and re-examine both our deeds and our motives.

Times changed however and the inquisitive spirit of the Greek philosophers became a distant memory during the Middle Ages. For centuries people were forced to have faith without inquiring into the makings of a good life; they were even told that wishing for the good life in this world was sinful. That pain and suffering in this world, in the context of absolute obedience to king and bishop, were essential for a successful afterlife. Naturally as the dark clouds of the Middle Ages began to lift, the winds of change caused a loosening of feudal authority (recall Chapter 1) and empowered the merchant classes of Europe and North America to celebrate a new-found belief in their right to be happy. Thus the notion of a market in which one pursues profit was associated with the notion of the freedom to be unapologetically happy. Moreover the accumulation of merchant, and later capitalist, wealth meant that this increasingly dominant social class were acquiring a taste for not only the right to happiness but also the economic and, therefore, the political power to exercise it. The American Constitution, with its explicit recognition of the citizens' right to pursue happiness, offers a poignant historical record of the rise of self-interest from the category of sins to which the feudal era had confined it.

Wanting to be happy thus emerged as a perfectly defensible philosophical ambition. In historical terms, it surfaced as part of the same ground-swell which produced the logic of the market, the steam engine but also the notion of people as citizens (as opposed to mere subjects): the emergence of the industrial, capitalist, society – recall Section 1.2. In Britain, the birthplace of market societies, the first influential writer to have revived the idea of the person as a sovereign individual, and therefore a precursor of modern utilitarianism, was Thomas Hobbes (1588–1679). In an attempt to justify the power of the State (or of the monarch), Hobbes wrote matter-of-factly about the selfishness of humans; of how they always strive to fulfil their desires even if this means brutally harming others. In this bleak narrative, people living outside a State (in a *state of nature*, as he called it) would be engaged in a 'war of all against all' and thus life would be, in Hobbes' own words, 'solitary, poor, nasty, brutish and short' (quoted from his major book *Leviathan*, 1651).

Thomas Hobbes on good and evil

For every man is desirous of what is good for him, and shuns what is evil, but chiefly the chiefest of natural evils, which is death; and this he doth by a certain impulsion of nature, no less than by which a stone moves downward.

Thomas Hobbes, *Philosophical Rudiments*, 1642

So Hobbes introduces a model of men and women as self-motivated (even downright selfish) creatures who will rarely restrain themselves from doing what hurts others if it gets them what they want. Where is the rationality in all this? Hobbes answers that, despite their selfish belligerence, humans' rationality manifests itself in their capacity to understand the benefits of peace and order and, therefore, in their willingness to agree to set up an association, a State, a government which will facilitate peaceful coexistence.

However, such an agreement does not suffice, Hobbes hastens to add. Even though people recognise that peace is better than war and universal respect of neighbours is preferable to feuding, each individual also recognises that his or her desires are best served by being unprincipled in a principled community. And if everyone prefers that all others are law-abiding while he or she cheats, steals, coerces and murders, then the agreement between people will be worthless and the 'war of all against all' will recommence. What is needed, Hobbes concludes, is something stronger than some agreement; individuals must agree to give up some of their rights to a higher authority (e.g. the State) so as to live in peace.

Recapping, in a society of free individuals motivated by selfishness no one has an incentive to behave well even though each prefers a situation in which all behave well to one in which all behave appallingly. Yet behaving appallingly they will. (Notice that this is an example of unintended consequences – see Section 1.2.2). Their only hope, thought Hobbes, lies in their capacity rationally to recognise all this and to authorise some powerful body (e.g. the Monarch, the State, the Law) to watch over them. Although it may be instrumentally rational to steal and pillage if you can get away with it, it is more (instrumentally) rational to agree to the presence of a police force stopping you from thieving and looting. The reason is that, otherwise, your personal benefits from villainy are outweighed by the horror of living in a society where everyone else can also mess with you. Thus the idea of the liberal State (liberal in that all citizens agree to its power) emerged as compatible with the selfish pursuit of individual gain.

The instrumental rationality of neoclassical economics is rooted in Hobbesian philosophy. However, since Hobbes its meaning was refined and its association with outright selfishness weakened by the Scottish philosopher David Hume (1711–76). Let us remind ourselves of the definition of instrumental rationality in order to assess Hume's contribution to its construction: Instrumental rationality is identified with the capacity to choose actions which best satisfy a person's objectives. Hume clarified and established the precise meaning of what it means to act in an instrumentally rational manner by spelling out the three determinants of action: *passions* (i.e. ends, objectives or desires), *means* (i.e. resources) and *reason* (i.e. a capacity to think logically, to assess the various options at our disposal). It is a very simple model indeed.

We have certain passions (e.g. a passion for chocolate, opera, fast cars, justice, whatever). Next we have means or resources which we utilise in order to satisfy our passions. These means are of course the instruments to fulfil our passions. Finally, we have the capacity to reason. For Hume, our reason is the slave to our passions. It simply helps us apply our means in the manner which serves our rulers, the passions, best.

Reason as a slave of the passions

We speak not strictly and philosophically when we talk of the combat of passion and reason. Reason is, and ought only to be the slave of the passions, and can never pretend to any other office than to serve and obey them.

David Hume, *A Treatise of Human Nature*, 1739

Does this mean that we are as selfish and potentially brutish as Hobbes feared? Not at all, says Hume. There are good people and evil. But their virtue or nastiness lies neither in their resources nor in their reason. It lies in their passions. The good have virtuous passions while the bad have wicked ones. One can be simultaneously instrumentally rational *and* disgusting (e.g. the Nazis were quite skilful in executing their horrific agenda) or irrational *and* good. According to Hume our ethos, our morality, resides not within our reason but in our passions.

Morality as separate from rationality

Morals excite passions, and produce or prevent actions. Reason of itself is utterly impotent in this particular. The rules of morality, therefore, are not conclusions of our reason.

David Hume, *A Treatise of Human Nature*, 1739

There are important repercussions from Hume's separation of passions from reason. If you happen to have a terrible passion, your reason is incapable of doing anything about it: it must serve your passion however disagreeable this may be. (So, we should not expect the Nazis to have had the capacity to *reason* that what they were doing was terrible.) Your reason, according to Hume, is a bit like a pair of scales: an impartial judge of the relative weight of whatever you place on them. Just like you would not blame the scales if one thing proved heavier than another, Hume argues that reason should be neither blamed nor commended for a person's actions. If you want to point a finger, point it at the person's passions. (Do you agree with this? Not everyone does. See box below.)

3.1.2 The birth of utilitarianism

Morality as genuine rationality

Not everyone agreed with Hume. For example, the German philosopher Immanuel Kant (1724–1804) thought that our reason gives us a capacity to restrain ourselves in a manner that makes life better. He distinguishes between enjoyment and duty and suggests that there are times when the two point us to different directions. When this happens, it is only the truly rational people who can ignore their urge to 'maximise' joy and, instead, do what they must:

> The majesty of duty has nothing to do with the enjoyment of life.
> Immanuel Kant, *Critique of Practical Reason*, 1788

Utilitarianism is a theory a stone's throw away from David Hume's model of rational men and women. Its main tenet was established by its founder, Jeremy Bentham (1748–1832), who started with the assumption that people have a passion for pleasure (broadly defined) and an aversion for pain: 'Nature has placed mankind under the governance of two sovereign masters, *pain* and *pleasure*. It is for them alone to point out what we ought to do, as well as to determine what we shall do' (*An Introduction to the Principles of Morals and Legislation*, 1789). Bentham was a well-meaning, radical humanist for his time. He believed strongly that people should be given the greatest scope for living an enjoyable life and that, therefore, in the final analysis, it did not matter what the bishop or the king thought – what mattered was how happy people felt.

Bentham's utilitarianism had two aspects: the first is a theory of individual behaviour (or psychology). He took Hume's model and where Hume had written passions, Bentham substituted utility. In other words, he placed all our passions under a single umbrella: the passion for more and more happiness, or utility. The second aspect was an ethical or political claim: that each should aim for the greatest happiness for the greatest number of people. That is, not only should we aim at our own utility maximisation but also want to build a society capable of achieving the greatest happiness for the greatest number. The economic theory of action we went over in Chapter 2 espouses Bentham's first aspect without much interest in the second. Whatever the reasons for this, it is worth noting here that Bentham did not, and could not, prove that those who act in order to maximise utility will also want to see the utility of the greatest number maximised. (We shall return to this interesting point later – especially in Chapters 9 and 10.)

Happy morons!

It is better to be a human being dissatisfied than a pig satisfied, better to be Socrates dissatisfied than a fool satisfied. And if the fool, or the pig, are of a different opinion, that is because they know only their side of the story.

John Stuart Mill, *Utilitarianism*, 1863

As you can imagine, Bentham found himself at the receiving end of a great deal of criticism. Hardline moralists heard of 'utility maximisation' and immediately imagined that Bentham was condoning sinful activities only because they produced pleasure. Intellectuals feared that the better things in life (like art, music and literature) would be deemed of equal importance to base instincts (e.g. beer drinking) if they generated the same amount of 'utility'. Left wingers thought that it was an apology for the reckless acquisitiveness of the new entrepreneurs. And so on.

A new generation of utilitarians attempted to amend Bentham's initial theory in order to address many of these criticisms. For instance, J. S. Mill (1806–73) and G. E. Moore (1873–1958) extended 'happiness' (or utility) to distinguish between deeper and shallower versions. In the meantime, economists had discovered utility. As outlined in Section 1.3.2 it was as if utility was designed for the purposes of building a science of society founded on the principle of classical mechanics. Utility became for the economist what energy was to the physicist: a central notion on which a general theory of behaviour (of individuals rather than atoms or celestial bodies) could be erected. The *Equi-marginal Principle* on which we have spent precious pages already (see Section 1.3 and the whole of Chapter 2) was a natural development of utilitarianism.

An ancient precursor to utilitarianism

'We say that pleasure is the starting point and the end of living bliss-fully. For we recognise pleasure as a good which is primary and innate. We begin every act of choice and avoidance from pleasure, and it is to pleasure that we return using our experience of pleasure as the criterion of every good thing ... When we say that pleasure is the goal we do not mean the pleasures of the dissipated and those which consist in the process of enjoyment ... but freedom from pain in the body and disturbance in the mind.'

Were these lines scripted by Bentham, or perhaps Mill in the nineteenth century? No, they were written by Epicurus (341–270 BC) in a letter to Menoeceus. Philosophy, like history, repeats itself.

3.1.3 From Bentham's utility to neoclassical economics

At first neoclassical economists adopted Bentham's utility as some property, or even psychological energy, contained within commodities or experiences. The moment we appropriate them, we are awash with their utility. So, we buy an apple because of the utility that we expect to get *out* of this apple; as if, in other words, utility is something *in* the apple itself. The more utility there is in an apple, the greater the enjoyment we get from eating it. This model required only a slight alteration to allow for different tastes: the sensory devices in each one of us are calibrated differently and therefore some people enjoy apples less than others. Yet in the final analysis utility was transferred from the commodity to the psyche and could be visualised as a kind of (potentially) measurable psychological energy.

However, that view did not last long. A standard problem with utili-tarianism (especially of this early version) is that it leads to political hot water. For example, provided utility is measurable then at least theoretically it is possible to answer the question: if I take X away from Jill and give it to Jack, how much utility will Jill lose and how much utility will Jack gain? And if I can show that Jack will gain a lot more utility than Jill will lose, is this not a justification for removing X forcibly from Jill in order to pass it on to Jack? Perhaps Bentham would have been happy with this; for it would have justified taxing the terribly rich in favour of the poor. None the less neoclassical economists were not interested in such comparisons of one person's utility with that of another. Therefore they ditched this early view of utility. There are two reasons why.

The first is that, by their own admission, they wanted to construct an apolitical economics. It is easy to see how these comparisons between Jack and Jill's utility from X are politically controversial (imagine for instance that X is not a jar of marmalade but Jill and Jack's child). And if political controversies were to be reintroduced through this back door which the concept of utility left open, what would the point be?

The second reason was that, in addition to not wanting to allow *any* kind of politics in economics, they were particularly averse to justifications of State intervention (with some exceptions where the market fails badly – e.g. when firms collude to avoid competition and subvert the market). If utility were indeed measurable across Jill and Jack, and if transferring X from Jill to Jack increased overall utility, then suddenly the State would be justified in taking X away from Jill. A very disturbing thought for those who wanted to create an economic theory proclaiming the dogma that the best State is one that keeps out of people's affairs.

Of course early utilitarianism was not only despised by those who leant to the political right. Those on the centre and the left also pointed out that the idea of measurable utility (also called *cardinal utility*) was generally dangerous since it made it possible to justify tyranny and other horrors. For example, consider the case where Jack tortures Jill. If all that matters is the maximum average utility, then if Jack's utility from torturing Jill is greater than the utility she loses as a result of being tortured, then her torture has been justified. More generally, this type of utilitarianism opens up nasty possibilities for condoning exploitation of the minorities for the sake of the majority.

Banning inter-personal comparisons: a failed attempt to rid utility of politics

Jack gets utility from X. So does Jill. But if Jack's utility is not on the same scale as Jill's then we cannot say who gets more utility from X: Jack or Jill? In this way, we will know whether Jack and Jill want X (they do if X gives them, individually, positive utility) but we will not know who wants (or needs) X more: Jack or Jill?

Has this theoretical move banished politics from utility theory? Not at all. It simply turned it into an arch-conservative theory. Suppose Jack is a multimillionaire, Jill is a pauper and X is $5. This amount of money would be enough to feed Jill for a day. Should Jack be taxed $5 so that Jill can be fed? This is a question the theory refuses to answer since it has been banned from comparing Jack's and Jill's utility from the $5. By default it supports the status quo.

In summary, Bentham's aim was to create a theory of the good society as the happy society in which utility maximising individuals would work out ways in which maximum utility would be possible for as large a majority as possible. The idea of utility maximisation as a model of individual behaviour appealed to the neoclassical economists of the late nineteenth century. However, they were not interested in Bentham's utilitarian theory of the good society. So, what did they do?

They kept the idea of utility maximising individuals without accepting the one assumption which made it possible for Bentham to talk about the good society: the assumption that my utility from an orange can be compared with your utility from the same orange. By dropping the claim that utility can be measured across individuals, economists rid themselves of many of the political controversies of the previous paragraphs (see box on previous page).

Of course they also jettisoned the possibility of knowing what the common good is since it is now impossible to add up people's utilities in an attempt to measure the community's well-being. In spite of the valiant efforts of economists such as A. C. Pigou (Professor at Cambridge) the only thing left from the original utilitarianism was a theory of individual action: a person does whatever maximises her utility, even though the latter cannot be compared across individuals.

3.2 Ordinal, cardinal and expected utilities

3.2.1 From Hume's passions to ordinal utility

David Hume thought that we are moved by our passions. Reason is simply a tool for finding out how best to serve them. Now the problem with passions, from the vantage point of the neoclassical economist, is that they are far too messy to put into equations and geometry. The passion to drink coffee can perhaps be quantified. But what about the passion for literature, justice, beauty, freedom? Too messy! Not surprisingly, economists preferred a notion of utility which can be rendered manageable more easily. Effectively they allowed us to have a single passion: a passion for utility.

But as we saw in the preceding pages, economists were keen to sanitise utility so as to avoid political controversies. Their solution was simple: suppose that individuals have preference orderings between different options; e.g. they prefer X to Y and Y to Z. The only passion they are allowed to indulge is a passion to reach the top of their preference ordering (X in our example). Utility then is a shorthand term for preference-satisfaction. It is not as Bentham and the early utilitarians argued that people derive utility as some kind of psychological energy from things/experiences; instead, they want to satisfy their preferences.

As they do so, we (the observers/theorists) imagine that they get more utility the higher up their preference ordering they end up. However, this is only in our imagination; it does not mean that they feel some particular psychological experience as they get what they want. In conclusion, utility is a term *we* use to relate the degree to which a person's preferences have been satisfied and not a term describing some *feeling* the person may be experiencing. Economists are keen to stress that theirs is a theory of rational choice, not a psychology.

In short, whereas Bentham's utilitarianism was a primitive psychological theory of choice culminating to a theory of the good society, neoclassical economists stripped it down into something almost unrecognisable: a calculus of private choice incapable of saying much about how good or bad society is. As for utility, from a psychological inner-energy form, it became a list of options ordered according to preference. The latter is commonly known today as *ordinal utility* because it conveys the order, as opposed to the strength of, preference. (Recall that strength of preference requires that utility can be measured. Earlier we called this type of utility *cardinal utility*.) Modern textbook economics assumes that people are maximisers of this ordinal utility.

3.2.2 The limits of ordinal utility and the partial return of cardinal utility

Suppose a person is confronted by a choice between driving to work or catching the train. Driving means less waiting in queues and greater privacy, while catching the train allows one to read while on the move and is quicker. The metaphor of ordinal utility maximisation works in the following way. Economists insist that every person has well-defined preference orderings: each one of us, after spending some time thinking about the dilemma, will rank the two possibilities (in case of indifference an equal ranking will be allocated). Hence if, all things considered, you prefer driving you will attach rank 1 to driving and 2 to catching the train. In choosing to drive, you will be maximising your 'utility'. For this reason this type of utility is known as *ordinal utility* since it conveys nothing more than information on the ordering of preferences. (Similarly in the indifference curve diagrams of Chapter 2, e.g. Figures 2.4 and 2.5, each indifference curve corresponds to some utility ranking with individuals wanting to go from a lower ranked curve to a higher ranked one. And since ordinal utility cannot be measured, the distance between indifference curves should not be taken as a measure of how much happier the person gets when climbing upwards.)

The point to remember about ordinal utility numbers (which are no more than indicators of rank) is that their arbitrariness denies the possibility of saying anything about the strength of preference. It is as if a friend were to tell you that she prefers Homer to Shakespeare. Her preference may be marginal or it could be that she adores Homer and loathes Shakespeare. Based on ordinal utility information you will never know. It follows from this that there is no way that one person's ordinal utility from Homer can be compared with another's from Shakespeare (since the ordinal utility number is meaningful only in relation to the *same* person's satisfaction from something else; it is meaningless across persons).

Ordinal utility is sufficient in many of the simpler decision problems in which solutions can be found without any information on strength of preference; e.g. the above case where you had to decide between driving and walking to work. (Or as in the case of Section 2.1.4 whenever there is full information on prices and available funds and the person tries to get to the highest indifference curve.) However, there are many other cases where ordinal utility is insufficient. For example, consider the problem in Section 2.2.1 in which our agent is not fully informed and has to decide how intensely to gather information. Ordinal utility cannot tell her how much information to search for. Consider a simpler example which demonstrates the point:

Imagine that you are about to leave the house and must decide on whether to drive to your destination or to walk. You would clearly like to walk but there is a chance of rain which would make walking unpleasant. Let us say that the chance of rain was proclaimed by the weather bureau to be fifty-fifty. What does one do? Well, the answer must depend on the strength of preference for walking in the dry over driving in the dry, driving in the wet and walking in the wet. If, for instance, you relish the idea of walking in the dry a great deal more than you fear getting drenched, then you may very well risk it and leave the car behind. For an observer to be able to predict this, information on the strength of preference is necessary (recall the ordinal utilities do not contain this; they only report on the order of preferences).

Cardinal utilities provide such necessary information. If 'walking in the dry', 'driving in the wet', 'driving in the dry' and 'walking in the wet' correspond to 10, 6, 1, and 0 cardinal utils respectively, then not only do we have information about what is preferred over what; but also of how much one outcome is preferred over the next. In this example walking in the dry is ten times better for you than driving in the dry. Therefore we find that cardinal utilities become necessary when the decision problem involves some *risk*. If you knew with certainty whether it would rain or not then your ordinal utility preferences (that is, the ranking of outcome alone) would be sufficient: you would walk. It is the uncertain prospect of rain that complicates things. Cardinal utilities allow the calculus of desire to convert the decision problem from one of utility maximisation to one of utility maximisation *on average*; that is, to the maximisation of *expected* (that is, average) *utility*.

Let us stick with the assumption that the chance of rain is fifty-fifty; i.e. the probability of rain is $\frac{1}{2}$ (where a probability equal to 1 means that it will certainly rain and a 0 probability means that it will definitely not rain). If you walk there is, therefore, a 0.5 (out of 1) chance that you will receive 10 cardinal utils and a 0.5 chance that you will receive 0 utils. On average your tally will be 5 utils (0.5 times 10 plus 0.5 times 0). If, by contrast, you drive, there is a 0.5 chance of getting 6 utils (if it rains) and a 0.5 chance of ending up with only 1 cardinal util. On average driving will give you 3.5 utils. If you act as if to maximise average utility, your decision is clear: you will walk. Hence in cases where the outcome is uncertain, cardinal utilities are necessary. The reason is that it would be nonsense to multiply probabilities with ordinal utility measures whose actual magnitude is inconsequential since they do not reveal strength of preference.

Notice however that cardinal utility takes us closer to nineteenth-century utilitarianism. I say this because strength of preference made a reappearance after many decades of having been banned by neoclassical economists. Suddenly something resembling a passion (other than the passion to satisfy preferences in general) has returned: one can like walking 1000 times better than driving! However, we are still a long way from Bentham's utilitarianism. The reason is that Jack's cardinal utility numbers are still incomparable to Jill's. Thus, when we say that your cardinal utility from walking in the dry is 10 this 10 is meaningless outside your person as it cannot be compared with a similar number relating to somebody else's cardinal utility from walking in the dry.

What is now interesting is whether we approve of the manner in which neoclassical economics models people's actions under circumstances involving risk. The importance of this cannot be underestimated. If we are not impressed by economists' attempts, their theories of Chapter 2 could be dismissed as next to irrelevant. Notice that uncertainty is everywhere. Even when it comes to purchasing a bar of chocolate, you may not be entirely sure prior to biting it about how much you will enjoy the experience. Thus a theory of choice (or even consumption) needs to work well under circumstances of uncertainty if it is to be useful. Economists argue that their theory does: all we have to assume is that individuals maximise utility *on average* or *expected utility*. This is interesting for many reasons.

First, it is of historical interest because it brings to mind memories of Bentham and nineteenth-century utilitarianism. Recall Bentham's motif: the most utility for the greatest number of people. Well, what is this if it is not maximising utility on average? Indeed they are one and the same thing! However, we must not forget that the neoclassicals have taken one crucial step that precludes the resurrection of Bentham: they have banned interpersonal comparisons of utility. So, when the modern neoclassical theorist speaks of *expected utility maximisation*, she is not referring to maximising the average utility across many different people. Instead she is talking about one person choosing the option which would give her the largest average utility across many repetitions, that is, if she had to make this decision many times over and over again. Still, it is an interesting echo of the earlier form of utilitarianism.

Second (and more importantly), because it gives us the opportunity to put the theory to the test in laboratory experiments. Unfortunately for the theory of expected utility maximisation, these experimental tests seem to cast a great deal of doubt on it. Actually an avalanche of research has shown that people do *not* behave according to the principles of expected utility maximisation. The box below gives an example. What conclusions should we draw from this? Two come immediately to mind.

1   Neoclassical economics may not offer as general a theory of choice as economists claim.
2   There is a profound difference between economics (or, more generally, social science) and the natural sciences.

The Ellsberg Paradox (named after Daniel Ellsberg who invented the following experiment)

Suppose you are shown an urn which contains 90 balls, 30 of which are red. The other 60 balls are either black or yellow; you are not told how many are black and how many are yellow. One ball will be picked at random from the urn. You are then offered a choice between two lotteries. **Lottery 1** will give you $100 if a red ball is drawn while **Lottery 2** will give you $100 if a black ball is drawn. Which lottery do you choose? To help you decide, here is a summary of the two lotteries:

	Red	Black	Yellow
Number of balls in urn	(30)	(X)	(Y) All we know is that X + Y = 60
Lottery 1	$100	0	0
Lottery 2	0	$100	0

Would you choose **Lottery 1** (in which case you will win $100 if a red ball is drawn from the urn) or **Lottery 2** (in which case you would win $100 if a black ball is drawn)? Now consider another two lotteries: **Lottery 3** and **Lottery 4**.

	Red	Black	Yellow
Number of balls in urn	As above		
Lottery 3	$100	0	$100
Lottery 4	0	$100	$100

In this case the only way of *not* winning $100 is if either (a) you chose **Lottery 3** and a black ball is drawn or (b) you chose **Lottery 4** and a red ball is drawn.

Expected utility theory argues that if you chose **Lottery 1** over **Lottery 2**, then you should also have picked **Lottery 3** rather than **Lottery 4**. Think about it. If you chose **Lottery 1** it means that, given the information that there are 30 reds in the urn, you think that there are fewer than 30 black balls in the urn. But if you think this, why would you ever select **Lottery 4**? For if you think that there are fewer than 30 black balls in the urn, **Lottery 4** is a bad choice (since if there are fewer than 30 black balls it makes more sense to choose **Lottery 3**). And vice versa.

However, a majority of people making this choice in laboratory experiments (including Leonard Savage, one of the founders of expected utility theory) chose **Lottery 1** the first time and **Lottery 4** later. What should we make of this? There are two answers:

1 *People are irrationally inconsistent.* This is convenient for those who wish to defend the theory but has long run implications for economics. Does economics create a theory of how people behave or of how they ought to behave? If it does the latter, then it cannot hold on to the claim of providing an objective analysis of society.

2 *People are rational but care about more than expected utility.* What do **Lotteries 1** and **4** have in common? The fact that when one chooses them one knows *precisely* one's chance of winning $100 ($\frac{1}{3}$ in the case of **Lottery 1** and $\frac{2}{3}$ in the case of **Lottery 2**). Could it not be that people are averse to not knowing their chances? Could it be that, because of an antipathy to ambiguity, they select the options that minimise it? If so, who is to say that they are irrational? But then if it *is* rational to defy the economists' model the latter is not a unique guide to rational choice.

In short, whichever answer we choose from the two candidates above, the economists' model is threatened.

The first conclusion in the above box seems obvious: if the theory does not predict how people actually choose, then how good is it? Many economists have claimed that they do not think that there is something wrong with the theory simply because individuals do not behave according to it. Their argument is that theirs is a theory of rational choice; perhaps it is not working as well as expected because people are *not* rational. Which brings us to the second conclusion above.

Why is economics profoundly different from, say, physics? Because, unlike economists in the previous paragraph, physicists could never defend a theory which does not work in the laboratory. If their theory does not work experimentally, physicists cannot turn around and blame atoms or planets for not behaving according to the laws of nature which ought to govern their behaviour! Which is precisely what the economists of the previous paragraph did (that is, blamed individuals for not behaving according to the laws of the economists' model of rational behaviour). But then economics has a problem: if we can blame people (rather than the theory) every time they do not behave according to the theory being tested, then no theory can ever be shown to be wrong. In that case, why experiment at all? (I shall return to this question in Chapter 11.)

3.3 Instrumental rationality and utility maximisation: the politics beneath the surface

So far we saw that neoclassical economics sees rationality as an instrument for satisfying desires. This identification was traced to David Hume who thought of the 'passions' as the sole source of motivation. Utilitarians of the late nineteenth century set the scene for the modern economist's philosophical base by identifying the one passion that supersedes all others: the passion for joy (however broadly or narrowly defined). This was a liberal political move. It told cardinals, princes, lords and the State to stop patronising the merchants, the shopkeepers, the capitalists whose power was growing disproportionally to their position of the social ladder (still dominated by the aristocracy in Britain): they themselves are the only ones who can decide what is best for them. And, yes, it is OK to want to be happy, to be nouveau riche, to find pleasure in ways of one's own choosing. Undoubtedly, this was a serious political challenge in its time.

Later, neoclassical economists appropriated the bits of utilitarianism which they thought would assist them in their attempt to create an apolitical economics. The result was that utilitarianism lost a great deal of its political agenda. Eventually economists turned utility to no more than a preference ordering. Out went Bentham's narrative of emancipation based on the notion of the right to happiness for the individual as well as for society. In came a mathematised theory of individual action (which we examined carefully in Chapter 2) which could explain all sorts of human deeds. Its final purpose: to illustrate the harmonious workings of markets populated by instrumentally rational people; by people whose logic coincided with the logic of the market.

The question then is: how apolitical is the economists' version of utility theory? Have they managed to sanitise Bentham's utility and turn it into an objective, scientific, apolitical tool? Is it a good idea to assume that everyone in society is rational (especially in the instrumental sense)? If we do make that assumption, are we (unknowingly) taking positions in the political debate? We already saw how banning interpersonal utility comparisons gave a conservative political flavour to utility theory. Such questions will occupy us again in Chapter 4 and beyond. For now it is interesting to note the views of some influential intellectuals on aspects of the economists' behavioural story featured in Chapter 2.

Let us start from a simple question: do philosophers agree that rationality is sufficiently widespread? Most would accept that, notwithstanding differences between people, a capacity to reason is available to almost everyone. René Descartes (1596–1650) – the French mathematician and philosopher – reflected this feeling when he wrote:

> Good sense is the best distributed thing in the world: for everyone thinks himself so well endowed with it that even those who are the hardest to please in everything else do not usually desire more of it than they possess . . . It indicates . . . that the power of judging – which is what we properly call 'good sense' or 'reason' – is naturally equal in all men.
>
> Descantes, *Discourse on Method*, 1637)

However, assuming that we are all *instrumentally* rational (i.e. maximise our utility) is not the same as acknowledging that most have the 'power of judgment'. Instrumental rationality requires more (or, as some would say, less) than that: it requires that we are committed servants of our preference ordering. It assumes that we have objectives which take the form of a list of preferences. Once this list is complete, all we must want is to use our means *in whichever way possible* to get to the top of our list. This is the idea of human beings on which neoclassical economics trades its theory of choice and, later, of society.

One of the earliest and keenest proponents of instrumental rationality in the context of political manoeuvring was Niccolò Machiavelli (1469–1527). He served as a high-ranking official in several administrations in Florence and wrote perhaps the first and most enduring manual (textbook?) on governing. In his advice to politicians of his time (to a hypothetical prince) he set out the project of working towards one's political objectives as follows:

> Thus it is well to seem merciful, faithful, humane, sincere, religious, and also to be so; but you must have the mind so disposed that when it is needful to be otherwise you may be able to change to the opposite qualities. And it must be understood that a prince, and especially a

new prince, cannot observe all those things which are considered good in men, being often obliged, in order to maintain the state, to act against charity, against humanity, and against religion.

(Machiavelli, *The Prince*, 1513)

Does he not sound like a proponent of instrumental rationality? His emphasis on the centrality of outcomes and the unimportance of means (as long as they serve the ends) resembles the economics textbook's message: it is what you get, not how you get it, that gives you utility (unless of course it is part of your objective to avoid or use certain methods). But is the tyranny of ends rational? Is it rational to be unable to pass judgment on your passions (in other words to be their slave)? Difficult questions.

What is certain, however, is that whichever way you answer, you take sides in important political debates. If you reject the primacy of ends, you are making a political statement (e.g. Americans arguing that it was wrong to bomb Hiroshima regardless of their government's ends). If you accept that ends justify means, again you take political sides. The interesting thing about economics textbooks is that they remain mute on this subject; their silence implying that it is possible to remain apolitical. Well it is not! For how could it be when, by definition, the model of Chapter 2 rules out a *rational* evaluation of preferences. Thus the desire of a millionaire to burn $1000 notes at a party in order to impress guests is as rational (or irrational) as the desire of a Third World mother to feed her starving child. George Bernard Shaw famously argued, ironically, that the reasonable adapt themselves to the way the world is while the unreasonable try to change both themselves and the world. Espousing the model of humans in the economics textbook makes it difficult to appreciate Shaw's irony. Thus it is political!

Finally, if we are to allow the world to look rationally back at us, as the German philosopher G. W. F. Hegel (1770–1831) suggests in the box below, surely it must be possible to look at ourselves and ask: where did I

Reason's narcissism

The sole thought which philosophy brings to the treatment of history is the simple concept of Reason: that Reason is the law of the world and that, therefore, in world history, things have come about rationally . . . In everything that is supposed to be scientific, Reason must be awake and reflection applied. *To him who looks at the world rationally the world looks rationally back. The relation is mutual.*

G. W. F. Hegel, *Reason in History*, 1837

get my preferences from? Are they any good? In a sense this would mean going back to Socrates (see p. 76) who suggested that we ought to assess our options not just in terms of our preferences but of how conducive they are of the 'good life'. Instrumentally rational people cannot do this. They are too busy satisfying them.

3.4 Summary

Before we examine these questions further in Chapter 4, it is useful to draw a balance sheet. On the one hand, we have the economists' model in Chapter 2. It offers a precise, simple, dazzling account of how people act, based on a notion of utility which has been de-politicised as much as possible. The idea is that economists have divested themselves of the role of judging what people want and created a theory of what they will do when trying to get it. It allows people to determine their preferences and it is as apolitical as it can get since it does not patronise them (e.g. it does not tell them 'you want X when you should want Y') and it does not allow anyone else to do so either (e.g. by banning interpersonal utility comparisons).

On the other hand, we have critics who see this model as dangerously political not only because of the conservative politics it promotes, but because it promotes its politics silently, disguised in a veil of scientific, totally apolitical endeavour. For them, teaching economics under the pretence that it is free of politics is a bit like teaching creationism as a scientific discourse free of religion. Consider for instance the following quote from Catherine Mackinnon, who writes from a feminist perspective:

> the state is male in that objectivity is its norm. Objectivity is liberal legalism's conception of itself. It legitimates itself by reflecting its view of society, a society it helps make by so seeing it, and calling that view, and that relation rationality. Since rationality is measured by point-of-viewlesness, what counts as reason is that which corresponds to the way things are. Practical rationality, in this approach, means that which can be done without changing anything.
> (Mackinnon, *Towards a Feminist Theory of the State*, 1989)

In conclusion, neoclassical economics can be viewed in two distinct ways: as an attempt scientifically to understand our society, or as an attempt to produce a theory which will under no circumstances recommend that those who currently have social and economic power should be stripped of it. Is the material in your economics textbook a rational theory of society or is it mere rhetorical ammunition in support of keeping things the way they are?

Chapter 4

Critique: do we maximise utility (even subconsciously)? Should we?

4.1 Humanity through the lens of economics textbooks

Imagine that some extra-terrestrials got hold of an economics textbook and used it in order to work out what we humans are like prior to paying us a visit. What would they come to expect? Neoclassical economic theory presents a model of men and women as cool, fastidious agents who get what they want and want what they get. As creatures ruled by something they call *self-interest* which they pursue via the meticulous application of their scarce means. And if these extra-terrestrials can read in between the text-book's lines, they will also know that this thing called *self-interest* is not the same as its nastier cousin *selfishness*. However, they will not be reassured fully by this. The only promise the textbook makes is that we can be counted on to be efficient in matching our means to our ends. Whether our ends are charitable or homicidal, the textbook does not say.

This chapter, like the last chapter of each part in Book 1, is of a critical ilk. It asks two sets of questions. The first scrutinises the descriptive accuracy of the picture of human beings painted by economists:

1   Are the extra-terrestrials in for a grave shock when they approach earth and observe us with their own eyes (or whatever sensory devices they may have)? In other words, is the economist's model of *Homo sapiens* (let us call this creature which inhabits the economics textbook *Homo economicus*) a fair approximation of real humans? Or is it totally off the mark?

The second set of questions takes us from description to prescription:

2   If it turns out that you and I do not think, behave, function or relate
     to each other as the economics textbook suggests, is this something
     that ought to worry us? Is it a sign of the fact that we are not as
     perfect as the economics textbook assumes? Should we perhaps try a
     little harder to become more consistent, less inefficient, more like *Homo
     economicus*? Or could it be that what the textbook dismisses as weak-
     nesses are, in reality, strengths which economists mistake for imper-
     fections because they are less sophisticated than the subjects they are
     writing theories about?

There is also a third question that will be left in abeyance until Chapter
11: does it matter to economists if their model of humans is unrealistic?

4.2 How like *Homo economicus* are we?

4.2.1 Behaving according to a theory even if we do not know anything about it

An objection often raised by newcomers to economics springs from the
latter's conspicuous austerity. Are we really being asked to think that when
we choose how much of two goods to buy we are equalising our marginal
rate of substitution with the ratio of the prices? Surely we are far more spontaneous, creative, even unpredictable than this. However, the neoclassical
economist sees these objections as fundamentally ill conceived. Consider a
tennis player serving for the tournament. A physicist can look at a slow
motion recording of the player's action and explain in full mathematical
detail the dynamics of the player's motion, the rotation of the arm, the swing
of the body, of how the initial posture maximised the power of the serve,
the effectiveness of the wrist's movement in giving the ball a wicked top spin
and so on. And yet all this scientific analysis does not depend on the player
being conscious of it.

Even if the player in question is ill tempered or erratic, the scientific
analysis is still the best explanation of what happens on court when the
player strikes the ball well, regardless of whether she is a natural talent with
no understanding of why she plays good tennis or a physicist-turned-tennis-
player. Indeed all we need to assume is that she is trying to win the point
(and, incidentally, maximise her prize money).

Similarly, the neoclassical economist is not arguing that when we
choose between combinations of commodities we do so by *consciously*
following the edicts of the *Equi-marginal Principle* (that is, reaching for points
of tangency between indifference curves and budget constraints); instead

---

Instrumental rationality as instinct

The English philosopher and mathematician Bertrand Russell (1872–1970) wrote: 'There is no more reason why a person who uses a word correctly should be able to tell what it means than there is why a planet which is moving correctly should know Kepler's law'. (Russell, *The Analysis of Mind*, 1921) A neoclassical economist would need to substitute only 'who uses a word correctly should be able to tell what it means' with 'who maximises utility should know what marginal utility is'.

---

economists try to emulate the role of the physicists, namely attempt to provide a scientific analysis for behaviour which is, primarily, instinctive.

The true assumption is not that the individual under consideration is actually following the steps prescribed by the theory but that, once she masters the skills involved in serving her objectives, she begins to behave *as if* she were following the theory. All along, however, she is most likely to be totally oblivious even to the existence of this or any other theory.

To illustrate further, the point here is that just as Martina Hingis needs to know no physics to play good tennis, the consumer can make rational choices without ever having heard of the *Equi-marginal Principle*. Take Figure 2.8 (see p. 72). One may naively argue that unless the worker in that example knows the location of her indifference curves she cannot make the appropriate choice (i.e. select the combination of leisure and income corresponding to the point of tangency at A). Such uninformed criticism is countered easily by pointing out that she will *gravitate* towards the tangency point A (even if totally untutored into economics) provided she tries to maximise her utility.

Suppose that initially she chose to work more than point A in Figure 2.8 recommends. One day her firm is short on orders and her boss sends her home early. To her surprise she finds that it is wonderful to return home at 4 p.m. and have lots more leisure time. On the following morning she negotiates a reduction in her hours at the expense of a reduction in her salary. Without realising it, she will have moved closer towards her best choice at tangency point A. In conclusion, even though totally unaware of economic theory, of the notion of marginal rates of substitution, of Figure 2.8 etc., but because of her inquisitiveness, our friend makes a choice *as if* on the basis of the analysis behind Figure 2.8 thus confirming the *Equi-marginal Principle*.

All the neoclassical theorist needs to assume is that the individual is smart, inquisitive and has a nose for what is good for her, that is, she is instrumentally rational. The point to remember is that the *Equi-marginal*

Principle is not meant to offer advice as to what we ought to do; it is, simply, a mathematical description of what instrumentally rational people do. Having sorted this one out, the question remains: are we instrumentally rational (i.e. utility maximisers) and, furthermore, should we want to be?

4.2.2 Suspect desires and the threat of rational idiocy

The quintessence of the human condition has troubled minds finer and sharper than those that spawned economic theory. Faced with choices that tear us apart, Sophocles' *Antigone* and Shakespeare's *Hamlet* continually demonstrate how much we do not know about ourselves. Can the neatness and simplicity of the *Equi-marginal Principle* put an end to millennia of existentialist angst? Could it hold the key to what we are about? Unlikely.

Choosing our character

The great nineteenth-century thinker John Stuart Mill, who took to economics because of his philosophical and political interests, wrote:

> A person feels morally free who feels that his habits or his temptations are not his masters, but he theirs; who even in yielding to them knows that he could resist . . . Or at least, we must feel that our wish, if not strong enough to alter our character, is strong enough to conquer our character when the two are brought into conflict in any particular case of conduct. And hence it is said with truth, that none but a person of confirmed virtue is completely free.
>
> John Stuart Mill, A System of Logic, 1843

One does not have to be a Shakespeare or a Sophocles in order to understand that there is more to wise choices than meeting objectives efficiently. Even in our more mundane moments we can experience a secret fear that what we desire is not worth desiring. When we begin to suspect our desires, the *Equi-marginal Principle* which is all about satisfying current desires (even if this includes the desire to satisfy future needs and wants) begins to look rather epidermic.

To make the point simply it will help to revisit an uncomplicated (but as you will notice slightly touched up) fable by the Greek story-teller Aesop, who lived in the sixth century BC.

It is summertime and the living is easy. However, whereas the grasshopper is lazing under the sun leaning against a fig-tree and playing his guitar, the ant is slaving away preparing for the coming of winter. As the ant passes by the fig-tree, he looks at the grasshopper with disgust and says: 'You are truly stupid. Instead of gathering food for when the snow comes, you waste your time singing and being merry. In my mind, wisdom necessitates a commitment to one's future self. This is why you should do like I do and invest everything in order to have as good a future as possible.'

The grasshopper smiles and replies: 'I may be stupid but I am perfectly rational. Indeed I am as rational as you. For my concerns are limited to the present moment and I am never interested in what the future holds. You may, naturally, be absolutely right in that when winter arrives I will be miserable, but since I am not interested in anything other than my present happiness, I will carry on singing.' The ant shakes his head and moves on muttering: 'When winter comes do not complain that I did not warn you.'

Does the grasshopper have a point about being rational even if stupid? It depends on how we define rationality. Since he has stated that he has no concern for future levels of utility, it is clear that, in the context of instrumental rationality and Figure 4.1, his best choice is to opt for maximum satisfaction today (the constraint reflects the feasible combinations of happiness today and in the future and is common for the ant and the grasshopper). Geometrically speaking, the grasshopper's preferences are such that his indifference curves are perpendicular to the horizontal axis and, therefore, his best choice is to sacrifice all future utility for present utility. Check that these vertical to the x-axis indifference curves imply that only additions to *present* utility can help the grasshopper climb on to a higher indifference curve (i.e. increases in anticipated future utility leave him on the same indifference curve).

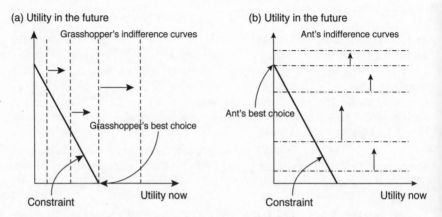

Figure 4.1   The grasshopper and the ant; two species of rational fools

By contrast, the ant currently assigns zero relative value to present utility (and maximum value to anticipating future utility) and ends up with horizontal indifference curves; thus unsurprisingly the highest accessible indifference curve yields zero present utility to the ant. In other words, because of their different preferences, the ant chooses to invest everything into his future whereas the grasshopper chooses the diametrically opposite strategy. On the grounds of neoclassical rationality they are equally rational since they both maximise their utility given their constraint. (Check also that the analysis employed here is identical to the model of time preferences and saving in Section 2.2.2.)

Winter came, the land froze, the trees lost their leaves. The ant stayed all snugly and warm in his hole consuming as little as possible of the stockpile of food (not because he feared that he would run out before spring but because, as Figure 4.1 explains, the ant has no *current* interest in present happiness and seeks only to survive in order to allow his future self, to whom he is so touchingly committed, to come happily into being!). The grasshopper, by contrast, was in a sorry state. Suffering from hypothermia and malnutrition he crawled to the entrance of the ant's hole and called out for help. The ant unexpectedly did not use this as an opportunity to remind him of their conversation but instead said: 'The terrible thing is that I cannot help you even though it would make me happy to do so. You see, I am only capable of enjoying the anticipation of happiness in the future rather than present happiness (note the shape of my indifference curves) and therefore I can give you no food. However, I can help in another way. There is a bush further down the road whose leaves are nourishing and rather appetising. Unfortunately, they are also poisonous. Ten days after you eat them you will die a very painful death. But given that you have no concern about the future, I presume that you will eat them.' 'Of course and thank you for the information,' replied the grasshopper and set off to find the bush.

Ten days later, the grasshopper was clutching his tummy in agony minutes away from death. Suddenly the ant appeared. 'It saddens me', he said, 'to witness the result of your rational stupidity. I bring you bad news and good news. Which do you want first?' 'The good news,' grumbled the grasshopper. 'Well, there is an antidote that will cure you within twenty-four hours. That's the good news. The bad news is that during those twenty-four hours you will be in greater pain than you are now. Knowing you and your preferences, you will rather not take it.' The grasshopper sighed in agreement. 'Farewell!' he exclaimed as it was not (in a neoclassical sense) rational for him to invest into his future (recall Figure 4.1).

Years later, the ant reached a grey old age and reminiscing he lamented: 'I envy that grasshopper. He wasted his life in the name of instant hedonism but at least he had some good moments. I, on the other hand, have wasted a lifetime investing into a future that never came. Not once did I enjoy the fruits of my labour as I enjoyed the anticipation of future satisfaction, never satisfaction itself.' And just before he expired, he admitted 'I envy that grasshopper; at least he lived while he was alive.'

The moral of the story: Knowing how to be wise is more diffi-
cult than knowing how efficiently to satisfy one's objectives. (Aesop always offered a moral at the end of each of his fables!)

Seriously now, this version of Aesop's *The Ant and the Grasshopper* brings into focus the partial nature of instrumental rationality. Put simply it reminds us that one can be, in the words of a contemporary economist (Amartya Sen), a rational fool; that is, a person who knows *how* to meet objectives but has no idea of *which* objectives are worth meeting. One hopes that we are not like this; that we can question our objectives rationally.

However, this species of rationality (one that helps us assess our objectives and character) is nowhere to be found in your economics textbook. Why? Because economics has developed a commitment to studying actions and choices without passing judgment on the desires that they serve. How then can the economist turn around and advise people to question their objectives (which is clearly what Aesop wanted our two friendly insects to have done)? To put the same point more technically, this would be like inciting people *not* to behave according to the *Equi-marginal Principle* when-ever one's utility is determined by suspect desires (see the box on the next page for an example). Is this a problem for economics?

Recall that the economists' great claim is that they are about descrip-tion (i.e. pure science) rather than prescription (which is left to ethics, politics, philosophy, religion and others). In this sense, the message from the fable of the *Ant and the Grasshopper* is not a problem for economics if people are as hopeless at questioning their objectives as Aesop's insects (although if this is so people are defective even if economics is not). However, if we all have the capacity to reason, occasionally, that our current desires are dumb and not worth acting on, then the theory has a problem because we may choose to behave in a manner that does not necessarily reflect our current objectives. So the theory will not be able to explain our behaviour unless it has some-thing to say about which objectives people are likely to reject as irrational. But this is something that economics has consciously chosen not to do; indeed the notion of rational or irrational objectives is not part of the economic way of thinking.

Summing up, the criticism occasioned by Aesop's parable has two cutting edges. The first was dealt with in the previous paragraph: neoclassical

Questioning one's objectives and the *Equi-marginal* *Principle*

Imagine that someone is prepared to pay $10 for a packet of cigarettes, $15 for two and $18 for three packets when the price of each packet is $5. How many should the person buy? The answer provided by the *Equi-marginal Principle* is two (since the marginal utility from the second packet equals its cost). Now notice the use of the word 'should' in the previous sentence. Its utilisation by economists reflects their assumption that people's objectives are their own business and that their recommendation takes them as given. So in so far as these objectives are not questioned, the person 'should' buy two packets; and this is indeed what economists predict the person will do. However, this is not to say that the rational person *must* (or indeed *should*) buy two packets of cigarettes. Perhaps what this person ought to do is decide to give up smoking after having successfully scrutinised his or her objectives. Of course economists would reply that it is not their job to tell people what they ought to want. True. However, they are running a risk of doing so indirectly, albeit very strongly, when they contend that the rational thing to do in this case is to buy two packets of cigarettes.

theory may not predict actual rational choices very well. There is, however, a corollary of this which brings us to the second criticism: neoclassical theory predicts too much! Let us be frank here. How did I touch up Aesop's story above to link it with the theme of this chapter? In order to present the ant and the grasshopper as rational, I drew up two sets of indifference curves so that both their choices became instrumentally rational.

Whatever foolish thing they had chosen to do I could always have drawn indifference curves which would have explained why their actions were (instrumentally) rational. Thus we see that when we observe others' behaviour we can always concoct certain objectives which would make that behaviour seem (instrumentally) rational. So if you were to witness me banging my head against the wall, you could justify that sorry sight by saying that my utility increases with every thump of my skull against the bricks. The worry here is that a theory which can explain everything under the sun as 'rational' is a theory which cannot distinguish between the rational and the downright foolish.

4.2.3 The utility machine

Criticism is cheap when unaccompanied by concrete alternatives. Section 4.2.2 can be seen as a tawdry shot at what is in reality a pretty powerful explanation of how people behave. Even if it gives rise to the paradoxical possibility of rational idiots (like the ant or the grasshopper) and although it raises interesting questions about rationality, wisdom and the importance of thinking carefully about what we want, it may be tempting to toe the neoclassical line and argue that, at the end of the day, the optimal choice model (i.e. the *Equi-marginal Principle*) is *about* right; that it captures most of what determines behaviour; that humans, most of the time, try to get what they want given their resources and that, even in the few cases when they do not, they behave *as if* they did. In the end, the argument goes, we are utility maximisers most of the time even if we do not want to be or know not that we are. Economics has figured us out as well as one could wish.

Has it? Are we utility maximisers? There is little doubt that the above is powerful reasoning. Yet part of us may still protest that human nature is not as trivial. Is this due to our vanity (our need to think of our selves as more than just computers mechanistically drawing up a balance sheet of utility and disutility), is it that we value the irrational parts of our character or is there some rational substance in these protests? Here is a way to answer this question for yourself – a hypothetical that will help you decide whether *you* are a utility maximiser or not.

Suppose a brilliant computer engineer comes up with the ultimate pleasure machine. You lie on a bed, its electrodes are attached to your head and your body is sustained artificially by means of intravenous drips and other state-of-the-art methods. Then the computer takes over your brain. However, there is no need to panic. This computer is totally benign; it is your friend rather than some mechanical monster eager to hijack your soul and render you lifeless. It reads your preferences, understands perfectly what you value, what causes you displeasure, and uses this information to create an imaginary life which is tailor-made to suit your wishes.

While you are connected to the machine, you have no idea that you are lying down with electrodes on your head looking quite pathetic: instead, you are convinced that the images created by the computer are true. You are surfing in Hawaii, winning the Monaco Grand Prix, proving Einstein's relativity theory wrong - whatever takes your fancy; such is the power of the machine. The question now is: assuming that you were satisfied that all the above is true and that your body would be taken excellent care of while attached to the computer, would you agree to be strapped to the machine for the rest of your life?

Think carefully before you answer. This machine is the ultimate utility maximiser: whatever experience you place at the top of your list of priorities (i.e. your ordinal ranking) is the experience that you will have. And since real life comprises a succession of experiences, the machine creates whole sets of life experiences for us in complete accordance with our wishes. Now for the big claim: *if you decline the invitation, then your decision is fundamentally opposed to the predominant economic view of the individual as a utility maximiser* (i.e. the neoclassical theory of Chapters 2 and 3).

So, will you join the 'utility machine' or not? If the answer is 'yes', you are effectively in agreement with neoclassical economics that you *are* a utility maximiser (since attaching ourselves to the machine is the perfect way of achieving maximum utility). For what it is worth, you will have discovered a theory of human nature which is simple, consistent and can be found in any economics textbook. But if the answer is 'no', you have problems! Let me explain.

One legitimate objection is that you may not trust absolutely the promise of the medical team that, while hooked on to the computer, your body will be in as good a state as it would normally be. Of course this is a legitimate reason for not agreeing to join the machine even if instrumentally rational. But would you still refuse if you *could* be perfectly certain that your body would not suffer any ill-effects while strapped to the machine? If the answer is yes, then you cannot be a utility maximiser. Why? Because by continuing to refuse you are acknowledging that there must be something other than utility (or 'getting what I want') which matters. (Otherwise you would have joined!) What is it? Could one be a utility maximiser and still not want to join the machine even if perfectly certain that one's physical condition would not deteriorate?

Consider the argument that you may be utilitarian but at the same time at the top of your preference ordering you place the well-being of |other people; that your utility is to be gained by helping others rather than through selfish pursuits. Not convincing! For even if you wish to help others, the machine will oblige you in the most efficient way. Remember that the machine creates the experiences in your brain/soul that *you* want it to. So, if you get your kicks from being nice to everyone, from helping the poor and needy, from altruistic deeds, then the machine will create such a life experience for you. Instead of feeling that you have just won the Olympics or made it in Hollywood, the computer, faithful to your preference ordering, will conjure up images of setting up path-breaking medical facilities in Central Africa, of looking after millions of desperate children and their families or whatever heart-warming images it takes to sooth your soul.

Still no one will *actually* be helped by you. Is this not a good enough reason to decline the machine's invitation to join it for the rest of your biological life? Not so if you are a utility maximiser. Recall the point that while you are attached to the machine you will have no idea that you are so attached. The images in your brain will be as real as the experience of reading these lines. Of course you may insist that, be that as it may, you still want to help *real* people instead of the fake images of real people that the machine conjures up even if the machine deceives you brilliantly that the ones you are helping are real.

But what is real and what is fake? What if someone suggests that you have no way of proving that your current reality is more real than the one the computer will create in your brain? How do you know that you are not attached to some computer as you are reading these lines which makes you think that you are, at this moment, reading a book when, all along, you are lying on a bed with electrodes sticking out of your skull? 'Fine, I do not *know* it,' you may respond, 'but right now, while in front of the machine, when asked to be joined to it forever, I have a choice between what I *think* is a real life and the virtual life that the computer will create for me. Even though the latter may promise a lot more utility, I may value enormously the current *belief* that the life I am leading now *is* real (regardless of my inability to prove it) so much so that I can explain my unwillingness to join the machine, and thus extinguish this valuable belief, in terms of utility maximisation.' Good point. What you seem to be saying is that you would be happy if suddenly the computer, without asking you, were to take over your brain (without allowing you to notice that it did so) and created a fake life that boosted your utility. However, if you are asked to *choose* the machine, you would not do so because of the large amount of utility that you enjoy currently by thinking that you are choosing reality over the machine's virtual reality. Fine. But then you would have to agree to a situation where the computer would use wireless techniques to take over your brain without your consent!

'Hold on a second,' you might, rightly, protest, 'Are we not getting a bit carried away here?' I think so too. Nevertheless please allow me to make the point again that if you choose to shun the machine on the grounds that you do not want to live a fake life (while attached to some machine) then you cannot be interested *uniquely* in utility. You are implicitly stating that you are also interested in something called *reality* however we may conceptualise this notion.

To sum up a rather complex argument, if you choose not to be linked to the machine for life, then you cannot care *only* about utility. Your textbook proclaims that the only notion of importance to the individual is utility, and since the computer admirably maximises utility, you must accept that utility is not all that matters to you if you are to argue against joining the machine either for moral reasons or because of a commitment to 'reality'. *You must concede that there is something outside utility that matters.*

But were most of us to think this way, the neoclassical model of rational choice would have failed at describing human behaviour. Moreover if we were to have a rational explanation of why we refuse to join the machine, economists can no longer claim that violations of their *Equi-marginal Principle* are evidence of irrationality. So, can we offer a rational explanation of why we would shun the utility machine? Is there anything other than utility that it makes sense to care for?

4.2.4 The first reason for shunning the utility machine: the fluidity of desires

Joining with the machine for ever would mean that we entrust our lives to our desires (since the machine does no more than to create a life in the image of our current desires). One reason why we may not want this to happen is a concern that our current desires are a bit naff – recall the *Ant and the Grasshopper*. Here is a similar example.

> Ronald does not attend classical music performances. Figure 4.2a explains why: the relative price of such tickets, in terms of all other prices, is shown by the slope of Ronald's budget constraint. The flatness of his indifference curves is indicative of how little classical music appeals to him and confirms that his optimal choice is to spend absolutely nothing on it (point A).
>
> One day his boss changes his constraint to that in Figure 4.2b; that is, the top part of the constraint (corresponding to the region between 0 and 1 concert) disappears. How? By demanding that tonight Ronald will take an important client to the concert hall. If he refuses, he loses his job and therefore his income (in which case his constraint collapses to the origin if Ronald chooses less than 1 concert). A disgruntled Ronald takes his seat at the concert hall when the curtain rises and, for the first time in his life, Ronald is immersed in the music of Mozart.

All other goods and services

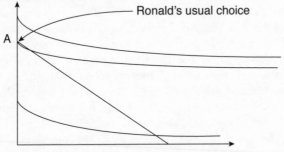

Classical music concerts

Figure 4.2a Ronald's choice before his boss forced him to go to the concert

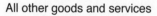

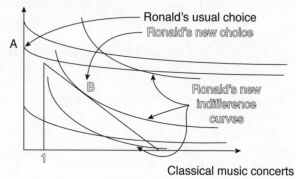

Figure 4.2b   Ronald's choice after his boss forced him to go to the concert and his indifference curves changed as a result of the experience

He is stunned! All of a sudden he realises that something has changed in him. Classical music is not boring and fit for geriatrics only; it is exciting and full of energy. He walks out of the hall and all night he can think of nothing else than that last movement. The next day he goes to his local record store and buys as much Mozart as he can afford. Then he checks the concert guide and books himself a seat for the next concert. To put the same story in economic language, his indifference curves have undergone a substantial rotation following the concert (see Figure 4.2b) which means that he is now a consumer of classical music (notice how his new best choice is point B in Figure 4.2b).

'So what?' you may ask. Well, when preferences and choices become interdependent, the neoclassical model finds it much harder to predict what we will do. In basic dilemmas (e.g. selecting different bundles of apples and bananas) we find what the individual will do given preferences, prices and income (via the *Equi-marginal Principle*). In this example, however, such information is inadequate. To predict that Ronald would buy classical music CDs we also needed to know the extent to which the (forced) consumption of one concert would affect his preferences. To put it briefly, when choice contaminates preference the theory (as presented in Chapter 2) is inadequate. This is so because the theory assumes that it is only preferences that affect choices and not vice versa. When the road linking the two becomes a two-way street, the theory is helpless unless it can say something about the second direction: that is, about how our experiences affect our desires. Unfortunately this is not something which the model in your textbook can handle.

Let us see how this point (the interdependence of preference and experience) offers the first reason for refusing the utility machine's invitation to join it for life: it is quite simple. Ronald had no desire for classical music (witness Figure 4.2a) initially. Had he submitted his body and mind to the machine, the virtual reality that the latter would create to make him happy would not include the experience of Mozart's music and the subsequent transformation. The computer, faithful to the preferences he came with, would continue to fulfil these preferences and would never expose him to the concert hall magic since its programming prohibits it to brainwash him (i.e. to create new preferences). However, some of us look forward to unexpected changes to our preferences; changes that it is impossible to anticipate. It is the delicious expectation of an ever-changing, developing self that gives us an important confirmation that we are not machines; that our human condition is pregnant with unpredictable possibilities. For those who value this feeling more highly than preference satisfaction it makes perfect sense not to join the machine; for they neither maximise utility nor do they think they ought to.

4.2.5 The second reason for shunning the utility machine: looking for happiness is not like looking for gold

The second reason why some of us would not join the machine for life is that the search for happiness presents problems unfamiliar to gold-diggers: when they find gold they have an objective test for testing whether it is real or fool's gold. However there is no such test for happiness! A fool can be genuinely happy for tragic reasons (recall J. S. Mill's words from p. 81 in Chapter 3). The second reason is that happiness is not only difficult to identify but also it is a pretty weird experience to boot. Take for example that evening back in the 1960s marked by a truly remarkable phenomenon: millions of Americans cried almost simultaneously. Lassie (the popular canine TV-star) had died in the final episode of the series. To have cried they must have been upset (clearly they had not shed tears of joy). Yet they had, of course, chosen to watch the programme and it is unlikely that they regretted that choice.

How can we reconcile their grief with the thought that they gained utility from watching the programme? Does grief produce utility? Surely no one places sorrow at the top of their list of priorities and seeks its attainment. Could it be that it was the unexpected grief, the shock, that they valued and that afterwards they wished that Lassie had not met her death? What if the next day the network were to announce that the final episode was not what the creator of Lassie had intended but, instead, that it was a pirate copy that was never meant to be screened? Would the grieving millions welcome such a development? Doubtful. What is interesting in this case is that viewers enjoyed the sadness the episode caused and were not willing to erase it.

Happiness is indeed a strange experience. Whenever we go to the movies, or read a book, perhaps we choose the author or director in a way the neoclassical model describes (that is, with a view to satisfying our senses or increasing our utility). However, the moment we start watching or reading, our enjoyment will be spoilt if we are in control of the plot. Effectively, we demand that we *do not have a choice* as to what happens in the movie or book. We may even choose to watch a horror movie because it paralyses us for two terrifying hours. Painful the scenes and passages may be but, if well written/made, we enjoy them.

I can't get no satisfaction

Mick Jagger and Keith Richards, *Rolling Stones*, 1965

So although we would love a machine that does our chores, lessens pain and alleviates suffering, we do not necessarily wish for a life of no pain, no suffering and no chores. Such a life would be dull and likely to end by suicide. Happiness is thus best supported by unplanned frequent excursions into its opposite (whatever that may be). Consequently a machine that simply filters out all that we place at the lower part of our list of priorities is incapable of generating a truly happy life because joy and pleasure may be parasitic on pain and grief.

Put differently, it may be impossible surgically to segregate the good from the bad experiences. However, notice that the utility machine needs such a separation as an input so that it can decide which experiences to expose you to and which to withhold. Unlike real life, which is not guided by a preference ordering, the utility machine cannot possibly tread the thin dividing line between pain and pleasure, utility and disutility, horror and edification. Thus life while attached to it may be free of pain but also devoid of the problematic pleasures of, say, a Dostoevski novel. Who is to say that choosing to shun the machine (i.e. caring about things other than utility generation) is irrational?

4.3 Happiness, freedom and creativity

4.3.1 Sour grapes and manufactured desires

The ant, the grasshopper and Ronald's concert hall experience have already shown us that there is more to the good life than preference-satisfaction. Lassie's TV death alerted us to the futility of attempting an all-purpose *and* globally meaningful definition of utility (i.e. a separation of utility from disutility). But if we do not maximise utility, what on earth do we do? Let us consider the opinion of Bertrand Russell, on this matter:

> All human activity springs from two sources: impulse and desire ... Children run and shout, not because of any good they expect to realise, but because of a direct impulse to running and shouting ... Those who believe that man is a rational animal will say that people boast in order that others may have a good opinion of them; but most of us can recall occasions when we boasted in spite of knowing that we should be despised for it ... When an impulse is not indulged in the moment in which it arises, there grows up a desire for the expected consequences of indulging the impulse. If some of the consequences which are reasonably expected are disagreeable, a conflict between foresight and impulse arises. If the impulse is weak, foresight may conquer (acting on reason); conversely, either foresight will be falsified, and the disagreeable consequences will be forgotten, or, in men of a heroic disposition, the consequences may be recklessly accepted. ... But such strength and recklessness of impact are rare. Most men, when their impulse is strong, succeed in persuading themselves, usually by a subconscious selectiveness of attention, that agreeable circumstances will follow from the indulgence of their impulse.

If Russell is right, behaviour cannot be explained by a model concentrating exclusively on desires. Even if we agree that impulses create desires, they cannot be *reduced* to desires. He makes two important points: first, there are many actions that are supported only by a drive, an impulse, an emotion (as opposed to a desire or the urge to happiness). Second, our rationality is not just an instrument for getting what we want: it is also a tool for convincing ourselves that we wanted what we got! This second point is a great threat to the economists' model which portrays choices as the rational responses to well-ordered desires. Russell, by contrast, suggests that we often

---

Sour grapes

As always very few thoughts are original. Russell's view was expressed brilliantly many centuries ago by Aesop's *Sour Grapes* fable. A fox is walking by a vineyard. She sees some grapes hanging above and she wants some. She jumps repeatedly but fails to reach them. Then she decides that she did not want them anyway: 'They must have been sour,' she muses. A typical case of altering our preferences in order to live with the fact that we cannot have what we want. (This is what is known today as *ex post* (after the event) *rationalisation*.)

act on impulse (without good reason) and only then subconsciously concoct a desire that *could* have motivated our choice. If this is how things work, a theory of choice putting preference and reason in the driving seat is a sad extension of our capacity for self-deception.

Children run and cry, adults laugh, both compulsively purchase commodities that they neither need nor really want, ignorant armies round up civilians, millionaires are caught shoplifting, students daydream: such behaviour cannot be explained in any deep sense by the economist's model. Yet the economist can, if pushed, create a list of desires that would have produced such behaviour.

Looking for reasons *after* the choice

A marketing study found that 93 per cent of those who had read the *whole* text of a full-page newspaper advertisement for a well-known brand of car were recent buyers of that make and model of car. Why did they read it? After all, they had just bought that car.

The answer given by psychologists is that after a hard choice people often want to find reasons for their choice (*ex post rationalisation*). Thus they read texts exalting the virtues of the car they have chosen.

Of course these lists are mere illusions of reasons, just like the reasons we often create in our heads in order to justify our actions. The big question is: how is the melange of desires, impulses and emotions manufactured? And this is a question that the economist's model has neither an answer for nor much of an interest in. One thing is certain: to argue that, in the end, our life is reducible to a list of priorities (called utility function) is unsatisfactory from both a philosophical and a psychological view. Economists can claim lots of things; they cannot claim, however, to have rendered philosophy and psychology obsolete.

4.3.2 Creative self-manipulation and identity

Faced with our own complexity (which economists unkindly, and arguably incorrectly, refer to as irrationality), we nevertheless often find amazing reserves of ingenuity with which to counter it. Homer tells the story of Ulysses who, while sailing home on his return from Troy, came across the Sirens. He knew of their magnificent song which had a reputation as the ultimate in melodic splendour. But he also knew of the harrowing fate awaiting those who, lured by the song, landed in the Sirens' trap. Not wishing to jeopardise his safety, but also unable to resist the temptation to indulge his ears, he instructed his crew to tie him tightly on the mast, plug their ears and ignore his protests until the ship was miles away from the Sirens' island. Thus, he shrewdly achieved the best of all possible worlds by restraining himself from doing what would have been, at the same time, utility boosting and fatal.

Soul-searching reveals that we all have at times attempted, mostly without Ulysses' proficiency, to bind ourselves on imaginary masts. When we deliberately leave home without our credit card, knowing that otherwise we will spend more than we ought to, we are retracing Ulysses' moves. What we attempt is to satisfy our desires taking into account the dangers of impulsive behaviour. Have we salvaged, at least partially, the utility maximisation principle? Consider the following application of the Ulysses strategy. I have an economics assignment to complete by tomorrow morning but before going home to work on it, you ask me to join you for a drink or two at the bar. I want to come but I fear that I cannot trust myself.

Although I would like to join you for a couple of drinks, I know that after the first two drinks I will want more and, for obvious reasons, the assignment will never be completed. Thus, I fear the impulse that will change my preferences in a manner that will lead to my intoxication. Enter the Ulysses strategy. What if I give you all my money and instruct you to buy me only two drinks? If I ask for more, you should say no! Supposing this ploy works, I will have creatively dealt with my impulse before it materialises and I will have thus maximised my utility. However, consider your position if I were to tell you the following after the two drinks:

> I know I have instructed you not to buy me a third drink. Thank you for being such a loyal friend but now the time has come for me to reveal the truth. The reason why I am studying economics is that I have always been a timid, pathetic person amenable to social and family pressure. In reality, I always knew that I should be an artist but never had the guts to take the risk. Now that I have had the first two drinks I have loosened up and I can safely say that this is it. No more economics! Thus, the real 'me' is now in command and instructs you to give me my money so that I can have a few more drinks in order to find the courage to do what is truly in my best interest: to drop economics and tell my parents that I want to be an artist.

Well, this puts you in a terrible dilemma. When I claim that the self with authority to speak on my behalf is the current, slightly intoxicated one, how do you react? Do you believe me or do you remain loyal to my previous self? The answer is that if we stick to the neoclassical story there is no answer. For how can we compare the relative merits of the two selves? Based on utility considerations alone it is impossible to know which self has more merit. (Note the similarity between this problem and the question of inter-temporal utility comparisons discussed in Chapter 3.) Something else, like moral judgment, is needed and utilitarianism is incapable of providing it. It is this missing link which may provide further explanation as to why I would feel reluctant to join the utility machine of Section 4.3.1.

Individuals and organisations

Economists acknowledge that organisations may find it difficult to have well-defined preferences in view of the diverse interests of their constituents (see Chapter 8). There is even an argument that organi-sations often thrive on this inconsistency. On the other hand, economics assumes that rational individuals must have well-ordered priorities which must guide their actions mechanistically. My friend and colleague Shaun Hargreaves Heap (1989) has argued that the economic theory of human choices would improve if economists treated individuals in the same way they treat organisations – as complex 'systems' with fluid and incommensurable motives.

4.3.3 Utility maximisation and freedom

Two competing views of human nature have emerged so far. One is the textbook's *Homo economicus*: a consumer of utilities whose optimal choice has nothing to do with preference creation and everything to do with prefer-ence satisfaction. The other portrays the individual as an exerter, a creator, a being whose character is shaped by her actions and by the actions of others. Although they are both interesting creatures, it is only the second type that qualifies in my eyes as autonomous, self-determining, real and (most importantly) as capable of being free. If this is right, to be free requires the capacity to differ from the model of women and men in economics text-books. Of course this is a big claim in need of justification. Let me try to provide it beginning with a simple question: what is freedom?

In our days freedom has (thankfully) made it big: the talk everywhere is of free speech, free trade, free markets. An obvious meaning of that short word 'free' is: the absence of constraints – one's ability to do what one wants. But is this a sufficient definition? If it were then the utility machine would be the ultimate liberator (since it is programmed to maximise your utility by removing all constraints). However, just as one can act foolishly while maximising utility (remember the ant and the grasshopper), one can be a happy slave. Thus untrammelled utility does not guarantee freedom. Consider the following example.

Suppose you and I are involved in a dispute about how to share 1 million dollars. You press a button and my brain is reprogrammed to loathe money. What will happen? It is then best for both of us that you receive all the money. By changing my preferences, you have set both of us free since both you and I can now get what we want (you get the money and I get the chance to avoid the money). According to the definition of freedom which equates freedom with the absence of constraints I am as free as you are. According to another account, however, you have turned me into a happy moron who gets what he likes and likes what he is getting.

On this account, instead of freeing me, by allowing me to maximise utility, you have turned me into the ultimate slave. This gives us yet another reason of why one may rationally decide not to maximise utility and shun the utility machine: we suspect that, rather than setting us free to 'enjoy', the machine will deny us the quintessence of our freedom. Whether this is what the machine does depends on how we understand the concept of liberty. If we think of freedom in terms of economics textbooks, the utility machine sets us free. If not it represents the definitive form of totalitarianism. Just imagine a world in which we all lie down in huge hangers attached to a vast pleasure machine!

4.4 Conclusion

As explained in the Preface, the third chapter in each of the three parts of Book 1 plays devil's advocate and criticises the economic textbook's contents. The current chapter fulfilled this task by taking plenty of shots at the textbook (i.e. neoclassical) theory of choice. Has it been a gratuitous exercise or is there a good reason for being critical? Obviously I would claim the latter. Take a look at any textbook. In a few brief paragraphs it dispenses with the central question which has been occupying philosophers, political scientists and intellectuals for centuries: what does it mean to act wisely in a social context?

The economist's answer to that momentous question is not only extremely narrow (see Chapter 2) but also annoyingly arrogant. Rationality is defined in often no more than one sentence, motivation is dealt with in terms of a preference ordering (culminating in indifference curves) and best actions (or choices) are expressed by means of the *Equi-marginal Principle*. The student will be excused to think that these are all technical issues to be learnt mechanistically.

Perhaps economics does not need to delve into more sophisticated philosophy or psychology in order to produce demand curves and economic theories of prices, purchases, etc. (I shall be returning to this question in Chapter 11). Nevertheless there is no excuse for textbooks to pretend that the questions on rationality, wise choices or the source of desire have been answered by the economic approach. Furthermore there is less excuse for not even mentioning the limitations of the offered approach or for marketing the economists' epidermic approach to human nature as the authoritative model of men and women.

The purpose of this chapter was to counter this arrogance. In Chapter 3 we saw how economists borrowed the concept of utility from political theorists (like Jeremy Bentham) in order to create a 'science of society'. Utility lost its humanist dimension (perhaps inevitably) and the warnings of early utilitarian philosophers like J. S. Mill (see box) were forgotten. In this chapter a series of parables illustrated the dimensions of humanity that have been left out of the economic approach.

Progressive utility

I regard utility as the ultimate appeal on all ethical questions; but it must be utility in the largest sense, founded on the permanent interests of man as progressive being.

John Stuart Mill, *On Liberty*, 1859

Why is all this important? Because of the power of indirect indoctrination. When we, the teachers of economics, tell our students that here is a model of how rational persons behave (and perhaps ought to behave), it is not unreasonable of them to think: 'If I am not that kind of person then I must be less than rational.' This would be a tragically misleading message which needs to be strangled at birth. For instance it is a favourite tactic of economists to concede that their model is not always accurate because people are not as rational as their theory assumes. Some concession! In reality, although it is true that humans may lack the computational capacity of a computer (and thus the ability to behave according to the *Equi-marginal Principle* with precision), often we do not behave according to the economists' theory because our rationality is *more* sophisticated than that which the economic model (or *any* computer) can understand.

Two simple examples of our superior rationality (as compared to economics' instrumental rationality): (1) we subject our desires to our reason; (2) we even manipulate them when we deem them unfit. Also we understand that our preferences are frequently manufactured and take steps to secure our autonomy from advertisers and other sirens who are after our minds and souls; in short, we do things that *Homo economicus* cannot even dream of (come to think of it, *Homo economicus,* being just a bundle of preferences, cannot dream, laugh, be embarrassed or feel shame). Thus if the economist's model does not predict our behaviour very well this is so as much because we are more clever than the model as it is because we are less skilled than a computer at calculating costs and benefits. And this is a message that needs to be broadcast loud and clear.

> **Debate as a precursor to free choice**
>
> Liberty, as a principle, has no application to any state anterior to the time when mankind have become capable of being improved by free and equal discussion.
>
> John Stuart Mill, *On Liberty*, 1859

In short this chapter has endeavoured to warn beginners that price-less virtues such as human autonomy, creativity and liberty (of the type J. S. Mill refers to in the box above) are not to be found in the economist's repertoire. Later (see Part 3) we shall find that the economic approach has serious problems in providing guidance on matters such as social justice and well-being. Could it not be that the root of these problems lie in the rather misanthropic model of men and women on which economics trades? We shall see.

In the meantime, it is useful to end this chapter by pondering a paradox. On the one hand, as already noted, economics is replete with eulogies to freedom (particularly of the market). However, on the other hand, the type of freedom that economics textbooks talk about is compatible with the science fiction image of rows and rows of persons attached to a pleasure machine which bombards them with utility (or, to be more respectful to ordinal utility, which keeps them at the very top of their preferences ordering). Less apocalyptically, it is consistent with a society in which individuals' ideals have been reduced to purchasing commodities in gigantic shopping complexes guided totally by cravings manufactured in elaborate marketing clinics. Perhaps the most helpful conclusion to draw from all this is that the economic textbook's model of rational choice is the culmination of the logic unleashed on the world by the emergence and domination of market societies (see Chapter 1 again). One question is worth keeping in mind when immersed in that logic: is a happy slave (a slave of feudal masters or, today, of the advertisers) capable of being free (whatever that person's utility level)?

So, if freedom is more than just desire-fulfilment what does it mean to be free? No one has the definitive answer but here is a suggestion: individual freedom may be the capacity to act freely, not only in order to satisfy the preferences that are there already (the utility machine can do this admirably), but in order to create new and better preferences – in order to improve one's self. We can do this only if we care about more than the indulgence of our current desires. This is of course not to say that we are masochists and that we derive utility from the *actual* sadness we get from reading a bleak novel or watching a melancholy film. Think of the bliss of the marathon runner who has just finished first at the Olympics. Could this bliss be the same had the pain been removed by some undetectable super-drug? No way. And yet this is not to say that the athlete enjoys the pain. Instead what seems to be happening is that grief, pain and sadness help us to reorient ourselves, to excavate parts of ourselves (even preferences) we never knew existed, to create new ones and to see the world through ever-changing eyes. The right to such a complex experience may be freedom.

The joyless ownership

During the 1993 bush-fires in areas of south-eastern Australia where forests were devastated but no houses or farms affected, the media often reported that 'thankfully no property was lost'. This is not incon-sistent with the general trend in market societies of forgetting how to derive satisfaction without direct consumption or ownership. For some this is a loss for humanity; a diminution of freedom even. Karl Marx, in his usual polemical style, had issued a warning which the econo-mists' model of human behaviour cannot heed.

> Private property has made us so stupid and one-sided that an object is *ours* only when we have it – when it exists for us as capital, or when it is directly possessed . . . the human being had to be reduced to this absolute poverty in order that he might yield his inner wealth . . . The *increase in value* of the world of things is directly proportional to the *decrease in value* of the human world.
> Karl Marx, *Capital, Volume 1*, 1867

Returning for the last time to the economic theory of rational choices, it seems that its main defect is an inability to recognise the richness of the human experience and thus to mistake appropriation of utility for freedom. It is true that animals act purely on desires created by impulse. And these desires guide their actions in a definite way. However, what distinguishes us from other animals is our capacity to base our choice, not only on prefer-ences over outcomes (e.g. consumption bundles), but also on preferences over preferences. Unlike cats and mice we have the capacity to think to ourselves: 'Should I want this?' or 'I do not like jazz music but I wish I did' or even 'Last year I was *so* immature! Thank goodness I no longer care about whether I lose another 3 kg or not.' So, be warned: the neoclassical economic model in your textbook cannot handle the complex motivation which makes life worth living. If this is right, then perhaps the economists' theory of behaviour is very well suited to mice and intelligent computers. We, humans, need a much richer theory!

Rat choice theory!

John Kagel and three collaborators proved that mice are keen followers of the neoclassical theory of choice. In their 1981 paper (published in the *Quarterly Journal of Economics*), they report on an experiment involving a male rat who was confined for days in a cage in which there were two levers. Every time the rat pressed one lever, a fixed amount of food was dispensed; each time he pressed the second lever, a fixed amount of water was made available. Pulling those levers was the only means the rat had to get food and water. The experimenters controlled the total number of releases of food or water so that, after say ten releases, no more food or water would be dispensed during that day.

This total number was the rat's daily 'income'. They also controlled the number of lever-presses it would take to release water or food. For instance, on some days the rat would have to press the food-lever twice to get some food whereas one press of the other lever would suffice for some water. Assuming that the rat preferred fewer lever-presses for a given quantity of food or water, the ratio of the lever-presses necessary to get food and water respectively was equivalent to the relative price of food and water.

After a few days of experimentation, the rat would discover his most preferred mix of food and water given his 'total income' and the 'ratio of prices'. Then the experimenters would alter his 'income' and 'relative prices' in order to discover whether the rat behaved in a manner compatible with the neoclassical model of choice. Their main finding is that, indeed, the rat's behaviour was consistent with utility maximisation! Whenever the ratio of prices changed, he would alter his consumption of food and water by consuming more of whichever became 'cheaper'.

Production and markets

Review: textbooks on firms, production and markets

1 Firms and the *Equi-marginal Principle*

Surprised that the *Equi-marginal Principle* is back? You shouldn't be. The theory of choice in Part 1 was designed to apply regardless of what is being chosen. We have already seen how consumers were modelled as boxes which digest commodities (or, more generally, experiences) as inputs and produce utility as output. If we think of these boxes as firms then the inputs are the 'commodities' used during the production process (e.g. labour, land, machines, raw materials) and the output is the commodities that come out of the production line (Figure 5.1). So, in exactly the same way that the *Equi-marginal Principle* relates how the first box (i.e. the consumer) can get the most output (i.e. utility) out of the inputs (e.g. commodities), it can also explain how the second box (i.e. the firm) can get the most output (i.e. commodities) out of its inputs (e.g. land, labour, machines).

1.1 The nature of a firm's inputs

> **Why do firms exist?**
>
> Why does a large firm like Ford have many different factories which exchange commodities (e.g. car parts) with each other but without using the market? For example the Spanish branch of the company produces gearboxes which are then added to a car made in Ford's

German factory. Yet the latter does not buy the gearbox from the former. In effect, the firm has substituted the market. But if the market works so well, why does the firm do this? Indeed, why does the firm exist at all? Why do people not do everything through one to one trading and, instead, work in groups called firms?

The answer given by Ronald Coase (who won the Nobel Prize in economics primarily for this thought) was that transacting at the market-place has its costs; e.g. the time it takes to haggle, the risk that you will purchase a good of inferior quality, the possibility that when you wish to buy some part it will not be available in sufficient quantity at the market etc. A firm, according to Coase, will expand until the cost of organising an extra transaction within the firm becomes equal to the cost of carrying out the same transaction by means of an exchange on the open market. It stops growing when the cost of organising internally the next activity (e.g. building a new gearbox) exceeds the transaction cost of buying it in from some outside supplier (e.g. an independent gearbox manufacturer). Notice how in the last sentence the size of the firm was explained by means of the *Equimarginal Principle*.

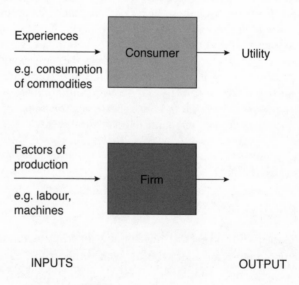

Figure 5.1   Firms as consumers

What are the inputs to a production process? At first we notice the raw materials (such as minerals, electricity, etc.) which are, clearly, commodities traded in markets just like apples and oranges. Then we observe the main factors of production which are also presented by neoclassical economists as commodities. For example, there are the workers who labour over the production line using machines in order to fashion final commodities out of raw materials. Are these people commodities? Are the machines, or the conveyor belt itself, a commodity? Is the land on which the factory stands a commodity?

As Chapter 1 suggested, these factors have not always been commodities. Indeed it was the transformation of these factors *into* commodities which coincided with the rise of industrial, market-based societies (that is, capitalism). Nevertheless one might say that, since the industrial revolution is behind us, we are free to treat factors of production as commodities. However, doing so introduces a small, yet significant, complication that we must attend to.

With reference to the diagrammatical analogy above between the models of the consumer and of the firm, the treatment of production factors as commodities necessitates that the firm is not thought of as the owner of these factors. Let me explain this subtle point: in the case of consumers, they buy commodities and then proceed to consume them. In effect the consumer acquires property rights over the consumption 'inputs'.

By contrast, the firm is not modelled as the owner of its inputs. Imagine the controversy the following statement would cause: 'Coca Cola owns its workforce.' No, firms *hire* units (or hours) of labour from its rightful owners: the workers. Although capital and land can be owned by the firms uncontroversially, again it is more helpful for the theory to imagine that firms are renting the land and the machines which they need. Why? Because the theory wants to pinpoint how much land or how many machines the firm should want to utilise at every point in time. If the firm already owns a fixed quantity of land and capital which it always uses, then what is the point trying to find out how much of these factors the firm ought to employ?

Of course you may point out that firms often *do* own their land or machines. Well, economists can live with this happily. Their objective is to remind us that land and machines have *opportunity cost*. Therefore, even if firms own their land, under-utilising it may be costly in the sense that the firm might increase its returns simply by leasing part of its land to someone else who could make better use of it. So even when a firm owns the machinery or the land it uses, economic analysis imagines that they are being leased by the firm (even if it is leasing them to itself!).

To recap, in economic theory consumers (excepting thieves) are assumed to own commodities before consuming them. Firms on the other hand do not own the factors of production which they 'consume'; instead they hire them. However, they *do* own the commodities churned out by the production line and traded at the market later. Why is this an important observation? For two reasons. First, because it helps us understand what the theory of the firm is trying to do: it attempts to tell a story about how firms select amongst different combinations of factors in order to minimise the cost of producing a certain quantity. The idea that firms make this choice amongst hired factors of production allows us to consider quantities of land, labour and capital which the firm might not presently own (or which it owns but chooses not to use and, instead, lease to others).

The second reason is political. As we shall see in Chapters 6 and 7, this conceptualisation of the firm as a non-owner of land, labour and capital creates a very specific image for business. If business does not own anything, what is its role? Quite naturally, embarking from this description of the firm, one comes to the conclusion that the role of business is to coordinate the activities of the factors of production; to be something of an orchestra conductor. Well, this is a pretty flattering image which I would not mind at all if I were, say, the European owner of a mine in Africa but which I would contest if I were one of the miners. However, we had better leave the politics to one side until the end of this chapter.

5.1.2 The firm's choice of input combinations

Remember how the consumer's best choice between different baskets of commodities was determined by the *Equi-marginal Principle?* Well, the same principles apply to the firm's choice between different combinations of factors of production. Firms like consumers have budget constraints. Their inputs are commodities and come at a price per unit. Moreover firms have a certain amount of money which they are prepared to lay out in order to purchase inputs. Naturally in the same way the consumer tries to extract as much utility as possible from a certain budget, firms try to ensure that for a given expenditure on inputs (e.g. labour, land) maximum output will be produced.

Of course there is an important difference between the consumer and the firm: Whereas the consumer craves utility for its own sake, firms are assumed to care about output only because of the profit they can make from selling it later. None the less provided the firm can count on being able to sell its output at a certain price (or range of prices), the choices of consumers and firms can be analysed using the same model. So, for our purposes, the analysis of how firms behave can proceed along the lines of diagrams which differ very little from the indifference curves and budget constraints of Chapter 2.

Looking at Figure 5.2 we find a picture very similar to that of Figure 2.4 in Chapter 2. Only here the axis depict not commodities to be consumed by some imaginary consumer but, instead, factors of production (e.g. labour and machines) to be *hired* by some firm. As for the curves resembling indifference curves, they are called *isoquant* curves (from the Greek word *iso* which

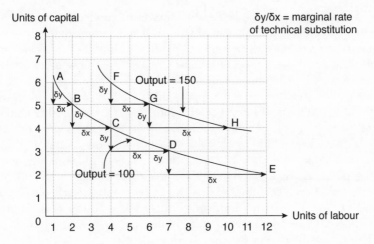

Figure 5.2   A firm's trade-offs

means 'equal') because they correspond to the combinations of the quantities of the factors of production (in our example labour and machinery) which give rise to the same quantity of output. Thus just as all the points of an indifference curve generate the same level of utility for the consumer, all the points of an isoquant produce the same output for the firm. For example, 6 units of capital (i.e. machines) and 1 unit of labour produce 100 units of output but so do 2 units of capital and 12 units of labour (see points A and E in Figure 5.2).

Isoquants and their slope: the marginal rate of technical substitution

The slope of an isoquant reveals the firm's production capabilities in the same way that an individual's indifference curves reveal her preferences. In Figure 5.2, at point A the firm produces 100 units making use of 6 units of capital and 1 unit of labour. If it were to reduce its capital by 1 unit without reducing its output, it would have to increase its labour util-isation by about 1 unit; a rate of 1/1. This rate (i.e. the rate at which it must increase its utilisation of one factor in order to compensate for the loss of a small amount of the other factor) is called the *marginal rate of technical substitution*. It turns out that the geometrical depiction of this rate is the slope of the isoquant. (Just as the consumer's marginal rate of substitution coincided with the slope of her indifference curve.) Check that at point D, for example, the *marginal rate of technical substitution* is $\frac{1}{5}$.

To sum up so far, the isoquants capture the production process of the firm by translating different combinations of inputs into different levels of output. The question now becomes: how does a firm choose between these combinations? Quite obviously it must first ask itself how much money it wishes to spend on inputs and what are the prices (rental prices, that is) of labour, capital, land and so on. Suppose that in our example the firm wishes to produce 100 units of output, each unit of capital costs $10 per unit per period to hire, a unit of labour is half as expensive at $5 per period and that the firm can afford to spend $60 per period on capital and labour. Since the planned output is 100 units, the firm needs to get on the isoquant joining points A, B, C, D and E. Consider each of these combinations in turn: A and D each costs $65 while B and C cost $60. Clearly combinations A and D cost more than the firm's budget while B and C are not only affordable but can also generate exactly the same amount of output (since all these points belong to the same isoquant).

Observing Figure 5.2 more closely we can discern geometrically the reasons for which combinations B and C make a lot more sense than A and D. Starting at A, if the firm were to reduce its utilisation of capital by one unit, how many more labour units would it need to employ in order to remain on the same isoquant? Answer: 1 extra unit of labour, that is the *marginal rate of technical substitution* equals $1/1$. But we do know that labour units are half as expensive as capital units to hire. Therefore the firm should definitely proceed with this substitution from A to B since it can replace an expensive capital unit with a cheaper labour unit without any loss in production. Similarly, if the firm were to begin at point D, it is easy to show that a move to point C would be sensible. Think about it. At D the firm would be employing 7 labour and 3 capital units. How many labour units would it need to give up in order to employ an extra capital unit while still producing 100 units of output? Answer: 3, that is, the *marginal rate of substitution* is $\frac{1}{3}$. This means that the firm could rid itself of 3 labour units (and thus save $15 per period) and in their place hire an extra unit of capital at two-thirds of the cost (i.e. at $10). A cost minimising firm would certainly do so.

In conclusion, capital–labour combinations B and C make sense while A and D are unacceptable. But which is better? B or C? The answer is that they are equally good since they cost the same ($60 per period) and produce the same output. This result is confirmed by, what else, the *Equi-marginal Principle*. Recall what it had to say in the case of consumer choices in Chapter 2: select the combination of quantities of two commodities such that the marginal rate of substitution comes as close to the ratio of prices as possible. Surprise, surprise this is also what is happening here. What is the marginal rate of technical substitution between points B and C? Figure 5.2 clearly shows that it equals $\frac{1}{2}$. And what is the ratio of prices of labour and capital? It is also $\frac{1}{2}$. No wonder combinations B and C seem better than the rest. They have the endorsement of the ubiquitous *Equi-marginal Principle*!

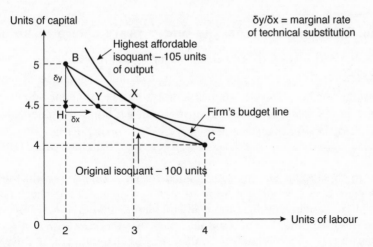

Figure 5.3   Efficient input choices

Is there perhaps a better combination than either B or C? Possibly. Figure 5.3 zooms in and looks more closely at the combinations lying between points B and C. One of these points is X.

Immediately we notice that X costs just as much as B or C. Thus there is no doubt that it is affordable. Is it preferable though? The answer is a resounding 'yes'. For it is clear that X lies above the red isoquant joining points B and C (which corresponds to output of 100 units per period); therefore X produces more output than either B or C even though it costs the same (notice that it lies on a higher isoquant which corresponds to 105 units of output per period). To see this another way, suppose the firm were to begin at B. Should it reduce its utilisation of capital by half a unit? If it were to do so, how much more labour would it need to employ to keep output constant? Answer: less than one unit of labour (i.e. an extra quantity of labour equal to line segment HY). But if it gives up this half a unit of capital (i.e. BH units of capital in our diagram), the firm can afford to purchase one whole extra labour unit (i.e. go from point H to point X); that is, half a labour unit more than it needs to keep output steady at the same level as at B. Thus by moving from point B down along its budget line (or constraint) towards X, the firm will be increasing output from 100 to 105 units per period at no extra cost. Under what circumstances will the firm have no opportunity to improve its situation further? The answer is: if it is at a point such as X where there is no room for further improvement of the sort we just described. Diagrammatically this means that, at the firm's best combination given its budget, one of its isoquants will be tangential to its budget line – as at X. Analytically, this is a restatement of the *Equimarginal Principle* which was fully developed in Chapter 2 (see box below).

The *Equi-marginal Principle* and a firm's choice of inputs

All we need here is a restatement of the *Equi-marginal Principle* from Chapter 2. Compare Figures 2.5c and 5.3: the best choice of inputs for the firm is achieved when the slope of the isoquant equals the slope of the firm's constraint. That is, when the firm's *marginal rate of technological substitution* equals the *ratio of input prices*.

In conclusion, the *only* combinations of factors the firm will consider, irrespectively of how much it wants to spend on inputs or how much output it wants to produce, will be those resembling X; that is, they will contain quantities of capital, labour, land etc. such that the *marginal rate of technical substitution* will equal the ratio of factor prices or, diagrammatically, they will be points of tangency between the firm's budget line (or constraint) and an isoquant. So, let us examine what will happen as the firm expands; that is as it spends more and more on inputs in an attempt to produce more and more output. In Figure 5.3 the assumption was that the firm had about $60 per period to spend. Suppose that was the case two years ago. Last year business boomed and it decided to spend $80. This year its expenditure increased further to $100 per period. How would its demand for capital and for labour units change from one year to the next? And how much should it produce at the new expenditure levels? Figure 5.4 answers these questions under the assumption that the price of labour and capital units have remained the same (at $5 and $10 respectively).

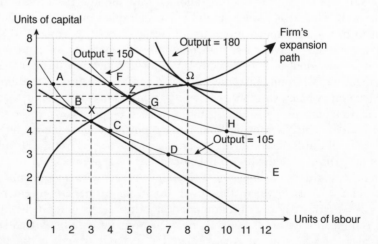

Figure 5.4 A firm's expansion path

Table 5.1 Input choice: a numerical example

Factor combination	Labour units	Capital units	Expenditure on factors	Firm's output
X	3	4.5	60	105
Z	5	5.5	80	150
Ω	8	6	100	180

Starting with the optimal combination when the firm has $60 to spend (combination X, already examined in Figure 5.4) all we need to do is shift the firm's constraint (up and to the right in the figure) with every increase in its budget and then observe the combination on the new budget constraint corresponding to a tangency point between that constraint and an isoquant. Table 5.1 summarises our findings.

So, according to Figure 5.4, the straightforward application of the *Equi-marginal Principle* suggests that by increasing its expenditure from $60 to $80 and then to $100, the firm can boost its output from 105 units to 150 and 180 respectively. Of course in order to do this it must be clever in the way it employs (or 'blends') its capital and labour; it must be *efficient* (see box on next page for a precise definition of economic efficiency). To achieve maximum output given its expenditure on these two factors, the firm must select the precise combinations above. If it does not (e.g. if it were to spend its $80 in the case of the second row on 4 units of labour and 6 units of capital – instead of 5 and 5.5 as in combination Z) it would fail to produce 150 units (notice that combination [4, 6] the firm does not manage to reach the isoquant corresponding to output 150 units).

The three combinations X, Z and Ω in Figure 5.4 are all recommended by the *Equi-marginal Principle* and, in this sense, are efficient (or optimal) in that they maximise output at a given cost (or minimise cost at a given output). Linking them up creates what is known as the firm's *expansion path*: as the firm increases its output it must stay on this path if it is to remain economically or Pareto efficient (see box below). To recap, a firm's expansion path comprises combinations which are tangency points between the firm's isoquants and its various budget constraints (one for each expenditure level).

Efficiency in economics: Pareto efficiency/optimality*

In the theory of the firm, a combination of inputs is inefficient if it is possible to alter it at no extra cost and, in so doing, boost output. And conversely: if a combination is such that any alteration of it will either cost more money or cause output to fall, then this combination is efficient. Diagrammatically, the combinations on the firm's expansion path (i.e. those conforming to the *Equi-marginal Principle*) are efficient while all the others are not.

This simple definition of efficiency is named after the Italian economist Vilfredo Pareto (1848–1923). Often it is referred to as *economic efficiency* in order to contrast it to *technical efficiency*. To illustrate the difference, consider a firm using input combination A in Figures 5.2 and 5.4: 6 units of capital and 1 unit of labour. According to the isoquant through A, the firm *can* produce 100 units of output at A. Well, this does not mean that it *will*. For example, the workers may be lax or the technicians may be operating the machinery less than perfectly. *Technical efficiency* implies that this will not be the case and that the firm will produce at every point in the figure of Figures 5.2, 5.3 and 5.4 the amount reported by the isoquant (i.e. the maximum possible given the combination of factors at that point). Economic or Pareto efficiency by contrast requires more: it requires not only the ability to work the factors that you have at your disposal as hard as possible, but also the capacity to select the right blend of factors of production given your firm's budget (i.e. point X in Figure 5.3 or the points on the firm *expansion path* in Figure 5.4)

* Note that the two words *efficiency* and *optimality* are used interchangeably in economics.

5.1.3 The firm's cost of production

In Homer's *Odyssey* there is a story about Penelope who spent ten years weaving a single garment in an attempt to stave off the pretenders to Ulysses' (her husband's) throne. She had promised the pretenders that when the weaving is over she would choose his successor from their ranks; and then proceeded weaving by day and spoiling her handicraft by night. If one is wasteful, either intentionally like Penelope or unintentionally, there is no limit to the cost of making something. Consequently, when economists

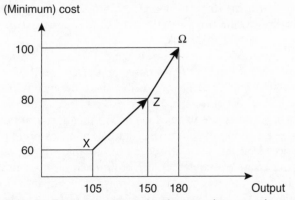

Points X, Z and Ω correspond to those on the expansion path

Figure 5.5   The makings of a cost curve

talk of the cost of producing a certain output, they mean the *minimum* cost.

For this reason, Figure 5.4 is invaluable. Once the firm's expansion path has been drawn, we can immediately read off it the minimum cost of producing different levels of output. Thus output levels of 105, 150 and 180 units will cost the firm $60, $80 and $100 respectively per period. But remember that these are minimum costs which will escalate if the firm chooses any combination other than X, Z or Ω. Why would the firm make such a mistake? Some times due to bad management; on other occasions because it cannot get its hands on the combinations it wants (e.g. a shortage of labour or a waiting list for tractors).

Figure 5.5 simplifies Figure 5.4 by reading off the latter the minimum cost of producing each level of output. While consulting it one must always keep in mind that the cost curve it depicts only applies as long as the firm sticks to its expansion path in Figure 5.4. One last observation is worth making at this stage: The average cost of producing a unit of output is not constant. As the firm's production increases from 105 to 150 and then to 180, the cost per unit (or average cost) drops at first from 57 cents to 53.3 but then rises to 55.5 cents.

5.1.4 Profit maximisation

So far the theory has explained how the firm wishing to produce a certain output, or equivalently to spend a certain sum of money on producing a commodity, will choose its inputs. *The time has now arrived to ask: how much output should the firm want to produce?* To answer this question, one must know what the firm's objective is. The standard assumption of neoclassical economics is that firms strive to maximise profits. The idea of *profit maximisation* is as central to the theory of the firm as the idea of *utility maximisation* was crucial in Part 1 of this book.

Profit, as defined by economists, is the difference between revenue and economic (or opportunity) cost. Consequently the level of output that maximises profit stretches as far as possible the difference between revenue and cost (provided of course the former exceeds the latter). Therefore the fact that a firm can increase its revenue by boosting output is not necessarily a good reason for doing so. Increasing output enhances profitability only if the extra units of output bring in more revenue than they cost.

In the language of economics, the profit maximising firm will increase output when marginal revenue exceeds marginal cost and vice versa. By deduction, the profit maximising output level is the one at which marginal cost equals marginal revenue. Figure 5.6 captures this latest reincarnation of the *Equi-marginal Principle* with output q′ maximising profit since at that level the slope of the revenue curve (i.e. marginal revenue) equals the slope of the cost curve (i.e. marginal cost). Notice that it is almost identical to Figure 2.2 (the only difference being that where we used to write 'utility' or 'disutility' we now have 'revenue' and 'cost'). For this reason the explanation of the geometry of the *Equi-marginal Principle* will not be repeated here (consult Chapters 1 and 2 for a revision).

In summary, Figures 5.2 and 5.3 solved the choice problem of a firm which knows how much money it wants to spend on inputs or, equivalently,

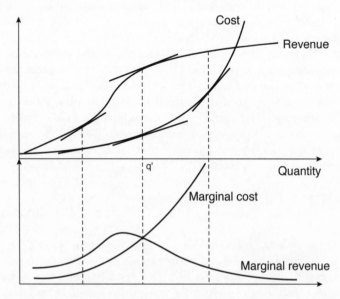

Figure 5.6   The geometry of the *Equi-marginal Principle* revisited

how much output it wants to produce. Figure 5.5 translated this solution into a cost curve reporting on the minimum cost of production at different levels of output. By matching this information to data on the firm's revenue at different levels of output/sales, Figure 5.6 completes the story by explaining what is involved in the choice of how much output to produce in the first place (or, equivalently, how much money the firm wants to spend on inputs).

5.2 Firms and markets

5.2.1 Competition as a determinant of a firm's revenue

You will have noticed that in the preceding pages we laboured over the derivation of the firm's cost curve whereas we threw its revenue curve into the picture (Figure 5.6) only at the last moment. Admittedly this was a bit naughty. Where did the revenue curve come from? Sure enough we learnt how to derive revenue curves in Chapter 2 as an extension of demand curves. However, back there we learnt how to obtain demand curves either for individuals or for groups of individuals (by summing up individual curves into curves for groups of consumers; into demand curves for whole markets). What we did not learn is how to derive a demand (or a revenue) curve for a firm.

Let us think about the problem. Suppose there are two ice-cream sellers on some beach: Jill and Jack. Jill charges $2 per cone. What will Jack's revenue be if he charges $3 (let us assume that there is no difference in the ice-cream they are selling)? Very little, one presumes. Why pay $3 if you can buy the same item for $2? Now suppose Jill got tired and went home, leaving the beach to Jack. With no competitor left, Jack will be in a position to raise the price to $3 without losing the revenue he would have lost had Jill continued to sell ice-cream at $2 a throw.

Granted that a firm's revenue is affected by the extent of competition it faces at the market, how can we work out what revenue it can expect at different prices? Before we proceed it is important to acknowledge the question's complexity. Imagine that you and I compete in some market. Before I decide what price to charge, or how much output to produce, I must try to anticipate your decision. But how can I do this? Predicting what you will do is not like predicting the weather. Unlike the weather which will be whatever it is meant to be regardless of my thoughts about it, your actions will depend on what you expect *me* to do just as much as my decision hinges on my expectation of your decision. We end up with a conundrum: my choice of output and/or price will depend on what I think that you think that I think that you think that I think . . . about this choice!

Competition breeds uncertainty about a firm's revenue at different prices and output levels. If a market is monopolised totally by some firm, there is no such problem: the sum of the consumers' demand curves will be the firm's demand curve (and there is nothing easier than deriving from that its revenue curve). However if there are two sellers we end up with the conundrum of the previous paragraph. And the greater the number of sellers the more complicated things become. Section 5.2.2 gives an example of a two-seller (or *duopoly*) market. Section 5.2.3 introduces more competitors, while Section 5.2.4 takes all of them but one away thus analysing the case of monopoly.

5.2.2 A market with two competitors: a duopoly

Consider the market for some specialised car component (e.g. a rare type of mechanical fuel injection suitable for a small number of 1970s exotic cars) and suppose that there exist six workshops capable of producing this unit. Every year, each workshop can produce 1, 2 or a maximum of 3 units at a cost of 8, 11 or 16 respectively (Table 5.2). Now suppose that two companies, Alpha and Beta, each owns three workshops. Neither firm will utilise more than one of its three workshops if it has orders for three units or fewer (notice than within the same workshop, once the first unit has been produced at a cost of 8, the second unit costs an extra 3 and the third an extra 5). However, if demand per firm ranges between 4 and 6 units, Alpha or Beta will utilise their second workshop; and if demand exceeds 6 units then all three workshops of the company will go into production. Thus let us assume that workshops come into stream sequentially. The first one operates when demand is less than 4 units; the second starts up production when demand exceeds 3 units; finally, the third begins to produce only if demand exceeds 6 units (i.e. when Workshops 1 and 2 are already working at full capacity).

Table 5.2 A workshop's cost of production

Units of output	1	2	3
Total cost	8	11	16

From the above we can derive the cost schedule for producing any output between 1 and 9 units for Alpha or Beta. For output levels 1 to 3, the cost schedule of the whole firm will coincide with that of the single functioning workshop. However, to produce 4 units, each company will need to use its second workshop in order to produce the fourth unit. Thus the cost of producing 4 units will equal 16 (the cost of producing 3 units in its first workshop – see Table 5.2) plus 8 (the cost of producing the fourth unit in the second workshop). And so on.

Table 5.3 summarises the cost schedule of either Alpha or Beta. Of course in real life firms have different cost schedules; however in order to keep the analysis simple let us assume that Alpha and Beta have identical costs because the three workshops they each own and run are identical.

Table 5.3 Cost and demand facing our two firms

Q	1	2	3	4	5	6	7	8	9
$	8	11	16	24	27	32	40	43	48

Example: Alpha's cost of producing 5 units = 16 (cost of producing three in one workshop) + 11(cost of producing two in its second workshop) = 27

> **The demand curve for the output of Alpha and Beta**
>
> Price per unit = 20 minus the combined output of Alpha and Beta

Now that we have data on cost we must turn our attention to the demand side: what prices are the customers of Alpha and Beta prepared to pay? Imagine that market research has shown that if only one unit were available in the whole market, an auction would occur and that unit would fetch a price equal to 19. Moreover if 2 units were to be auctioned off, each would be go under the hammer for 18. Again for simplicity let us suppose that the price for each unit would approximately equal 20 minus the number of units in the market. Thus if Alpha were to produce 3 units and Beta 4, then the price the market would be able to bear (provided all 7 units were to be sold) would equal $20 - (4 + 3) = 13$.

Notice how the information made available by market research, although precise and of interest to our two firms, does not tell them how much to produce. The reason is that the price of Alpha's product depends not only on how many units Alpha makes but also on how many Beta produces. But the same applies to Beta. Thus the earlier conundrum: Alpha's output decision depends on what it expects Beta will think that Alpha anticipates Beta to ... What a mess! However, there is a way in which to disentangle all these beliefs, expectations and projections.

Suppose that you are Alpha's managing director. You do not know how much Beta will produce and as a result you cannot know what price you can sell your output at. What do you do? Your problem resembles that of a chess player: without any firm idea as to your opponent's next move, you are forced to consider various scenaria of the form: 'If Beta does X, which of my actions is a best reply to X? And if Beta does Y, what is the best reply to Y? Etc.' Like a grandmaster of chess, the more scenarios you consider in this way, the better prepared you will be for all eventualities and the better the chance that you will make the right moves.

Given that the maximum output of each company is 9 (3 from each of its three workshops), Beta has nine possible options from which to choose. It may decide to produce 1 unit, 2 units, ... or 9 units. What *you* can do is to treat these nine possibilities as nine different scenarios. 'Suppose', you say to yourself, 'Beta were to produce X units. What would my profits be if I produced Y units?' Although time consuming, this is not too hard a calculation. For example, take the scenario were Beta produces 3 units altogether when your company produced 4. The total output (by both firms, that is) being 7, the price that each unit would fetch at the market would be 13 (recall that market research showed that price would equal 20 minus the total output).

So since you produced 4 units, your revenue would equal 4 times the price (13) = 52. Subtracting the cost of producing 4 units from this revenue (which according to Table 5.3 is 24) leaves you with a profit of 28. In the same way, you can calculate your profits from all possible decisions of the two companies. To spare you the anguish of so much arithmetic, Table 5.4 reports on the profits you ought to expect from different scenarios (involving 9 possible choices by each company).

With all this information available to you, it has become possible to gain a better insight into which output is more likely to maximise your profits. Looking at the first five columns, it is easy to see that provided Beta produces an output no more than 4 units, your best strategy is to produce 6 units. Why? Remember that each column corresponds to one output strategy by Beta. Thus the first column applies if Beta is to produce a single unit, the second if Beta produces two units, the third if it produces three units and so on. In each of the first four columns, your highest profit is located in *your* sixth row; that is, provided Beta produces no more than 4 units, your best decision is to stick to 6 units. (In Table 5.4 the maximum profits per column are shown in bold. Note that the first four lie on Alpha's sixth row.)

Table 5.4 Alpha's profits in each of eighty-one possible scenarios

		Beta's ouput								
		1	2	3	4	5	6	7	8	9
	1	10	9	8	7	6	5	4	3	2
	2	23	21	19	17	15	13	11	9	7
	3	32	29	26	23	20	17	**14**	**11**	**8**
Alpha's	4	36	32	28	24	20	16	12	8	4
output	5	43	38	33	**28**	**23**	**18**	13	8	3
	6	**46**	**40**	**34**	**28**	22	16	10	4	<0
	7	44	37	30	23	16	9	2	<0	<0
	8	45	37	29	21	13	5	<0	<0	<0
	9	42	33	24	15	6	<0	<0	<0	<0

Each column represents the output of Beta and each row the output of Alpha. So, as in the example of the previous paragraph, if Beta produces 3 units and Alpha 4 units, we look at the cell defined by the fourth row and the third column to confirm that Alpha will earn a profit of 28.

Now if for some reason you expect Beta to produce 5 or 6 units, clearly your best reply is to produce only 5 (notice how your maximum profit – in bold – is in your fifth row when Beta has selected its fifth or sixth row). And if Beta is expected to produce between 7 and 9 units, you are better off producing only 3 units. Looking at the overall picture, it is obvious that your profit is highest when Beta produces as little as possible (see the first column) while it will fall dramatically (to values less than zero) if your competitor floods the market with its produce. How much output should you produce now that you know all this?

If you are *very* cautious, you may stick to only 3 units anticipating that Beta may produce 7 or more. If not, you will produce between 5 and 6 units (5 if you expect Beta to produce between 4 and 5 units, 6 otherwise). Economics textbooks in this case suggest that you will produce 5 units for the simple reason that you have no reason to expect your competitor to produce a quantity different from yours since the two companies are so alike (recall that they have the same costs). Therefore in the same way you should not expect your competitors to produce more than you intend to produce, they will not expect you to produce more than them either. The only exception is the case where one firm has been in business for a while, before the second one comes in. Then the firm that was there first, by some historical accident, will always produce more and enjoy higher profit than the other even if they face the same costs. To see this clearly check that if Beta was operating before Alpha entered the market and had already settled on an a steady output of 7 units per period, then Alpha's best strategy would be to produce only 3 units. In that case, Alpha's and Beta's profits would be 14 and 30 respectively. As economists say, Beta would be benefiting from a *first mover advantage*.

To summarise, in this simple case of duopoly one would expect each firm to produce 5 units on average. In aggregate, output would hover around 10 giving each firm an average profit of 23. Finally the price of these components would, if this theory is correct, averages $10.

5.2.3 Collusion, cartels and monopoly

You are still Alpha's manager. Both you and your competitor have settled at 5 units of output and $23 profit each. At this point you notice something interesting. If you and the manager of Beta can somehow agree on reducing output to 3 units each, your profits (and thus Beta's profits) will climb from the current 23 to 26 (consult Table 5.4). Why not come to such an agreement? There are two reasons why such an agreement may be difficult to reach. The first one is that most countries have legislation which forbids such agreements amongst competitors. Of course if this was the only obstacle to collusion between firms, it would be unlikely to stop them from colluding.

However, there is a second, much more compelling, reason: although it is in Alpha's interest to agree with Beta to an output of 3 units each, it is also in its interest to break the agreement and produce 6 units once Beta has produced 3 (notice from Table 5.4 that when Beta is sticking to the agreement and produces only 3 units, Alpha's profits will increase from 26 to 34 if it cheats and raises output to 6 units). But because this is a temptation afflicting Beta as well (i.e. the urge to cheat on Alpha), it may undermine the trust between the two companies without which such an agreement would not occur.

This does not, of course, mean that collusion is impossible. For example, wise managers may learn to resist the temptation to cheat because the payoffs from cheating are short term while those from collusion are long term. If this happens, then competition between the two companies will end and the two will function like a merged company: explicitly as a merged monopoly or implicitly as a cartel. What would the result be? Aggregate output would fall from about 10 units to 6 units (3 each) and price would rise to 14 (recall again that price equals 20 minus total output). Evidently the end of competition would increase prices, boost the sellers' profit and reduce the number of car components available to consumers. In a nutshell, collusion and monopoly increases profit *because it makes it possible for producers to organise a reduction in the level of output.*

5.2.4 Expanding competition

In our example collusion between Alpha and Beta reduced output almost by half. But even if collusion had not occurred, output would still be relatively low: each firm's output would be around 5 or 6 units, which would leave one workshop per company idle (each firm owns three workshops each with a capacity to produce three units). Suppose the government takes a look at this situation and concludes that something needs to be done about this waste in productive capacity. It takes Alpha and Beta to court for restrictive practices and succeeds in breaking them up. The two companies are forced to give up their idle workshops which are then put together into a free-standing company Gamma, the new player in the market with a capacity to produce as much output as either Alpha or Beta (since now all three own two workshops each).

How much should Gamma produce if Alpha and Beta together produce 10 units (Alpha produces 5 and Beta 5 units), and therefore the price is set at 10 (price = 20 minus total output)? One thing that Gamma ought to keep in mind is that the price will be affected by its output decision. Assuming that the earlier market research is still valid, i.e. in this market price equals 20 minus the total number of units supplied to consumers, Table 5.5 relates Gamma's decision problem.

Table 5.5 The effect of a third firm entering the market

Gamma's output	Total output	Price	Gamma's revenue	Gamma's cost	Gamma's profit
0	10	10	0	0	0
1	11	9	9	8	1
2	12	8	16	11	5
3	13	7	21	16	5

The first row refers to the situation prior to Gamma's entry into the market. Total output equals the sum of output by Alpha and Beta. Recalling that in this case price would equal 10 (20 minus total output), when Gamma enters the market producing 1 unit total output rises to 11 and the price falls to 9 (otherwise the extra units of output produced by Gamma will not find a buyer). As for profit, 1 unit produced at a cost of 8 fetched 9 at the market; a profit of $1. However, if Gamma were to produce two units, even though price would now drop to 8, it would be selling them for a sum of 16 when the cost of production is only 11. This profit of 5 is due to what economists call *economies of scale*, the situation where you increase your cost by x per cent (as a result of producing more) but your output (and revenues) increase by more than x per cent. In this case, Gamma increased output by 100 per cent (from 1 unit to 2 units) while its cost increased only by 37.5 per cent. This is the reason why 2 units bring in higher profit than 1 unit.

Economies of scale usually apply when a company is producing far below its capacity. As output rises to near the maximum capacity of the workshop, squeezing yet another unit of output out of the production line causes a rapid escalation of costs. So we see that the marginal cost of producing a third unit rises to 5 (cost goes up from 11 to 16; a difference of 5). In summary, Gamma comes into a market in which the existing companies, Alpha and Beta, produce 5 units each (total output = 10) and sets its own output at 2. The effect of this new competition for the incumbent firms is that their profits are curbed as market-wide production increases and, consequently, price falls. To be precise, Alpha's and Beta's profits will decrease from 23 to 13 as the price will fall from 10 to 8. And all this because of the extra 2 units that Gamma supplies to consumers.

Why does Gamma not produce 3 units? Although according to Table 5.5 its profit would be the same ($5), it may not wish to provoke Alpha and Beta. Notice that if Gamma produces 3 units, it will be pushing Alpha's and Beta's profits down to $8 for no benefit to itself. Why provoke them in such a way unnecessarily? (Notice that if Alpha and Beta agree to set their output equal to 7 each Gamma will be driven out of the market.) Thus we can predict with some confidence the following market structure:

> Output: Alpha and Beta producing 5 units each and Gamma 2
>   units; total supply of 12 units.
> Price: $20 - 12 = 8$
> Profit: Alpha and Beta 13, Gamma 5; total profit equal to 31.

How do we know that this will be a stable situation? A strong indication that things might stabilise at this state can be had from the observation that none of these firms has an incentive to change its output. We have already seen why Gamma might refrain from producing more. Consider Alpha and Beta. If either of them reduces its output from 5 to 4, its profit will fall from 13 to 12. Thus none of them have an incentive *individually* to change their output. Of course, as before, they may prosper if they get together and decide to cut their output in unison; that is, collude.

Just like in the case of duopoly (before Gamma was created), if the firms manage to coordinate their action in order to restrict production, they will increase their profit at the expense of consumers. For example, suppose that the three agree to reduce their individual output by 1 unit, that is Alpha and Beta to cut production from 5 to 4 and Gamma from 2 to 1. Then Alpha and Beta would boost their profit from 13 to 20 while Gamma would see its own fall from 5 to 3. However Gamma might agree to this if Alpha and Beta were to pay Gamma, say, 50 per cent of their extra profit due to this agreement (i.e. 50 per cent of $7 + 7 = 7$). Then the agreement would mean an extra 3.5 profit for Alpha, another 3.5 for Beta and an extra 7 for Gamma – all due to the reduction in total output by 3 units (and thus the increase in price by 3).

On the other hand, as mentioned previously Alpha and Beta might decide there is a better course of action: boost output to 7 units each so that it is never profitable for Gamma to produce even a single unit. After a while, Gamma might go out of business at which point Alpha and Beta could resume their cosy duopoly. Even though this strategy is costly for the incumbent firms (since they will be making a profit only of 2 while keeping their output at 7 units each), it might prove tempting enough in view of the long-term benefits of having rid themselves of a third competitor.

In conclusion, Gamma enters the market and spearheads an increase in supply, a concomitant reduction in price and a fall in the profit of the incumbent firms. The new competitor drives price down and expands the quantity available to consumers. However the increase in the number of firms from two to three cannot by itself guarantee this. As we just saw, there are two other possibilities: (1) Collusion between the incumbent firms and the newcomer; (2) collusion between the incumbent firms in order to kick the newcomer out of the market.

5.2.5 Perfect competition

Have you ever heard mathematicians defining two lines as parallel if their intersection is an infinity away? What is the point of saying this? Well, it is of theoretical interest even though when one is building a bridge, or simply trying to find the quickest route to the Post Office, it suffices to say that two parallel lines never meet. Economists also have a way with theoretical statements which have no obvious practical value but which are interesting from a theoretical point of view. The most famous is the idea of a *perfectly competitive market*.

In Section 5.2.4 we saw how the addition of a third firm had a capacity to enhance competition, reduce price and increase supply. Imagine that starting from a market with only a few firms, more and more firms enter without any restriction. Suppose further that they all sell the same commodity (not even different brands of the same commodity) so that no firm can claim that its product is better than anybody else's. Finally, assume that consumers have equal access to all these firms (e.g. they are all located in the same district) and know the prices that each one of them charges. You are beginning to get the idea of what a perfectly competitive market is supposed to look like.

To get a preliminary flavour of perfect competition, suppose that each of the workshops of our earlier example was a separate business with four of them operating. With all four producing at full capacity (3 units each), cost for each firm is 16 and price equal to 8 (since total supply to this market is 3 times 4 and price equals 20 minus total supply). Thus each firm retains a profit of 8 and the level of total profits is 32. Now the question is: does it make sense for the fifth workshop/company to start producing as well? If it produces one unit, price will decline from 8 to 7 and, therefore, given that the cost of producing one unit is 8, the fifth firm will lose money. However if it produces 2 units, even though price will decline further to 6 (for the simple reason that in order to convince consumers to buy the extra units suppliers must reduce prices), its revenue will equal $2 \times 6 = 12$ while the cost of producing 2 units is only 11. So, by producing 2 units the fifth firm will be making a modest profit. But look at the profits of the other four firms: With price down to 6, their revenue will collapse to $3 \times 6 = 18$ and their profit will fall from 8 to only 2 (i.e. $18 - 16$).

To recap, in a market where entry by new firms is free, the profitability of incumbent firms attracts newcomers. This increase in supply reduces overall profit by boosting supply and reducing price. This is no more than the basic idea that motivated Adam Smith's faith in the market's capacity to expand production as far as possible while keeping price just above cost (and thus cause profit to hover around zero) – recall Section 1.2.2. Notice too the workings of Adam Smith's *unintended consequences*: in our example,

Table 5.6   Profit, revenue, price and cost as competition intensifies

Output	1	2	3	4	5	6	7	8	9	10	11	12	13	14	15
Price	19	18	17	16	15	14	13	12	11	10	9	8	7	6	5
Revenue	19	36	51	64	75	84	91	96	99	100	99	96	91	84	75
Cost	8	11	16	24	27	32	40	43	48	56	59	64	72	75	80
Total profit	11	25	35	40	48	52	51	53	51	46	40	34	19	9	5

no entrepreneur *intends* to reduce price or aggregate profit. Exactly the opposite is the case actually: in an attempt to boost their own profit, they reduce profit for everyone; including their own. Table 5.6 and Figure 5.7 demonstrate.

As long as there is profit to be made, more firms will come into the industry. As we just saw, with four firms producing 12 units altogether, the fifth firm had an incentive to come into the market and produce 2 units thus forcing the profit curve of the industry as a whole down. Figure 5.7 illustrates how free entry into a profitable market by profit hunters will, eventually, all but eliminate profit – a diagrammatic perspective on Smith's *unintended consequences* also reveals the significant incentive firms have to collude. For if they could agree to cut down total output to about 8 units, their collective profits would sky-rocket (observe how the profit curve reaches its peak at about 8 units of total output). You may then ask: why don't they limit their collective output to 8 units then? The answer is, as mentioned

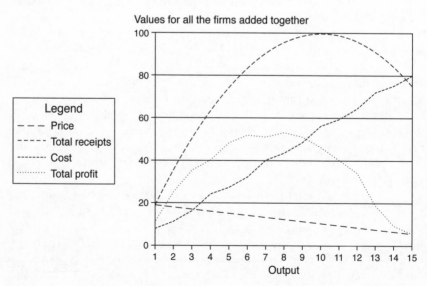

Figure 5.7   Aggregate revenue, cost and profit for all firms in the industry

earlier, that the incentive to collude (however strong it may be) has a mortal enemy: the incentive for any individual firm to cheat on whatever collusive agreement is struck.

To understand this point better, note that Figure 5.7 refers to *aggregate* profit, revenue, etc. This is why it makes so clear the benefits to firms from collusion. However, if you look at things from the perspective of individual businesses (rather than from that of the whole industry), a different picture emerges. For example, suppose that there are four firms operating each agreeing to produce 2 units of output, a total output of 8 which maximises collective profits. There are two reasons why this agreement may be infeasible: (1) a fifth firm has an incentive to enter producing 2 units (this will give it a profit of 9), and (2) even if there is no entry, any of the existing firms will increase its profit by boosting output provided the others stick to the agreement.

Whether the agreement will stick or not in this example involving four or five firms is unknown; it depends on the kind of communication that exists between them, how long they expect to be in that market together, each firm's relative valuation of future as compared to present profit and so on. Nevertheless economists (especially economics textbooks) assume that the larger the number of firms the less likely that they will manage to collude. And this is were the notion of *perfect competition* emerges as a sort of benchmark. *Perfect competition* is thought of as the limiting case in which there are so many, many firms that it is impossible for them to coordinate their actions. So many, that each one firm is like a tiny drop in a vast ocean and thus incapable of influencing anyone and anything; not even the price of the commodity.

In our example above, the market was pretty small (at most six firms with maximum total output of 18). In this setting it was natural that whenever a firm increased its output, this had a significant effect on price (to be precise, we assumed that with every increase in output by 1, price came down by 1). The reason was that each firm's output was a significant proportion of total output. However, when the firm's output is minuscule in comparison to the whole industry's, changes in its production level may have a negligible effect on price. This is what is assumed to be the case under *perfect competition*. Firms accept the price that is determined by the market (economists refer to such firms as price takers) and simply strive to select their output in such a way that their profit is maximised. So as long as firms are profitable, new entry into the industry will mean new entrants from outside (presumably those abandoning other less profitable markets), an increase in output and a subsequent decline in the industry's profit. When will this migration end? Whenever the industry's profit falls to such a low level that stops attracting new firms (diagrammatically, see Figure 5.7: this will happen when total receipts by firms edge close to the cost line or, equivalently when the profit line hits the horizontal axis).

5.2.6 The significance of perfect competition

Is there such a thing as a perfectly competitive market? One in which no firm has the power to change prices, all firms sell an *identical* product, there are no distances to be covered or transport costs, information is bountiful and therefore consumers can never be cheated into buying that item for $2.10 if it sells somewhere else for $2.05? Unlikely. So why is it that economists use the idea of perfect competition so much in their theories? The most common answer is that it is useful as a limiting case; an extreme diametrically opposed to that other extreme case of pure monopoly or collusion.

Looking again at Figure 5.7, it is simple to locate the two extreme cases of monopoly and perfect competition. The former coincides with a level of output such that total profit is maximised (about 8 units). The latter corresponds to the level of output at which profitability has been reduced to almost nothing as a result of fierce competition between profit maximising firms (15 units). These two cases can be thought of as 'markings' (or limits) against which to project an actual market situation.

For example, take the scenario explored in Section 5.2.2 according to which there were two firms producing 5 units each – a total output of 10. By comparing this total output to that which would obtain under monopoly (i.e. 8 units) and under perfect competition (i.e. 15), one can work out at a glance the extent of competition in the market under observation. For instance, our duopoly example seems evenly perched between the two extremes. And the lower the degree of collusion, or the larger the number of competitors, the closer we get to perfect competition. Even if we are certain never to get to a perfectly competitive market environment, it is useful to know our distance from it.

5.2.7 The market for factors of production

Firms sell commodities (or services) at markets whose structure determines, together with the cost of production and the level of price, output and profit. However, firms are not only sellers but buyers too. To be more precise they buy raw materials, electricity and other consumables (that is, commodities from other enterprises) and hire factors of production (such as labour, capital and land) – recall Section 5.1.1. How are these rental prices determined? The theory of the firm presented in this chapter can be adapted rather simply in order to provide answers. Table 5.7 gives an example.

Like other markets, there are sellers and buyers, only this time individuals sell to firms rather than vice versa, e.g. workers selling their labour. Suppose that at the measly price of $10 per day only 10 (rather desperate!)

Table 5.7 A market for a day's labour

Number of workers hired for a day	Wage necessary to attract this number of workers (Assumption: each worker receives the same wage)	Total daily labour cost to employer	Marginal cost to employer (cost of the last worker hired)	Wage employers would be prepared to pay for this number of workers
10	10	100	10	100
20	20	400	30	90
30	30	900	50	80
40	40	1600	70	70
50	50	2500	90	65
60	60	3600	110	60
70	70	4900	130	45
80	80	6400	150	30
90	90	8100	170	20
100	100	10000	180	10

Under a perfectly competitive labour market, the wage workers get paid by the employer is such that the number of workers who offer their labour to the firm at the wage is identical to the number of workers the firm wishes to employ at that wage; that is, we seek the row coinciding with an equality between the elements of the second and fifth columns. Thus we should expect a wage of $60, 60 workers to be hired daily and a total daily labour cost to employers of $3600.

Under a monopsonistic labour market, the single employer hires a number such that the wage she would be willing to pay equals her cost of hiring the last bunch (of 10) workers; i.e. her marginal cost (that is, we seek the row at which there is equality between the employer's fourth and fifth column). So, 40 workers will be employed at a wage equal to $40 and the total cost of labour to the single employer will be $1600 (notice that marginal cost to single employer is $70; contrast this to the case of a perfectly competitive labour market in which each buyer faced a marginal cost of only $60).

workers would wish to work. To attract 20 workers, employers must pay $20; to lure 30 workers they must fork out $30 per day. This information is contained in the first two columns of Table 5.7. The third column multiplies the first two and generates data on the total wage bill for all employers in this market at different levels of labour utilisation. The fourth column reports on the cost to the employers from having hired the last worker on average (e.g. when 40 workers are employed, the cost of having increased employment from 30 to 40 equals $700; $700 divided by these extra 10 workers is $70). Finally the last column (ostensibly put together after some market research) tells us what wage employers are willing to pay to each worker at different levels of employment. So, when there is a terrible labour shortage, and only 10 workers are available, employers are willing to part with $100 per worker per day. But as the supply increases, their generosity declines (can you explain this in terms of diminishing marginal returns?).

Given the identical structure of this mode of analysis and of the preceding theory of the firm's output and price decisions, it is hardly surprising that there is no difference in the conclusions. As in the commodity market, the largest 'quantity' will change hands under conditions of perfect competition. These conditions include that labour units for sale are identical (that is, no worker is more dexterous or lazy than others), information is plentiful (so that wages offered by different firms are known to all workers), and there is a very, very large number of small-scale employers (so that none of them has the capacity to alter the market-determined wage). If all this holds, the level of employment will be such that the wage necessary to give workers the monetary incentive to work will equal the wage employers are prepared to pay. In the example above, this happens when 60 workers are employed (see how the wage in the second and the fifth columns coincide).

But what if the market is not competitive? And what is the opposite of perfect competition in this case? The term used is *monopsony* (from the Greek root *pson-* which means 'to purchase' and therefore implies a market with a single buyer). If all workers are trying to sell their labour to a *single* employer (or equivalently to a cartel of employers), then the wage will be lower than if there were many employers competing against each other for the workers' services. The reason for this is that a single employer can push wages down by hiring fewer workers than would have found jobs in a competitive labour market.

To see this in terms of the example above, note the main difference between a monopsonistic and a competitive labour market: as stated already, in a competitive market there are many employers and therefore each one of them is too insignificant to have a sizeable effect on the wage. (Whether an employer hires an extra worker or two will not affect the wage since the effect of that on overall employment is tiny.) By contrast, single employers have the whole labour market to themselves and therefore, whenever they alter employment, these alterations affect the wage directly. In this sense, employers operating in a competitive market can safely assume the wage to be independent of how many workers they wish to employ; they take the wage as constant.

However, notice that things are different in a monopsonistic labour market. Imagine for instance that you take over all the firms in this market and remain the sole employer. At first you will be employing the 60 workers that you inherited from the firms that you took over. Would you keep them in your employment? Let us think about it. If you were to fire 10 workers, how much money would that save you? From the fourth column (sixth row) we know that these 10 workers added to your cost $110 per worker ($60 as their wage plus an extra $50 which is the cost of having to keep paying the remaining 50 workers a wage of $60 rather than the $50 you would be paying them after firing these 10 workers). How much money were you prepared to spend on these 10 workers? According to the fifth column (sixth row) you were prepared to spend $60 for each one of them; yet they are costing you a whole $110. Conclusion: you must fire them.

Should you stop there or should you fire more workers? Answer: you must fire another 10 workers (a total of 20 workers). Why? Because, looking at the entry in the fifth row, fourth column, the last 10 of the remaining 50 workers cost you, per head, $90 when all along you were prepared to spend on them only $65 per person (see the entry in the fifth row, fifth column). They must therefore go. When should you stop firing workers? The answer that Table 5.7 gives is: when total employment equals 40. Why? Because at that level the marginal cost of labour (i.e. the cost to the single employer of each of the last bunch of 10 workers – see the fourth column – equals the wage this monopsonist is willing to pay – see the fifth column).

In summary, the take-over of this competitive market by a monopsonist reduced the wage from $60 to $40 and, simultaneously, cut employment from 60 to 40. As a result, the total income of workers diminished from $3600 to $1600.

Recapping, just as monopolists profit from their capacity to restrict production, monopsonists in the labour market benefit from their ability to restrict employment. The only difference is that in the first case the victims are the consumers whereas in the latter they are the workers (of course often these two categories are the same people) who, as we just saw, suffer a reduction in wages and fewer jobs.

Minimum wages: do they increase unemployment?

The answer provided by this theory is: it depends! If the labour market is competitive, minimum wages will increase unemployment. However, if there are strong monopsonistic elements (and this includes the equivalent of oligopoly, i.e. oligopsony), imposing minimum wages may actually create more jobs.

The reason is that, under competitive conditions, increasing wages from $60 to, say, $70 will reduce the level of employment from 60 to 40 (see the fifth column which shows that employers are prepared to buy only 40 units of labour at $70). However, under monopsony, we start at an employment level of 40 and a wage of $40. Now if the government introduces a minimum wage of $60, the monosponist has no reason to maintain employment at a level less than 60 since the only reason for doing so is to reduce wages from $60 to $40. Now that this would be illegal (the legal minimum being $60), the monopsonist employer will simply choose the level of employment which sets the minimum wage ($60) equal to the wage she is prepared to pay; that is, find the row in the fifth column of Table 5.7 which is closest to $60 (notice that this happens in the fifth row implying a chosen level of employment equal to 60 workers).

In effect the minimum wage can force the monosponistic market to behave as if competitive. Of course for this to be so, the minimum wage must equal the level which the competitive market will have reached. If it is set at a higher level (e.g. wage = $70), then the monopsonist will settle on an employment level (40 workers) below that of a competitive market.

5.3 Summary

The businesses, firms and corporations which live in economics textbooks are not unlike consumers. Instead of consuming whisky, hamburgers and cinema tickets, they devour units of capital, labour, land and raw materials. Rather than generating 'utility' for the individual, these consumable 'inputs' produce commodities for the firms which hire them. None the less in the final analysis it is, once more, 'utility' that they give rise to: After the commodities have been produced, they are sold at the market-place and the revenue is used to reward the owners of these factors (the landowners who rent the land, the workers who 'hire-out' their labour units, the entrepreneurs who invest their capital units, etc.). These rewards are, finally, used in order to purchase commodities whose consumption yields utility for the individuals. The circle has been closed.

At the heart of the neoclassical theory of production is the idea of firms as brokers which organise the swapping of capital units for labour units (and units of other inputs). Production is perceived as no more than such an exchange. Rational (or efficient) firms are those which select their combination of inputs and make output or pricing decisions according to the *Equi-marginal Principle*. The extent to which they profit depends on the extent of competition which is often assumed to depend entirely on the number and size of the firms in the industry.

History of textbook models

The intellectual road to perfect competition

6.1 Production: from classical narratives to neoclassical models

In pre-industrial societies most production occurred close to, if not within, the household. Thus consumption and production cohabited in a way that would have made it impossible to separate analytically – as modern textbooks do – the activity of 'making things' from that of consuming them. Only after the establishment of explicitly market-societies in which people produced not goods but commodities (i.e. goods whose whole reason for being produced was so that they could be traded in some market), and the subsequent emergence of the factory (see Section 1.1), was production moved far from where people lived and slept. Indeed it took the whole might of the industrial revolution to create the distinction between the private and public spheres that we take for granted today and which encouraged economists to spend much time analysing production outside the context of the *ekos* (*ekos*, the root of the word *economics* emanating from the Ancient Greek οἶκος which means 'home').

Thus in contradistinction to feudalism, capitalism was based on economic units in which goods were produced not in order to be used or eaten by those who produced them, but almost exclusively in order to be sold to strangers in impersonal markets. Economists (also a product of the emerging capitalist market society) spent most of their time studying this new wave of industrial production of commodities. However, it was only after the growth of neoclassical economics towards the end of the nineteenth century (i.e. at least one hundred and fifty years later) that the private sphere of the household and the public sphere in which industrial production took place gave rise to the formal separation (common in modern textbooks) between the Theory of Consumption and the Theory of Production.

6.1.1 The classical view: firms as blocks of capital

The first economists, the classical economists referred to in Chapter 1, did not spend much of their mental energy devising complex theories of the individual firm (just as they were not particularly interested in theories of individual consumption). Fascinated by the bigger picture of the market economy as a self-organising system they explored keenly the mechanics of competition in interlocked markets and the fluctuations of whole industrial sectors. For example, Adam Smith saw firms as organisations built around blocks of capital (i.e. machinery) employed by entrepreneurs for the purpose of fashioning commodities at ever reduced cost per unit before entering the emerging circuits of national and international trade.

For Adam Smith (as mentioned in Chapter 1), the dog-eat-dog aspect of capitalism was significant because it forced entrepreneurs to amass machinery so as to reduce costs and stay in the game. It was the accumulation of these machines (or capital) that would raise the productive capacity of society as a whole leading to a plentiful supply of the commodities which would make life more bearable for the masses. In this sense, the firm was a block of capital (of steam engines, sewing machines, etc.) and the entrepreneur the coordinator of this build-up. Production was understood as the conversion of raw materials and intermediate goods into finished products ready for the retail market; a process which required the blending of machine power (capital) and human effort (labour).

The other classical economists shared this perspective: production was associated with industrial activity involving the physical creation of something tangible that did not exist before. While they disagreed with each other on many aspects of capitalism, they were united in their regard of production as a process during which a powerful boss oversaw the labour of relatively powerless workers who utilised machinery in order to create commodities. Their analytical and ideological differences transcended this common perspective and touched upon other, more subtle, issues. To give a flavour for these differences I will refer briefly to the views of the two other classic economists mentioned in Chapter 1: David Ricardo and Karl Marx.

Ricardo, as you will recall, was a worried man. Unlike Smith, he did not think of all the ingredients of capitalist competition as desirable. As explained in Chapter 1 (see Section 1.2.3) he feared that the energy of capital accumulation would be sapped by those who managed to appropriate

---

Material goods please: spare us the moralising

One does not have to be a supporter of capitalism in order to espouse Adam Smith's belief in more worldly goods. George Bernard Shaw (1856–1950), the outspoken socialist playwright, wrote:

> The crying need for the nation is not for better morals, cheaper bread, temperance, liberty, culture, redemption of fallen sisters and erring brothers, nor the grace, love and fellowship of the Trinity, but simply for enough money. And the evil to be attacked is not sin, suffering, greed, priestcraft, kingcraft, demagogy, monopoly, ignorance, drink, war, pestilence, nor any other of the scapegoats which reformers sacrifice, but simply poverty.'
>
> G. B. Shaw, Preface to *Major Barbara*, 1905

---

large segments of produced wealth even though they had not helped create it. Thus he was concerned that if this appropriation continued unabated (or even with increasing fervour), the economy's engine of growth would stall. To use the term that Ricardo introduced, if a large portion of society's surplus produce ended up as economic rent (recall the definition of rent in Section 1.2.3: a return to some factor of production or person *over and above* the worth, or opportunity cost, of that factor's or person's productive contribution), the society's capacity to generate future surplus would be impaired.

The explanation is simple: if those who have the incentive to invest into machinery (i.e. industrial firms in competition against each other) receive a decreasing portion of the pie, they will slow down their rate of investment and thus the pie will not rise as fast (it may even start shrinking). But how could this be the case? Why would some be in a position to appropriate a share of the pie not justified by their contribution to its creation?

Take two firms: one is an industrial company making nails. The other is a farm cultivating corn on rented land. The former competes against many other nail-producers in an open market. The latter is also trading in a competitive market but is situated on a prized piece of land. As the economy grows the demand for nails and corn increases. However, whereas in the nails industry this increase in demand translates into more firms producing nails with more or less similar costs, in the market for corn, our farm is in a privileged position since the amount of fertile land is finite. Therefore as the demand for corn rises, other less productive land is brought into operation and the costs of these new farms lies above that of the original farm. The difference between the two enterprises is now clear.

On the one hand, we have the original farm which benefits from economic growth because the extra demand for corn increases the price of corn without affecting its cost. This happens because, in order for the market's increasing appetite for corn to be satisfied, new farms have to be set up on less fertile soil than that gracing our original farm. But for the new farms (with higher production costs than our farm) to start producing, the price of corn must rise so that it covers the extra cost of cultivating poorer soil. Meanwhile, our original farm happily continues to exploit its fertile land, producing at the same low cost as before but now enjoying the higher price. Under these circumstances, what is the landlord who owns the farm likely to do? Clearly he will increase the rent (since he knows that the tenant can afford to pay more given his success at the market for corn). When will he stop increasing the rent? When the rent is such that a further small increase will make the tenant quit producing corn and leave for the nearest town. So, Ricardo exclaims, *without investing into any new machinery*, without trying harder, the landlord who owns the fertile land will be raking in more revenue at no extra cost. And the greater the increase in demand for corn, the larger the share of the pie that he will appropriate for no extra effort or investment. ⸺

On the other hand, both our farmers who do not own or work on fertile land, as well as our nail-producing firm, are not in the same privileged position. When the demand for nails grows, after an initial period of rising prices profit, new nail-producers will enter the market driving profit down to zero again. Similarly, the profit of our working farmers will be eaten away by increases in the rent charged by the landlord. However, and this is the difference between landlords and capitalists, economic growth create more competition for producers but not for landlords since the quantity of land is more or less fixed. Thus while the capitalists (industrialists or tenant-farmers) have to find ways of reducing their costs in order to survive (e.g. invest whatever profit they have made into new cost-reducing machines), landlords have no such concerns. Indeed they are guaranteed more rents for no greater effort as long as the economy grows. In conclusion manufacturing firms as well as farmers who rent land from landlords, invest into new technology, more efficient production methods, etc. and in so doing help mechanise and modernise society. Yet their profit is constantly eaten away by increasing competition. By contrast, the owners of the sought-after land make more and more profit without so much as lifting their little finger. This is why Ricardo was so worried: because those who invest into society's infrastructure (the capitalists) end up with little to show for it whereas those who do little or nothing at all (the landlords) cream off the surplus.

Ricardo's conclusion (first stated in Chapter 1) was that unless something is done (e.g. taxation) to keep in check the portion of surplus appropriated by the first type of producers (i.e. all those who happen to own a resource in short supply), the producers who are genuinely responsible for capital accumulation and growth will run out of the resources necessary to keep the show on the road.

Leaving to one side the general implications of Ricardo's work, it is clear that he distinguishes between two kinds of revenue: (1) that collected by firms in return for entrepreneurial effort, investment in technology, etc. and (2) that received in return for nothing other than the mere historical accident of owning (usually through inheritance or chance) a resource in short supply which, as the economy grows, becomes increasingly valuable and able to furnish its owner with more and more economic rent. Following up this distinction, firms can be segregated between those whose profits reflect their productive contribution to the economy's surplus and those which receive a lot more from society than they contribute to it (that is, rent). Unsurprisingly Ricardo identified (at least psychologically) manufacturing industry with the former and landowning, estate agents, mining, housing (amongst other) with the latter.

Karl Marx both utilised and amended significantly Adam Smith's portrayal of firms as organisations based on blocks of capital and Ricardo's distinction between productive and unproductive activities and economic roles. Adopting the view of production as the physical creation of goods to be traded at the market, he distinguished between those activities involved in the production of value and those which redistributed existing value. For example, the farmer, miner and manufacturer produced value in so far as they fashioned corn, coal or nails out of nature's raw materials. The value of their activities was in direct proportion to the value of these commodities (which in turn was determined by the amount of human labour required to produce them – see Section 1.2.4).

By contrast the bookmaker or equally the stockbroker produce no new value; they just help reassign already produced value to different people and, in the process, retain some of that value in the form of fees for themselves. Just like Ricardo, Marx thought that the dynamism of capitalism hinged on its capacity to minimise unproductive activities and channel more resources into productive ones. Consequently Marx also saw the factory owner, the manufacturing capitalist (as opposed to the landowner or banker), as the most significant agent of capitalism.

Productive versus unproductive labour

A more moderate but equally interesting way of distinguishing between the two kinds of labour is to consider the question: Can the production of commodity X help society increase its surplus (i.e. its production during a year over and above what was necessary in order to replenish the resources, goods etc. that it consumed during that same year)? If it can then the labour that went into producing X was productive. Otherwise it was unproductive.

Karl Marx on the capitalist's drive to accumulate capital

. . . what appears in the miser as the mania of an individual is in the capitalist the effect of a social mechanism in which he is a cog. Moreover the development of capitalist production makes it necessary constantly to increase the amount of capital laid out in a given industrial undertaking, and competition subordinates every individual capitalist to the immanent laws of capitalist production, as external and coercive laws. It compels him to keep extending his capital, so as to preserve it, and he can only extend it by means of progressive accumulation.

Karl Marx, *Capital*, Volume 1, 1867

Although it was the worker alone who created value (by putting her effort into commodities), the capitalist was the despot who orchestrated the process of its creation and collected the resulting surplus value (by paying workers the value of their labour time while retaining the significantly larger value of the products they produced – see Section 1.2.4 again). What happened to this surplus value? After paying off the landlord for the use of the factory space and the bank for outstanding loans and interest, the rest remained as profit to be converted into more machinery (capital accumulation) – see box above.

One of the most original aspects of Marx's theory of the capitalist firm concerns the production process which he sees as distinct from the market. At the market people exchange apples for oranges, money for car stereos, holiday packages for credit, and so on. However, *within* the firm, according to Marx, the relation between workers and bosses is not anything like that of buyers and sellers. Instead their relation is more like a contest: the boss trying to extract as much labour (or effort) from the worker for the given wage and the latter resisting. In this sense the rules and traditions of the market-society end at the factory gate. Once workers have traded their labour time for a given wage, they enter the gates daily and are involved in a continual power struggle (e.g. how many minutes they are allowed to stay in the toilet, the pace of work which is considered acceptable, the right to stay at home and nurse a sick child, etc.). According to Marx, to understand the goings-on within the firm one needs to be a sociologist, psychologist, political scientist as well as an engineer all wrapped in one. Mere knowledge of the supply and demand model does not help.

Moreover, starting from his assumption that only labour produces value, Marx develops an interesting theory of the firm's capital: capital is no more than *crystallised labour*; that is, the embedding of layers of labour into machinery which, combined with the intellectual labour of the inventor, contribute to the improvements in productivity. And since it is the value produced but not claimed by the worker which is used in order to purchase these machines, labour and capital are one and the same factor of production. Workers have sweated on the factory floor to produce the value that gives rise to capital accumulation and the capitalist has used her social power (due to the asymmetric ownership of factories, tools etc.) to extract that value out of workers. In one short sentence, capital is crystallised labour reflecting the social relation between workers and capitalists.

Notice that, once workers have sold (say) 40 hours of their time per week, there is no limit to how much effort (or actual labour) the employer can want from them during those 40 hours. And as the market pressurises the employer, the employer passes that pressure on to workers by demanding more effort. Therefore labour is the major factor of production within the firm while capital is the product of that labour or, to put it in a more abstract manner, it is a reflection of the way bosses and workers relate to each other.

Finally, the hallmark of Marx's view of capitalist production is an intentional contradiction. On the one hand, we have his enthusiastic recognition that the emergence of the capitalist firm was essential for the creation of capital and the liberation of society's productive forces from the strait-jacket of feudalism. On the other hand he claimed that the capitalist organisation of production, once established, is unable to utilise society's productive energy further. In today's jargon, capitalism is inefficient.

Marx's explanation is that private ownership of factories, and the subsequent retention of the firm's surplus by owners, perpetuates a conflict between workers and owners which forces managers to adopt not the most efficient production technique but the one which will maximise their power over the workers. Moreover the workers, alienated from the product of their labour, have little incentive creatively to develop new techniques and ideas. Put simply, Marx saw the coming of capitalism as a decisive yet incomplete step in the direction of efficient production.

6.1.2 The neoclassical view: production as exchange

Classical economists were mesmerised by images of the factory, the conveyor belt, the steam-engine, the mass creation of commodities, the division of labour which cut costs spectacularly. They were the children of the brave new industrial society. Even though they disagreed on many things (ranging from the prospects of capitalist societies, to the ethics or efficiency of the boss–worker relation and the different degrees of concern that unproductive people were receiving large shares of the wealth), they shared a common vision: society progressing through the wonders achieved in smoke-filled industrial sites. For them contemporary terms such as the 'entertainment industry' would seem ridiculous. Entertainment is great, Smith and Marx would agree, but it ain't no industry folks! Production is the act of creation of physical objects. Music, theatre, hair-cuts, parties are all wonderful things but they lie outside the sphere of industry. To put it differently, they can occur and flourish only in countries underpinned by either a strong industrial sector or ownership of very scarce resources (e.g. oil).

Enter neoclassical economics with its urge and enthusiasm for a unifying principle which would turn economic analysis into something very much like Newtonian physics. Having adopted 'utility' as the universal currency which would help them achieve this end, neoclassical economists initiated their grand break from the classical tradition. Everything was to be reduced to utility (in ways mirroring the Newtonian explanation of all physical phenomena by an appeal to the notion of energy). Thus consumption was to be thought of as the human being's response to a craving for 'utility' and production as the creation of that 'utility' (since humans did not lust for commodities or experiences *per se*, but for the utility they would derive from them).

Actually we have already come across in this book the basis of neoclassical production theory as part of the second chapter's presentation of consumption theory: recall the example of someone walking in the fields picking berries. When should she stop picking (i.e. producing)? The answer (courtesy of the *Equi-marginal Principle*) was that she should stop when her dis-utility from picking the last berry just about equalled her utility from it. Therefore neoclassical economists, so as to promote the concept of utility as the one which unifies all economic analysis, *had* to insist on a definition of production as the costly generation of utility.

This definition took them far away from the classical economists' identification of production with heavy industry, the accumulation of machinery, the sound of the factory whistle and the sight of mineworkers' blackened faces. For neoclassical economists a stand-up comic was as much a 'production' worker as a miner. The immediate repercussion of this position was that, all of a sudden, the classical economists' distinction between productive and unproductive activities disappeared. So did their conviction that production was a rich process of physical transformation of intermediate goods into material commodities. Moreover their prime concern and yardstick for the success of an economy, i.e. strong capital accumulation, gave its place to 'utility'. Whereas for Adam Smith *et al.* showing that a particular measure would enhance the build-up of machinery was sufficient for demonstrating the superiority of the measure in question, in neoclassical eyes the only test was whether it would enhance utility.

Having identified production with the creation of utility (as opposed to the creation of physical products), neoclassicism proceeded to its second major step towards homogenising production and consumption: it identified what happens in the firm with a pure exchange between owners of different factors of production (recall that, unlike Marx who thought only of labour as a factor, neoclassical economists recognised three: land, labour and capital – perhaps four if we include 'entrepreneurship'). According to this view, capitalists exchange with workers units of capital for units of labour as if they are at a market place trading apples for bananas. They also exchange units of capital for units of land with landlords. Then, once the trade is complete (e.g. once 4 units of labour have been blended with 3 units of capital), the resulting combination of the traded units translate into a certain amount of output – recall the isoquant curves in Chapter 5. How this happens is not explained. It is simply presumed that it is a technical matter; that a combination of so many workers and so many machines will or can produce so many units of output.

There are some crucial implications of this theoretical position. First, the politics and sociology internal to firms is taken out of the theory: just like buyers and sellers at the local fruit-market need have no relation with each other beside the actual, impersonal transaction, neoclassical economics models the labour process as a simple transaction between workers and bosses. It is as if workers and their employers are not involved in any fluctuating power/social relation with each other.

Second, along with the social relations within the firm, the neoclassical model dismisses the actual process of production. Indeed the whole complex process of producing a commodity is collapsed to that one instance during which workers and firms agree to exchange labour for capital at a given price. It is as if production is a procedural, automatic matter that occurs in some unspecified manner after the exchange between workers and employers. Third, the neoclassical theory of capitalist firms does not require capital at all; e.g. employers could be exchanging units of land for units of labour. Unlike classical economics which reserves a privileged position for capital and its accumulation, the neoclassical model of production as exchange is so abstract that the presence of capital is not obligatory for the model to make sense.

What is the conclusion one should draw from these three implications? It depends on one's point of view. One possible conclusion is that neoclassical economics has succeeded in unifying the two strands of economics (the theory of consumption and the theory of production) and to take the politics and sociology within firms out of the analysis. According to this (neoclassical) perspective, economics has ridden itself of its non-scientific aspects and allows us to look at firms and production through an objective lens. The opposite conclusion is that, in its urge to turn production into a species of consumption involving an exchange between different factors of production, most of the interesting aspects of production under capitalism (especially those discussed extensively by the founders of economics) have dropped out of the scene.

In summary, the neoclassical portrayal of the firm, which incidentally coincides with that of contemporary textbooks (see Chapter 5), is that of a small market in which owners of capital trade with owners of labour, land, raw materials, etc. Once the trade is complete output springs from the production line quite miraculously. Moreover the level of output bears a one-to-one relation with the particular combination of the various factors of production (that is, 3 units of labour and 5 units of capital combined with 2 units of land produce a *given* amount of corn; and all this regardless of the particular relationship between workers and employer, or the social and economic conditions outside the factory gates). And since the firm does not own its inputs but instead only hires them, the entrepreneur is a mere coordinator of factors of production the output of which she claims on the basis of her initial ownership of the funds necessary to hire the factors.

6.2 Markets and competition

6.2.1 Classical theories of the market: their origin in Natural Law philosophy

As the product of the same intellectual movement which gave rise to modern physics and biology, the founders of economics were excited by the possibility of discovering the ways of the world without the need to rely on explanations afforded by some higher authority (e.g. the Church, the king or even the philosophers). Their contemporary natural scientists, children of Isaac Newton and Charles Darwin, were already writing down the laws of the cosmos and of the species. One of things that early economics had in common with other elements of this wave of scientific endeavour was a background in Natural Law philosophy. According to this philosophy 'good' meant that toward which each thing tends by its own intrinsic principle of orientation. Anything which forces some thing or person to go against its 'natural' predisposition was deemed 'bad'. As you can imagine, Natural Law tradition can be traced back to theology.

For instance the Italian theologian St Thomas Aquinas (1225–74) states in his text *Summa Theologiae*: 'Good is what each thing *tends* toward . . . Good is to be done and pursued, and evil is to be avoided'. So, when Newton discovered the mathematical laws of the pendulum, or the solar system, he discovered the state towards objects or even planets were *tending*; a state that was natural, safe and good. And when Adam Smith alerted the world to the *tendency* of prices to reflect costs provided the market was competitive, his enthusiasm reflected St Thomas' identification of the state towards which things *tend* with the 'good'. Therefore competitive markets produced 'good' outcomes.

The following box reveals how Adam Smith, influenced by the Natural Law tradition, saw in market forces an invisible hand capable of guiding human beings in a way that no individual could. Thus if any individual (or group, e.g. a government) were to try to assume the role of the market forces,

they would be *forcing* the system out of its 'natural' state. Such an interference with Natural Law not only would lead to inferior economic outcomes
but also is described by Smith (see box) with words such as 'dangerous',
'folly' and 'presumption'.

Adam Smith on market regulation as an interference with Natural Law

The statesman, who should attempt to direct private people in what manner they ought to employ their capitals, would not only load himself with a most unnecessary attention, but assume an authority which could safely be trusted, not only to no single person, but to no council or senate whatever, and which would nowhere be so dangerous as in the hands of a man who had folly and presumption enough to fancy himself fit to exercise it.

Adam Smith, *Wealth of Nations*, 1776

The classical economists who followed Adam Smith shared his belief
that society ought to be allowed to tend towards its natural, harmonious,
state (such was the optimism of those born and bred during the European
Enlightenment). Even those who opposed untrammelled capitalist markets
based their opposition on something akin to the Natural Law tradition. They
may have criticised parts of Smith's analysis but did not stray significantly
from the belief that 'good' things spring from a tendency toward balance
and equilibrium. They just disagreed on what *is* a natural state for an
economic system.

To illustrate this point further, let us return for one last time to the
other two classical economists referred to in this book. David Ricardo's
problem with rentiers (that is, with those who acquire wealth by amassing
economic rent) was that they were weakening the invisible hand; that they
got in the way of market forces and slowed down, or even made impossible,
the establishment of Smith's happy equilibrium. It is not much of an exag-
geration to say that even Karl Marx's contribution, although admittedly
more radical than Ricardo, falls within the same sphere: for Marx the
problem with capitalism was its ferocious contradictions and incurable insta-
bility. An economic and social system based on the asymmetrical ownership
of factories, farms, machines, etc. could not generate a stable equilibrium.
Thus Marx's critique of capitalism can be interpreted as the view that free
markets lead to unstable social conditions at odds with Natural Law. To put
it differently, chronic unemployment, economic crises and inflation were the
symptoms of a system unable to procure balance, harmony and equilibrium
because of the fact that a certain class (the owners of factories, farms, etc.)

stubbornly held on to a monopoly on the means of production for their own enrichment.

6.2.2 Classical theories of the market: rivalry and profit equalisation

If one had to summarise the classical view on markets in one word, one would have to settle for *process*. Just like Newtonian physics set out to discover the equations determining the *motion* of planets in the solar system, classical economists attempted a similar description of the market process. To give an example of their approach, take the objectives of a firm. Modern textbooks simply assume that firms maximise profit. Period. Given this assumption, it is then claimed that the pursuit of profit brings firms into conflict. By comparison, classical economists did not take the firm's objectives as given and static but as the product of constant evolution.

To illustrate this dynamic perspective on what firms are about, suppose that some new firms come into an existing market. The resulting competition forces the older firms to pursue profit more ruthlessly than before in order to compete successfully. In that way, the pursuit of profit and competition feed and reinforce each other. On the other hand though, when competition leads to a profit crisis, firms start thinking of ways to reduce antagonism and collude with each other. Then they realise that in order to do so they must avoid the temptation of reaping short-term profit by price-cutting; learning to be abstemious (i.e. to settle for less than maximum profit) underpins the spirit of cooperation amongst them and, ironically, boosts their profit. The upshot is a cyclical, dynamic picture in which the firm's anxiousness for profit fluctuates in relation to the competitiveness of their environment.

From the above we glean a fundamental aspect of the classical economists' view of the market: the contradiction between profit-seeking and competition. Firms are forced into a state of rivalry because of their interest in extracting as high a profit as possible. However, collusion between firms can bring higher profit than competition. Having said that, collusion is also unstable because if all of a firm's competitors refrain from aggressive tactics, then that firm may succumb to the temptation to corner the market. But if it does so others will follow and a cut-throat price war will ensue. (See box on the next page for an example of how profit may accrue more readily when it is not the sole objective.) Thus rivalry at the market-place causes firms to oscillate between conflict and cooperation. It is the depiction of such a dynamic process which characterises the classical economists' view of the market.

The next most important aspect of classical views of markets is that the pursuit of profit leads firms to migrate from one industrial sector to another usually abandoning the ones which have become too 'crowded' and cut-throat. This movement would tend to reduce the profitability in the areas into which they have moved but would only end when profit rates become almost the same in different sectors of the economy. Capital flows from one area to another like water between communicating bottles. The flow ends the moment the level of profit is equalised across sectors (just like the water flow ends when its level is the same in each bottle). This became known as the principle of profit equalisation.

How is the flow of capital realised? As capital equipment wears out in the areas of low profitability, it is not replaced. Instead new capital is brought into use in the more profitable sectors of the economy. The result is that profit per firm is reduced in the profitable areas (as more firms compete for that market) and increased in the less profitable ones (as rivalry is reduced there) until profit rates are about the same in both types of area. However this equilibrium, this state of balance in which profit rates are the same economy-wide, is rarely reached. Before the tendency for the equalisation of the rate of profit has been exhausted, the economy may have changed.

For example, technological innovations or changes in consumer preferences may have boosted profitability in a hitherto unprofitable sector thus instantly reversing the flow of capital away from it. Consequently classical economists recognised that the position of equal profit towards which the market is tending changes constantly with the result that it is never reached. It is in the context of this dynamic view, of this *process*, that the principle of profit equalisation is compatible with an observation that profit is unequally distributed in the economy.

Profiting from a healthy disregard of profit

Suppose that if you promised *sincerely* to drink a glass of pig urine tomorrow morning, I would hand over to you $1 million *immediately* and regardless of whether you actually drink the hideous liquid in the morning. Assuming I could tell whether your promise is honest (e.g. I have plugged you into a super-efficient lie-detector), what are your prospects of collecting the $1 million? The answer is that you would not collect a penny if the *only* thing you cared about was the money. The reason is this: to get the money, you must convince my lie-detector that you will drink the urine. And the only way of doing so is to convince yourself that this is what you intend to do. But then again, how can you believe this when you know damn well that once you have collected the money you will have no reason to drink the urine tomorrow?

However, things may be different if you care about something more than money: *wanting to keep your word for the sake of keeping your word.* For if you develop a commitment to not lying then you may convince yourself that a pledge is a pledge and that, if you promise to drink the urine then this is exactly what you intend to do. In that case you will pass the lie-detector test and collect the money. But you will fail if your honesty is due to an exclusive interest in the $1 million rather than to a genuine commitment to being honest. Honesty may very well reward you handsomely but it cannot be acquired by you (at least not genuinely) when your reason for doing so is that it pays to acquire it.

The moral of this story for firms is that profit will be boosted when rivalry gives its place to collusion but that collusion cannot rely only on the urge of firms to profit. Firms also need to develop an interest in collusion for reasons that are unrelated to money making (just like you would have to develop a genuine interest in truth-telling in order to collect the $1 million). For example, managers of different firms may develop a moral code in their dealings which allows them to collude; an ethical code which they want to follow regardless of profit. Although it is difficult for such codes to emerge and survive, it should not be assumed impossible. After all even thieves (and Mafia bosses) take 'honour' seriously!

To give a further example of the classical economists' analysis of the market as a *process* consider this: the invention of a new product gives its inventor a monopoly position and high profit. Inevitably other firms develop similar products with the effect of reducing the inventor's high profit rate. Since this process characterises most markets, the rate of profit fluctuates constantly. It declines in the sectors of the economy relying on ageing products and rises in the other sectors which are spawning new products. Unsurprisingly profit rates may never become equalised even though a proper description of what is happening requires us to recognise the *tendency* towards profit equalisation.

6.2.3 Neoclassical theories of the market: perfect competition as the ideal market

As witnessed in Chapter 5, the neoclassical approach to the market differs from the classical perspective. Where classical economists speak of chaotic market processes (which oscillate between collusion and cut-throat competition), the neoclassical approach of contemporary textbooks focuses at stable market conditions. To coin a metaphor, the classical view of the market process resembles a roaring mountain river whose water flows unpredictably towards the tranquillity of the ocean. By contrast, the neoclassical economists' models bring to mind a serene snapshot of a calm lake representing equilibrium, i.e. a state of balance from which the water has no tendency to depart.

The difference lies in the emphasis. The classicists focused on the flow itself and only thought of the equilibrium as something towards the market tended but never reached. The neoclassicists, by contrast, focused on the equilibrium itself without much concern about the path the market would have to follow in order to reach it. This difference in emphasis meant that the classicists (in view of their interest in *processes*) created stories about the emergence of competitive pressures or, vice versa, about the birth of monopoly conditions in sectors where some firms acquired market power either by driving other firms into the ground or even by taking them over. In comparison, the neoclassicists (in view of their interest in a state of market equilibrium or stasis) created descriptions of what stable markets would look like (recall Chapter 5).

To understand the perspective brought to economics by neoclassicism, let us examine the notion of competition. Which is the highest form of competition in a typical economics textbook? Perfect competition: the ideal form of market in which the powerlessness of firms is such that none have the capacity to alter prices or make profit and where the (large) number of firms stabilises precisely at the moment profit collapses to minuscule levels. The moment profit starts rising, new firms come into the market and it falls again. Why is this thought of as ideal? Because prices fall to the level of cost and output is maximised; with consumers reaping all the benefits.

Of course there are many similarities between classical and neoclassical views. In both cases it is the movement of firms from one industry to another in search of higher profit which regulates the rate of profit and the distribution of resources. Nevertheless the differences are real. Whereas the classical narrative on what one ought to expect of intense competition is inextricably bound with a tumultuous and multifaceted rivalry between firms (price conflict, technological innovation, temporary alliances, mergers and take-overs), in the textbook model of perfect competition there is no actual competition – in the real meaning of the word. For if no firm can influence the market, and each knows this, they accept their lot and keep functioning passively, without attempting to out-manoeuvre their competitors. In this sense perfect competition is an imaginary market in which there is no actual competition whatsoever!

Of course this does not mean that the neoclassical economists believed such a placid market could ever exist. As the box reveals, they are acutely aware that perfect competition is an extreme hypothetical, and unrealistic, model to be used for pedagogical and analytical purposes only. How is the

---

Perfect competition as an imaginary, impossible market

Perfect competition

> is not intended to be a description of any real economy or even a description of any realistically attainable end. Its role is to enable one to derive a set of theorems that define the conditions under which the productive resources of the economy are optimally allocated in creating the various goods and services that are desired.
>
> Scott Gordon, *The History and Philosophy of Social Science*, 1991

---

idea of perfect competition used then? The aim is to work out a theoretical case in which prices are as low as possible, output as high as it can be and the resources used in production are the minimum required. Neoclassical economists thought that if they could study this theoretical case (i.e. perfect competition), they would then gain insights into what an ideal market would look like *so as to assess the merits or demerits of observed markets*. Notice the difference in method between classical and neoclassical economists. The former attempt to understand real markets by describing them (and the chaos inherent in them) as well as they can. The latter do it in a more roundabout way: they create an extreme model of a market which cannot possibly exist in order to use it as a yardstick for real markets which they hope to understand better by means of this comparison.

Why this difference? Recall Chapter 1 and the way neoclassical economics came to the fore. In contrast to the non-professional enthusiasts known as the classical economists (who were driven by an urge to produce theories of the momentous events around them), the neoclassical economists had an interest in emulating classical mechanics (the number one science at that time). They set out to create *models* of ideal economies in the same way an engineer would build a model of the ideal bridge in the process of thinking about what bridge to construct. And just like bridges are static, immovable (one hopes) things, the economists' model shared a static outlook.

We can see the effect of the different outlooks by examining, for the last time, the way the two strands of economics analyse competition. Classicists see it as an ever fluctuating process hinging on technical innovation and changes in demand but also on the norms and conventions (as well as the politics and sociology) governing the relation between entrepreneurs (conventions which make collusion between them more or less feasible and sustainable). A look at a modern (neoclassical) textbook tells a different story. Two extreme snapshots are first discussed: monopoly (i.e. a single firm) and perfect competition (a large number of tiny firms producing a homogeneous product with no restrictions on the entry or exit of firms from the industry). Then the extent of competition in an actual industry is determined by trying to locate it on this continuum between the two extremes of monopoly and perfect competition. The actual location (and thus the degree of competition) eventually boils down to the number of firms in the industry.

6.3 Summary

Modern economics textbooks define production as the generation of anything capable of creating utility. In other words production equals the creation of utility. This definition allows neoclassical theory to unify its analysis of production (the creation of utility) and consumption (the hunger for utility). As for production itself, firms undertake to coordinate the three factors of production (land, labour and capital); to act as islands of non-market coordination of economic activity in the oceans of a market society; to let owners of capital, labour power and land, under the shrewd supervision of the entrepreneur, engage in exchange. The outcome of this exchange is commodities to be sold in the market at large. Finally the ideal market (that is, one characterised by perfect competition) is a stable one where no one can set prices, profit is kept to zero (after opportunity costs are covered) and output is maximised.

Before this (neoclassical) approach became dominant, there was the classical view: firms as 'blocks of capital' and production as the physical transformation of intermediary into final products within these 'blocks of capital'. The market mechanism was portrayed as a ceaseless cauldron where nothing ever stood still, a jungle which forced capital not only to accumulate but also to spread around the economy in search of profit. The sign of a well-functioning market mechanism was more machines (i.e. capital) well distributed around the economy with the distribution pattern reflecting a permanently unfulfilled tendency towards profit equalisation.

What are the fundamental differences between the textbook analysis and the classical one? Could they be saying the same things using different narration techniques? Three things are certain: whereas classicists turned the spotlight on change, flow, process and dynamics, the neoclassicists spent their time analysing states of rest, balance, equilibrium. While classicists saw production as a social process involving simultaneously power games, exchange, cajoling, threats, even exploitation, neoclassicists pictured production as a type of pure exchange. And where the classicists tried to understand markets by painting an accurate and wholistic picture of the markets they observed, the neoclassicists tried to do the same by painting a model of ideal markets one at a time.

Chapter 7

Critique: is the textbook's theory of production good economics, good politics, both or neither?

7.1 Work and production

7.1.1 Difficulties in distinguishing between production and consumption

If production is to be defined as the costly generation of utility (which is how economics texts define it), professional comedians are producers. But what about the friend who makes us laugh around the dinner table? The textbook rules her out of the set of producers because her jokes do not cost her anything, unlike the professional comedian who had to give up other money-making ventures in order to stand up in front of the audience. So, it turns out that, according to (neoclassical) economics, for a comedian to be recognised as a production worker, she must produce laughter *at personal cost*. Interesting. But what of the mother who tries to make her sick child laugh? Is this work? Or is it a form of consumption (e.g. the enjoyment of motherhood)?

On the one hand, this is a clear case of production. In order to create utility for the whole family, she stayed at home looking after her sick child (thus forgoing income) and now has to come up with funny jokes (when she is not necessarily in a humorous mood). On the other hand, she may not be able to imagine that she would be wanting to do anything else. In this case her work is akin to the friend who entertains you over dinner. Both generate utility (for themselves as well as for others) without a significant opportunity cost.

Nevertheless it seems strange to define a mother's child-care as production only if she considers the time spent nurturing her child as something she had to forgo. To extend this point further, the neoclassical definition of production (as the costly generation of utility) opens the way to the criticism that people who love their work, and who would still do it for free if they had to, are not considered to be producers (because work in their case is indistinguishable to leisure).

The counter-argument is that everything has its opportunity cost (that is, one always has to give up something in order to do something else). So the loving mother who feels that she is not giving anything up in order to stay at home, or even the workaholic architect who would rather die than go on holiday, are both giving things up in order to do what they love. Everything comes with an opportunity cost. Fair enough. But then every utility generating activity, normally associated with consumption, would constitute production: from listening to music to building a bridge.

7.1.2 Difficulties in distinguishing between work and leisure

Anthropologists who studied aboriginal cultures have often commented on how little members of hunting and gathering societies used to work. Only a few hours a day were spent seeking food and building shelter. The rest was time spent on discussions, tribal dancing and other communal pursuits. Notice what the anthropologists had done: they distinguished between work-related and non-work-related activities. How did they do this? By defining a number of tasks as essential (e.g. hunting) and others (e.g. rain-dancing) as inessential. But who are we to say what is essential for these people? Or to put it differently, what if they were to send their own researchers to our cities and classify pursuits such as Parliament sittings, advertising, banking and the bravura in the stock exchange as inessential pursuits?

Textbooks (reflecting the method of neoclassical economics) try hard to define consumption and production in terms of the same idea: utility. Consumers eat utility up (so to speak) while producers generate it for others and at a cost. However as we just saw (in Section 7.1.1) economics ends up without a convincing definition of how consumption and production differ. This failure echoes the same theory's earlier difficulty in separating utility from dis-utility (recall Chapter 4). Just as it is impossible to segregate the satisfaction from reading a sad, yet brilliant, novel from the real pain and sadness it caused, it is absurd to draw a dividing line between the fatigue incurred when doing a job from the job satisfaction one may derive from it.

And yet the textbook *must* pretend there is no problem (if it wants to convince readers that the choice model at its heart is unproblematic)! Recall a whole theory of work was erected (turn back to Section 2.2.3) on the grounds of a trade-off between income (or equivalently consumption) and leisure. The idea was that people want both money (because of the commodities it provides) and something called leisure which, apparently, is the opposite of work. The individual worker's problem then is how to select the best combination of the two things she likes: income and leisure. In the end, having taken into account the offered wage and how much she dislikes working, she decides to give up X amounts of leisure in return for a sum of money $Y. Therefore the textbook (or neoclassical) theory of work begins with the assumption that, for a given amount of income, people want to minimise work (or, equivalently, maximise leisure).

Work and leisure

'If you don't have work you have no leisure.'

Anonymous unemployed person

But what is leisure? The opposite of work, we are told. OK. Let's say we agree on this. Now consider an unemployed person who has given up looking for a job simply because there do not seem to be any in her region. According to the textbook, she is enjoying maximum leisure at the cost of not having much money (excepting social security or savings). Therefore if only someone gave her the money that she would be earning normally (as an employed person) she would have been much happier than if she had been given her job back. Yet sociological studies show, time after time, that people get a sense of self-worth from working without which their lives end up in ruins. The social bonds created at the workplace are, in many cases, irreplaceable. Yet this does not mean that workers rise happily every morning looking forward to crossing the factory gates. The human condition is too complex for such black and white analyses.

In summary, economic textbook definitions of work and production are problematic. (1) Work is defined as the opposite of leisure (non-work) and individuals are assumed to prefer leisure (non-work) to work other things (e.g. income) being equal. This is too simplistic and misrepresents the true nature of work as well as the true nature of leisure. (2) Production is defined as the costly generation of utility. However, this is too broad a definition: watching a horror movie (to the extent that the fear involved in watching it constitutes a cost) qualifies as production. Bluntly speaking, the economics textbook seems to be rather hazy about both work and production.

7.1.3 The modern invention of work and production

For the aboriginal cultures examined by western anthropologists, a rain-dance was as essential for 'production' as gathering food. Even the rituals that, to western eyes, looked like a bit of communal fun, were instrumental in preserving the social division of labour. In those societies, therefore, the western distinctions between work and leisure made little sense. Indeed this remained the case world-wide until fairly recently; until, that is, the creation of market societies in which the majority of the population had *no option but to sell their labour* in order to make a living (recall the discussion in Chapter 1). Before the emergence of industrialised market societies, goods were mostly being produced and consumed within the household, the community or the feudal estate by the same people. Work and leisure occurred in the same space and, often, it was impossible to distinguish one from the other. While consumption and production were confined within the same community, it made no sense to define them as strictly separable activities.

Is sport work or play?

Until recently sport was deemed to be a non-work activity; hard and tiring perhaps, but not the equivalent of working down a mine or for a bank. While it remained so, it was possible to invoke the ancient Olympic spirit of virtuous amateurism (e.g. it is participation that counts, not victory). When commercial television coverage made it possible for audiences to be captured by sporting achievements and 'sold' to advertisers for specific sums of money, things changed. A full monetary valuation of sporting endeavours became possible for the first time, sport became a commodity and sports-people entrepreneurs. The abandonment of amateurism by the International Olympic Committee was then only a matter of time.

In order to reach the stage at which we can speak sensibly about work and production as the opposites of leisure and consumption, humanity had to experience the industrial revolution and the consequent creation of factories in which strictly work-activities were performed (by contrast to the household and the estate). In this sense, the economics textbook has difficulties understanding work and production in all places and at all times *because it tries to define them independently from the prevailing social conditions*. It is as if the models in the textbook can be applied with equal force to aboriginal Australia prior to the European invasion, ancient Greece and contemporary Japan. They cannot. Work and leisure are meaningful concepts only in an industrialised society were people make a living by selling their time to employers who use it in order to fashion commodities which are to be sold at the market. The act of selling one's labour time gives rise to some conception of alternative uses of time which make notions of leisure and, even, productive work meaningful. In this sense, only when the development of industrial production takes shape does the notion of work (as separate from activity) materialise.

Have you noticed the common historical theme running through this book? In Chapter 1 I argued that before the industrial revolution there existed no factors of production (as we know them today; that is, as *commodities*) and, therefore, there was no great 'demand' for pure economic thinking. It was the unleashing of the industrial revolution which created labour, land and capital as marketable inputs in the production process. To this I am now adding the argument that the industrial revolution *created* the idea of work as different from other tiring activities (e.g. hobbies, rituals, nurturing the young and the old). By extension, production became associated with the term 'industry', that is with the process that occurred inside those ugly factories whose creation signalled the distinction between work and nonwork activities.

Unfortunately the economics textbook (also an indirect product of the industrial revolution) does not recognise these subtleties. Instead it defines, rather crudely, work as the opposite of non-work and production as the opposite of consumption. Why does it do this? In my (biased) opinion, it does so because of the urge to abstract from history; to create 'scientific' definitions independent of historical change. In the process, it produces (I think) bad definitions. However, one may argue that these disingenuous definitions may be necessary for a good theory of markets. Are they? Read on.

7.2 Production as exchange

7.2.1 Labour as more than a commodity

Economics textbooks treat labour like any other commodity. They use the *Equi-marginal Principle* to model the determination of its price (i.e. of the wage) and of its sold quantity (i.e. of the level of employment measured in working hours or days). Having internalised the modern conversion of work into a *commodity* (again you may want to turn to Chapter 1 to revisit the story of this conversion), it assumes that labour can be purchased in a manner similar to the way bananas change hands in some fruit market. This is the first serious assumption: labour can be *quantified* and purchased just like any other commodity. 'I will have 5.6 units of labour,' the employer is supposed to be able to announce when entering the labour market. The second crucial assumption is that units of labour, once purchased, combine with other

The discovery of women's unpaid work in the home

For centuries housework was considered a woman's *duty*. In recent times, however, we have been made aware that women actually *work* in the household as hard, if not harder, as anyone else. Feminists put it bluntly when claiming that women were called housewives so as to hide the fact that they were unpaid housekeepers. Why is it however that we have only 'discovered' this now? Sue Himmelweit (1995), a feminist economist, answers this question:

> My argument is that the willingness to talk about domestic work, using tools designed for the analysis of paid work, and even to debate whether household labour should be included in national accounts statistics, stems from tendencies within the economy itself, which have put paid and unpaid work into much closer and obvious comparison with each other . . . Substitutes for the results of nearly all the activities that go on in the home are available for purchase on the market, providing an immediate way in which they can be valued.

Thus the emergence of a market for domestic services (e.g. laundry, ironing, house-cleaning, baby-minding, etc.) allowed us to recognise women's domestic efforts as work!

factors of production to produce *specific* quantities of output. It is as if the matter of how much output a certain combination of labour and other factors can produce is of a singularly technical nature; a little bit like a recipe: take a cup of milk, add three teaspoons of flour, etc. and you will be able to serve six people. (This is effectively what the isoquant curves of Chapter 5 assume.)

Of course neither of these two assumptions have much connection with the reality of workplaces. First, workers cannot sell their labour at the time when the employment contract is signed. All they can do is sell a promise to report to work at particular times and work 'diligently'. What does 'diligently' mean however? Who is to interpret its meaning? How hard is hard enough?

Compared to the fruit market in which it is easy to quantify how much a seller sells *before* the transaction, the labour market is characterised by an impossibility of explicit contracts between employers and employees. The 1979 general election slogan of the British Conservative Party captures the

> **Labour isn't working . . .**
>
> British Conservative Party election campaign poster, 1979

difference between labour and other commodities nicely (even though this was never its intention). In the case of all other commodities, the signing of the contract between buyers and sellers ends the negotiations and the contest between the two sides. In the case of labour, however, the opposite is true.

But if the first assumption (that labour can be quantified at the moment of purchase) is threatened, the second assumption (that given employment translates to given output) collapses. For how then can we speak of a combination of X units of labour and Y units of capital producing Z units of output? What are these units of labour? Are they measured in the number of hours workers have been contracted to work? If so, how do we know how hard they will be working, with how much enthusiasm, or with what intensity? Surely the intensity and enthusiasm during the working day are not constants that the employer has purchased together with the workers'

Monitoring work, labour effort and the wage contract

Neoclassical economics has begun to acknowledge that imperfect monitoring of workers causes problems for its analysis. For example it is easy to show that if the employer cannot know how hard workers labour (because the nature of work is such that they cannot be watched *and* because output may fluctuate for reasons unrelated to workers' effort – e.g. fluctuations in the weather or in demand) the best solution is to charge workers a flat fee for the right to work and let them collect any profit. In this case (which is known by economists as the *Principal–Agent Problem*), the workers pay the employers for the right to work and collect the proceeds minus the employers' fee. Indeed this is usually the case with taxi owners and taxi drivers: the latter pay a fixed sum to the former and in return collect the day's takings. (Notice how this scheme transfers all the risk due to variations in demand to the worker.)

Of course this does not explain the enforcement mechanism when monitoring *is* possible. How do employers enforce a certain work-pace when there can be no prior contract which specifies the agreed pace in advance? The answer is: by the threat of dismissal and other psychological methods. It is these important determinants of the profit/wage link that the textbook theory does not account for.

time. They are, instead, variables which depend on a host of circumstances only one of which is the wage.

Indeed they depend crucially on the precise relationship between employers and employees, between employees themselves, on the threat of dismissal etc. And since human relations, relations between rich(er) employers and poor(er) workers, not to mention the culture of the work-place, are complex and unquantifiable variables, how intelligent is it of economists to assume that the level of output is a mathematical function of how many units of labour have been purchased by the employer *independently of these unquantifiable variables?*

Work effort in a firm and the economic links with the rest of the economy

The employer can prevent workers from slouching only if they are monitored and threatened with dismissal – see previous box. However, the 'value' of this threat depends on how easily workers can get jobs elsewhere; that is, on the level of unemployment. Thus labour productivity depends on economic variables pertaining to the whole economy (macro-economic variables, as they are called). But if this is so, it is impossible to draw a firm's isoquant curves (as we did in Chapter 5) without a complete model of how the whole economy works.

Only if this host of social variables is included in the production function (i.e. the mathematical rule which converts inputs into outputs) will the isoquant analysis in Chapter 5 reflect reality. But since these variables are by their very nature impossible to quantify, it may not be at all possible to do so. Then it may be inevitable that any theory of production along the lines of the analysis in Chapter 5 is unconvincing. To see this point from a different angle, consider the centrepiece of the neoclassical theory of the firm: the *Equi-marginal Principle*. It breaks down the moment the social nature of production is taken into consideration.

To see why this is so, let us recount how it produced a theory of the firm. In Figure 5.3 the optimal utilisation of capital for the firm was given by point X. How was this derived analytically? Simple. By altering the combination of labour and capital *while maintaining the same output level* (i.e. while remaining on the same isoquant curve) until the marginal rate of technical substitution (that is, the slope of the isoquant) equals the ratio of the wage and the price of capital.

Given that the marginal rate of technical transformation is defined as the ratio of the marginal product of labour and the marginal product of capital (i.e. the extra output that will be produced by employing one more worker or one more piece of capital respectively), to know the slope of the isoquant (or the marginal rate of technical transformation) requires that we know the marginal products of labour and capital. But if the argument in this section is correct and labour input (or its effect on output) cannot be quantified straightforwardly (by measuring hours of work alone), then it is not possible to know the marginal product of labour or how different combinations of labour and capital *can maintain the same output level*. In summary, the firm's isoquants cannot be defined.

For example, travelling along an isoquant curve means reducing labour input while simultaneously boosting capital use. In general this will involve firing workers. This development, however, may affect the productivity of the remaining workers directly. Labour productivity might increase if those who keep their jobs become more fearful and, in response, accelerate their work-pace. However, it may decrease if the remaining workers are so incensed by the dismissal of their colleagues that they reduce their effort (or even strike) as a protest.

Notice the theoretical headache that this complication causes for neoclassical economics. Geometrically speaking, it makes it hard, even impossible, to draw legitimate isoquant areas. The reason is that, all of a sudden, the relationship between labour inputs, non-labour inputs and outputs is no longer self-contained: it depends on non-quantifiable (e.g. sociological, psychological, political, etc.) factors characterising the employer–worker relation. Even though the effect of trading off 100 workers for 1 extra industrial robot might be measurable after the event, its magnitude depends on factors which are neither exclusively 'economic' nor specific to this particular firm (e.g. it may depend on the rate of unemployement economy-wide). Returning to the geometry, the above means that it may be hard to explain isoquants such as those in Figure 5.4 if sliding down one of them (e.g. a firm trading workers off with machines) may lead to many different directions in a manner that is difficult (perhaps impossible) to explain by means of this theory. And if it turns out that isoquants, are ill-defined functions then the same applies to the firm's expansion path and, by extension, to its cost curves (see Figures 5.5 and 5.6).

If this is so (and I believe it to be), why is it that (neoclassical) economics insists on production functions, isoquants, cost curves, and so on? Why does it continue to treat labour and bananas as if they were analytically equivalent (i.e. mere commodities)? The answer is that, unless labour is treated this way, production cannot be analysed using exactly the same tools (e.g. the *Equi-marginal Principle*) as those used in the theory of choice and consumption.

'So what?' you might ask. Well, recall Chapter 1 in which the proposition was put that neoclassical economics was characterised (from its conception during the later part of the nineteenth century to date) by an urge to create one large mathematical model capable of explaining all economic behaviour in a manner which shuts out of economics all sociological, historical and political arguments; the perennial attempt to turn economics into a kind of social physics.

Now, consider what would happen if economists had to accept that production cannot be examined properly without a theory about the social relations between bosses and workers, between workers themselves or about the social environment in which firms operate. It would be like admitting that history, sociology, politics, etc. ought to have a say in the theory of the firm. If economists know one thing it is that monopoly pays. And after having spent a hundred years creating one in the sphere of economic theorising by shutting the door on other social scientists, it would be madness to let them in again!

7.2.2 Keeping politics out of the picture: the covert role of isoquants

Another reason for the single-mindedness with which textbook economics insists on treating labour like a mere commodity is political. Before neoclassical economics, economists did not hide their politics behind equations: their analyses were replete with their political views.

Positive economics

In a bid to proclaim economics as a pure science, neoclassical theorists divide their economics into two types: positive and normative. *Positive economics* is meant to be the analysis of how the economy *is*, objectively. *Normative economics* comes in as an after-thought and studies how we would *like* things to be; a subjective, value-laden view. Following this distinction, the vast majority of neoclassical economists claim that their work is positive economics (that is, objective science).

However, whenever we encounter a social theorist, or politician for that matter, who tells us that their views of society or their recommendations about policy are beyond politics, we should beware. The best way of pushing one's political agenda is to convince others that one does not have one!

Adam Smith made it quite clear were he stood on most political issues of his time; David Ricardo took an active role in Parliament (by buying a seat in it!), haunting the landlords, whom he had depicted in his economic theory as the main threat to growth, and championing the cause of the industrial capitalists; Karl Marx devoted his life to working-class politics. It was not until the emergence of neoclassical economics that economists began to pose as scientists above politics and invented the myth of 'positive economics' – see previous box.

How does this determination to keep politics out of the theory explain the economic textbook's devotion to the idea of labour as a mere, quantifiable, commodity and of production as a simple market exchange of labour units for money? Let me answer with another question: when two *consenting* adults do mutually beneficial things without harming anyone else, is there any justification for the rest of us to intervene? Of course not, is the liberal answer. Politics is what happens in the public arena but not within such a relationship. Thus if economists could convince us that the employer–employee relationship is of that nature (i.e. mutually beneficial and consensual), then it should be accepted on face value and not as something that needs to be questioned or analysed. The only thing that would then matter, from an economic point of view, is the price and quantity of the labour traded between employers and employees.

Notice how the analysis of Chapter 5 guarantees precisely such a view of production which renders political, social and ethical aspects irrelevant: by insisting that, because workers voluntarily sell their labour for a price labour is like any other commodity on the market, it implies that what applies to the fruit market must also apply to the labour market. Under this scenario, no exploitation or exercise of power by employers is remotely possible and, by deduction, there is no politics at the shop-floor. The economics textbook's monopoly on wisdom regarding production is thus assured!

When arguments like those of Section 7.2.1 make an appearance (e.g. that labour is more than a commodity; that it cannot be quantified happily; that *because* it cannot be quantified, and because the worker cannot promise a specific quantity of 'labour units' at the outset, the employer–employee relationship is one characterised by power-plays as the employer tries to extract as many 'labour units' as possible after the contract has been signed . . .), they threaten the project of keeping economics free of politics. It is no great wonder that economics textbooks do not pay much attention to these ideas. We must never forget that textbooks were written by people with vested interests which often clash with the pure pursuit of truth (and this *must* include the present author!). Of course there is no question of a conspiracy of silence. All that is necessary is a definite disincentive towards questioning the textbook's authority which ultimately takes the form of a financial incentive to write textbooks which one's colleagues will recommend to their students. Textbooks that challenge the profession's authority are unlikely to make money and therefore, following the rule of the market, unlikely to be published!

7.2.3 The covert politics of isoquants

Isoquants (see Chapter 5) are simple curves depicting how every different combination of labour and non-labour inputs *automatically* translates into certain amounts of output. Can they have politics? Not as such. However, the argument that firms purchase at the market particular quantities of labour which are then put in the production process and, hey presto, out comes a *pre-specified* amount of output, *is* a political claim. To illustrate this, contrast this model of production with the following ghastly image: pregnant women and small children working in a tin mine for hours on end, abused by unscrupulous supervisors so that they keep working at an inhuman pace. Sounds extreme? Well, maybe. But these scenes did occur during and after the industrial revolution in Britain and do occur (as you are reading this) in the Third World.

Carpet factories in the Indian sub-continent are notorious for working young children in conditions of quasi-slavery for 14 hours a day and in return for pitiful amounts of money. But even if these practices no longer existed, they still act as a poignant reminder of the isoquants' political implications. The point is simple: *from the textbook's point of view, there is nothing really that helps us distinguish between the horrors just described and the more civilised working conditions experienced by western workers.* For example, the owners of the carpet

---

The personal IS political

At the beginning of Section 7.2.2 you came across the liberal position that what consenting adults do behind closed doors is not political but private or personal. Granted that this is an appealing principle worth defending (who after all wants others to meddle with their private affairs?), women came to notice something strange about it: their second-rate status in and out of their homes, their exploitation in the hands of often violent husbands, the under-valuation of their work . . . all these beastly aspects of women's lives were mostly consented to by women. Indeed the worst kind of enslavement is one accepted by the slave as natural; as something that could not be otherwise. Thus the feminist movement's rallying call in the 1970s, in an attempt to eradicate exploitation by consent, was 'The personal is political'. From our point of view, this acts as a reminder that the mere fact that individuals may have agreed to some exchange does not by itself render that exchange apolitical, free or acceptable. The nastiest dictatorship is one to which all consent.

factory above could justify themselves by arguing that they did not force these children to work for them; that these children and their families consented to working under such conditions and for low pay. 'To have consented they surely benefit from the employment we give them,' they are liable to claim.

Any theory that does not have the tools to look at this carpet factory and see the rampant exploitation which goes on in there, is a blind theory. And when this blindness is *designed* into the theory so as to keep politics at bay, it is not only bad economics that results but also barbaric politics. In this context, some critics of neoclassical economics see the textbook's attempt to keep politics out of economics not as just a theoretical *mistake* but, instead, a conscious attempt to impose a particular type of politics: to be precise, the political view that anything employers can get away with is OK! If this is true, isoquants represent a specific political position; one that makes exploitation and coercion at the workplace invisible.

7.2.4 Consenting to exploitation

If workers sell labour units to employers, in the same way that the newsagent sold you a paper this morning, can they be exploited? Did you exploit your newsagent? Surely, just like the newsagent, they would not agree to the sale if it is against their better judgment. This is the political excuse the economics textbook implicitly uses in order to justify its treatment of production as an uncontroversial, technical process. The answer, of course, is that they may have had no other alternative. Granted that no one forced them to take the offered job and that their employer did not chain them to the work-bench, this does not rule out exploitation. Let us not forget that desperate people will agree to do desperate things. If you were dying of thirst in the desert you might have consented to paying $10,000 for a glass of water. Similarly if your children were dying of malnutrition you might have consented to working 18 hours a day for some bread and water. In that case the employer would not *need* to chain you to the work-bench.

The point here is that the extent to which a market exchange is truly consensual depends on the seller's opportunity to turn down a customer; to say 'sorry, I don't want to sell'. In the case of the fruit-market or the newsagent, the fact that the seller has ample opportunity to reject your offer protects her from being coerced into a disadvantageous trade.

She is protected by the presence of many buyers other than your good self willing to purchase fruit or newspapers. Equally you, the prospective buyer, are immune from exploitation because you can turn your back to her and buy your bananas or magazines elsewhere (if she tries to charge you an exorbitant price). The next box contains two definitions of a fair trade. The first is that implied by economics textbooks: exchanges are free, or pure,

---

Free trade: two conflicting definitions

1   A transaction (or contract) is free and fair provided it was agreed to by all parties.
2   A transaction (or contract) is free and fair provided all parties had viable alternatives to it and yet decided to go ahead with it.

---

if they are voluntary. The second definition goes further by demanding that those who agree do so from a position of *some* equality. That no party can exploit the other's lack of an option to turn down an offer.

But is this what happens in the firm? Is the capacity of the sellers of labour to turn down job offers (or quit) evenly balanced with that of the buyers of labour to fire workers and replace them with others? Perhaps such balance can exist during periods of exceptional growth when demand for commodities is so buoyant that there is a shortage of labour. However, it is far-fetched to assume that this is always (or even usually) so.

For as long as there is unemployment, finding another job is always going to be more difficult than finding another worker. This imbalance in the opt-out opportunities of workers and employers means that their relationship is not as consensual as that witnessed in your local fruit-market. An asymmetrical distribution of options between firms on the one hand, and workers on the other, translates into an asymmetry in the relative power of the two sides. The greater the level of unemployment the greater the capacity of bosses to coerce workers at the workplace regardless of the fact that workers have the right to walk out if they so wish. In our harsh world, rights translate into capacities rather infrequently.

Is this different from any other market? Can we not also say that in the fruit market the seller can be 'exploited' by the buyer if, say, there is a glut of fruit in the market and few people want to buy it? Then you could approach a hapless seller who will consent to handing over the fruit at a price even below cost. Is this not exploitation? Perhaps it is. However, once the fruit has changed hands the exploitation is over. It is a one-off incident.

By contrast, labour units cannot be passed on from seller to buyer in the way bananas can. Once the price of labour has been agreed, workers have to bring *themselves* into the workplace day-in-day-out in order to impart their labour units. Furthermore they cannot even have the fruit-seller's privilege of knowing exactly how many units they agreed to sell. Recall that the employer can always demand that the employee coughs up more labour units (i.e. works harder) during the contracted office or factory hours. More menacingly, there is no limit to how hard is hard enough (that is, how many labour units will satisfy the firm's appetite).

> ## Power struggles and productivity
>
> . . . capitalists may often implement methods of production which enhance their power over workers rather than those which raise productive efficiency. For this reason, the technologies in use in a capitalist economy . . . cannot be said to be an efficient solution to the problem of scarcity, but rather, at least in part, an expression of class interest.
>
> Samuel Bowles, *American Economic Review*, 1985

In conclusion we see that labour is a strange commodity. It cannot be measured at the point of sale and comes attached to human beings who are paid by other human beings (the employers) whose purpose it is to separate them from as many labour units as possible. To pretend that this process is a technical matter that can be adequately described by means of isoquants is to use mathematical tools in order to hide the true nature of the production process; to obfuscate rather than to illuminate.

7.3 The source of profit in competitive markets

7.3.1 The political dimension of profit

Often the most difficult questions to answer are the seemingly easy ones. 'What is profit and where does it come from?' is a good example. Textbooks (see Chapter 5) define profit as the difference between revenue and economic cost (which differs from accounting cost in that it takes into account all the *opportunity costs* of production). The problem with this definition is that it does not tie in profit tightly to some productive activity. For example, a successful Mafia protection racket (that is, charging shopkeepers a weekly fee in return for *not* destroying their shops) is usually highly profitable. But surely such 'profit' is plain theft of other people's wealth and has nothing to do with the *generation* of wealth.

If you talk to a Mafia boss he will undoubtedly defend his profit as a legitimate payment for the risks and work he put into his 'business'. Indeed most Mafiosi work hard and do take great risks. However, this does not change the fact that their 'profit' is wealth produced by others and 'claimed' by the Mafia. Ruling out Mafia gains as a form of economic profit is a first taste of how our perception of profit is determined (perhaps unwittingly) by our politics, ideology, ethics, etc. This may be an extreme example yet not a misleading one of how economists, depending on their ideology, adapt their view of what constitutes legitimate profit and what does not. Economists have done this from time immemorial!

As an example, recall David Ricardo's disapproval of the economic role of landlords (see Chapters 1 and 3). To his mind, receiving increasingly large sums of money solely because one happened to have inherited desirable real estate, dilutes the incentive mechanism of capitalism and undermines its energy. Moreover the received money is the result of other people's (i.e. capitalists' and workers') efforts; a form of theft. Clearly if this political bias in favour of entrepreneurs and against landowners was to be maintained, Ricardo needed to show that profit (i.e. the entrepreneurs' reward) can be distinguished decisively from the landowners' loot. Subsequently Ricardo formulated his theory of rent so as to distinguish the worthy return to capitalist endeavours from the unworthy rent collection of profits and thus maintain his anti-landlord agenda.

Another political economist who made no bones about his political agenda was Karl Marx. Just as Ricardo wanted to castigate landlords for extracting, in the form of rent, the wealth generated by others (that is, the capitalists), Marx endeavoured to prove that capitalists extracted, in the form of profit, the wealth produced by workers. So profit for Marx, just like rent for Ricardo, was seen as the byproduct of exploitation of a productive class by an unproductive one.

Quite naturally, economists with political sympathies for landlords tried to rebuff Ricardo's theory of rent. And those who sympathised with capitalism, felt an urgent need to show that Marx was wrong and that profit was a legitimate payment to capital for its productive contribution.

7.3.2 Profit as a just payment

The standard (neoclassical) defence of the ethics of profit-making in the face of Marx's critique is that capitalists, like all owners of commodities or of other factors of production (e.g. land, labour, etc.), need to make a return in order to keep 'supplying' the market economy. Put bluntly, every commodity has its price. For example, unless apartments command the right amount of rent, they will remain untended and will crumble down. Without wages reflecting workers' productivity, workers will choose unemployment and thus labour will not be supplied. In exactly the same way, argue neoclassical economists, if capital does not return a profit to those who have accumulated it, then it will wither. Each factor receives its price and, provided the market for each of those factors is competitive, there is no exploitation and no extraction by one group of the products of someone else's labour or application.

The most ingenious defence of capitalist profit along the lines of the previous paragraph was that founded on the ubiquitous *Equi-marginal Principle* at the heart of the neoclassical analysis. Let me rehearse the argument once again. Question: what determines the value of X for person Y? Answer: the amount of money Y is prepared to pay for the next (or the last) piece of X. Thus, according to neoclassical theory, the best measure of labour's value is the amount one additional worker will add to a firm's revenue if employed. That is, employ an extra worker and see how much more output will be produced. Then value that output, depending on the price you can get for it, at the market. That value, generated by hiring an extra worker, is called the *marginal revenue product* (MRP) *of labour.*

As long as this MRP exceeds the wage of the additional worker, the firm will employ an extra worker (since doing so will bring in more revenue than the additional labour cost it will create). On the other hand, if the MRP of the last worker to have been employed is less than the wage, then that worker will be fired. Consequently the firm will employ a number of workers such that the wage is exactly equal to labour's MRP. In this sense, workers will receive the full value of their labour; not a penny more or less – see the box for an example.

The value of labour according to neoclassical theory

Consider a company making beds and suppose that if it were to hire an extra worker the firm's output would increase by one bed per week without any extra costs (i.e. the extra bed will not require additional raw materials, electricity, etc. in order to be produced). If the firm can sell an extra bed each week for $300 then it follows that the firm will be happy to hire an extra worker and pay up to a maximum of $300 per week. Now suppose that prices drop and the firm cannot sell that extra bed for more than $280. Then the newly hired worker will be fired or the wage will be reduced to a maximum of $280. In conclusion, the theory claims that, in competitive labour markets, wages reflect the value of labour measured by labour's marginal revenue product; that is, by the arithmetical product of (1) the last worker's output, and (2) the price that output can fetch at the market.

The same analysis is used in order to explain profit as the price of, or the return to, capital. Hire an extra unit of machinery and see how much the firm's revenue changes by. This change is the *marginal revenue product* (MRP) *of capital* (which is calculated by multiplying the change in output, following the employment of one extra unit of capital, with the price that output commands at the market). As long as the price of capital is less than its MRP, more capital will be employed. The firm will stop employing more capital when capital's MRP equals the price of each capital unit. Thus, if we think of profit as the price of capital, profit is determined by capital's marginal productivity.

The above analysis of profit adds a fascinating angle to the discussion in Section 7.2 in which a number of criticisms were made of the textbook assumption that labour is just another commodity. Given that the weight of argument in Section 7.2 tilted so heavily in favour of the conclusion that labour is more than a mere commodity, why are economics textbooks so keen to carry on describing the labour market as if it were no different to the market for bananas? The previous paragraphs may contain the answer.

For if it were accepted that labour is a commodity like all others, then all would agree that its value corresponds to the marginal utility it offers its buyer (like all other commodities). And if capital were also thought of as a commodity, then all would agree that its value can be explained with regard to the marginal utility it offers its buyer. Then, by default, everyone would agree that in a (competitive) market economy labour and capital, just like all other commodities, receive payments consistent with their marginal productivity. It takes a tiny step to travel from this conclusion to the belief that, under capitalism, labour and capital receive their just rewards.

Is this not a grand defence of capitalism from the attacks of subversives, like Marx, who claim that profit is the result of the exploitation of workers by capitalists? Construed as a commodity which receives its full value in direct proportion to its productive contribution, the proposition that labour is exploited sounds nonsensical. Furthermore, by showing that profit is a natural reward for the productive contribution of the services of capital's suppliers, profit is cleared of any association with theft, exploitation, coercion and the like.

In summary, neoclassical theory portrays profit as just payment; a fair reward to those who invest in capital goods instead of spending on luxuries, holidays, etc. To bolster this claim, the theory explains the size of profit (i.e. the rate of profit) by yet another application of the *Equi-marginal Principle*: the profit rate equals the value produced by the last (or marginal) unit of capital employed. In other words employers receive a reward in proportion to the marginal productivity of the capital they invested in.

However, this neat definition raises a thorny question: how can the quantity of capital be measured so that profit rates can be explained by quantities of capital (as the neoclassical theory demands)? This question attracted a great debate which became known as the Cambridge Controversy (as it involved heated exchanges between economists in Cambridge, England, and Cambridge, Massachusetts). The outcome of this debate was that the quantities of different bits of machinery (i.e. of capital) could not be measured unless the rate of profit was known. Put differently, it is impossible theoretically to determine the rate of profit by first measuring the quantities of capital and then measuring the value that each of those quantities could produce.

But this is a devastating blow to the neoclassical defence of profit as a fair payment reflecting the marginal productivity of capital. For if we need to know the rate of profit *before* measuring the quantity of capital, what is the determinant of profit? Where does it come from? Even more ominously for defenders of capitalism, this theoretical twist opens the door to Karl Marx and his followers who answer: 'Profit results from the exploitation of workers.' Is it therefore terribly surprising that neoclassical economists are in no mood to be reminded of the Cambridge Controversies?

7.3.3 Capital as a social relation

Suppose one abandons the notion that labour is a commodity like all others and accepts the arguments in Section 7.2. What happens then? First, the idea that labour units can be purchased at given prices (or wages) disappears. With a given wage and given working hours, how much effort the worker will put into the production line depends on a host of factors, not only the incentive mechanism, the degree of surveillance, the probability of being fired, the fear of unemployment, but also the social norms prevailing in the firm and in society at large (for instance note the difference in the work ethic between Japan and a Mediterranean country like Greece). Second, isoquant curves disappear since there is no longer any strict correspondence between the amount of labour time purchased by firms and output. Third, capital and profit take on a whole new meaning.

To explain the last sentence, consider the hypothetical case where a firm manages to work its labour harder for no extra pay (e.g. recent increases in unemployment cause greater insecurity and heighten the threat of being fired). Naturally its output and profit will increase. Is this increase in profit due to a rise in the marginal productivity of capital (recall that according to economic textbooks profit is a reward for capital's productivity)? Of course not. Profit increased because workers were 'convinced' to generate more labour units for no more pay. At least part of the firm's profit is due to the exercise of social power by employers over their employees. Thus the moment we recognise that labour is not a traded commodity (as bananas are), we recognise implicitly that profit is not just a reward for the productivity of capital. At least partly, it is also due to the exercise of social power!

Slowly yet steadily, the admission that labour is a human activity irreducible to the status of commodity leads us to the subversive thought that capital may not be a plain commodity either. Let us think about this. If profit is invested by firms in order to accumulate capital so as to increase productivity further (since this is the only way of keeping the firm's competitors at bay), then capital is the realisation of previous profit. But if profit is the product (at least partly) of the firm's social power over workers, then capital is a manifestation of that power too. In this sense, capital encapsulates value that was extracted from workers as opposed to value that was traded between equals. Capital suddenly emerges as a social relationship (or at least the manifestation of the social relation between employers and employees).

'Fair enough,' you might say. 'If we agree that the transfer of labour is a contested transfer, rather than a pure exchange, profit will begin to smell of exploitation and capital will emerge as the product of a social, as opposed to a purely economic, relation. So what? Would this make any real difference in how we understand the value of bread, the price of personal stereos, the productivity of Jack or Jill?' It does. Let me illustrate how in two steps. The first step elaborates the nature of the relationship between worker and employer. The second step shows how the value of bread or personal stereos reflects the whole web of social relations in society.

Step 1: If workers do not sell labour units to employers, what *do* they sell? One possible answer was given by Karl Marx: they sell their time (e.g. 40 hours per week) for a price (the wage). The buyer of that time then uses it in order to extract as much *actual* labour (or effort) from the workers during the purchased time. The worker effectively transfers her 'energy' from her person to the commodity in hand and thus bestows economic value to it. But she does not get paid for that 'energy'; she gets paid for her time. Profit then results from the fact that her 'energy' is worth more than her time. It is this difference that the employer retains and from this difference springs profit.

But why does the worker agree to part with her 'energy' for a price which reflects only the market value of her time spent at work (but not the value of the work itself)? Because she has no other alternative, is the answer. The employers, given their monopoly on means of production, are holding all the cards. If you own no tools, land, capital, etc. and you decline to work for the price of your time (which is less than the worth of your efforts), then too bad: you starve. As mentioned earlier, according to this left-wing view it is the asymmetry in the options of employers and employees that makes profit possible .

Step 2: Consider the statement 'The value of bread depends on the "energy" expended by those who baked it.' The idea here is that competition amongst bakeries forces the price of bread to a basement reflecting the cost of making it. Other things being equal, this basement value is proportional to the amount of effort, or human energy, necessary to bake it.

Suppose now that Jack and Jill are two workers, one working for the Sliced Bread Co., the other for the Wholesome Bread Co. Imagine that the Sliced Bread Co. is antiquated and uses old coal-fired ovens whereas the Wholesome Bread Co. uses modern electric ones. There is only one way Sliced Bread Co. can survive: by having Jack work harder than Jill in order to compensate for the slower, more expensive, ovens. At the end of the day one of them works harder than the other yet the products of their labour have the same value at the market. At this stage, effort of the same magnitude has different economic value because of differences in the machines used. Thus it is clear that the value of a loaf of bread cannot be determined just by labour's contribution; it depends also on the technology used.

Of course in the long run the Sliced Bread Co. will have to upgrade its ovens (or close down). When it does upgrade, then Jack and Jill will be working as hard as each other in order to bake bread of similar market value. As technology improves, the amount of labour needed in order to produce a loaf of bread falls. Thus the value of a loaf of bread depends on society's overall technological advances. Moreover how much labour effort, or 'energy', will be put into bread production by workers depends on how successful the managers of Sliced Bread and Wholesome Bread are in making workers labour harder as well as in employing the latest technology. And since they are likely to be more successful the greater the overall rate of unemployment, it also transpires that the value of bread will also depend on the level of unemployment. If this were not enough, it will also depend on the *distribution* of unemployment; for if there is a lot of unemployment in the mining industry and very little in the bread industry, then (given that those working in bakeries will be less worried about losing their jobs than miners) the bread manufacturers will not be able to increase labour productivity as much as mining firms.

The moral of the story for the philosophical reader is simple: if one accepts the proposition that labour and capital are not simple commodities but, instead, they represent social relations then it turns out that it is impossible to talk about the value of bread (or of any other commodity) without a theoretical analysis of the technological and social structure or even the history of the entire society.

The political implication of this is even more controversial: if we cannot understand the value of simple commodities like bread without first examining the whole web of social relations (e.g. the relation between classes, sexes, races, etc.), it cannot be true that the only thing that matters from the economic point of view is that we understand the movements of demand and supply in individual markets. Furthermore if profit and capital accumulation depend on how successfully extra (and unpaid) labour units can be squeezed out of workers, then it transpires that unemployment (and its related ills) are not mere accidents or failures of capitalism. Since it is the fear of unemployment that enhances the gap between (1) the economic value of the effort workers put into production and (2) the value of their time (their wages), unemployment is central in generating profit and thus capital.

You can now see in full colour the repercussions of espousing this analysis:

1   wasteful unemployment is an essential aspect of a *successful* capitalist economy (rather than a problem which can and should be addressed within such an economy)

2   profit is not a payment for some productive activity but more like a
     rent charged by those who monopolise the factories and the land for
     no other reason than the fact that they have the social power to do so
3   demand and supply are powerless to explain the value of bread which
     can only be explained by looking at the totality of social and economic
     relations.

What is the natural implication of this explosive brew? That capitalism is
inefficient in its use of human and non-human resources and it must be
replaced by a more rational system where economic activities are coordinated centrally and growth/profit for the few is not sustained by the immiseration of the unemployed and the exploitation of the many.

For the economists who wanted to derail such socialist ideas, reliance
on neoclassical theory came naturally. Their argument was that all the social
facts relevant to economic analysis of production could be encapsulated
within isoquant curves and, thus, production functions. Thus, even though
the weaknesses of these neoclassical theories were widely acknowledged by
many economists who used them, they received very little attention outside
the small circle of radical or left-wing economists. In summary, the domination of the textbooks' analysis of firms and markets by neoclassical models
is best interpreted (in my biased opinion) as a political phenomenon, rather
than a scientific one. Neoclassical economics served admirably as a set of
models defending the free market economy.

7.3.4 Saving capitalism from its neoclassical defence

At times the defenders of a political ideology inadvertently end up doing more
damage to it than its enemies. Witness for instance the damage inflicted on
Christianity by the fanaticism of the Inquisitors, or the plight of the socialist ideal in the hands of socialist zealots. Some economists, totally support-
ive of free market economies, suggest that the ideal of capitalism is under
threat from neoclassical attempts to defend it. Best known amongst them is
the twentieth-century Austrian economist Friedrich von Hayek (1899–1992).
He took a look at neoclassical theory, and decided that it contained neither
a good description nor an intelligent defence of free markets.

Economists, of all political persuasions, cannot count!

All economic theories, whichever their political orientation, have problems with arithmetic! It is not, of course, that economists are innumerate.
Rather, the problem lies with a difficulty in *identifying*, and therefore
measuring, variables which are crucial to the integrity of their theories.

Neoclassical theory

We have already seen how neoclassical theory would find it hard to measure labour input (as opposed to the number of working *hours* purchased by the firm). An even greater problem for this type of analysis (which dominates economic textbooks) concerns the measurement of capital. In Chapter 5 we drew diagrams in which one of the axis represented the number of capital units. Yet how can we measure capital? If capital is machines, there are all sorts of different machines, some big some small, some brand new some ageing. How can we add them together and come up with a number as to how many capital units a firm employs? And what about the price of capital? How is it to be determined unless we can add all capital together and say: 'The supply for capital in the market as a whole equals X units.' Thus neoclassical theory has a problem measuring the most significant inputs into the production process: the amounts of *actual* labour and of capital that are fed into production. In that case, it becomes impossible to use the *Equi-marginal Principle* (since it relies on measuring the effect of an extra unit of labour or capital on revenue) in order to determine the economic values of labour and capital.

Marxist economics

The left-wing approach initiated by Karl Marx, and featured in the previous section, faces its own measurement difficulties. When we talked of the value of bread, the value of labour's efforts, the value of labour time, this 'value' notion was not the same as price. By referring to values rather than prices, this approach tries to dig deeply into the causes of price changes; to look beneath the surface of ephemeral prices and unearth the under-currents which influence prices in the long run. Thus this whole analysis is carried out in terms of values with the hope that actual prices will, in the long run, come to reflect these values. The problem with this idea is that, whereas prices can be measured, values cannot. Moreover it has been shown that, theoretically, prices are unlikely ever to reflect these values. Thus one cannot even claim that the movement of prices gives us a rough indication of the changes in the value of commodities, labour, etc.

In conclusion, it seems that economic theorists cannot measure the variables closest to their hearts (e.g. marginal productivity for the neoclassicals, value for Marxists). Yet another reason on why they cannot *prove* each other wrong.

Hayek seems to ask: why do we teach newcomers to economics that the model of perfect competition (recall Section 5.2.5) is the ideal description of the free market? (Unlike this book, most economics texts begin with perfect competition as the main instrument for introducing students to the theory of markets and firms.) Do we do so because we think that they will be inspired by it? That they will recognise in it the splendid qualities of capitalism? What *are* these qualities anyway? Hayek's answer is that markets are remarkable institutions because they are so anarchic and so irrepressibly fluid. No one can really tell what will happen next in a real market. No one is sufficiently informed about what consumers want (not even consumers themselves), or what is the cheapest way of producing things. The resulting uncertainty causes everyone to be on their toes and to try to insure against the multitude of lurking dangers. How can they do this? Through perpetual innovation, is Hayek's answer.

The impossibility of knowing what is about to happen in the market feeds into itself as people respond to uncertainty by creating new products and new production methods. Compare this jungle-like scene with the textbook's model of perfect competition: a tranquil world in which everyone knows everything there is to know and therefore no one can outwit anyone. Since each knows this too, they all realise how futile it would be to do anything other than accept passively their unimportance. More tranquillity results. In Hayek's mind, this is not a model of a dynamic capitalist economy: it is rather a hellish picture of stagnation.

It is not only that textbook models misrepresent the true nature of capitalism which angered Hayek. He was worried primarily for political reasons. At the time he was formulating his most important critique of neoclassical theory (the 1930s and 1940s), the greatest of debates centred on the question of whether it is best to rely on free markets or to plan an economy centrally (as was the case then in the Soviet Union). Hayek felt that neoclassical arguments in favour of the market were a gift for the supporters of central planning.

Briefly, his position was this: textbook economics presents perfect competition as the ideal to which capitalist markets must aspire. In that model it is accepted that every bit of economic information *can* be known (e.g. the firms' marginal costs, the demand curve for each commodity, etc.). But if this is so, Hayek exclaimed, is it not true that we can plan an economy? Rather than leaving it to the market, we can decide that the Ministry of Economic Planning will determine prices for each commodity depending on demand and cost conditions for each industry. Additionally such a planned economy would be immune from the dilution of competition which often occurs in capitalism through the emergence of large corporations with significant monopoly power.

Hayek is adamant that the neoclassical models which appear in such glossy diagrams in today's textbooks offer excellent ammunition to those who want to wreck the free market. His suggestion is this: if you want to claim that markets are irreplaceable, focus on the *impossibility* of double-guessing the economy. People change their minds all the time about what they want, fashions come and go, technology is an ever-accelerating roller-coaster: there is just too much economic information around us and no planner or economic model, however clever or well meaning, can digest it and respond intelligently to all these wants and capabilities.

The anarchic market is the only institution that can create some order out of this chaos. Nevertheless order which is thus created is created *spontaneously* or, otherwise phrased, *unpredictably*. Unsurprisingly no economic model (that is, a human being's design) can capture this process. For if it could, then the market would not have been spontaneous (and, by deduction, irreplaceable).

Another great Austrian defender of unregulated capitalism was Joseph Schumpeter (1883–1950). He also turned on the model of perfect competition, just like Hayek did, for idealising perfect competition and for demonising monopolies. His simple point was that innovation cannot be pursued by companies making next to nothing. Only large corporations with significant market (i.e. monopoly) power can afford to indulge into research and development. So, what is all this rubbish about perfect competition being the ideal market in which profit tends to zero? If capitalism is to be celebrated, we should be playing up (rather than down) its tendency to spawn monopolies. As for any fears that monopolies will be too powerful and will exploit consumers, he dismissed them by claiming that monopoly power is like fashion: here one moment gone the next. As new products are developed by small firms, today's dinosaurs will die off and new firms will rise to take their place. He called this process *creative destruction*.

In summary, the perspective of Hayek and Schumpeter is very appealing to those who have a high regard for the genuinely free market. It is not however as popular amongst theoretical economists because it results into an admission that no economic model can capture that which makes markets indispensable. Although diametrically opposed politically, this criticism of textbook (or, more generally, of neoclassical) models of firms and markets shares many common features with the criticism waged by socialists. Socialists criticise what they see as indefensible neoclassical assumptions (e.g. labour and capital being commodities like all bread and butter, the firm has no power, competition is static) whose role is to portray capitalism as natural and just. Free marketeers like Hayek and Schumpeter criticise the same assumptions but for the opposite reason; namely, that the end result is a poor defence of capitalism.

7.4 An alternative approach to production

Criticising theories is always easier than improving upon them. In this section the criticism gives way to a constructive suggestion. Suppose that we were to reject the isoquant approach to the firm's behaviour as well as the neoclassical model of markets (i.e. the contents of Chapter 5) and individual choice (i.e. Chapter 2). What could we then say about how prices and profit are generated? What would a non-neoclassical theory of production look like?

For a start, it ought not treat labour as another commodity, or assume that profit is a mere price (of capital), or insist that capital is homogeneous (i.e. that it can be measured in the same way pounds of sugar or kilowatts of electricity can). Moreover it would have to avoid the modelling practices for which neoclassical theory has been criticised. For example, the practice of habitually assuming that firms maximise profit incessantly when it is clear that managers often pursue a *blend* of objectives (including maximising market share, profit, control of the organisation or the market, even political objectives). Or the practice of specifying the way the market is structured before analysing it (that is, how many firms there are, how they choose to compete, whether they try to undermine each other or collude). A model faithful to these criticisms would have to avoid some assumptions central to the neoclassical models. The question then is: is it possible to tell a story about how prices, wages and profit are determined *without* any such assumptions?

7.4.1 A pure production model (proposed by Piero Sraffa)

Imagine a totally hypothetical economy comprising only two industries: the grain and the cattle industry. It is quite clear that the two industries are interrelated: cattle farms need to buy grain to feed their animals and grain farms need cattle to plough the land. This is not unlike our modern world in which one industry uses the products of other industries in its production process (e.g. computers being used by steel and concrete factories while computer companies are housed in buildings made of steel and concrete). Let us now suppose that in order to grow 10 tons of grain, farmers require 2 cows to pull the plough, 4 tons of grain as seed and as feed for cows, and 1 person working full time for a certain period (e.g. 6 months). Turning to the cattle farmers, in order to 'produce' 10 healthy cows during the same period, they require 3 tons of grain, another 4 cows (to act as parents to the calves) and 2 persons working full time.

Let us summarise this information in Table 7.1.

Suppose that the price of each ton of grain and each cow are p_g and p_c respectively. Producing 10 tons of grain can be viable only if their market

Table 7.1   Joint production

Industry	Output per period	Input per period
Grain	10 tons of grain	4 tons of grain, 2 cows and 1 worker
Cattle	10 cows	3 tons of grain, 4 cows and 2 workers

value is greater (or at least not less) than the cost of producing them. Now, the market value of 10 tons of grain is 10 times p_g (i.e. $10p_g$). What is the cost of producing 10 tons of grain? From Table 7.1, the farmers will need 4 tons of grain (cost = $4p_g$), 2 cows (cost = $2p_c$) and 1 worker. Letting the worker's wage be denoted by w, the total cost of production is:

$$\text{Cost of producing 10 tons of grain} = 4p_g + 2p_c + w \tag{1}$$

Similarly,

$$\text{Cost of producing 10 cattle} = 3p_g + 4p_c + 2w \tag{2}$$

For these two industries to be financially viable, the value of the 10 tons of grain (i.e. $10p_g$) and of the 10 cows (i.e. $10p_c$) must, at the very least, cover the production cost of these quantities (see expressions (1) and (2)). In other words,

$$10p_g \text{ must be greater than or equal to } 4p_g + 2p_c + w \tag{3}$$
$$10p_c \text{ must be greater than or equal to } 3p_g + 4p_c + 2w \tag{4}$$

If profit is to be made, the revenue on the left hand side must be greater than the cost on the right-hand side in (3) and (4). However, the economy can generate profit only if it is producing a surplus. Let us see whether it does. In each period if the two industries are to produce the 10 tons of grain and the 10 cows, they must 'consume' *together* 7 tons of grain (4 to be used in the grain and 3 in the cattle industry). Thus this economy uses 7 tons of grain to produce 10 tons; a surplus of 3 tons of grain per period. Looking at the cattle industry, the two industries 'consume' 6 cows per period: 2 cows are used in the grain industry and 4 in the cattle industry itself. The output of the latter being 10 cows (or calves), there is a surplus of 4 cows per period. Consequently this economy manages to create, during every productive cycle, a surplus of 3 tons of grain and 4 cows. So, if there is a surplus someone can appropriate it. Who? It will either be the employers or the workers. Who gets which part of this surplus will depend, as we shall shortly see, on the wage.

Since, as we have just established, there is room for profit in each of the two industries, (3) and (4) can be rewritten as equalities:

$$10p_g = 4p_g + 2p_c + w \quad + \quad \text{Grain-industry-profit} \tag{5}$$
$$10p_c = 3p_g + 4p_c + 2w \quad + \quad \text{Cattle-industry-profit} \tag{6}$$

Rearranging we get

$$[\text{Grain-industry-profit}]/(4p_g + 2p_c)$$
$$= [10p_g - (4p_g + 2p_c) - w]/(4p_g + 2p_c) \tag{7}$$
$$[\text{Cattle-industry-profit}]/(3p_g + 4p_c)$$
$$= [10p_c - (3p_g + 4p_c) - 2w]/(3p_g + 4p_c) \tag{8}$$

On the left-hand side of equations (7) and (8) we find the ratio between an industry's profit from producing 10 units of output (tons of grain or cows) and the amount it spends in order to do so on these two commodities. If we think of each industry's expenditure on cattle and grain as an investment essential to the production process of each commodity, then the ratios on the left-hand side of (7) and (8) are best thought of as the *profit rate* in each of the two industries. Therefore equation (7) captures the amount of profit grain growers should expect for each $1 they spend on cattle and grain. Similarly equation (8) relates the profit cattle producers should expect for each $1 they spend on cattle and grain.

Let these *profit rates* be denoted by PR_g = Grain-industry-profit/$(4p_g + 2p_c)$ for the grain and PR_c = Cattle-profit/$(3p_g + 4p_c)$ for the cattle industry. So far nothing has been said about the behaviour of individual producers. For instance no assumption has been made about how much they choose to produce, or whether they maximise profit. In order to push the analysis further, some behavioural assumption needs to be made. However, nothing as drastic is required as in the neoclassical model which has to specify the firm's objectives fully. Here we need only suggest that when individuals or firms decide where to invest (that is, invest money either in businesses producing grain or cattle), they select the industry with a higher profit rate.

The industry which attracts more investment money will experience an increase in its output brought about either by the establishment of new firms or the expansion of old ones. This rise in supply will mean more competition amongst suppliers and an eventual decline of the price and, consequently, of the industry's profit rate. By contrast the other industry, the one with a lower profit rate, will suffer a decline. However, and this is the irony, as investment money departs for greener pastures the industry from which it fled will produce less, competition amongst the remaining firms will decrease and thus they will be able to charge a higher price. Thus the industry with the lower profit rate will experience a rise in profit. The end result of both these tendencies (that is, the tendency of the profit rate in the more profitable industry to rise and that in the less profitable to fall) will be an equalisation of the profit rates across the two industries.

When, and of course *if*, the two profit rates PR_g and PR_c equal each other, the two equations (7) and (8) can be combined into one:

$$[10p_g - (4p_g + 2p_c) - w]/(4p_g + 2p_c)$$
$$= [10p_c - (3p_g + 4p_c) - 2w]/(3p_g + 4p_c) \qquad (9)$$

Equation (9) is impossible to solve because it contains three unknowns: the two prices and the wage. However, suppose we set one of the two prices equal to 1. For example, let us set the price of each ton of grain equal to 1. Furthermore, let us set the wage also equal to 1. Equation (9) then becomes:

$$[10 - (4 + 2p_c) - 1]/(4 + 2p_c)$$
$$= [10p_c - (3 + 4p_c) - 2]/(3 + 4p_c) \qquad (10)$$

Equation (10) contains only one unknown (the price of each cow) which can now be given a numerical value. Solving for p_c we get the value 1.323. But what does this mean? Why did we set the other prices (the price of grain and the wage) equal to 1?

The reason we set these prices equal to 1 is that it was the only way we could find a solution to our 'economic system', albeit only a partial one. But what does this solution mean? Since we set $p_g = 1$ arbitrarily, the derived value of $p_c = 1.323$ can mean only one thing: that for the amount of money which buys you 1 ton of grain, you cannot afford to buy a cow! Indeed each cow is 1.323 times more expensive than a ton of grain; or, to put it differently, 1 cow is worth the same as 1323 kg of grain. Although we are not much wiser about how much either grain or cattle will cost in actual money, we *do* know the relative worth of the two commodities. So, although we cannot derive actual prices from this simple model, we can still deduce what economists refer to as *relative* prices (that is, the price of grain relative to the price of a cow).

Similarly with the wage: we set it, without knowing anything about it, equal to 1. Doing so was an admission that we cannot work out the level of the wage. However, setting $w = 1$, $p_c = 1$ and $p_c = 1.323$, and substituting these values in equations (7) and/or (8) gives us a value for the profit rate:

$$PR_g = PR_c = 0.354$$

(Check that the profit rate above is the same value whether we substitute the values $w = 1$, $p_g = 1$ and $p_c = 1.323$ in equation (7) or (8). This is, of course, not surprising since we have assumed – see equation (9) – that the profit rate in the grain industry is the same as that in the cattle industry.)

What does this profit rate mean? Nothing much *by itself*, in the same way that finding out that the price of a ton of grain equals 1.323 did not mean much *by itself*. Just like $p_c = 1.323$ was only meaningful relatively to the price of cattle, a profit rate of 0.354 makes sense only in relation to the set value for the wage ($w = 1$). It states that, if a worker collected $1000 for a period's (e.g. 6 months) work, the owners of the firm made a profit of $354 for each $1000 they invested in their firms.

7.4.2 Wages, prices and profit

To get a whiff of the implications of this model, suppose that some recent improvement in the way cattle are raised halves the amount of direct labour required in order to produce 10 cattle. Arithmetically speaking this means that equation (8) becomes

$$[\text{Cattle-industry-profit}]/(3p_g + 4p_c)$$
$$= [10p_c - (3p_g + 4p_c) - w]/(3p_g + 4p_c) \quad (8')$$

The only difference between (8) and (8') is that in the latter the cost of labour for producing the 10 cattle is only w (i.e. one worker times the wage) whereas in equation (8) it equalled 2w (since two workers were needed prior to the introduction of the new method of raising cattle). Reworking our numerical example on the basis of (8') generates the following results: setting $w = 1$, $p_g = 1$, we end up with $p_c = 1.196$ and a profit rate of 0.408.

Observe how this simple model has thrown light on the effect of technological change in the cattle industry on the relative price of grain and cattle as well as on the profit rate: As a result of a reduction by 50 per cent in the amount of labour required in the cattle industry, cattle is now relatively cheaper (its price relative to that of grain has diminished from 1.323 to 1.196, that is a cow is worth about 127 kg of grain less than before) and the profit rate has risen from 0.354 to 0.408 (that is, for every $1000 invested in production of either grain or cattle, firms earn $408 in profit). Happily this makes perfect sense. Since the same surplus is generated with less labour, and given that the wage has not changed, employers reap the benefits in the form of increased profit.

Let us now turn to the effect of changes in the amount of money workers are rewarded with (that is, the wage). Starting from the original situation (equations (7), (8) and (9)) we found that when the wage is 1 (and setting the price of a ton of grain equal to 1 as well), the rate of profit equalled 0.354 (or 35.4 per cent of expenditure on raw materials). Suppose the wage were to be doubled. Setting $w = 2$ in equation (10) the price of cattle increases from 1.323 to 1.414. Why? The answer is that cattle production is more labour intensive than grain production (recall that while it took

1 worker to produce 10 tons of grain, 2 workers are needed to 'produce' 10 cows) and therefore when the price of labour increases, cows cost relatively more than grain.

Substituting $p_c = 1$ and $p_c = 1.414$ in either (7) or (8), the new profit rate emerges as 0.172. The meaning of this is that the doubling of the wage has led to a reduction of the profit rate from 35.4 per cent to 17.2 per cent of expenditure on raw materials. This result reflects the basic idea that, when the economy produces a surplus, the wage rate determines the proportion of that surplus to be appropriated by workers. The higher the wage the greater the workers' share of that pie and, conversely, the lower the wage, the greater the employers' profit. This relationship between wages and profit can be worked out explicitly (see Figure 7.1a) by setting the price of grain equal to 1 (as before) in expression (9) and then trying out a sequence of wage rates in order to observe the profit rates and relative prices which will emerge.

In this example we have allowed the wage to take the values 1, 1.5, 2 and 2.5. Figures 7.1a and 7.1b present the effect of these wage rates on profits and on the relative price of cows (relative to grain).

As Figures 7.1a and 7.1b suggest wage rises force the rate of profit to fall and the good whose production is more labour intensive to appreciate in value. In summary, the surplus generated at the end of each period can be distributed in any which way between workers and employers in the form of wages and profit. Who will get what depends on the relative social and institutional power of the two sides. Whether this inherent antagonism will spill over in industrial conflict (e.g. strikes, lock-outs, go-slows) will depend on the political environment, the legal framework for mediation, the nature of the State and so on.

7.4.3 The strengths, weaknesses and politics of the pure production model

Strengths

Starting with its strengths, this model offers simple yet powerful insights. It explains readily how prices, wages and profit are interlinked; of how changes in the production process of one good filter through to changes in the prices of other commodities as well as in the profit rate across the economy. For instance we saw how an improvement in the method of producing cattle (a reduction by half in the amount of labour required to produce 10 cattle) caused the relative price of cattle to drop and the profit rate to rise throughout the economy. Moreover these insights can be extended in uncomplicated ways to reflect a more realistic economy. If we wish to add other industries all we need to do is include more equations like (7) and (8) one

(a)

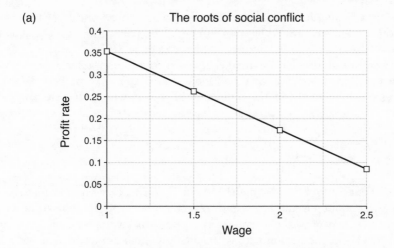

(b)

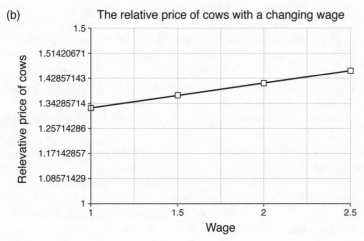

Figure 7.1a   Wage–profit trade-off
Figure 7.1b   Wage effects on prices

for each additional industry. The resulting system of equations will return prices for each commodity in relation to the price of a ton of grain (which, as in the above, will have to be set equal to 1) and will resemble a model of a complex, interdependent, multi-industry economy.

Perhaps the greatest strength of this model is due not to its ingredients but to those things that it can live without. For instance the lack of the assumption that firms maximise profit, or the fact that it does not need to specify the degree and type of competition between firms, or that labour is a commodity whose price and quantity are determined like any other commodity. This way, and unlike the theory in Chapter 5, the analysis does not incur criticism from those who argue that the objectives of firms can never be neatly expressed by simple mathematics; or that markets experience waves of acute competition followed by waves of collusion as new firms enter industries and struggle for market share before being 'accommodated' by existing companies. The only behavioural assumption made here was that investment gravitates to the industry with the higher profit rate and thus there is a tendency for that rate to be the same across different industries.

Weaknesses

Take another look at the model presented above. Can you see that some-thing rather important is missing? Yes, consumers are nowhere to be seen. This is of course why it is known as a *pure production model*: it analyses only the process of production without paying any attention to the demand side. So, what kinds of prices are we talking about if there are no consumers to pay them or indeed to influence them through their purchases? The answer given by economists who wish to defend this approach is this: they are long-term prices towards which *actual* prices must tend if the profit rate is to remain roughly equal across industries and the economy is to remain balanced. The point here is that the derived prices reflect the costs of produc-tion and unless the prices paid by consumers at the market match them, then the costs of production will not be covered. So, for the economy to remain viable and capable of producing the surplus sustaining the wages and prices depicted in Figures 7.1a and 7.1b, equation (10) must hold in the long run.

There are two main reasons why actual prices may differ substantially from those computed by the pure production model. First, because invest-ment may not be migrating fast enough from the less profitable to the more profitable industries, in which case the profit rates may vary between indus-tries. (For example this would occur if some industries are more heavily monopolised and therefore perpetually more profitable than others.) If this happens equation (10) will not be realised. And since the computed prices spring from that equation (10), there is no reason to expect real relative prices to tend towards the computed ones.

The second reason why prices may differ from those of our model is that consumers may alter their purchasing pattern consistently favouring one commodity over another. If this happens, and unless the change in consumer preferences is reflected in the costs of production (e.g. how many units of good X is necessary in the production of good Y), the favoured commodity's price will exceed the price computed by the model since the latter takes cost but not demand into account. This failing of the theory points to a larger weakness: the model's static nature. Think of the Sony Walkman for a moment. Until it arrived there was no industrial sector producing it. Then suddenly the Walkman made its appearance and, because of a massive build-up of demand for the product, a new industry for personal stereos was created. A theory that does not include a demand side can never account for a phenomenon of this sort. Having said that, and in defence of the pure production model, no economic theory (neoclassical or not) can claim to be in a position to accommodate dynamic change convincingly.

The last weakness that cries out for discussion is that there is no room in this economy for non-produced commodities (with the exception of labour which is discussed under 'politics' below). For instance, neither land nor antiques can be thought of as output of the productive system. Technically speaking we cannot add an equation for each of them to equations (7) and (8) since, in reality, no one produces land or antiques. They just happen to be there either as a gift of nature or as products of past societies. But if we do not include them in our system of equations we cannot derive a price for them. Of course this is not at all surprising since we have already realised (see the previous paragraph) that this theory only attempts to model production; and since land is not produced how could we expect the poor model to say anything about its price? If land or antiques have economic value, it is only because there is demand for them (i.e. there is no cost involved in their production) and they cannot be produced. The lack of a demand side to this theory make it impossible for it to assign prices to such resources or goods.

Politics

From a political viewpoint the most interesting aspect of this model is the one which appeals to those who emphasise the distinct nature of labour (recall Section 7.3.3). Notice the difference between labour on the one hand and grain or cattle on the other. All three are inputs into the production process; this much they have in common. However labour, unlike grain or cattle, is only an input, not an output; it enters the production process but is not produced by it. To put it another way, there is no industry producing labour. Labour is a human resource, an inextricable part of human beings which enters the process of production and is paid for it. But a mere commodity it is not. Evidence of this is that its price, i.e. the wage, is not determined in the same way the price of grain is.

Instead, the amount of money workers receive in return for their contribution to production is inversely related to the profit retained by employers. Put differently, the magnitude of the wage is determined by a tug of war between employers and employees. *The wage is fixed by a social, political and institutional process which decides the distribution of income between owners of firms and workers.* Compare this to the neoclassical analysis of Chapter 5 which claims that workers and employers are renumerated depending on how much they contribute to the firm's output. The only conclusion from this is that whatever employers or workers make in a competitive capitalist economy they must have earned every penny (the flip-side being that they deserve not one penny more).

Judging the two types of models in terms of their political message, it is clear which one suits which political agenda. If you want your economics to leave no room for arguments that profit is the result of exploitation of workers by powerful bosses, the neoclassical model fits the bill to perfection. If on the other hand you embark from a conviction that the ratio of profit and wages reflects social power and class conflict, the pure production model is your theory. The fact that the two models are so different in complexion, and that it is virtually impossible to prove which is correct and which not, ensures that one's choice of economic theory is probably more of a political than a 'scientific' dilemma.

7.5 Conclusion

This chapter orchestrated a feisty critique of the model of firms, production and markets purveyed by economics textbooks. By questioning even the very definition of what constitutes production or leisure, this chapter set off to show that nothing is uncontested in economics (see Section 7.1). Everything from the least convincing assumption of the textbook to the seemingly uncontroversial can be (and should be) the source of fascinating debate.

While examining the *process* of production (see Section 7.2), we encountered the argument that textbooks enter a slippery slope the moment they describe the goings-on in workplaces as a pure market exchange between owners of different factors of production. The reason is that selling one's labour is *profoundly* different from selling one's car. If this is so, the manner in which this difference is (or is not) taken into account determines one's economic interpretation not only of labour but also of the wage and, by association, of profit. But then our understanding of capital (whose price *is* profit) must also be affected by an acknowledgment of labour's special nature.

Next I claimed that competing models of the production process appeal differently depending on one's politics. Indeed the dominance of the textbook approach is not unrelated to the fact that it lends the free-market system rather flattering theoretical coverage. Treat labour and capital as commodities conceptually indistinguishable from bananas and you end up with the conclusion that in competitive economies employers exploit employees just as much (but never more) as employees exploit employers. Pretty attractive as a theory if you are an employer paying staff $1 an hour! And rather debilitating a theory if you are the trade unionist trying to organise these workers in the union.

Unsurprisingly the political influence works both ways: Just as sympathy with textbook models is not down to pure logic, antipathy towards them also springs, not purely from logic, but from political opposition to capitalism (see Section 7.3). Sometimes it even springs from defenders of capitalism who think that the neoclassical celebration of the free market found in textbooks is a botched job (see Section 7.3.4).

Last, Section 7.4 gave a hearing to an alternative analysis of markets; one not often found in textbooks. The purpose was to derive relative prices and the profit rate without taking any of the steps which reduce labour and capital to the status of mere commodities. The result was a theory with a great deal of emphasis on the links between (1) the distribution of society's surplus between employers and workers and (2) the relative prices of commodities. However, the fact that this model had its own drawbacks reveals clearly the impossibility of settling the dispute between economists of different views by recourse to pure logic.

Non-neoclassical economists of a left-wing bent will continue to criticise the mainstream for failing to capture the essence of production as well as the model of Section 7.4 does. The mainstream, on the other hand, will accuse its critics that they espouse a type of model which contains no consumers; that they spend too much time modelling the intricacies of production and the special nature of labour while totally ignoring the importance of consumer preferences and capitalists' entrepreneurship.

The fact of the matter is that they are both right. Neither economic model has a monopoly on truth. Yet there is no way one can agree with both because doing so will mean that one must accept, simultaneously, two (or more) utterly contradictory interpretations of capitalism. A recipe for fudging and confusion. Things are not made easier by the fact that, more often than not, when economists argue about technical problems (e.g. the problem of measuring capital), they are too coy about the political dimension of their disagreement.

Instead of coming out and bravely admitting that their position is largely influenced by a clear political agenda (e.g. a wish to reduce taxation of the rich, to expand the State's role, to promote privatisation, or even to disparage capitalism), they dress up their arguments as purely scientific claims. Thus economic debates are modelled on the Royal Society meetings of yesteryear in which learned, politically disinterested, physicists debated the nature of electro-magnetic fields. In reality, economic debates echo a titanic (often left-versus-right) political battle raging in the shadows.

So, what are *you* left with? A wonderfully exciting detective project, is the answer. Study the various competing economic theories and see whether you can unmask them by bringing their hidden politics into the light of day. Your task will become even more electrifying when we move on from a discussion of firms and markets to one about the constituent elements of a good society. Part 3 shows the way to this mesmerising playground.

Markets, the State and the Good Society

Markets, the
State and the
Good Society

Review: textbooks on markets and social well-being

Welfare economics and its three theorems

.1 The icing on the cake

The rational person maximises utility. What should the rational society do? Neoclassical economics seizes on Adam Smith's most famous claim: that the merchant 'by pursuing his own interest he frequently promotes that of the society more effectually than when he really intends to promote it' (see the box on 'Trade and virtue' on p. 17). Since, according to neoclassical economics, everyone is a merchant (even manual workers or comedians), if Adam Smith is right then utility maximisation by each may lead not only to maximum personal utility but also to maximum benefits for society as a whole. Intriguingly Smith adds that this is most likely to happen when merchants do not really care about the common good. To put it slightly differently, no one needs to care or even know what is in the public interest. All they need do is pursue their own and, hey presto, the public interest may be served.

Of course Smith made a mere allegation which he qualified by using the word *frequently*. One presumes that he had some doubt about whether selfish pursuits will *necessarily* produce public virtues. Neoclassical economics, by contrast, set itself the task of reaching precise conclusions. Under exactly what conditions will Smith's miracle come about? Already we saw how neoclassical theorists went beyond Smith's wordy description of the self-interested economic agent. In Chapter 2 they gave us a complete mathematical model of such a person. In Chapter 5 the agent was modelled as entrepreneur, again mathematically, and the conditions under which a market would qualify as maximally competitive and socially efficient were spelled out (i.e. the model of perfect competition). Imagine now that the same mathematics could *prove* that, given similar conditions, consumers and producers who maximise utility or profit in a free market environment *unconsciously* engender a social reality which is the best society could hope for (given its resources and private preferences). Such a feat of logic would constitute the ultimate vindication of Adam Smith. It would be the icing on the neoclassical cake.

To produce this proof however, the public interest (or common good, or general will) must be defined. Otherwise there is no way of showing that it is served (or maximised) by one rather than another socio-economic system. Here lies a central difference between Smith and the neoclassicals. They both feel that a free market in which self-interested agents pursue their objectives will produce the most successful society. But unlike Smith who is content to state this point without trying to prove it, neoclassical economics seeks proof. However, as the box below suggests, trying to prove the brilliance of the market may involve steps which detract from such brilliance (e.g. the need to 'measure' the common good). If this sounds too convoluted, set it aside and enjoy instead the three basic steps neoclassical thought has taken in order to deliver its proof. Which proof? That the free, perfectly competitive market is the social mechanism which can satisfy social wants most effectively.

Knowing what is in the public interest

Adam Smith exalts the market for having the capacity to serve the public interest even though no one cares or knows about what this is. Actually he may be telling us that it is *impossible* to know what is in the public interest; that since the common good can only be brought about by decentralised, uncoordinated acts, no *one* person can conceive of what is in the interest of all. If this is so, perhaps the market's capacity to serve the common good cannot be proved since none of us know what it is.

8.1.2 The first theorem: the *Equi-marginal Principle* and economic efficiency

The *first theorem* says that an economy in which every industry is perfectly competitive and in long run equilibrium (i.e. price equals marginal cost) will be efficient (see Sections 5.2.5 and 6.2.3 in Chapters 5 and 6 for a reminder of what perfect competition means). Before exploring this claim, it is worthwhile recalling the economists' definition of efficiency.

The first fundamental theorem of welfare economics

Competitive markets in long-run equilibrium are efficient.

In Section 5.1.2 of Chapter 5 a chosen combination of inputs into a firm's production line was defined as inefficient if it were possible to alter it at no extra cost and, in so doing, boost output. At the level of society, a distribution of resources or commodities is, again, inefficient if an alteration of it could potentially make some member of society better off without making anyone worse off.

Pareto* efficient distributions

A distribution of commodities or resources is efficient provided there is no possibility of altering it and in so doing make someone better off without making somebody else worse off.

(* Named after Vilfredo Pareto who defined economic efficiency in this manner.)

To give an extreme example, suppose all the cinema tickets in the world are given to people who love the theatre (but dislike the cinema) and all the theatre tickets are handed over to those who hate the theatre (but would happily go to the movies). Clearly this is a silly distribution. Simply by taking some of the cinema tickets from the first group and swapping them with some of the theatre tickets of the second group, we would make some people better off (at no extra cost) without leaving anyone with the feeling that they were cheated. In this sense, the possibility that such an improvement could be made (without making anyone worse off) proves that the original distribution of tickets was inefficient.

Notice that this definition of efficiency (see previous box) offers a neat explanation of why people meet at markets in order to trade. For if we start off with an inefficient distribution of commodities, attributes (e.g. skills, assets, etc.), this distribution can be improved upon (by the definition, since it is inefficient). In other words, there is room for making some people better off (without making anyone worse off) through swapping theatre for cinema tickets (or, equivalently, apples for oranges, money for labour units, etc.). This is indeed the origin of trade.

Trade occurs when there are benefits for both buyers and sellers and its result is a redistribution of commodities, attributes or assets such that the traders all become better off; for if they did not, why did they agree to trade? The moment they stop trading (e.g. there is no offer of trade anyone will accept) one presumes is the moment when there is no longer room for making some better off without jeopardising the well-being of anyone. And if there is no such room, it must be the case that the resulting distribution is efficient (again see the previous box).

The conclusion is inescapable. Provided efficiency is defined in the manner above, market exchanges are a response of utility maximising persons to inefficient distributions of commodities, attributes and assets. When exchange stops of the buyer's and seller's own volition, this must mean that an efficient distribution has been achieved (since they will not stop trading until no one can be made better off without someone sees no further benefit from trade). It is therefore not a great surprise that the *first theorem* of Welfare Economics turned out as it did: as long as markets are competitive and have reached long-run equilibrium, they must generate efficient distributions of commodities. Let us think about this for a moment. What does it mean to say that a market is perfectly competitive? It means that no producer is powerful enough to prevent the production/sale of a commodity for which *some* consumer would pay a price that covers its cost. And what does long-run equilibrium mean? It means that the size of each industry has adjusted to the level of demand so that prices are neither higher nor lower than marginal cost. In that case, the consumer who buys the last unit of some commodity is *only just* prepared to pay the price for it; equally the producer of that last unit is *almost* reluctant to produce and sell it. Under perfect competition in each and every market no productive capacity will be wasted as no consumer who is prepared to pay a price for a good that covers the cost of being produced will remain unsatisfied.

To highlight the above discussion, consider the following three examples of markets which fail the test of efficiency:

1   *External impediments to competition*: suppose that the government imposes a minimum price on commodity X of $10, at which price a maximum of 100 buyers wish to buy X. Suppose further that some sellers *would* be prepared to sell a further 20 units of X at $9 each while there are buyers who would happily purchase these 20 units at $9 (but not at $10).With an imposed minimum price of $10, these sellers will *not* be able to sell the extra 20 units (since maximum demand at $10 is 100). Thus the government's intervention means that there will be some sellers who could be made better off (if they were allowed to sell 20 units at $9 each) and some buyers who would also be made better off (if they were allowed to buy these 20 units at $9 each). Thus controlling price in this way stops these people from engaging in mutually beneficial trade and therefore prevents the elimination of some inefficiency (the inefficiency which is due to the government's regulation which prevents the prospective buyers and sellers of the extra 20 units

from trading). (Note that sellers who sell the 100 units at the regulated price of $10 are extremely happy with the government's intervention. Efficiency is not in everyone's interest!)

2   *Monopoly*: if a market is monopolised, the monopolist will stop producing before price equals marginal cost (i.e. the cost of producing the next unit of output) – see Section 5.2.5. But this is wasteful. By cutting production off before marginal cost equals price, the firm is refusing to produce units whose cost would be less than the price buyers are willing to pay. Put differently, it is refusing to exploit the potential of profiting from these extra units of output (since they would cost less than the price it could have raised at the market) while simultaneously denying customers units which they would be happy to buy. (Exactly why the monopolistic firm does not exploit this opportunity to eliminate such inefficiency is discussed below – see also Section 5.2.3.) Therefore this is the reason why our *first theorem* of welfare economics insists that markets must be competitive (as opposed to monopolistic or oligopolistic) in order to be efficient.

3   *Disequilibrium*: but why should competitive markets be 'in long-run equilibrium' before they can be shown to generate efficiency? Suppose a competitive market is not in long run equilibrium. For example, imagine that demand has increased suddenly and each firm is making positive profit. In the long run (economics textbooks tell us) more firms will enter the industry attracted by its high profitability. As they do so they will push price down to the level of average cost and no firm will profit (over and above their opportunity cost of producing). But what if this influx of new firms does not happen? Then we have disequilibrium since a shift in consumer demand in favour of commodity X will not be met by a surge in the number of production lines making X. Disequilibrium thus means that the market is not responding to consumer demand as well as it ought to. Again, as in the case of monopoly above, consumers will be willing to pay more for extra units of output than they would cost to producers and yet the latter refuse to supply these extra commodities; another case of inefficiency since buyers and sellers fail to exploit all the possibilities of mutual benefit.

This is the moment to point out the connection between our *first theorem* and our trusted friend, the *Equi-marginal Principle*. Take example (1) above. A government intervention like this one means that the price is not allowed to adjust until the *Equi-marginal Principle* is properly satisfied. Let me explain. What did the *Equi-marginal Principle* teach us? That instrumentally rational agents will stop acting when the marginal benefits equal the marginal cost of an action. Thus, trade would stop naturally at the moment when the benefit from buying (or selling) one unit of X equals the cost of doing so. Now, if some sellers were prepared to sell a unit of X for $9, it must mean that their benefits from this sale would exceed their cost. If the government stopped them from selling at $9, effectively it has stopped them from following the edicts of the *Equi-marginal Principle*: they will have been forced to stop transacting *before* the benefit from buying (or selling) one unit of X became equal to the cost of doing so. In summary, the government would have prevented an efficient outcome through an intervention (price control) which hinders the workings of the *Equi-marginal Principle*!

A similar link can be drawn between the inefficiency of monopoly (example (2) above) and the *Equi-marginal Principle*. Monopolistic firms produce less than under perfect competition because this is their way of generating profit: choke off supply and thus push your customers up and to the left of the market demand curve until your profit is maximised – this is the bible of the monopolist. However, in so doing, the monopolist forgoes potentially profitable sales (which consumers would welcome) if it could have told new consumers this:

> OK, here is the deal. So far I have been charging $10 per unit, a price that I know you will not pay. However my marginal cost at the moment is $6. Thus I am happy to charge you, say, $8 for some extra units. However you must promise not to re-sell these extra units to my existing customers (who are paying $10 per unit). What do you say?

This occurs often. It is called *price discrimination* (firms with monopoly or oligopoly power) charging different prices for identical commodities solely because some customers are keener than others to pay high prices. However, firms cannot do that in every case. For instance booksellers cannot be certain that the new customers will keep their promise not to resell books to existing customers. When it is impossible to keep new customers apart from older ones, monopolistic companies will not charge different prices and will not produce the extra units of output. In this sense, they and their customers will have failed to exploit all the possible gains from trade.

To recap, if firms with monopoly or oligopoly power can negotiate over the price with each customer separately, all agents (firm and consumers) would stop transacting at the point suggested by the *Equi-marginal Principle*, all inefficiencies would be eliminated and every mutually beneficial trade would take place. If this happened, there would be no reason to call monopoly inefficient. However, in practice monopolists cannot know how much each client is prepared to pay. Even if they do know, it is hard to separate their clients from each other and charge them different prices (e.g. Jill could ask Jack to buy her a few units of X if Jack were to be charged a lower price). As a result monopoly tends to be identified with inefficient outcomes. In analytical terms, monopolists conspire to obstruct customers (as well as themselves) from following the *Equi-marginal Principle* to the full because this is the only way of making profit in the absence of means for separating customers and charging them the maximum price each would be willing to pay. (Another case where efficiency is not in everyone's interest.)

Turning to example (3) the fact that, following an increase in the demand for X, the rise in the price of X failed to attract new firms in the industry means that opportunities to profit by firms outside the X-industry will have been wasted. If the X-industry has become so profitable, then firms from other industries in which the profit rate is lower ought to realise this and move into the market for commodity X. Indeed this is what the *Equi-marginal Principle* suggests: keep moving from industry to industry until the cost of the next move is the same as the extra profit. If firms' movements fail to respect the *Equi-marginal Principle* (e.g. because they are too slow, they did not notice how lucrative the X-market is, existing producers ganged up on them collectively in order to prevent entry into their market, etc.) not only will they have lost an opportunity to increase their profit but also they will be preventing the consumers of X from improving their utility level. Why?

Because by not entering the market for X, the supply of X will have failed to rise following a surge in demand and the price would remain artificially high and output artificially low. This is why, in analytical terms, disequilibrium in competitive markets is considered a source of inefficiency: it translates into a situation where, because entrepreneurs stop their migration from industry to industry *before the cost of moving into the next market (i.e. market X) equals the benefit from such a move*, consumers continue to suffer a higher price.

But why is this a case of inefficiency? After all we defined a situation as inefficient if it could be improved without making anyone worse off. However, in this situation the existing producers would be made worse off if new firms entered the industry; their profit would fall. Although this is true, it can be shown that the benefits from the entry of new firms will outweigh the losses (i.e. that consumers will benefit from the influx of the new firms more than the existing firms will lose out). Let me offer a simple numerical example to demonstrate this: suppose that there is an industry producing personal stereo headsets (and assume that no consumer will want more than one). Initially, total output equals 1000 units per period, price is $10 per unit and cost per unit is fixed at $8; thus consumers are forking out, in total, $10,000 per period and producers make a total amount of profit equal to $2000.

Under the assumption that profit attracts entrants, new firms ought to come into the market and boost the total supply beyond 1000 units, thus pushing the price below $10. Suppose however this does not happen and no new firms appear. Has anything been lost? Yes, is the answer. For if the new firms had materialised, not only would the existing customers enjoy a saving (following the price drop) but also new buyers who will not buy new headsets now (because $10 is too steep for them) would have gained. For example, suppose that the new firms would have produced an extra 100 units thus bringing the price down from $10 to $8. Existing buyers would save a total of $2000 (1000 units times the saving of $2 per unit) and new buyers would be happily spending their $8 on the extra 100 units (which reveals to us that they receive utility which is worth to them at least $800 altogether). In total consumers would have benefited to the tune of at least $2800 had new firms entered.

Naturally the existing producers would be very unhappy to see the new firms enter the industry (since such entry would reduce their profit from $2000 to nothing). However, it is interesting to notice that the loss to the producers from the entry of new firms ($2000) is less than the gain of the consumers ($2800 at least). In this sense, society as a whole loses out if new firms are not attracted into a profitable industry. And what of the existing firms? Does the fact that they are happier without the extra competition count? No it does not, say the economists. But, one may insist, does the economic definition of efficiency state clearly that for a change to be efficient no one must be made worse off? Why is the entry of the new firms thought of as a move towards greater efficiency even though the poor firms, who have been happily producing headsets at a profit, will see their profit wither?

The economist's answer is simple: imagine that consumers could band together, collect a bit more than $2000 amongst them, and hand that sum over to the existing firms in exchange of their consent to the new firms coming in. Will a deal be struck? Definitely, is the answer (since that 'gift' is worth more to the existing firms than the profit they would lose through enhanced competition). But why would consumers do this? Why collect more than $2000 and pay it to these firms for no return? Well, because there *is* a return which, as calculated earlier, is at least worth $2800: the benefits to consumers from the extra 100 units and the lower price brought about by the extra firms. In conclusion, when entry does not occur into a profitable competitive industry, it is *as if* significant potential gains from trade have been wasted.

For this reason, the *first theorem* maintains that efficiency requires that competitive markets are in a state of long-run competitive equilibrium. (Once more notice that, because in reality consumers are unlikely to band together in order to bribe existing firms into accepting the new firms happily in their midst, the firms already in the industry would be very happy with a disequilibrium (inefficient) situation in which new firms, for some reason, have failed to flock in. This is the third example of how efficiency can be unpopular amongst many.)

This last example offers us a helpful overview of snowball welfare effects resulting from violations of the *Equi-marginal Principle*. Some firms failed to follow our *Principle* by staying out of an increasingly profitable market and, as a result, society missed out on a great opportunity to experience lower prices (and thus, via the *Equi-marginal Principle* lower marginal utility, more output and inevitably more total utility).

Summary of the first theorem

What it says   It can be proved that an economy comprising only perfectly competitive markets each in long-term equilibrium (i.e. price equals marginal cost in each market), generates an efficient distribution of productive effort and output in each of its various industries and markets. This state is also referred to as a *general equilibrium*.

What it does not say   That competitive markets will *necessarily* reach a long-run, general equilibrium. Simply put, there is no proof that they will. At best the mathematics can prove that (under restrictive conditions) such an equilibrium *can* exist; that *if* a perfectly competitive economy finds itself in a long-run equilibrium it will then be efficient. However, it is one thing to prove that something is possible and quite another to show that it is likely, let alone certain (for example, though it is possible that England will win the next World Cup it would take a leap of faith to assume that it will).

Its logic   If all agents maximise utility, and the cost of making a small change to what each is doing equals the benefit from such a change, then as long as there are no impediments to acting and trading, each person's utility will be as high as possible *given* the utility of everyone else. But this is simultaneously the definition of economic efficiency and the definition of a general competitive equilibrium in which price equals marginal cost and demand equals supply in all markets.

8.1.3 The *Equi-marginal Principle* and society's budget constraint: the Production Possibility Frontier (PPF)

The *Equi-marginal Principle* was designed as a rule determining whether some individual action (e.g. consumption of bananas) should take place and when it ought to stop (i.e. when the marginal benefits or utility equal the marginal losses or cost). In Section 8.1.2 we saw that it is central to the examination of the efficiency of markets (as opposed to the efficiency of individual actions). Figure 8.1 offers a clearer perspective on how the *Equi-marginal Principle* must be elevated from the private to the social level if it is to help neoclassical economics present a model of what rational societies (again as opposed to rational individuals) do.

Imagine that our economy produces two goods only (the multi-good case is a simple extension of the two-good case). The concave line (commonly referred to as the Production Possibility Frontier – PPF) is meant to represent all the efficient combinations of goods X and Y society can produce. In terms of our *first theorem* this means that to be on the PPF an economy must be in a perfectly competitive long run equilibrium.

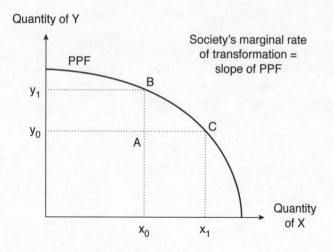

Quantity of Y

Society's marginal rate of transformation = slope of PPF

PPF

B

y_1

y_0

C

A

Quantity of X

x_0 x_1

PPF = Production Possibility Frontier

Figure 8.1   Society's production possibility frontier

To see why, consider point A at which the economy produces x_0 units of commodity X and y_0 units of Y. Now imagine that the market for X is perfectly competitive. Why would this economy ever be on point A when it could be on point B? Something must stop it from generating the maximum output of Y possible given its X output. What? We have already discussed a few examples. For instance, it could be that the government has intervened by setting a minimum price for commodity Y in which case Y-producers do not produce as much as they would otherwise. Alternatively, the market for Y could be monopolised by some firm (or oligopolised by a small number of firms – see Section 5.2.1). In this case, the supplier(s) will be using their market power (emanating from the fact that competition is limited) to boost their profit by restricting the output of commodity Y. It is clear from Figure 8.1 that the effect of such uncompetitive interventions (either by government or by firms) will push the economy below its PPF, that is it will force it into an inefficient situation.

Why inefficient? Because any point below the economy's PPF can be improved upon. Moving the economy from point A to point B increases the output of Y without jeopardising the production of X. In principle, since at least one person values additional Y units, there is room for improving the utility of one person without jeopardising that of others (i.e. by making the change from point A to B). For example, the government (presumably representing the public interest) could negotiate with the monopolist producer of Y as follows: keep your existing monopoly profit, produce an extra $y_1 - y_0$ units of commodity Y and share the value of this extra output with the consumers. (Alternatively of course the government could step in and abolish monopoly either by encouraging more competition or by setting the price of Y equal to what it would have been under competition, thus forcing the monopolist to produce y_1 – see the box on p. 147).

In summary, an economy comprising only perfectly competitive markets will lie on some point on its PPF (Figure 8.1). To understand why, recall that in Chapter 5 perfect competition was described as the market format which maximises output and minimises price. No wonder if *all* markets in an economy are in perfect competition, the level of output of each commodity will be at a maximum given the level of output of other commodities. Notice that this translates into a point on the PPF: points B and C (unlike A) are such that the output of Y is maximum given the level of output of X – and vice versa. Once at B (or C) the only way of producing more Y is to produce less X. By contrast, starting with an inefficient situation (e.g. point A) it is possible to produce more X *and* more Y – e.g. by moving to some point on the BC segment of the PPF.

Another interpretation of the PPF resulting from the previous paragraph is that it acts as society's budget constraint. Provided the economy is efficient, it can choose any point on the PPF but none beyond it. Once on the PPF, say point B, it can consume $x_1 - x_0$ extra units of X only at the expense of $y_1 - y_0$ units of Y (i.e. travel from B to C). This is the rate at which the economy as a whole *can* trade units of Y for units of X. It is called the society's *marginal rate of transformation* (the rate at which it can transform 1 unit of Y into more units of X) and its geometrical equivalent is the slope of the PPF. Analytically it is not at all different to the slope of the individual's budget constraint in Chapter 2.

8.1.4 The second theorem: the *Equi-marginal Principle* and redistribution

The difference in people's preferences means that a society's location on the PPF (see Figure 8.1) will favour some people at others' expense. For example, consumers who love X and hate Y will prefer point C to point B and vice versa. Similarly, producers of Y will prefer that society settles on B rather than on C. In view of the fact that all points on the PPF are all equally efficient from an economic standpoint, is there any way of finding out where the 'public' wants to be?

To rephrase the problem, instrumentally rational individuals choose the point on their budget constraint which maximises their utility; that is, the point of tangency between one of their indifference curves and the budget constraint (see Figure 2.5c on p. 61). How do instrumentally rational societies choose?

Looking at Figure 8.1, if the PPF is thought of as society's constraint, it is natural to think that a set of indifference curves capturing society's

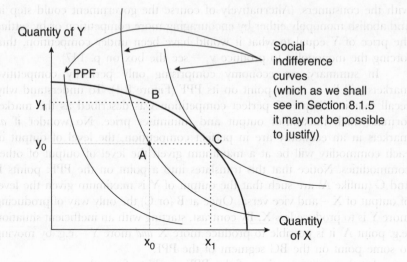

Point C: Society's best choice on its PPF

Figure 8.2   Society's optimal choice

collective preferences would complete the model – see Figure 8.2. If such *social* indifference curves were available, then the *Equi-marginal Principle* would solve the problem. The optimal social choice would be the combination which sets the *marginal rate of transformation* (i.e. the PPF's slope) equal to the *social marginal rate of substitution* (i.e. the slope of the social indifference curve) – see Figure 8.2 in which society's preferences have been presumed to be such that point C is society's optimal choice.

The second theorem of welfare economics

Any Pareto efficient economic [out come] can be attained by a suitable redistribution of resources.

* See below for a discussion of what constitutes a 'suitable' redistribution of resources.

The *second theorem* of welfare economics says that society can select any Pareto efficient outcome via a careful redistribution of resources. For instance, in the context of Figures 8.1 and 8.2, society can steer itself from B to C by diverting more productive resources from the firms which produce commodity Y to those producing commodity X. However, this redistribution must be executed carefully. Recalling that efficiency was achieved in the context of the *first theorem* by perfectly competitive firms in long-term equilibrium, any redistribution should respect the competitive market mechanism if the points on the PPF are to remain feasible.

Two examples of legitimate redistributions of resources:

1   The public increases its demand for X and reduces its interest in Y. As a result, firms abandon the Y-market and enter the X-market with the immediate result of pushing the economy down along its PPF.

2   The government confiscates land (or some other resource, e.g. energy) used to produce Y and gives it to producers of X on the understanding that they will use it to produce more X. This has, again, the effect of shifting resources from one industry to another. But why is this a legitimate transfer of resources?

The answer is that the word 'legitimate' is not used here in a moral or juridical fashion. A redistribution is deemed legitimate (or suitable according to the phraseology of the *second theorem*) provided it is a direct redistribution of resources. In example (2) above the government redistributed land from one industry to another. This was a *direct* redistribution of resources which did not involve any tampering with the market mechanism. The following example of an illegitimate (or unsuitable) redistribution clarifies matters further.

An example of an illegitimate redistribution of resources: the government subsidises the price of commodity X. That is, for every unit of X produced, the government hands over to its producers a certain amount of money. Why is this illegitimate (by contrast to example (2) above which was legitimate)? Because in this case the government tampers with the price mechanism rather than with the distribution of resources. When the government takes a plot of land or some unit of energy, or some machinery, and transfers it from one industry to another, it is not meddling directly with the price or output decisions of any firm. In contradistinction, when it subsidises the price of the X industry's product it intervenes directly in the price mechanism and, in so doing, drives a wedge between cost and price. This wedge attracts new firms to industry X because of an artificially high price and results in a situation where units of X are produced at a cost exceeding what consumers are prepared to pay. At the same time, these firms have abandoned industry Y where, as a result, supply will have fallen and the price of Y will exceed marginal cost (that is, some consumers of Y who want to pay prices that cover the cost will find that no one wants to sell them such units). Thus such intervention undermines the capacity of competitive markets for an efficient matching of demand and supply and, not surprisingly, the economy fails to reach the PPF in Figures 8.1 and 8.2.

Summarising, the *first theorem* of welfare economics says that an economy comprising competitive markets in which price equals marginal and average cost (i.e. in long-term equilibrium) are efficient. The *second theorem* takes neoclassical economics further: it suggests that if as a society we want to produce a different, yet still efficient, bundle of commodities to the current one, there is nothing stopping us. All we need do is redistribute resources between industries in a manner that does not jeopardise efficiency. And since efficiency was associated (recall the *first theorem*) with a system in which prices and output are determined by competitive market forces, the redistribution which is deemed safe (i.e. the redistribution which will not lead to inefficiency) is that which only shifts resources from one industry to another without tampering with the firms' price or output decisions.

For instance if society wants more water-melons and fewer bananas, it ought to take some land from banana-growers and pass it on to farmers producing water-melons. It should not, however, try to generate this shift in production by subsidising water-melons or taxing the consumption of bananas. The latter is tantamount to an intervention with the market mechanism which is essential for an efficient economy whereas the former is a mere (yet direct) shifting of resources from one industry to another.

Finally perhaps the easiest way of relating the *meaning* of the two theorems so far is in terms of a metaphor. The *first theorem* identifies the competitive (and in long-term equilibrium) market mechanism as a machine which transforms brilliantly certain inputs into maximum output; where the inputs are a society's factors of production (or resources) and the output is some bundle of commodities on its economy's PPF. Enter the *second theorem* which says that if we wish for an output containing a different mix of commodities (i.e. a different location on the economy's PPF) then we can have it by means of a suitable alteration of the inputs which go into the machine (i.e. the distribution of resources between different industries). However, we must *not* tamper with the internal workings of the machine; we are just not clever enough to open the machine up and alter its inner mechanisms. If we try this we shall break it and end up with lower output whatever the input (i.e. on a point in Figure 8.1 below the PPF – such as A). In conclusion, society is free to choose the final distribution of output on the PPF. However, the way of bringing it about is by a suitable choice of the initial distribution of the inputs which will enter into the process of production. Once the initial distribution is selected, we ought to let the market turn inputs efficiently into outputs without any further intervention.

8.1.5 The first two theorems and the distribution of utility amongst society's members

In Section 8.1.4 society's dilemma was portrayed in terms of which combination of commodities it should produce. There is however another crucial angle to this question: how is the produced bundle of commodities to be distributed among individuals? The obvious answer is that, when market transactions end, each will be left with what they happen to own. However, the market can be very cruel. If you enter it with nothing to sell, you are unlikely to leave it with very much at all.

This is where the *second theorem* makes an interesting contribution. It tells us that if we think the distribution of commodities (and the resulting utilities) is unfair, we can alter it without compromising the efficiency of the market mechanism. As long as the redistribution does not tamper with the market mechanism (i.e. prices) and simply takes some assets from person A and gives it to person B before the market opens for trade, the outcome will still be efficient but B will end up with more utility.

As in Section 8.1.4, where redistributing resources from one industry to another was OK as long as it was a direct reshuffling of initial resources and not an intervention in the workings of the market, here too a redistribution of wealth is fine provided the terms of trade between buyers and sellers is unaffected. To illustrate briefly, a tax on inherited wealth or on assets to be used in order to increase the wealth of poorer members of society meets these criteria. On the other hand, taxing the consumption of luxury goods for the same purpose constitutes an illegitimate intervention with the price mechanism (since it will affect the relative price of commodities).

The *second theorem* offers us a glimpse of an opportunity to alter the current distribution between the 'haves' and the 'have-nots' without damaging the efficiency of our economy. Yet this proposition may harbour more problems than it solves. To see this, imagine that society has selected a point on its PPF yielding 3 units of X and 3 units of Y. Suppose also that this society consists of three people: Tom, Dick and Harriet. Table 8.1 presents nine potential distributions of the produced goods along with the utility that each distribution gives our three friends.

The nine distributions in Table 8.1 leave our three individuals with different levels of utility. For instance distribution (i) leaves Tom and Harriet with the greatest utility while Dick enjoys only his fourth best distribution. At this point it is worth reminding ourselves of the concessions neoclassical economics had to make regarding the meaning of utility (return to Chapters 3 and 4): the utility numbers in our table cannot be compared between persons (remember that interpersonal comparisons of utility were disallowed – see Section 3.2.1). In other words, these utilities are of the ordinal type relating order of preference for an individual but totally empty of meaning across persons. To give a telling example, the fact that Tom's and Harriet's utility index is 1 (i.e. their first preference) when distribution (i) is awarded does not mean that they are equally happy. Indeed one may be happy while the other suicidal. All it means is that, from the available menu of distributions in Table 8.1, Tom and Harriet prefer distribution (i) to all others.

Which of the available distributions is best? Recall our definition of efficiency (see the box on p. 207: *a distribution of commodities or resources is efficient*

Table 8.1 Tom, Dick and Harriet's well-being

	Tom			Dick			Harriet		
Distribution	X	Y	Utility*	X	Y	Utility	X	Y	Utility
(i)	3	0	1	0	0	4	0	3	1
(ii)	2	0	2	1	1	3	0	2	3
(iii)	*1*	*1*	*3*	*1*	*1*	*3*	*1*	*1*	*5*
(iv)	*0*	*2*	*5*	*1*	*1*	*3*	*2*	*0*	*7*
(v)	*0*	*3*	*4*	*0*	*0*	*4*	*3*	*0*	*6*
(vi)	0	1	6	3	0	2	0	2	3
(vii)	0	0	7	3	3	1	0	0	8
(viii)	0	0	7	2	1	2	1	2	2
(ix)	*0*	*0*	*7*	*1*	*2*	*2*	*2*	*1*	*4*

Note * The utility numbers indicate order of preference; e.g. 1 stands for the distribution a person prefers most, 2 for his/her second preference, etc. From these we observe that Tom has a preference for X over Y, unlike Harriet who gets more utility from Y. Dick's utility, on the other hand, seems proportional to the sum of X and Y units at his disposal (that is, he values X and Y more or less equally). Highlighted distributions are inefficient (for an explanation see below).

provided there is no possibility of altering it and in so doing make someone better off without making somebody else worse off. Are there any inefficient distributions in Table 8.1? The answer is affirmative. Distributions (iii), (iv), (v) and (ix) are inefficient; that is, there are other distributions which are better than these in the sense that they make at least one person better off without making anyone worse off.

To see this, compare (ii) and (iii): moving from (iii) to (ii) makes Tom and Harriet better off without affecting Dick's utility index. Thus (iii) is inefficient. Next compare (iii) and (iv). Again moving from (iv) to (iii) makes Tom and Harriet better off without any ill-effects on Dick. Distribution (iv) must therefore be inefficient. Now let us compare (i) and (v). Once more Tom and Harriet would benefit from a move to (i) starting at (v) without Dick minding. Distribution (v) is thus ruled out as inefficient. Finally distribution (ix) is disqualified as inefficient since a move to (viii) would make Harriet better off without altering Tom's or Dick's situation.

Fair enough. Some distributions are inefficient while others efficient. But who will weed out the inefficient ones? The answer is: the market mechanism! This is why economists are so excited by the market: it has a capacity to weed out economic inefficiency without any need for government (or other types of heavy-handed) intervention. To illustrate, suppose that at the beginning there was distribution (iv). Harriet could then approach Tom and put this proposition to him:

'Tom, I can see that with distribution (iv) your utility level is quite low; indeed you are at your fifth most preferred distribution. I am not doing much better; distribution (iv) is my seventh best. Now, here is my suggestion: I will trade one of my units of X for one of your units of Y. This will take us from distribution (iv) to (iii) which is your third best and my fifth best.'

Tom thinks about it and replies:

'You are absolutely right; why should we accept distribution (iv) when we can trade ourselves into one which is better for both? Come to think of it, let us go further: I shall hand over to you both of my units of Y in exchange of your two Xs. That way we will be moving to distribution (ii) which is your third best and my second best'.

Harriet has no reason to disagree while Dick is totally uninterested since his utility is left unaffected by a move from distribution (iv) to (ii).

Efficiency (as defined by neoclassical economics) can be pretty awful

Consider a distribution in which one person owns *everything* on earth whereas everybody else is wretched, starving and hopeless. Given the economic definition of efficiency, this is an efficient distribution of resources (since moving away from it would make one person – the Gargantuan owner of the whole world – worse off).

Thus the market mechanism can take an inefficient distribution and, provided individuals like Harriet and Tom strive to achieve higher utility, generate an efficient one. However, it is crucial to note that the resulting efficient distribution will depend on the starting position. For instance we just saw that were these people to start with distribution (iv), trade would steer them to efficient distribution (ii). By contrast, were they to start at distribution (ix), trade would take them to distribution (viii). Whereas in the first case Dick and Harriet will enjoy their third best distributions, with Tom being on his second best, in the second case poor Tom will be stuck on his seventh best with Dick and Harriet enjoying their second best distributions.

This is *exactly* what the *second theorem* tells us: any efficient distribution can be attained by means of an appropriate selection of the *starting position*; that is the appropriate initial allocation of resources, commodities, wealth, and so on. In this example, if we want to favour Dick and Harriet while damning Tom, we should start them at distribution (ix). The result of trade would then be distribution (viii) which is pretty good for Dick and Harriet and abysmal for Tom. If we wish to favour Tom and Harriet, we can start them at distribution (v); then they will trade themselves to their favourite distribution (i) at the expense of Dick who will get the worst possible deal. Finally, if we wish to favour Tom only a trifle more than Dick and Harriet, we shall start them at (iv) since trading would subsequently take them to (ii) at which distribution Dick and Harriet attain their third best and Tom his second best.

OK, granted that society (courtesy of the *second theorem* of welfare economics) can achieve *any* efficient distribution it wishes for, which one should it select? Were we to ask Tom or Harriet, they would have a vested interest in promoting (i). Dick on the other hand has a strong incentive to avoid (i) like the plague and to lobby for (vii) instead. Of course there is also distribution (iii) which society may select on the grounds of equity (since (iii) gives one unit of X and one of Y to each person) but which will result into distribution (ii) as Tom and Harriet trade a unit of Y for a unit of X). One thing is certain: notions of economic efficiency cannot help here since there are many equally efficient distributions. So, how do we decide?

Economists used to think that such decisions can be made by society in the same way that individuals make choices: by maximising *social utility* or *social welfare*. Indeed if we could show that there exists a social welfare or social utility function that can be maximised like an individual's utility function was in Chapter 2, then neoclassical economics would be able to claim that the social choice problem is solvable by means of another extension of the *Equi-marginal Principle*. The diagrammatic representation of such a solution would be none other than the tangency point C in Table 8.2. I started this paragraph with 'Economists used to think that . . .' Why 'used to think'? Because since then Kenneth Arrow (b. 1921) proved a monumental theorem in 1953 (part of the reason why he was awarded a Nobel Prize in economics) which shows that such a social utility or social welfare function cannot exist in a liberal democratic society. This theorem has come to be known as the *third theorem* of welfare economics.

8.1.6 The third theorem: the impossibility of aggregate preferences

> ### The third theorem (Kenneth Arrow's Impossibility Theorem)
>
> It is impossible to sum up the preferences of individuals in order to come up with an idea of *society*'s preferences while simultaneously (1) no one person's opinion overshadows the opinions of the rest on what they all want, and (2) the resulting social preferences are useful in deciding what society should do.

Kenneth Arrow's theorem is a wonderful piece of logic. He lays down four properties that a 'proper' social utility or social welfare function ought to have (see below). Then he shows that no such function can exist. End of story!

But what does this mean? It means that there is no such thing as a social utility function whose maximisation would be evidence that the public interest (common good, general will, etc.) is served. Put differently, it means that drawing indifference curves as in Figure 8.2 is illegitimate; that unlike the individual whose preferences can be depicted by means of indifference curves, the public's preferences cannot. Indeed Arrow proved that we cannot talk about a social utility or social welfare function; that social preferences cannot be constructed using individual preferences as raw materials.

This was a major blow to welfare economics. The *second theorem* told the world that society can have any efficient mix of commodities (or individual utility levels) it wants; all it needs is to decide *which* one it wants. That question would be answered if we could find a rule (or a mathematical function) for aggregating individual utility functions into a social utility (or welfare) function. Then finding out what society wants would be a simple matter of discovering which distribution of commodities and utilities maximise that social utility (or welfare) function. At that moment of optimism, seconds before the cornerstone was put into place, Kenneth Arrow walks in with the *third theorem*, stunning the economics profession into morbid silence: 'No such social utility (or welfare) function is possible'.

Arrow's proof is beyond the scope of this book. However, it is possible to relate its logic sufficiently for the purpose of grasping its meaning and implication. Recall Arrow's objective: to show that we cannot synthesise individuals' ordinal utility functions into a social utility (or welfare) function. Arrow begins thus: suppose it were possible to devise a rule which aggregates Tom's and Dick's and Harriet's ordinal utilities (or utility functions) into some overall (or social) ranking of preferences. Let us call this rule (or social welfare/utility function) R. Do you agree that we would like R to respect the following five conditions?

1   *Universality*: that is, R must work equally well whatever the individuals' preferences. Effectively this is like saying that a country's constitution should be designed to work well irrespectively of which political parties stand in the general election, of their policies and their electoral strength. Similarly Arrow suggests that R must be in a position to synthesise successfully all sorts of private preferences.

2   *Efficiency*: that is if painting all pavements pink would improve the utility of some people without affecting adversely the utility of the rest, R should report that it *is* in the public interest to paint the pavements pink and not some other colour. If this condition is not met by R then R does not really aggregate people's preferences but, rather, it violates them.

3   *Transitivity*: that is, if R reports that social utility would rise faster as a result of building a new Opera House than a new football stadium *and* it also reports that the football stadium will boost utility more than a new prison then it must *not* report simultaneously that a new prison would be preferable (from society's viewpoint) to a new Opera House. Unless social preferences are transitive in this sense (i.e. if X is preferred to Y and Y to Z then X must also be preferred to Z), they are useless. For if they are intransitive there is no way of knowing what society wants: a new Opera House or a new prison? Or indeed a new football stadium?

4   *Independence from irrelevant alternatives*: that is, imagine that R reports society to prefer pink rather than grey walls inside public lavatories *and* more public money spent on swimming pools rather than on golf courses. Now imagine that for some reason (e.g. a scare involving the health effects of chlorine), public preferences change and society suddenly wants more money spent on golf courses rather than swimming pools. Arrow suggests that this change alone is no reason to suppose that the public's preference for pink rather than grey lavatory walls will have changed. Thus the public choice between options X and Y should not depend on the public valuation between two other options Z and W which ought to be irrelevant.

5   *Non-dictatorship*: that is, no individual's preferences should have more gravity than everyone else's. Imagine that only one person in society prefers pink pavements, pink lavatory walls, pink taxis and a plethora of golf courses. Everyone else loathes this prospect. If R were to report that pink pavements, golf courses, pink taxis, etc. were in the public interest, R would be placing that one person's interests above everyone else's. For instance if government policy was determined by R and R was biased in this manner in favour of the one individual whose tastes conflict with everyone else's then the end result would be a dictatorship. Kenneth Arrow, very wisely, insisted that this ought not to be the case.

Arrow's *third theorem* of welfare economics (also widely known as Arrow's impossibility theorem) can be restated simply: *There can exist no rule R which respects all five of the above conditions simultaneously.* Bluntly, there is a trade-off between (3) and (5) above. *Either the social preferences emerging from an aggregation of individual utilities will be intransitive* (and thus useless – see the next box) *or one person in society* (i.e. an effective dictator) *will be in a position to overrule everyone else's preferences.*

An example of intransitive social preferences

Imagine that Harriet, Tom and Dick wanted to go out together tonight. They have three options: X = cinema, Y = theatre, Z = pub. Suppose that their preference orderings are Harriet: (Y, Z, X), Tom: (Z, X, Y) and Dick: (X, Y, Z). What should they do? Democracy demands that they put the matter to the vote. Between X and Y, a two-to-one majority would see X prevail (Tom and Dick against Harriet). Between Y and Z again a two-to-one majority would back Y (Dick and Harriet against Tom). Between X and Z another two-to-one majority would win it for Z (Tom and Harriet against Dick). In other words, an intransitive social preference! Notice how the result of the vote suggests that this group of friends prefers the cinema to the theatre (first vote), the theatre to the pub (second vote) and, extraordinarily, the pub to the cinema (third vote). In other words, as a group these people cannot really make their minds up.

8.1.7 A brief summary

At the end of Section 8.1.3 I summed up the first two theorems as follows: the *first theorem* depicted competitive markets in long-term equilibrium as a wonderful machine for transforming a society's resources into the most plentiful basket of commodities. The *second theorem* suggested that any of these baskets as well as any efficient distribution of these commodities *between* individuals could be had. We can have more equality between individuals, great differences between rich and poor, various degrees of inequality . . . anything goes. Just select the initial distribution of resources with which different industries and individuals will be endowed before reaching the market and then let the market generate an efficient basket of commodities as well as an efficient distribution between individuals. This is the message from the first two theorems. The question then became: how do we know which of all these efficient distributions society wants? The answer, courtesy of the *third theorem*, was: we *cannot* know on the basis of individual preferences!

Things are actually a bit worse than that. Not only do we have no way of knowing which of all efficient market outcomes we desire as a community of citizens but, actually, we cannot be sure that markets will produce efficient outcomes. The reason is that the *first theorem* (which talks of the efficiency of markets) is not sufficiently reassuring. It says that markets, if perfectly competitive and in long-run equilibrium, will be efficient. Still no market can be declared perfectly competitive *and* in long-run equilibrium.

What about imperfectly competitive markets? Will they also be efficient? Or will they fail us on that count?

8.2 Market failures

8.2.1 Productivity linkages and over-production

This section offers an example of how perfect competition, even in long run equilibrium, could be grossly inefficient. Recall how Chapter 5 assumed that a firm's productivity (i.e. the relationship between its inputs and output) was a private affair independent of anything its competitors did. Suppose however that this is not the case; that one's *productivity* (not production) is affected by the output of one's competitors. In terms of geometry this would mean that the firm's isoquants *move* with every fluctuation in the output of some other firm. But how could that be? Consider the following example: fishermen often find that the size of their catch is not just a function of how many hours they toil at sea, or how skilful or capital intensive their operation is, but also on how much effort has been put into fishing by other fishing vessels. The reason is, of course, that the greater the total volume of fishing the more exhausted the stock becomes. Thus the greater the total volume of fishing the more time and effort you have to expend in order to catch the same number of fish; that is, the lower one's productivity.

The above example is one in which the productivity of one firm is negatively related to the output of its competitors. Such linkages cause competition to generate inefficiency or market failure. Let's see why: if the fishing industry is competitive, this means that there will be no limit to the number of operating firms (or boats). In turn this means that as long as some profit is forthcoming from a little more fishing, some new firms/vessels will fill the gap and enter the industry. But as they do, the productivity of the other boats will fall (as the fish stock becomes depleted). To maintain their output, they will fish more intensely and extensively. The result will be that the productivity of the new boats will fall and, in response, they will also work longer hours.

At some point the market will find an equilibrium. Then no one will be making much profit (which is always the case with perfectly competitive markets anyway) but the most important aspect of this market equilibrium is its monumental waste of resources. For if they could reach an agreement to limit their efforts (e.g. to fish 40 per cent fewer hours each), then the total volume of the catch would probably rise as the fish stock would be replenished. In this sense, untrammelled competition reduces the industry's total output (to the horror of Adam Smith) and wastes valuable human effort (not to mention the ecological damage it causes). Funnily enough, this is one case where monopoly could be more sensible since it would limit fishing in order to boost profit. Perhaps a sensible compromise would be for the fishermen to get together and form a cooperative which would police the fishing practices thus preventing over-fishing. Notice however that this is no more than a type of State intervention in the free market explicitly designed to limit competition. Moreover the State agency empowered to police the agreed fishing quotas must be endowed with substantial resources and with the right to apprehend fishing vessels exceeding their quotas since it is clear that the incentive to over-fish remains; if anything the agreement strengthens it (the reason being that a cheating fishing boat's catch would be greatest if every other boat respected the agreed quotas).

How common is this problem? Currently the question of fishing quotas and the manner in which they ought to be policed is taxing the minds of the European Union and threatens to develop into a major clash between Britain and its partners (especially Spain). Besides this example many more similar cases involving productivity linkages which threaten exhaustible resources could be mentioned. However, the recent proliferation of the 'information' sector brings to mind examples that do not seem immediately related to the fishing example. Consider one such example beginning with the assumption that the mind of the consumer has limited storage and computational capacity. Thus attempts by competing interests to 'inform' us (e.g. advertising, marketing, etc.) suffer similar negative productivity linkages: the effectiveness of an advertisement depends not only on how cleverly it was made, but also on how many advertisements we, the audience, have had to suffer already. The more advertisements we have seen the less attention we will pay to the next one.

Thus the greater the output of an advertising company's competitors the lower its own productivity and, therefore, the greater the volume of advertisements it needs to bombard you with in order to pass the same message. At the end of the day, advertisers and audience alike end up exhausted. If only they had come to an agreement and limited their collective assaults on our brains, we would all be better off. Alas, how can such an agreement be reached?

The unintended consequences of competition as menace rather than virtue

An agreement between the fishing companies may not be, by itself, sufficient. This is so for the same reason why firms in competitive markets fail to collude even though they prefer collusion to outright competition: because even though they would like their competitors to stick to the agreement, they have an incentive to break it. And since this is the case for each firm, agreements are short-lived.

> Generally speaking, this is a trap that economists like Adam Smith want firms to fall into so that they reduce their prices, produce more and thus serve the public (see the boxes on pp. 16 and 232). However in this case, the trap means ecological damage and much wasted social effort. For this reason it has been argued that the State is needed to put legislation and police mechanisms into place which will force agents to do what is good for them.

8.2.2 Exploitation of public and natural resources

Some resources do not belong to anyone in particular. They are public property. The problem with the market mechanism is that it is designed to assign to privately owned commodities prices which reflect their value. However, when some resources are not privately owned, the market is notorious for undervaluing them. The result is low prices for valuable public resources. And since their price is much below their real value, they are consumed, or indeed, destroyed much more quickly than they ought to. For example, clean rivers have traditionally been used by industry as a cheap repository of waste. If dumping waste in rivers is cheaper than buying the machinery for proper disposal, then the rivers will become clogged with waste. Even if society as a whole valued clean rivers, spotless beaches and breathable air, the fact that these resources are not privately owned commodities means that the market will consistently fail to value them properly.

In Chapter 1 a brief history of the rise of industrial society was attempted. The central facet of that story was that, for the first time in human history, productive land, human labour and machinery (i.e. capital) were transformed into *commodities*. It was not, of course, that land, labour and capital were not valued prior to the industrial revolution. Of course they were. What marked the end of the pre-industrial era was the creation of extensive markets for these resources. Labour was no longer simply an activity of generations of peasants; land stopped being exclusively the reward for conquerors and the object of inheritance. Labour and land were commodified. However, not every resource was commodified. The sea, the air we breathe, the great rivers were too cumbersome to become objects of trade in some market-place. Thus they remained as valuable non-commodities untouched by the market. The fact that they were undervalued and exploited to destruction was a natural repercussion of the limits to commodification.

'What can be done to limit exploitation of public resources?' asks the neoclassical economics textbook? As we shall see in Section 8.3 there are two main neoclassical answers:

1   Institute active State policies for protecting public resources.
2   Complete the commodification process which started with the indus-
     trial revolution; namely, auction off property rights to individuals or
     companies so that public resources are privatised in such a way as to
     enable the market to value them properly.

8.2.3 Non-provision of public goods

In the previous section we discussed how markets fail if the inputs into a
firm's production or an individual's consumption are publicly, rather than
privately, owned. Markets fail too when the output of some production
process is freely accessible to the public (as opposed to being sold piece by
piece to paying customers). For example take the first radio broadcasts.
Audiences all over the country warmed to them; they saw them as a window
to the outside world. Nevertheless these broadcasts were a weird type of
commodity. Unlike a banana which will be eaten either by you, or by me
or by someone else, *but not by all of us simultaneously*, radio broadcasts can be
listened to by an audience of one or of one trillion. When I 'consume' one
more unit of it (i.e. one more programme) this does not mean that, unless
the broadcaster increases output, someone else will have to consume one
less unit. This type of commodity is called a *public good*.
     The problem with public goods is that producers cannot charge
consumers directly. How will the radio station know that I am listening and
charge me while I am running along the beach plugged into my personal
stereo? But if producers cannot charge consumers then they will not produce
the programme even if there is an audience out there which *would* (if it had
to) pay good money for it. This would be an instance of market failure
because we would have:

1   a group of consumers willing to pay money for a commodity
2   one or more producers who would be willing to produce this
     commodity for the money the public could be convinced to pay
3   no production because there is no mechanism for making consumers
     pay a sum reflecting their own valuation of what they are consuming.

Initially radio and television was provided, at least in Europe, by governments which used tax-income in order to pay for them. However, soon afterwards, private radio and television stations emerged, having found a way
around the problem of 'selling' a public good. Instead of charging their audiences for the programmes they are consuming (something they could not
do), they used their programmes to capture audiences' attention in order to
sell them to advertisers peddling various commodities to the station's audience. Thus in the end consumers are made to pay in two ways: by having

to suffer advertisements and through the higher prices they pay at the market
for the advertised commodities due to the extra advertising costs (which are
typically passed on to consumers). Although the market failure has been
ameliorated partly by the introduction of advertising, the outcome is still
inefficient if it can be shown that audiences and broadcasters would be better
off if a mechanism was found for transacting directly (rather than via advertisers). The development of Pay-TV is a step in this direction; that is, in the
privatisation of a public good.

Indeed in many cases of public goods the market has managed to overcome its failings by privatising them. Look at football stadiums. Football
used to be played on village greens and anyone who wanted to watch could;
football was a public good. Then walls were built around the playing field
and the spectacle was privatised. However, many other goods simply disappeared because the market could not provide them and had no means of
privatising them either. Large national parks to be enjoyed by visitors and
indigenous people are an example. The cost of upkeep for them, or keeping
greedy developers out, was huge and so in many parts of the world (especially the Third World) it was simply uneconomical to charge entrance fees
that would cover the cost. The sad result was that they were privatised as
resources for the production of other commodities (e.g. the tragedy of the
Amazon jungle in Latin America where tropical forests are expropriated to
produce beef and timber) or were left unkempt. In the end, the commodity
'national forest', 'clean air' or even 'public library' ended up either not being
provided or under-provided.

So, what can be done to address this market failure? As in Section
8.2.2 there are two answers:

1   The State ought to take over and provide the valuable public good
     financing its production through a mixture of charges and taxes.
2   Privatise them.

8.2.4 Summing up: externalities, market failure and the free-rider problem

All three cases of market failure discussed in Sections 8.2.1, 8.2.2 and 8.2.3
are referred to in economics as examples of *externalities*. What do they have
in common? The following feature: in all three cases agents make decisions
without the luxury of knowing that the outcome will depend *entirely* on the
decision that they make. In Section 8.2.1 the decision of a fishing vessel on
how intensively to fish was not enough to determine how much fish it would
catch; it also depended on something else; something *external* to its decision.
What was that *externality*? The answer is: the decision of other fishermen as
to how intensely to fish.

In Section 8.2.2 we had another case of *externality*. The utility of people who enjoy clean beaches, fresh air and unpolluted rivers was determined not by a decision of their making but by the decision of a chemical factory manager to dump toxins in the river and the atmosphere. Finally in Section 8.2.3 the provision of a public good was prevented by yet another *externality*: the fact that, even if you are prepared to make a contribution for the maintenance of your local public library, you may choose not to fearing that few others would make a similar contribution (in which case your contribution would be wasted). Moreover if you thought that everyone else would contribute, perhaps you could save some money by not contributing yourself (since the rest would have already contributed enough). In the end, the fact that the viability of the public library depends more on what others do than what you do (i.e. it is a matter *external* to your decision) means that it is unlikely you or anyone else will make a contribution even *if you all want to see the public library carry on and would be prepared to pay for it.*

Neoclassical economists have thus concluded that whenever there are *externalities* (i.e. one's well-being depending not only on one's decisions but also on those of others) competitive markets fail to provide an efficient outcome. Furthermore it is very hard for people to get together and find a collective solution because of what is termed the *free-rider problem*. For example, in Section 8.1.1 we saw that a fisherman would have an incentive to break any agreement to limit fishing. Why? Because, although each would prefer a situation in which all (including himself) would limit their fishing effort to a situation without any rules, he would be best off if he over-fishes while everyone else was sticking to the agreed limits. Of course if this is true for one fisherman then it is also true for all and the agreement will be short-lived as everyone will attempt to take a free-ride on the back of others (thus the *free-rider problem*).

The same *free-rider problem* impedes a simple solution to the externality-induced market failures of Section 8.2.2: in the case of pollution it could very well be in the interest of each citizen that no one pollutes since the opposite would bring about environmental catastrophe from which everyone would suffer. However, it may be that limiting pollution costs money and effort (from fitting expensive filters in factory chimneys to taking the effort to carry one's empty can of soft drink to the nearest bin) and what you prefer above all else is that others pay those costs and keep the environment clean while you carry on polluting (if you are the only one who pollutes this is not much of a problem since your rubbish will be very limited in quantity and you are unlikely to come across it again once you have swept it, so to speak, under the carpet). But if everyone tries to *free-ride* in this manner, then environmental catastrophe beckons.

Finally, it is precisely the problem of free-riding which prevents the provision of public goods in Section 8.2.3: although everyone prefers that they are provided (even if they have to pay money for these goods/services),

The free-rider problem: an experiment

Suppose your teacher comes into class one day and tells you that your percentage grade for a full semester will be decided as follows: each one of you will select an integer between 1 and 9 (including 1 and 9). You will write your chosen integer on a piece of paper with your name. Then the teacher will calculate the average of the chosen numbers and your individual grade will be set equal to:

11 times the AVERAGE of all integers chosen in class minus your OWN choice of integer

So, for instance, if there are 50 of you in class and everyone chooses 9, then the average is 9. Since you have chosen 9 also, your grade (and everyone else's grade) will equal $11 \times 9 - 9 = 90$ per cent – a pretty good one. In this sense, it is in everyone's interest that all 50 of you select integer 9.

However, imagine that you thought that all of your 49 classmates would, indeed, write down 9. If you were to choose a smaller integer, say, 1, then the average would diminish from 9 to 8.82 ($49 \times 9 + 1$ divided by 50) but your grade would rise to $11 \times 8.82 - 1 = 96.02$ per cent. By contrast all your other classmates (who we have presumed chose 9) will receive $11 \times 8.82 - 9 = 89.02$ per cent. You will be at the top of the class! This is a typical case of *free-riding* – you would be taking a 'ride' on your mates' back. Notice further that this is so whatever you expect your colleagues to have chosen: whatever you expect the average choice of integer to be, your grade will be greater if you choose 1. The tragedy here is that, if each thinks in this manner, then each of you will select integer 1 yielding a grade of 10 per cent for everyone in class!

From a theoretical point of view, there are three important features of this experiment in *free-riding*: first, each one of you prefers that all select 9 to everyone selecting 1. Second, each will have an incentive to select 1. Third, a prior agreement to choose 9 will be violated unless you and your classmates care about things other than this one grade (e.g. your friendship, the fact that people may not speak to you again if you select integer 1, etc.). In summary, the *free-rider problem* reveals how groups of instrumentally rational people may act in a manner which is detrimental to everyone's interests.

the fact that they do not have to pay makes them think that the best outcome is one in which someone else pays while they are *free-riding*. Of course if everyone thinks that way, no public good will be provided (and ironically no one will end up free-riding).

8.2.5 Market failures due to ignorance and uncertainty

Imagine that there is a commodity X which some seller wants to sell for price P. At the same time there is a buyer who wants to buy X at price P. One would expect that the two would get together and transact in a mutually beneficial manner. However, imagine that commodity X is a one-year-old car in excellent condition. Yet the buyer cannot be sure about this. She has heard terrible tales of people who bought one-year-old cars which after a few months developed all sort of problems (either because they were the 'rotten apples' of the production line or because of the way they were abused by their first owners).

Suppose that quite a few buyers harbour a similar fear. The result will be that the price of one-year-old cars drops as the fears of prospective buyers translate into lower demand for such cars. As this happens, some sellers who offer pristine cars for sale may not be interested in selling at the new, lower, price (e.g. they may decide to keep their good one-year-old cars rather than sell them at a price below their valuation of their car). Thus the better examples of one-year-old cars will be withdrawn from the market thus increasing the proportion of the 'rotten apples'. As prospective buyers hear more and more stories of trouble afflicting those who have bought second-hand cars, they gradually abandon the market (e.g. by borrowing money from the bank in order to purchase new vehicles). The result is that the demand for second-hand cars will fall further and so will the price. The new fall in price will further reduce the number of good second-hand cars for sale, boosting once more the proportion of 'rotten apples' on sale. And so on until the bad second-hand cars have driven most of the good ones out of the market.

Why is this a market failure? Because in the end we shall have owners of slightly used cars that would like to sell their cars and buyers who would like to take them off their hands but there will be no sale because the buyers cannot identify the sellers of the good quality vehicles. The reason for this failure is ignorance coupled with the fear of deception. To put it differently, information is asymmetrically distributed (sellers know their cars better than the buyers do) and one group which are not easy to identify (the sellers of 'rotten apples') have an incentive to take advantage of that asymmetry and try to deceive buyers. Unfortunately the sellers of good quality products as well as the buyers are submerged in a dark cloud of deceit which prevents them from recognising each other and trade profitably.

Price as a sign of quality

A few years ago my department offered high school teachers a two-week refresher course (during the summer holidays) on recent theoretical developments in economics. Fully aware of the difficult financial position of schools, we decided to offer this service for free. Seven teachers expressed an interest and, as a result, we did not offer the course. Next year we offered the same course for $1000 per head. We had sixty-five applications. Why? The only explanation is that when uncertain about the quality of an offered commodity or service, price is used as an indicator. If it is too low, the buyer leaves the market.

Looking back at the model of perfect competition in Chapter 5, the reason why this type of failure was not envisaged back then was the assumption that buyers care only about quantity; or equivalently that they can recognise quality instantly. When buyers cannot do so, the result might be excess supply which becomes permanent when reductions in price do not boost demand. Why not? Because they are interpreted as a sign of deteriorating quality (as in the second-hand car market – see also the box).

Market failures due to uncertainty have been a hot issue in economic theory for some time now. One can think of a multitude of examples of markets failing to coordinate the activities of agents sufficiently. Take the labour market for instance; a market which seems to have been out of equilibrium for ever. Why are there hordes of unemployed people (a clear case of persistent excess supply)? Of course the answer depends on one's particular point of view and this is not the place to have this debate. Nevertheless it is interesting to investigate the capacity of the second-hand car example above to offer a possible explanation.

Imagine that employers are uncertain about the skills, character or productivity of prospective workers. Furthermore suppose that they cannot know how good they are until months pass and they show their true colours (by which time the firm will have spent significant time and money training them). Notice how this situation resembles, analytically, the second-hand car market. Buyers are uncertain about quality which they cannot recognise until after they have made the costly purchase. The result is that demand is lower because of this uncertainty and as a result price falls.

But as price falls two things happen: (1) buyers, who are already uncertain, see the diminishing price (i.e. wage) as a signal of deteriorating quality ('For her to be offering to work for so little she can't be that good,' thinks the wary employer); (2) as price (i.e. the wage) falls the better workers migrate to other industries (or even countries) and leave behind only the less skilled/committed to apply for jobs. If employers catch on to (2), the effect described under (1) strengthens. At the end of the day, employment is lower than it ought to and a number of skilled/committed workers remain unemployed while, simultaneously, there are employers who would love to employ them but do not. A clear market failure!

Keynes and the power of prophesy

John Maynard Keynes (1883–1946), perhaps the most celebrated twentieth-century economist, argued that the mere existence of opportunities for efficiency gains is not enough to motivate markets to work well. In an uncertain world something else is needed: *trust*. Thus it is perfectly possible for producers not to invest and to cut production for no other reason than an irrational fear that the demand for their products will not be there. Consequently workers will not be employed, investment will not take place and thus the level of demand for commodities will indeed be low. In the end, the producers' fears, driven more by their psychological state than by objective reality, will have been confirmed by the low level of demand!

The previous paragraph captures, to some extent, the point that the British economist John Maynard Keynes first made in the 1930s while trying to explain the crises to which a capitalist free market is prone: uncertainty is capable of throwing markets into downward spirals which may prove irreversible (without some outside help). Blind faith in the market will lead only to the perpetuation and perhaps deepening of market failure.

Uncertainty and the coordination problem: another experiment

Suppose that the *free-riding* experiment in the box on p. 232 was amended slightly. Your grade is determined by:

11 times the MINIMUM choice of integer in the class minus your OWN choice
(Notice that the only difference is that AVERAGE has been substituted with MINIMUM.)

In other words, everyone writes down an integer between 1 and 9, as before, the teacher makes a note of the *lowest number chosen* (as opposed to the average in the earlier *free-rider* experiment), multiplies it by 11 and then subtracts from that your own choice of integer. The resulting number is your grade. Thus if everyone chooses 9, again everyone in class will receive a 90 per cent grade. However, it takes only a *single* person to choose a lower number to wreck that prospect. So if you think that the minimum choice in class will be X ($1 \leq X \leq 9$), the integer that will maximise your grade is X! Unlike the earlier case of the *free-rider problem* in which you had an incentive to select the lowest integer possible, here you have no such incentive. You will be best off if you select an integer equal to the lowest chosen in the class.

This is what economists call a *coordination problem*. It is called this because everyone wishes to coordinate; each wants desperately everyone to choose 9, in which case they will also choose 9. Moreover there is no deception or conflict involved (unlike in the case of the *free-rider problem*) since no one has any reason to cheat on others by choosing less than the class minimum (whereas in the *free-riding* experiment, each had an incentive to choose 1). In this situation economists have traditionally expected rational people to choose 9. 'Why shouldn't they?' they asked. 'If they are rational, they must see that this choice would make everyone better off and, in the absence of any incentive to cheat (in contrast to the *free-rider* case) they will make that choice.' This prediction reflects the faith that economists have in the combination of rationality, self-interest and free choice to produce maximum benefits. However, it is not supported by the facts.

In a class comprising 113 mature MBA students (most of them highly accomplished professionals with years of managerial experience), more than 80 selected integer 1 when I asked them to play this game to determine part of their assessment mark. Why did they fail to coordinate so spectacularly? The answer is: lack of trust caused by uncertainty. If one believes that there is a strong chance that someone in the group will pessimistically expect that there is a person who will choose integer 1, then one has every reason to select 1. If others anticipate this, they will choose 1 too. In the end the group fails to coordinate on the choice that would benefit all even though, unlike the *free-rider* experiment, no one had an incentive to cheat (i.e. choose a small integer).This experiment captures nicely the spirit of

Keynes' argument in the previous box: markets may fail because of coordination problems; that is, due to uncertainty, people (like my students in the above experiment) predict the worst and as a result the worst happens. For example, firms may fear that future demand for their commodities will be low and, as a result, cut investment and fire workers. Consequently workers lose their income and demand for the firms' commodities declines, as predicted.

8.2.6 Monopoly as social failure

Last but not least, firms with a capacity to affect price have a degree of market power. The less the amount of competition they face, the greater that capacity. Thus market power springs from one's relative monopoly position. As it grows the firm can boost profit by cutting production and thus pushing its customers up on their demand curve to the point at which profit is maximised. This is great for the monopolist but a market failure nevertheless. We have already explained why this is so in Section 8.1.2 (see also Chapter 5). In brief, monopoly power is identified with market failure because of the lost units of output. Output that would have benefited both firm and consumers had it been produced never materialises; a clear case of inefficiency. The way to undo this loss is either to force the monopolist to produce more (e.g. the State could force a maximum price which would induce monopolies to produce more – see the box on p. 147) or for consumers to form an association with large buying power so that their representative can enter into direct negotiations with the monopolist.

8.3 Correcting market failure

8.3.1 Correcting markets by extending them

One response to market failure was foreshadowed in Section 8.2.2. If the market has failed because of public ownership of resources or public access to output then one solution is to privatise them. In the case of public goods, privatisation entails a system which enables producers to charge individual consumers. Pay-TV has already been mentioned as a case in point. Through the development of suitable technology, the television signal is coded so that access to it is restricted only to those who pay a subscription fee. Turning to the case of hitherto undervalued (and thus exploited) public resources, privatisation means the transfer of enforceable property rights to individuals. Here is an example: a factory pollutes a river by pumping waste into it.

The importance and fragility of collective action

Giving residents property rights will be an effective policy only if they have a strong collective voice; e.g. a well-organised and funded council. Otherwise even if it is in their interest to form an association in order to negotiate with the polluting firm, they may never do so – a classic *free-rider problem*. For example, if there are private costs involved in participating in the running of an association (e.g. the long hours of debate and deliberation in the local town hall, monetary contributions, etc.), each resident may want an association to be formed but may leave it to other residents to put it together. If all do the same they will be no association. Moreover, there is an ever present danger that the firm will be able to divide the residents, and in so doing continue to pollute with impunity.

Local residents complain that their quality of life suffers and that *they* bear the cost of pollution rather than the firm generating it. The government can pass legislation prohibiting the disposal of untreated effluent into the river. This would constitute a non-market intervention.

Alternatively the government could pass a law giving residents the right to a clean river. If the firm continues to pollute, the residents' association can sue. Thus the firm will have an incentive to talk to the association or local authority about the problem. The ensuing bargaining will, one hopes, lead to an arrangement involving an acceptable level of pollution by the firm bought at the expense of some monetary compensation. In summary, giving residents property rights over 'clean water' will, according to this scenario (see however the box above), put a price on pollution which the firm must pay and therefore limit it.

The problems with this solution extend beyond the real danger that residents may not have the social power necessary to stand up to a rich conglomerate whose top lawyers are capable of stealing the most stunning victories out of the jaws of certain judicial defeat. Another important worry is that if this solution (namely, giving residents a legal right to clean rivers) is logically sound, so is doing nothing. Consider this: if the residents have no legal case against a polluting firm, they may still band together in order to approach the firm with a view to bribing it into stopping the pollution of their backyard. The only difference here is that, instead of the firm bribing them to accept some pollution, it will be the residents that will bribe the firm in order to limit its pollution. What is the difference between the two situations?

The main difference, of course, is that in the one case the polluter will be paying the victims whereas in the second case the opposite will occur.

Nevertheless note that this is not of interest from a neoclassical economic viewpoint since there is no notion of fairness or justice in our economics textbooks (only instrumental rationality, efficiency and maximisation feature). We cannot even say (because of the *third theorem* which denies the possibility of aggregating private into social preferences – see Section 8.1.5) that it is not in the public interest that the victims compensate the culprits. It is quite telling that the argument more likely to sway economists against the solution of letting victims of pollution bribe the polluting firm is a reminder that the *free-rider problem* which may stop residents from coordinating their actions is made worse because they must reach deep into their pockets in order to amass enough funds to bribe the firm into polluting less.

The same free-rider problem threatens to damage the chances of letting the market address its own failures in the case of productivity linkages as in Section 8.2.1. Rather than asking the State to intervene and impose fishing quotas (or advertising quotas), adherents of market-based solutions would suggest a self-regulatory, informal system. Of course this is perfectly possible as producers realise that it is in their interest to curtail their efforts. Nevertheless the *free-rider problem* remains because it is still in the interest of each to break the agreement especially if everyone else is sticking to it. Ironically the best guarantee that the agreement will not be broken is that people keep their word, not because of the material benefit from keeping it, but because they like to keep it anyway (see the box on p. 161). In this sense, market failure will be avoided provided producers are not profit maximisers!

What about informational asymmetries as in Section 8.2? Again there is a suggestion, by those who wish to see market failures addressed by markets rather than by extra-market intervention, that left to their own devices self-interested agents will find a way to sort out the inefficiencies caused by uncertainty. In the case of second-hand cars, for example, extensive warranties may be introduced making the purchase of such a car a safer proposition. As for the labour market example (see the end of Section 8.2), various schemes have been mentioned. For example, workers take qualifications (e.g. economics degrees, MBAs, etc.) which are hard to obtain not because they will learn things that employers value enormously but as a signal to employers that they are capable of hard work. Indeed these courses may be known by all to be utterly useless. It does not matter, though. As long as it takes perseverance and commitment to plough through them, employers may seek people with such qualifications during their recruitment drives in order to reduce their uncertainty about candidates' capacity for commitment.

Turning to the last market failure discussed in Section 8.2.6, namely monopoly, again followers of market solutions suggest an extension of markets rather than direct government intervention. Instead of nationalising monopolies or imposing price controls on them, they recommend breaking monopolies up in order to create some competition. On the other hand, some of the greatest minds to have defended the market mechanism have gone further: they (recall Joseph Schumpeter and Friedrich von Hayek from Section 7.3.4) suggest with great intellectual vigour that we ought to stop worrying about monopolies. If it were not for monopoly profit, there would be no progress since the vast technological advances from which we all benefit today were financed by monopoly profit. In any case, monopolistic firms do not last long; they rise and fall like empires and their reign only continues as long as they have something to contribute.

Less zealous free-marketeers admit that there is room for government intervention to lessen the inefficiencies caused by too much market power in the hands of few firms; especially those which, because of very high fixed cost and decreasing average cost (e.g. electricity grid companies, railways, etc.) are 'natural' monopolies. Their argument is that competition can be introduced even if it is artificial. For example, railway franchises can be auctioned off periodically whereby the bidding companies offer the public the lowest fare schemes at the time of the auction. This way competition takes place, not at the customers' end of the market, but between firms who struggle against each other as to who will run the service for the lowest possible monopoly profit.

In summary, whenever markets fail there is a pro-market answer as to how society ought to respond. Distribute property rights, allow for spontaneous agreement for limiting damaging activity, introduce more competition through clever means, etc. Yet none of these solutions are comprehensive. Giving property rights to residents may not work if polluting firms learn to rule by dividing; self-regulation of the fishing or advertising industry may fail because the incentives from cheating often outweigh moral codes as well as the vision of the common interest; second-hand warrantees are unsafe, costly and can be offered only by notoriously untrustworthy second-hand dealers; MBAs and other degrees are costly on the individual and on society and, once everyone has one, they cease to send to employers useful signals; auctions over public utilities are open to corrupt practices by colluding bidders. Thus there are doubts about the efficiency with which extending the market (rather than pushing it aside when it fails) is the answer to market failure.

8.3.2 The inadequacy of approximations of the public good: the compensation principle

Extending the market to address its failures invariably raises questions about the distribution of benefits and burdens resulting from such extensions. Indeed different extensions of the market affect the distribution of utility (and income) between individuals differently. We have already seen one example in the case of pollution control in Section 8.3.1. If society gives residents the right to clean rivers, the reduction in pollution will be accompanied by a transfer of income in their direction as the firm will be prepared to bribe them so as to avoid prosecution. If, on the other hand, the firm retains an implicit right to pollute, it might receive a stream of income from the residents (or, more likely, from the local council or central government financed by taxpayers' money) as a payment for limiting pollution. The two different 'rights' will thus result into two different distributions: one benefiting residents the other the polluting firm. Which one should society select?

Perhaps you, my kind and sensitive reader, have no doubt whatsoever about who should pay whom. However, neoclassical economics is in a bind. Recall the *third theorem* which states that we cannot compose a notion of common preferences out of private desires. If this is so, and in the total absence of any well-defined economic notion of fairness, who is to say what society considers fair, proper and in the public interest? In the absence of a working notion of the common good, how should we select the particular extension to the market necessary to address market failure?

For instance, when a railway franchise is being auctioned off, should the government accept the bid involving the lowest level of monopoly profit or should it also pay attention to the bidders' promises about unprofitable services that are essential for some small and remote communities? In other words, is it in the public interest to aim at the outcome that is best from the viewpoint of consumers as a whole (by minimising monopoly profit at all cost)? Or is it in the public interest to subsidise some groups at the expense of the community at large? Without a notion of the public interest, these questions cannot be answered.

Or can they? Some neoclassical economists refused to remain paralysed by the *third theorem*. They claimed that it is still possible to approximate the 'public interest' even though they concede that the *third theorem* makes it impossible to talk of collective objectives. One idea that received much attention as a possible escape from this dead-end is that of compensating the losers. It works simply: suppose the government is considering a certain policy which will benefit some and upset others; e.g. building a new runway at the main airport with a view to developing tourism and business links further. As the local residents who live under the proposed new flight-path will certainly lose from such a policy, it cannot be recommended unequivocally on strictly economic (Pareto efficiency) grounds (recall that any change is Pareto efficient only if it benefits some without upsetting anyone).

Of course the problem is that if a government were to adopt only policies that made no one worse off then it would hardly ever do anything. It would take only one person to declare dissatisfaction with the proposed change to veto it: a recipe for non-action even if every one other than that sole individual would benefit enormously. One way around this problem is to compensate that one individual in order to remove her veto. For example, those residing close to the proposed airport could be paid damages sufficient to undo any loss of utility from aircraft noise. If society at large is set to benefit so much from the airport, surely it can afford to compensate those living nearby. Practically however there is a problem. First, it is difficult to know how much compensation has to be paid to each 'loser' in order to make them as well off as before. Second, who will pay this compensation? The average taxpayer or those more likely to benefit from the new airport (e.g. business travellers, hotel owners)?

A third difficulty with the idea of compensating those who lose out as a result of some State policy, is that there are many cases in which compensating the loser clashes with the very purpose of that policy! For example, suppose that a community comprises one multi-billionaire and lots of poor people. It may be argued that taking a mere $1 million from the former, to use it in order to buy food and medicine essential for the poor, is a good idea because the benefit to the poor will outweigh the loss to the tycoon. However, the latter cannot (and should not) be compensated by the poor.

To avoid these practical difficulties, and in order to untie government's hands in the area of policy making, some economists suggested the *compensation principle* stating that when considering the implementation of some policy X, then we do not have to have a global social utility or welfare function, or a general picture of what is in the public interest: if the beneficiaries from policy X *could* compensate the losers, then that policy should be given the go-ahead. Simple! Note that this principle does not involve any actual compensation and therefore avoids the complications in determining exactly who needs to be compensated, by how much and who should pay for it; instead it says that *if* the losers' losses are less than the gains of the winners, then the latter *could*, in principle, compensate the former. In this case, policy X should be adopted without asking the winners to compensate the losers.

You can see how this thought comes naturally to an economist's mind: if the aggregate gains from some policy exceed the aggregate losses then it is a good policy. Is this a brilliantly simple way to cut through the *third theorem* and find a way of knowing which policies a government ought to implement? To find out, we need to consider the problem more carefully. Imagine that some clever economist measured the gains and losses (see Figure 8.3) of Ms Jill Resident and Mr Jack Traveller, representatives respectively of those who live under the proposed flight-path of the new runway and of the business community who stand to gain from extra tourism. At present the combination of Jack and Jill's utilities is given by point A on the current utility frontier in Figure 8.3.

If the new runway is to be built, new possibilities open up. Diagrammatically these new possibilities are given by the new (thick) utility frontier. Moreover our economist predicts that B is the combination most likely to materialise on the new frontier if the government does not intervene following the building of the new runway. Should the new runway be built? Should

Ms Jill Resident's utility

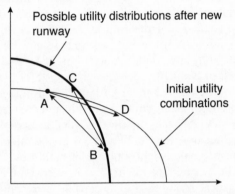

Arrows: direction of compensation

Figure 8.3   The inadequacy of compensation principles

'society' move from A to be? According to the *compensation principle*, it should since Jack's gains are such that Jack could, at least in principle, compensate Jill and still be better off after Jill's loss of utility has been eliminated.

To see why this is so geometrical, notice that although B is much worse for Jill than A, the new (thick) frontier contains points such as C which make both Jack and Jill better off. So, in principle, Jack could offer Jill to move from A to C provided she rejects her objections to the new runway; a proposition Jill has not reason to turn down. How would this work? Well after the runway is built and Jack makes more money and/or utility, he will pay Jill an amount that will reduce his utility and increase hers (until they reach point C). In the end, both Jack's and Jill's utility will have increased as a result of the new runway. If this Pareto improvement is *possible* then the *compensation principle* recommends that the runway be built without, of course, any actual compensation for Jill (recall that determining who would pay Jill and how much would have complicated things to such an extent that no one would bother building the runway anyway).

In summary, as long as it is possible to show (or argue) that new policies or projects (e.g. the new runway) would make points such as C *feasible*, the *compensation principle* recommends that they are endorsed even though, in reality, society would be moving from point A to point B. The beauty of this solution to the problem of selecting between policies which will always be opposed by some is its simplicity. However, there is a serious snag. Now that the runway has been completed, the *same* compensation principle can be used to recommend that it is demolished! How can this be?

Return to Figure 8.3 and let us consider the suggestion that the new runway should be scrapped now that we are at point B (to which society has just moved through building the runway following the *compensation principle*'s recommendation). Surely it is absurd to think that the same principle that recommended its construction will now recommend its demolition. And yet this is what happens. For if the runway is closed down, and Jack and Jill move from B back to A, Jill could now (in principle) compensate Jack for his loss of utility and, in so doing, move to point D. At D they are both better off (compared to point B) which means that, according to the *compensation principle*, the new runway should be mothballed immediately!

One thing becomes clear through all this: policies cannot be intelligently and impartially selected on the basis of a partial compensation principle which ignores a general notion of the public interest and, instead, concentrates on mechanical comparisons of gains and losses by those immediately affected. The example of Figure 8.3 revealed how inadequate such a *principle* is in practical terms since it is capable of recommending that a new project should go ahead and that it should be abandoned immediately.

In conclusion, we are back were we started: in desperate need of some idea of what is in the public interest, provided of course we want our governments to 'do things'. Unfortunately it seems increasingly likely that there is little chance of legitimate collective decision-making which reflects the common good.

8.3.3 Conclusion: neoclassical economics on rational societies

This chapter started with the question: according to neoclassical economics rational people maximise utility. What do rational societies do? The (honest) answer is that there is no answer. The *first theorem* seems to suggest that the rational society which wants efficiently to convert resources into commodities should set up competitive markets and, somehow, ensure that there are in long-term equilibrium. However it is not that easy. Section 8.2 outlined a long list of reasons as to why markets may fail – even when competitive. Moreover, and even if all the institutional causes of market failure are removed (e.g. public goods and resources are fully privatised), there is no guarantee that markets will reach an equilibrium (efficient) state if left to their own devices. For reasons similar to those expressed by Keynes and discussed in Section 8.2.5, markets may fail to reach an efficient balance of demand and supply only because of the fear and recoiling caused by uncertainty. To put it differently, markets may fail simply because a sufficient number of people fear they will. Consequently it seems inevitable that some form of government intervention will be necessary.

The problem with State intervention is that it always benefits individuals or groups differently. Who should benefit more? The *second theorem* confirmed that it is up to society. Any distribution of utility is possible provided the State redistributes resources. This means that there are two major reasons for State intervention. One is that the market requires a helping hand when its invisible one falters. The second reason is that the distribution of resources, income, utility and opportunities in society is to a large degree arbitrary and could be different. 'Why should some people be condemned to be poor just because their parents were poor?' ask some. The *second theorem* offers society a means for altering this distribution.

So far we find that there is a significant role for State intervention either for the purpose of helping markets get along or in order to alter the social division of the pie. The problem for neoclassical economics is the stubbornness of the *third theorem* which, in no uncertain terms, tells us that, if individuals are utility maximisers as in Chapter 2, there is no possibility of deriving a working notion of a common interest. So, how is society to decide *which* of the many interventions at the market-place it ought to pursue? Which income distribution should it select (recalling that choosing not to do anything in this regard is to make the highly political decision that the current situation is OK)? The *third theorem* denies the possibility of an answer to that question. But if there is no well-defined public interest, what on earth is the State doing? On whose behalf does it act?

Economics textbooks took years to acknowledge the *third theorem*. It seems that the better ones have now bitten the bullet and admitted to students the inevitable: economics cannot tell you what policies serve the common good. This is why political democracy is irreplaceable. The political process, with all its idiosyncrasies and imperfections, has the task of fashioning some *political* equilibrium (see box) which determines what is to be

---

Political equilibria: neoclassical economics' view of democracy

Voters have different interests and they vote in favour of the party whose policies reflect them best. Parties adopt policies which maximise votes *given* the policies of their competitors. A political equilibrium emerges not when parties agree with each other but when none of them has an incentive to change their policies. As economic and social reality changes, the equilibria shift yielding different government coalitions. Meanwhile voters form lobby groups to influence the government of the day. Thus a complete political equilibrium is one at which no agent has an incentive to change what they are doing; e.g. lobbyists continue to lobby at a given pace, party manifestos remain unchanged, etc. To put it in a familiar way, everyone follows the edicts of the *Equi-marginal Principle* only this time their choice is between combinations of various political programmes.

done at the level of society. Of course you cannot teach an old dog new tricks. Thus many textbooks indulge themselves with an analysis of these political equilibria which are reminiscent of those in Chapters 2 and 5: political parties are portrayed as vote-maximising firms, citizens as self-interested agents who select amongst different parties with a view to maximising their utility, and the democratic process as a market in which parties try to 'sell' their policies in competition to each other.

This market of votes-for-policies produces an equilibrium set of policies which, according to neoclassical theory, characterise the current type of State intervention in society. Neoclassical economics may have failed at providing a blueprint as to what the rational State ought to do but it has still exacted its revenge by providing its own explanation as to what States do in the absence of such a blueprint.

History of textbook models

The concept of a legitimate State in economics: origins, the dead-end and two escape routes

9.1 Chronicle of a failure foretold

The failure of neoclassical economics to provide a blueprint for the rational society was foretold in Chapter 3. It was there that the origins of neoclassical models were traced to the nineteenth-century utilitarian philosophy of Jeremy Bentham (see Section 3.1.2). Bentham, you might recall, made one simplistic assumption about human beings (that they seek pleasure) in order to present his major ethical and political claim: each person ought to aim for the greatest happiness for the greatest number (i.e. maximum average utility). Of course he could not prove that utility maximisation by each would lead each to want maximum average utility. This failure was no doubt a precursor to the problems neoclassical economics encountered (see Chapter 8) when it tried to construct a social utility or welfare function.

Bentham's political philosophy had an unmistakable practical edge: he wanted to use it in order to justify a progressive redistribution of wealth from the rich to the poor. In effect he was arguing that spreading resources more evenly would raise average utility which would, in turn, indicate a movement towards a better society. As you may imagine this blueprint for taxing the rich proved controversial; especially amongst those who would lose out as a result of such a redistribution.

In its haste to qualify as a scientific (and thus apolitical) discipline, neoclassical economics had to steer clear of these controversies. It did so by banning interpersonal utility comparisons (see Section 3.2). The moment it accepted that Jack's utility from an apple cannot be compared with Jill's from the same apple, it avoided having to take sides as to who deserves the apple more. However it also ruled itself out of any discussion about who *should* receive the extra apple: Jack or Jill? By default, it was forced to accept that the one who can pay more gets it

In Chapter 3 this point was made as follows:

> By dropping the claim that utility can be measured across individuals, economists rid themselves of many ... political controversies ... Of course they also jettisoned the possibility of knowing what the common good is (since it is now impossible to add up people's utilities in an attempt to measure the community's well being).

In essence the early utilitarian project of articulating a concept of the common good was sacrificed in order to construct a general, uncontentious, model of individuals. Re-reading the history of the economists' model of individual choice in Chapter 3 illuminates our current discussion of the problems that economics has in determining what society might want as a whole:

> Whereas utilitarianism was a primitive psychological theory of action whose main purpose was to culminate into a theory of the good society, neoclassical economists stripped it down into a calculus of private choice at the cost of rendering it incapable to judge how good or bad society is/was.

Once interpersonal comparisons were banned, following the conversion to ordinal utilities, it was hardly surprising that it was difficult to synthesise individual concerns into common objectives. Indeed Kenneth Arrow's *third theorem* of welfare economics – which explains the impossibility of a (legitimate and useful) social utility function built out of the ordinal utility functions of individuals (see Section 8.1.6) – seems inevitable when we take another look at some of the things we have already discussed.

In Section 3.3 the point was made that, to retain neutrality in relation to people's deeds, the neoclassical model had to ban any rational evaluation of preferences. Subsequently the millionaire's urge to burn $1000 notes in a nightclub to show off his wealth could only be seen as equally legitimate as the pauper's desire for a piece of bread. But if the State or the community is to agree with this, there will be *no* room for any State action; for instance, taxing an unwilling billionaire to provide some food for the pauper will be hard to justify.

Chapter 3 concluded with the warning that attempting to remain apolitical and above controversy (as to who deserves how much, etc.) is not at all to remain neutral. When witnessing an injustice, choosing to remain neutral when you have the power to intervene is to become an accessory to the unfolding injustice. Thus neutrality is apolitical only if the scene unfolding in front of your eyes is also apolitical. Economists used to understand this. This is why they took comfort from the *second theorem* of welfare economics (see Sections 8.1.5 and 8.1.6) which leaves the door open to all sorts of reallocations from one efficient distribution of resources and utilities to another. The problem was that economists wanted society to pinpoint its preferred redistribution as an instrumentally rational social choice. In other words, society had to have something to maximise; a utility function (yielding indifference curves) just like the one individuals were assumed to have back in Chapter 2. (This social utility function is commonly referred to as a *social welfare function*).

Of course this dream was shattered by the *third theorem* which proved the impossibility of such a collective utility function. Therefore neoclassical economics discovered that it cannot have an objective view of what is in the common interest even if the utility functions of every individual citizen are fully known. An ugly dilemma became inescapable: either oppose all collective decisions (since there is no collective preference to be served) or support collective decisions to re-distribute resources *in the absence of a common utility function* (or social welfare function). This is the great dilemma around which all sorts of debates and disagreements rage. Interventionists argue for collective decision making; for State action to alleviate poverty and injustice; for the construction of universal education and health systems outside the market. Free-marketeers argue against any such intervention.

The economists' change of heart about democracy

Once upon a time (e.g. before the 1980s), economics students were being taught that the role of government was to maximise social welfare through the 'right' blend of policies. Since then the economics profession has swung from that naïve presumption of a government maximising social welfare to an anti-government mentality, a preoccupation with how politics is by definition corrupt and no government can be trusted. Could it be that the *third theorem* is to blame, at least partially, for this? Whatever its causation, one manifestation of that change of heart is the campaign for taking many decisions away from elected officials and bestowing them upon unelected ones (e.g. the regulation of monopolies, monetary policy and the call for a totally independent Central Bank, etc.)

9.2 The great liberal debate: efficiency versus equity

9.2.1 Rationalising wealth and privilege

Once upon a time, the powerful did not have to justify their wealth. They celebrated their fortune and used their power to take the heads of those who refused to join them. Nevertheless, even back then the powerful had a strong desire to legitimise their affluence. For centuries they justified their fortunate position by appealing to some deity: 'It is God's will that I shall rule over you' was a favourite refrain of many a despot. However, with the passing of slavery, feudalism and the emergence of capitalism, economic power passed to those who did not have direct political power (i.e. the merchant class) while political power itself became more dispersed as the democratic State began to take shape (see Section 1.1 for more on the emergence of industrial societies).

In this new social environment, people started asking questions and demanding answers. Scientists like Galileo showed that no authority should command automatic respect. Through experimentation and logic they discovered that the earth moved against the edicts of the Pope. No longer was it enough for the king to proclaim a divine right to rule over his subjects. The historical phase during which the masses could be herded by strong warriors had been terminated by the emergence of the factory, the steam-rolling capacity of capital accumulation and, of course, a series of popular rebellions which claimed quite a few aristocratic heads. The time had come for those in authority to find a convincing case as to why they ought to remain in their positions.

Perhaps for the first time the wealthy faced the need to explain why society should accept a scandalously unequal distribution of resources. Their ingenious answer was that inequality acted as an incentive to the lower

---

Parallels with Thomas Hobbes' legitimation of the State

In Chapter 3 (p. 78) we saw how Thomas Hobbes provided the first liberal justification of a strong State in modern times. His argument was that citizens would see that it is in their interest to surrender their right to violence to a higher authority (e.g. the Sovereign) so that they will no longer suffer the temptation of waging war against each other. That is, rational individuals would *want* the Sovereign to rule over them so that they can live in peace. Similarly, the wealthy sought to justify their wealth by claiming that it was also in the interest of the poor that they were wealthy!

classes to work harder in the hope that, if they did, then they could also adorn themselves with the material trappings of opulence. Thus everyone benefited indirectly from an unequal distribution of wealth. 'If everyone is to earn the same, what is the incentive to work hard?', they would ask. In other words, it was in the interests of all that some are absurdly rich while many are poor; the so-called *trickle-down effect*.

Adam Smith's defence of the wealthy

The rich, Smith writes,

> divide with the poor the produce of all their improvements. They are led by an invisible hand to make nearly the same distribution of the necessaries of life, which would have been made, had the earth been divided into equal portions among all its inhabitants.
>
> Adam Smith, *Wealth of Nations*, 1776

To couch this argument in the language of neoclassical economics, whenever asked to justify their wealth, the affluent pointed to the tension between the wish for an efficient economy and the desire for an equitable society. Their argument was straightforward: if society chooses to redistribute wealth in order to foster more equality, then it runs the risk of discouraging hard work or investment by those who fear that their rewards will be taken away by the State – the so-called *levelling-down effect*.

9.2.2 Liberal thinkers and the efficiency-versus-equity debate

Liberal thinkers (including economists) found themselves in a tight bind. Being products of the industrial revolution, and thus apostles of the liberation of the productive forces brought about by capitalism, they remained enthusiastic about Adam Smith's notion of an end to world poverty and destitution through continuous increases in the social surplus. They dreamt of a vibrant, dynamic economy, capable of generating high growth rates so that everyone in society could become better off. The prospect of an interfering State, merely redistributing a tiny pie amongst the population, or even worse the possibility that the pie would shrink as the State's intervention discouraged investment and hard work, must have seemed appalling to them.

Nevertheless, this concern for efficiency did not prevent some of them from being sceptical about the claims put forward by the wealthy. The latter had every incentive to overemphasise the importance of efficiency over equity

---

Redistribution without inefficiency

In Section 8.1.4 the *second theorem* of welfare economics carefully specified the conditions under which redistribution can occur without losses in efficiency. Recall the requirement that only inputs to the market process are reassigned. Any interference with the market process itself would lead to a loss of efficiency; that is a point in Figure 8.1 below the economy's PPF.

---

because doing so reduced the political pressure to tax them. Even if redistribution were perfectly compatible with efficiency, they would still announce from the roofs of their elegant villas that, in effect, they were heroes who suffered opulence for the good of the poor.

The dilemma of liberal thinkers is there for all to see. On the one hand, there is a desire for spreading resources around more evenly; for greater solidarity with the suffering and less tolerance for the hideously rich. There is also the thought that redistributing opportunities more evenly may unleash new talents which would otherwise be too stifled by poverty to make a significant contribution to society. On the other hand, there was the concern that a pro-active State would distort the market's incentive mechanism and create a culture of dependence thus slowing down Adam Smith's escalator which was lifting everyone upwards, albeit at different rates (see p. 16).

For at least three centuries the conflict between efficiency and equity has characterised liberal politics and economics. It still does. Conservative thinkers place more emphasis on efficiency and are prepared to see large doses of inequity as the price society should be willing to pay for a long-term increase in its capacity to produce wealth. They feel that the State ought to intervene only when a person's income falls below certain terribly low levels. And even then, the State must ensure that its support does not destroy the person's motivation to pick up the pieces and try again. By contrast, more liberal thinkers see a much greater role for the State (for example, as a provider of basic goods such as education and health that should not be left to the market) and are less worried about the effects of such intervention on efficiency.

The difference between most conservative and interventionist liberal economists, political theorists, sociologists, etc. is a matter of degree. They agree that efficiency and equity are important but, often, antagonistic objectives. Their disagreement lies on what is the best blend of the two and how it can be achieved. Conservatives feel that the best blend sacrifices as little efficiency as possible and involves the State only when it is absolutely necessary. Their foes regard the optimal blend as one that contains significant amounts of equity and is brought about by a significant State presence in social life. That the two camps are separated only by the degree to which they value efficiency relatively to equity can be gleaned from their interchangeable labels in different countries. Whereas to be a member of the Liberal Democratic Party in Japan or the Liberal Party of Australia is to be on the conservative right of those countries' political spectrum, being a Liberal in Germany, Britain and the USA is to be regarded as a centrist who favours wide-ranging State intervention in pursuit of equity.

9.2.3 The efficiency-versus-equity debate and the dead-end of welfare economics

One hope liberal economists had was that the tension between equity and efficiency would be one that society could negotiate for itself (recall Section 9.1). If a social utility (or welfare) function could be shown to exist, then at least in principle society could rationally decide which blend of efficiency and equity it desired: the blend which maximises social utility (or welfare). Of course even then it would take a great deal of debate, disagreement and outright conflict to decide what that blend was and how society could achieve it. But, at the very least, we could all go to bed at night safe in the thought that there was such a thing as a degree of redistribution and State action which was firmly in the public interest. All we would have to do is pin it down.

However, the *third theorem* proved that even this hope is too optimistic. If we cannot generate a social utility (or welfare) index out of our private utility indices, then there simply does not exist an optimal blend between the market and the State, between equity and efficiency. Not even theoretically! What should we do then? Should the State do nothing? Or is there an escape from this dead-end?

There are two escape routes for liberals, both of which emerged in the 1970s, and I will discuss them in the next two sections. They share one common feature: the view that the efficiency-versus-equity dilemma is unhelpful or even false; that it merely distracts us from what really matters: justice. The first escape (see Section 9.3) focuses on what is termed social or distributive justice. It suggests that there is a degree of equity without which society is inefficient and a degree of efficiency without which society is unfair! The second escape route (Section 9.4) also turns on the notion of fairness but chooses to focus not on social justice but, instead, on the injustice inherent in taxation. One's conclusions on what constitutes the good society will differ vastly depending on which of the two escape routes one chooses.

9.3 The first escape route from neoclassical economics' dead-end: John Rawls' theory of distributive justice

9.3.1 Towards a rationally compassionate society

The French Revolution, whose rhetoric and ideas marked the dawn of political democracy for humanity, was inspired by three heart-warming calls: one for liberty, one for equality and one for fraternity. Economists talk a great deal about liberty (free markets, free trade, etc.) much less about equality and not at all about fraternity. Indeed the neoclassical model of individuals (see Chapter 2) leaves very little scope for even a definition of equity or fraternity. If utilities cannot be compared across persons, what does equality mean? And if individuals maximise utility, the only way fraternity makes sense is if my utility rises and falls in proportion to yours; possible but too hard to model in any convincing manner. In contradistinction, freedom is dead essay to define: the absence of constraints.

As this and Chapter 8 have made abundantly clear, this view of individuals does not allow economics to say anything plausible about the Good Society; about what is and what is not in the public interest. Liberal thinkers who were concerned about this failure recognised immediately that the problem lay in the economists' model of human beings. Some even predicted the problem before it occurred (see J. S. Mill's point in the boxes on pp. 114–15).

It is indeed no great wonder that individuals like those in Chapter 2 (who aim exclusively at scaling some utility ordering) fail to have common objectives. How could they? If common objectives are to be allowed back into the picture, persons must be given back their capacity to care about more than satisfying their preferences (echoes of the argument in Chapter 4 that life on the utility machine would be a poor substitute for the real thing). If, for example, they care also about non-quantifiable things such as justice and solidarity with others then the common good *can* be envisioned. These liberals even went as far as to argue that the tension between efficiency and equity (or social justice) is exaggerated intentionally by those who simply want to preserve their privileges. The next box offers a glimpse of such a liberal's view.

Views like that of J. K. Galbraith are as old as capitalism (recall that they resemble the egalitarian and humanist views which led Jeremy Bentham and J. S. Mill to develop utilitarian ideas during the nineteenth century). What motivates me to link the current section (Section 9.2) with the name of the US philosopher John Rawls (b. 1921), rather than with Mill or Keynes or Galbraith, is that in his *A Theory of Justice* (published by Harvard University Press in 1971) Rawls attempts a monumental feat: to prove that compassion, a concern for justice, for fraternity, for an interest in those who are worse off, is not only ethical and nice but also rational. This is a major

---

**A liberal who places compassion above all else:
J. K. Galbraith (b. 1908)**

Andrew Marr [of *The Independent* newspaper (8/1/1995)]: 'To what extent [does the creation of the Good Society] involve a return to the principle of the redistribution of wealth . . .?'

JKG: . . . *I think we have to conclude that the modern market system . . ., by its nature, distributes income very badly, very unequally. And therefore progressive income tax in one of the great civilising forces of our time. And there's always the possibility that if one has high marginal rates (of tax), people will work harder to maintain their after-tax income.*

Andrew Marr: 'Returning to the size of the State, one of the big arguments that you hear these days about the reasons why the State must shrink, both in terms of its share of national wealth, and in what it does, is that we are all part of a global market, that we are facing above all the Asian tiger economies which don't have large Welfare States and which have relied upon a more familiar structure of social support. Easternisation . . . requires the West to cut back the size of its State and to carry on cutting back. Now is that just an excuse by people who used to be called the capitalist class?'

JKG: *This is an excuse. This is a justification for what they want to see happen in their favour. One of the curious things of our time is that the rich in the United States, and I think this is true of Britain and Europe, do not want to defend themselves as rich. They want to have a larger moral case, and the idea that Taiwan, Singapore and China are threatening Western economies is a wonderful way of escaping from selfishness into something that seems on the whole vaguely plausible.*

---

claim. One that eluded liberals before (recall how Bentham failed to show that rational utility maximising individuals would care about average utility in society). Has Rawls pulled it off? If the answer is yes, then a State which intervenes to correct market failure but also to redistribute income, provide health care, educate its citizens, is a rational State which achieves maximum liberty, justice and efficiency simultaneously.

9.3.2 Rational but selfless deliberation on what is just: Rawls' veil of *ignorance*

Rational and selfless? How can this be possible? In Chapter 2 neoclassical economists defined rationality as the capacity to pursue efficiently one's self-interest. We labelled this *instrumental rationality*. How can somebody be rational and selfless? Rawls argues that, though difficult to achieve, it is a blend of rationality and selflessness that we must strive for if we are to be able to say anything sensible about our society. The reason why, so far, we have failed to conceptualise the common good is that we have been too caught up in our own desires and interests. If only we could take a break from our self-interest, rise above our petty little concerns and see society dispassionately, then we would be in a position *rationally* to decide what is and what is not good for society.

To put the same point slightly differently, imagine that all members of society could be assembled in a large theatre. Rawls addresses us all and asks us: 'Are you happy with your social arrangements? Is yours the Good Society? Or do you wish that some aspects of it (e.g. income distribution, the assignment of political and economic power) are changed?' His problem is that he cannot trust us to tell him what we really think. There are those of us who are, currently, extremely well off. They have an incentive to keep things as they are; to answer that our society is as good as it can get. They have an incentive to say this *even if, deep down, they know that ours is an unjust, ugly society*. Additionally, there are some who are poor but who have no one to blame other than themselves, their laziness and their lack of drive or application. They are in the opposite situation: *even if, deep down they feel that this society is pretty fair*, they still have an incentive to tell Rawls that it is unjust and horrible in the hope that a redistribution of income will occur in their favour.

So, poor Rawls is standing up there in front of us receiving information that he cannot trust. His problem is, as mentioned earlier, that we are far too caught up in our own self-interest to be truthful in our assessment of what society should be like. And it is not just a matter of being untruthful to Rawls and others. It is also a matter of being untruthful to ourselves. History has repeatedly shown that those who end up as rich and powerful soon afterwards manage to convince themselves that they deserved to become so and, therefore, that the society that brought them riches, power and fame *must* have been just and beyond criticism or reform. Rawls, thus, realised that to unleash our rational capacity for assessing our society something drastic is needed; some trick which will divorce us from our current, debilitating, self-interest.

Suppose that, standing next to Rawls on the podium, there is a machine which can stop time without interrupting consciousness. (You have

seen enough Hollywood science-fiction movies to be able to imagine this!)
At the touch of a button, Rawls stops time, everyone freezes in the theatre
but, soon after, we all rise in spirit form from our frozen bodies and join
Rawls at the front of the theatre. Looking back we can see our frozen selves
exactly as we were the moment Rawls hit the button. In a trance-like state
(imagine also a mesmerising soundtrack in the background), we are asked:
'Look back at yourselves. Think of the society that you make up. Now that
you can see yourselves from some distance, what do you think? Is your
society a good one? Is it just? Or do you wish to reform it?'

Before you get a chance to answer, the cunning Rawls adds:

> To give you a reason to answer my questions rationally and truthfully,
> let me say this. If you decide that your society is indeed fair and that
> you wish to return to it, then I shall oblige you. All I have to do is
> hit the same button once more. However, when this happens you will
> not be returned to the body/self whence you were extracted. This
> machine will assign you to *some* body/self randomly. Now decide: is
> your society a fair one or is there some need for reform, for a redis-
> tribution of social roles, etc.?

What a shock! All of a sudden we are told that the chances of returning to
our original self are practically zero (to be precise they equal $\frac{1}{N}$ where N is
the size of the population). And yet we must decide whether we wish to
return to that society without knowing who we are to be upon our return.
In effect, we are being asked to judge rationally between different types of
society, distributions of roles, wealth, etc. *without the faintest idea as to who we
shall be in that society*. Rawls looks on our puzzlement with glee. For he has
achieved his aim: to make us assess our society rationally yet selflessly.

His point is that, if we decide to go back to our society even though
we do not know which role we shall have in it, then ours must be the Good
Society. The idea is simple. Now that the rich or the poor have no guarantee
that they shall be rich or poor after Rawls pushes the button; now that the
hard-working or lazy persons have no guarantee that they will be hard-
working or lazy; now each citizen has a strong incentive to choose between
different social arrangements objectively, without being guided by their
personal interest. Why? Because the best way of serving their private interest,
when uncertain about who they shall be, is to try to select the Good Society;
the one which maximises everyone's chances of prosperity and happiness.

Of course Rawls, being a serious philosopher, does not make any reference to time-stopping machines and science-fiction movies. This was my
idea for conveying his theory to you. Rawls' own term for the state of uncertainty about one's personal position is the *veil of ignorance*. Individuals are
asked to decide which is the Good Society as if behind a *veil of ignorance*
which prevents them from seeing which position they will occupy in the

---

The veil of ignorance

A hypothetical scenario according to which individuals select, from a menu of alternative socio-economic arrangements, the society which they want to live in *without* knowing which social role, preferences, income distribution, gender, race, etc. they will have in that society.

---

society of their choice. It is this ignorance about our own position in the chosen society which motivates us to conceive of the public interest.

To recap, Rawls plays a trick on us in order to force us to look at ourselves objectively. He reminds us that we are shackled by our self-interest so much so that we have lost sight of what we really think about our society. He then offers us a helping hand in distancing ourselves from our petty concerns and taking a broader, more objective, look at the social arrangements which our ancestors and we have created. Of course he does not have access to a time-stopping machine which can maintain our consciousness and then reassign us back to different individuals at random. Nevertheless what this hypothetical does for us is to alert us to the *theoretical possibility* that, as rational individuals, we may assess our society; that we may perceive the public interest. And that is all Rawls needs: an escape route from welfare economics' *third theorem*; from its gloomy conclusion that, *even theoretically*, there is no such thing as a public interest.

Our problem so far has been that we could not expect the State ever to serve the public when the public cannot have a common objective *even in theory?* Rawls' point is that it *is* possible to conceive of the public good in theory. Moreover he shows that his theoretical (or hypothetical) concept can have very practical, highly applicable, policy implications about what the State ought to be doing.

Rawls' theory as a secular alternative to religious definitions of the Common Good

Liberalism has been influenced by religion from its inception. Recall Adam Smith's celebration of the market as a miracle of coordination. It is as if by an *invisible hand* that the market synthesises selfish behaviour into public virtues. A secular form of divine intervention. Similarly with Rawls. His *veil of ignorance* allows individuals to look squarely at the Good without being blinded by their self-interest. A secular solution to the problem that religion solves by invoking a benevolent almighty.

Table 9.1 Rawls' theory of justice: a numerical example

	Distribution 1	Distribution 2	Distribution 3
Group A	20	140	100
Group B	20	25	26
Group C	20	15	24
Per capita income	20	60	50

(Numbers denote thousands of dollars per year; each of the three groups A, B and C contain the same number of individuals.)

9.3.3 From theory to practice: redistributing according to the Maximin Principle

If Rawls is right, then behind the *veil of ignorance* (that is, with no knowledge of our social position, power, income, gender, colour, etc.) we can make, as a group of people, a rational (and thus objective) choice between different social arrangements, income distribution and so on. But how shall we decide? To motivate the discussion, imagine that we are considering three different income distributions amongst, roughly, three different income groups or classes (for simplicity let us assume that each group contains the same number of people): see Table 9.1

Our task is to judge which distribution (1, 2 or 3) we favour *as a group*. Suppose that Distribution 2 is current. Rawls then asks us to compare Distribution 2 with 1 and 3. Which is better? Of course, those of us who are fortunate enough to belong to Group A will have a vested interest to proclaim that the current arrangement (Distribution 2) is excellent. Notice that any shift from Distribution 2 (to either 1 or 3) will mean that Group A members will lose money ($40,000 if we move to Distribution 3 and a whopping $120,000 from a move to Distribution 1). Similarly, Group C people will have a vested interest in denouncing Distribution 2 as unfair, unjust, disgusting, etc. Therefore vested interests make it impossible (echoes of the *third theorem* of welfare economics) to decide which distribution of the three in Table 9.1 serves the public interest best. Indeed no public interest is discernible due to the antagonistic interests of our divided society.

This is where Rawls' *veil of ignorance* ploy delivers the goods. For if these people were told that they will be assigned *randomly* to one of the three groups, then suddenly they lose their self-interested perspective. Group A members who currently enjoy an income of $140,000 per annum must now realise that there is only a 1-in-3 chance that they will retain this high income. Indeed there is a 1-in-3 chance that, if society rules in favour of keeping Distribution 2, they may end up with a measly $15,000 a year. So, how should rational people choose when faced by ignorance about the

---

John Rawls' *Maximin Principle*

'Choose the income distribution which *maximises* the *minimum* income' (thus, *maxi-min*). Societies applying this principle in order to decide on the best distribution of income will organise themselves in such a way as to boost the well-being of the worst off.

---

income level they will end up with? Rawls' argument is simple; rational people must agree that the best distribution is the one which *maximises the income of the poorest*! He refers to this argument as the *Maximin Principle*.

Let us first see what the practical implications of this principle are before letting Rawls defend it. Looking at our three distributions above, the *Maximin Principle* selects Distribution 3 as the one that rational individuals ought to choose behind the *veil of ignorance*. It is easy to see why: the worst off (i.e. Group C) make $20,000 under Distribution 1, $15,000 under Distribution 2 and $24,000 under Distribution 3. Thus they are better off under Distribution 3. The latter is thus selected by a principle which maximises the income of the worst-off in society.

But why would rational individuals, even behind the *veil of ignorance*, choose to maximise the income of the worst off; why would they opt for the *Maximin Principle*? Rawls' answer is that when uncertain about your social position you must think of what will happen to you if luck is unkind to you and decides that you will be in the worst social position; that you will be one of the less privileged members of society. With this thought in mind you will, if rational, want to ensure that the worst off are as well off as possible. The reason? Simply that you may end being one of them!

Thus the *veil of ignorance* encourages everyone to think of the poor, the underprivileged, the needy; it does so by making people imagine that they face the same probability of being one of them. It is, after all, a ploy to force us all to assess our society by stepping outside our own shoes and into those of others. However, some may argue that individuals may still choose Distribution 2 even if placed behind the *veil of ignorance*.

For instance, people may be of a gambling disposition and choose Distribution 2 not only because it rewards the rich more than the other two but also because it involves the highest average income (60 as opposed to 50 in the case of 3 or 20 in the case of 1). They may, for example, fancy that a 1-in-3 chance of earning $140,000 rather than $100,000 (if they end up in Group A) outweighs the 1-in-3 danger of earning $15,000 rather than $24,000 (if they end up in Group C) plus the 1-in-3 chance of earning $25,000 rather than $26,000 (if they end up in Group B). If they think this way, they may spurn the *Maximin Principle* and select Distribution 2 instead of Distribution 3. Rawls argues that it is not rational to think this way.

He implores us to realise that this is not a lottery and it is silly to treat it like one. Instead it is a one-off, irreversible, decision of monumental importance. After all, we have been given a chance to redesign our society; to determine our collective future. Imagine he says that we do decide to gamble and we select Distribution 2 in the hope that we will be assigned to Group A. Now suppose that the gamble does not pay off and, instead, we end up as members of Group C. After the event we are bound to regret our decision; for if we had chosen Distribution C our annual income would be $24,000 rather than the $15,000 we have now.

Of course, we may be good sports and accept that we gambled and lost. But for how long? One year, two years, ten years? And what about our children and grandchildren whose opportunities will be limited by our mistake to gamble their future away? In the end, those in Group C will experience discontent. They will beat their breasts admitting that they were silly to choose Distribution 2 in a gambling fit and call for a redistribution. Discontent is bound to rear its ugly head. Thus, Rawls argues, rational individuals will not gamble when behind the *veil of ignorance*; instead they will espouse the *Maximin Principle*.

9.3.4 Rawls on the efficiency-versus-equity dilemma

If we do choose according to the *Maximin Principle* then the elusive public interest will have been defined: whatever policy boosts the well-being of the worst off serves the public interest. Is this a moralistic conclusion? Rawls argues that it is the result of pure logic, not emotion. We ought to fashion society in this manner because it is rational to do so. The fact that our choice of income distribution will be socially just is a reflection of the fact that we chose it rationally. In other words, Rawls' answer to the question 'What should the rational society do?' is: 'It ought to be just by placing maximum emphasis on improving the well-being of its neediest members'.

Interestingly Rawls' theory of justice and distribution seems to have resolved the perennial conflict between equity and efficiency. Notice that

---

Rawls' definition of just inequalities

Inequalities as defined by the institutional structure or fostered by it are arbitrary unless it is reasonable to expect that they will work out to everyone's advantage and provided that the positions and offices to which they attach or from which they may be gained are open to all.

John Rawls, A *Theory of Justice*, 1971

Rawls' mechanism does not side either with traditional calls for equality nor with the demands for cold-hearted efficiency-at-all-cost. Indeed Distribution 1 is far more equitable than Rawls' favourite Distribution 3. It may be more equitable but it is not fairer, according to Rawls. He asks: where is the fairness in making everyone poorer than they have to be in order to bring about less inequality?

In this sense, Rawls supports a degree of inequality which is in *everyone*'s interest. If the introduction of some extra inequality increases the income of the worst off, then it is fair to introduce it. But, if inequality comes at the expense of lower living standards for those at the bottom end of the distribution, then it is deemed unjust.

Just like Rawls rejects the proposition that equality is *by definition* just, he also denies the claim that it is *always* rational to strive for greater efficiency. Compare Distributions 2 and 3 in Table 9.1: the former corresponds to a higher per capita income (average income is $60,000 under Distribution 2 compared to $50,000 under Distribution 3). However, this does not mean that a rational society ought to opt for it. For Rawls, rational individuals deciding objectively (that is, behind the *veil of ignorance*) will choose Distribution 3 in spite of the fact that it yields a lower per capita income (or total income) than Distribution 2.

9.3.5 Summary: Rawls and the Good Society

In conclusion, Rawls' theory of justice begins with a theoretical trick (the *veil of ignorance*) in order to furnish some far-reaching, yet down-to-earth, policy recommendations. The theoretical trick was to ask us to imagine that all social roles would be reassigned randomly. Would we want to keep the current distribution of privileges, roles and income when we do not know which we will be assigned? Or would we want to change it into some other distribution? If we rule unanimously in favour of some distribution, then we will have arrived at our destination: the Good Society. Free of the blinkers which vested-interest plants into our heads, we will have stood on common ground (since behind the *veil of ignorance* we are all equal) and will have pinpointed our preferred socio-economic distribution. Unanimity, combined with an equal starting position for all rational individuals, means one thing: that the distribution thus chosen cannot possibly be unjust or irrational.

The next question is: which socio-economic distribution will be chosen? His answer is: The one which maximises the well-being of the worst-off. Why the worst-off? Because, not knowing at the point of decision which position we will occupy in society, it is rational to ensure that, if it so happens and we are unlucky enough to be assigned the worst possible position, we should be as content as possible. This is known as the *Maximin Principle* which recommends that the welfare of the poorest becomes our first and only priority.

> 'I like to pay taxes. With them I buy civilisation.'
>
> Oliver Wendell Holmes

The policy implication is clear: the State must intervene by taxing the rich, transferring income to the poor, creating a safety net with minimum health and education provision; in short, the rational State fosters social justice. But, there is a limit beyond which any further intervention is itself unjust. This limit is reached when any additional re-distributive intervention reduces efficiency to such an extent that the people it is meant to assist are harmed. The State should leave alone any inequality which can be eliminated only if the income of the poorer members of society suffers.

Of course, a central question remains unanswered: why should individuals *want* to participate in Rawls' thought experiment? If he could forcibly place us behind the veil of ignorance and thus put us in a situation which gave us no alternative other than to make a choice between distributions unaware of our ultimate position, then perhaps he is right; perhaps we *will* choose according to the *Maximin Principle*. But given that he cannot do this in reality, why would we agree to go along with his thought experiment? Some of us, for instance, may turn around and say to Rawls: 'I don't give a damn about which distribution is best, just, rational, etc. I am happy as I am. On your bike Johnny boy!' Rawls must, therefore, concede that his method for finding out what the Good Society looks like works only if everyone is interested in finding out.

Still, Rawls has a significant claim under his belt: if society *wants* to discover the socially just socio-economic distribution, there is a way of doing it. Let us all forget for a moment our social position and imagine that we could end up, at the touch of a button, in *anyone's* shoes (from Rupert Murdoch and the Queen to the homeless person freezing under a bridge). In what sort of society would we worry about this prospect least? For it is that society which features maximum social justice. And if we want to have a State that works towards realising that Good Society, then we know what it ought to be doing: Intervene in such a manner as to raise the life prospects of the worst-off.

Rawls admits that one cannot simply expect society to *want* to achieve social justice. Why would the rich happily espouse a theory which results in a State that taxes them as part of the *Maximin Principle*? In this sense, Rawls' theory is not predictive. He is not *forecasting* that his scheme will be adopted provided people are intelligent. On the contrary, his theory is prescriptive. He is *telling* us what to do if we want a State that serves the public interest without necessarily expecting that we will be interested. His simple point is that, unless the State acts to boost the well-being of the poor, it is an unjust State; and human history is replete with them and their remains.

Nevertheless, Rawls is not just moralising. He believes that unless the State serves the public good, discontent will brew and turn into social conflict which is never conducive to an efficient use of human resources. In this sense, injustice is never rational and therefore a rational society will *want* a pro-active State which busily pursues justice. Rawls trusts that individuals will recognise this need if sufficiently rational. However, this is not the type of rationality that we encountered in Chapter 2. Rawls' rationality requires more than a capacity to serve desires; it demands also a faculty for reflection (Rawls speaks of a *reflective equilibrium*). In his mind the rational person must be able to put herself in other people's shoes; a view akin to Immanuel Kant's notion of rationality (see p. 80). If Rawls managed to create a concept of the public interest he did so because he moved away from the utility-maximisation model of human beings that economics textbooks insist on.

What does this mean for economics? If we were to accept Rawls' arguments, we would have to agree that when society acts in order to correct market failures, or in order to undo unjust distributions, something more than utility is at stake: justice. Thus there is an excellent, additional reason for being sceptical about the instrumental rationality of economics textbooks (in addition to the many reasons mentioned in Chapter 4): unless rationality is given a wider interpretation (i.e. more than a capacity to serve private desires) there is no possibility of the public interest being recognised, let alone served!

Rawls and Rousseau's Social Contract

Rawls' ideas are the culmination of a very old tradition within liberalism. It stems from J.-J. Rousseau's ideas as featured in his eighteenth-century classic *The Social Contract* according to which the legitimate State is one that could have come about only as the result of a rational bargain amongst equals. Unless the State can be shown to be a social institution whose authority over them individuals accept, it will be illegitimate and thus unstable. The *process* of getting together, through direct political activity, in order to reach an agreement about what the State ought to do, is one which simultaneously shapes the rational State *and* the rational individual. In this sense, the State is not just an institution created to serve the desires of individuals. It is much more than that. As individuals get together, argue, reach agreements, hold elections, change their minds, etc. they evolve into citizens; they become rational. In the end, the creation of the State and the shaping of the rational citizen are two symbiotic processes. The Good Society has created the rational person and vice versa.

Rawls demonstrated how, the moment the meaning of being rational in a social setting is rescued from the aridity of the economics textbook (that is, from the strait-jacket of its instrumental guise), two ideas which have been thought of by economists as antagonistic, all of a sudden, become allies: rationality and justice (or, equivalently, efficiency and equity). By rejecting the neoclassical economists' narrow view of rationality, Rawls shows that the rational (as opposed to the moral) society will choose to be guided by the principles of social justice. This has been the finest moment so far in the tradition started just before the French Revolution which sees the Good and Just Society as a grand agreement between rational citizens.

9.4 The second escape route from neoclassical economics' dead-end: Robert Nozick's entitlement theory of justice

9.4.1 Process, not outcomes!

Hold on a second! – shouts Robert Nozick, another contemporary American philosopher. If you think that you can legitimise so easily a State which bursts into people's lives, grabs fistfuls of money against their will and passes them around at the whim of some bureaucrat, think again. In his brilliantly scripted 1974 book *Anarchy, State and Utopia*, Robert Nozick (b. 1938) puts up an argument against anyone who entertains an interest in an interventionist State – ranging from John Rawls to the socialists. His dismissal of the claim that the State's job is to monitor, and to improve upon, the prevailing distribution of income, privilege, need and social power is short and swift.

Nozick asks: suppose I were to tell you that last year Jill's income was X. Was this fair? Should she have earnt more or less? Naturally you cannot answer this question without further information. You will need to know what Jill does for a living, how hard she worked, how much income she had to forgo during the past decade while training for her current job, what risks she had to take in order to make X, etc. In other words, you need to know whether she was *entitled* to an income of size X. Given that information, you can then pass judgment on whether it is fair that she received X. By contrast, passing judgment on Jill's income *in the absence of such information* is callous and irrational. More than this: it is unjust! And yet this is exactly what Rawls asked us to do in the previous section.

Indeed Rawls devised a scheme for selecting between different distributions of income; that is, the income level of each individual in society. And he asked us to do so without a word on *how* these individuals would be generating that income. Nozick thus claims that *any* theory seeking to select between different income distributions cannot pay attention to *how* each person generates her living but, instead, focuses on *what* she makes.

This is just as callous, irrational and ultimately *unfair* as it was in the previous paragraph in Jill's case. Only this time things are worse because (1) *everyone* (and not just Jill) in society is judged unfairly, and (2) such a travesty is marketed as an exercise in social justice.

In summary, if social justice is what we crave, Nozick makes the interesting point that, rather than judging people and societies on the level of income that each has, we ought to ask: are they *entitled* to what they got? Or should they have earned more (or less) given their attributes and activities? Put bluntly, it is not outcomes that determine whether an income distribution is fair. It is the process which brought it about.

9.4.2 The three rights that individuals are entitled to in the Good Society

---

Nozicks' three entitlements

1   *Justice in acquisition*
    Individuals are entitled to assets they discover or invent themselves.

2   *Justice in transfers*
    Individuals are entitled to assets they acquired through voluntary market transactions.

3   *Correction and compensation in cases where entitlements 1 or 2 are violated*
    Individuals are entitled to compensation whenever one of their assets acquired in accordance to entitlements 1 or 2 above has been forcibly removed.

To make his point more sharply, Nozick asks us to accept that in a free society, in a Good Society if we wish, individuals must be entitled to the three rights in the adjacent box. First, comes the entitlement to keep assets (that is, things of value) that one discovers (and which are not owned by anyone else) or assets resulting from an invention. Second, one is entitled to assets that one has acquired through legitimate transactions with others. Third, is the entitlement to a system of justice (police, courts, the Law) which corrects any violations of one's first or second entitlements or rights.

For example, if someone steals from you (a violation of the first or second entitlement, since the thief will have acquired an asset illegitimately) then the Good Society must respond by apprehending the thief and returning the stolen asset to you. Similarly, if someone makes unauthorised use of an invention of yours (i.e. breach of copyright) again you are entitled to compensation since your first entitlement has been violated.

No reasonable person can surely dispute that, in the Good Society, people should be entitled to these three basic rights. Nozick confidently expects that we shall all nod in agreement. Then, he thunders, there is no way you can justify a State which re-distributes income! Why? Because Nozick has enshrined three rights, or entitlements, which rule out taxation. Since taxation is involuntary (that is, the tax office does not ask for your consent before it collects your income tax), it violates one of your first two entitlements.

For instance, according to the first entitlement you have the right to keep assets that you created through a process of invention. According to the second entitlement you have a right to assets acquired through legitimate trade. And yet the interventionist State of Rawls (or of any other theorist who supports forceful redistribution through the tax system) violates these rights since taxation is equivalent to grabbing part of these assets; assets that you are *entitled* to and which you are unhappy giving up. So, if you have agreed with Nozick's entitlements in the previous paragraph, he insists that you must agree with him that it is the duty of the police to arrest the tax officers (since the third entitlement calls for a State which apprehends those who violate your first two entitlements)!

And since we cannot have the police apprehending government officials who carry out the policy of the State, there are only two options: either individuals must lose their basic rights (as enshrined in Nozick's three entitlements) or the State must give up the policy of re-distributing income through the tax system. Make your choice. If you still think that redistribution is crucial, then fine; go ahead. Just keep in mind that you will be sanctioning continuous violation of basic human rights, acts which are hardly compatible with notions of social justice.

Nozick's own choice is simple: the basic human rights which he codified in his three entitlements ought to be treated as inalienable. Any vision of a just society, of a grand social contract amongst equals, which is built on violations of human rights will inevitably turn into a nightmare; into a totalitarian State which savages its citizens' rights in the name of some theoretical Common Good. The only Good and Rational State is one that understands its limits and keeps out of people's lives. Its only legitimate role is to provide security, law and order so that individuals can live, work and relate to each other freely.

9.4.3 Summary

Whereas Rawls gave us a blueprint on how to re-distribute income when searching for the socially just distribution, Nozick undermined the very reasons for searching in the first place. Both of them attempt to describe the type of society individuals would be happy to live in. However, whereas Rawls is concerned about the outcome, Nozick focuses on the process. Rawls spends sleepless nights over the degree of contentment in society once an income distribution has been reached. Nozick, on the other hand, does not think we can afford to worry about that. As long as everyone got the income that they deserved, this is all the justice we can afford. Trying to tamper with the income distribution for the purpose of promoting justice is like pursuing freedom by building concentration camps.

9.5 Rawls and Nozick: an assessment

9.5.1 Rawls and Nozick as contractarians

When the three musketeers swore allegiance to one another they entered into a kind of contract: all for one and one for all! Similarly life-long friends obey an unwritten code of behaviour according to which one will drop every-thing in order to rush to the other's assistance in moments of crisis. It is possible to think of such unspoken accords as unwritten contracts binding people together.

Imagine that all members of society entered into such an implicit contract. Since we are talking about a huge number of people, solidarity amongst them requires formal institutions (e.g. the police, an ambulance service, etc.) which can 'rush' to someone's assistance when necessary. Thus the State would then be seen as the realisation of a grand contract amongst all citizens. If its activities and institutions reflect accurately a contract that each citizen would have entered into happily, then the State must be legit-imate. Otherwise the State is acting arbitrarily against the interests of society.

Contractarian theories of the State and their foes

This is a tradition which goes back at least to Pericles' speech *Epitaph* (Pericles was the leader of Athens during its Golden Age – fifth-century BC) in which an authoritarian and a liberal State were distinguished on the basis of *consent*. During the European Enlightenment (recall the box on p. 264) the liberal State was defined as the kind of State that all citizens would approve of had they been given the opportunity to participate in a large Convention whose purpose would be to negotiate the type of State that they wanted.

Under this hypothetical scenario, individuals would negotiate around a table until they decided unanimously which type of State they wanted. Of course in reality no State has been instituted that way. But, contractarians argue, if we look at our current State and find it *possible* to imagine that it *could* have resulted from such a Grand Bargain, then it may indeed be a Good State. If, on the other hand, we cannot even begin to imagine how citizens would have ever approved of the State under which we currently live, then it cannot be defended; it is an illegitimate, authoritarian State.

However this 'tale' has not convinced everyone. Some have dismissed it not just as a silly fairy-tale but as a nasty fiction. For example, Carole Pateman, a contemporary political theorist, notes in her book *The Sexual Contract* that one of the most important, yet hidden, aspects of the Grand Bargain underpinning the creation of modern States during the past two centuries was the meticulously designed (as opposed to accidental) exclusion of women. That the Social Contract was an agreement amongst men which could come about only if it was based on a hidden Sexual Contract forced by men on women. Men's citizenship (and their participation in the creation of the modern State) was founded on the exclusion of women from the public sphere and their confinement to the home as non-citizens; as unpaid workers. Men of different background and social class found it in themselves to reach an agreement because they had something in common: they 'owned' women collectively. Thus the Social Contract can be portrayed as a story of the subjugation and oppression just as much as a story of liberation and consent.

Pateman's attack on the social contract tradition reflects an earlier left-wing attack (e.g. that by Karl Marx) which proclaimed that, if the modern State reflects some large-scale agreement, it reflects the agreement between the owners of capital (i.e. the employers) to coordinate their actions via State institutions in order to maximise the effective exploitation of the working class.

The box (as well as the preceding paragraph) relates an approach to the State known as *Contractarianism*. Both Rawls and Nozick sketched their theories on a contractarian canvas. Rawls went to great pains to describe how we may conceive of the Good Society as the result of a grand negotiation (behind the *veil of ignorance*). Nozick too believes that the Just Society is one in which it can be shown that individuals, given a chance, will have unanimously approved of the principles which govern their State's activities. Where they disagree rather violently is on the nature of the citizens' unanimous agreement. Whereas Rawls thinks that the citizens' convention, if rationally conceived, should result into a Welfare State whose purpose is to correct the distribution of opportunities and income, Nozick is convinced that rational individuals will limit the scope of the State solely to the defence of rights over life and property.

The cause of the disagreement is twofold: first, Rawls focuses on social outcomes (e.g. the distribution of prevailing income) and not on the process that brings them about (e.g. *how* individuals earned their income). By contrast Nozick is not interested in outcomes but in processes. Second, Rawls believes that people have the *right* to live in a society in which inequality is allowed only if it benefits everyone. Nozick, on the other hand, proclaims another *right* as paramount: the right to keep whatever asset one has acquired or created without violating the same right of others.

9.5.2 Internal contradictions of Rawls' and Nozick's theories

Rawls and Nozick, in their very different ways, have offered neoclassical economics escape routes from the impasse at the end of Chapter 8. Suddenly they made it possible for economists to speak of society's interests again in spite of the *third theorem* (see Section 8.1.6). Nevertheless it is not all plain sailing for those who wish to follow the routes opened up by Rawls and Nozick. Both theories suffer some serious internal problems. Starting with Rawls, there are three obvious problems.

First, it is difficult to see how persons can acquire a dispassionate, objective, standpoint from which to pass judgment on their society – even if they follow Rawls' advice and imagine that they are behind the *veil of ignorance*; that is, that they are divorced from their current physical reality *and* social status with no knowledge as to which status they will be reassigned to. For example, when deciding between two socio-economic distributions, one in which women continue to have the lesser social roles, the other refusing to discriminate on the basis of gender, it may be hard for people (both men and women) to abandon in one stroke the prejudices which have shaped them.

By this I mean that some prejudices (e.g. the view that women are inferior) are so deep-seated (in men and, curiously, in some women too) that at least some people (particularly men) may opt for the discriminating distribution because it is so deeply ingrained in their conscience; and they may do this *even if they know that there is a good chance that, after the selection of some 'society' as best, they may end up as women*. In short, we cannot liberate ourselves from the norms and prejudices which have formed our being simply by convincing ourselves that our social role (and even body) could have been different.

Second, in Rawls' scheme for discovering the Good Society, there is a presumption that, behind the *veil of ignorance*, we shall consider all possible options and therefore get the chance to select the one which satisfies our collective criteria thus qualifying as socially just. But how can we know *all* possible options? Who will tell us? What if, during our deliberations, we fail to consider the *truly* Good option? To illustrate, consider a society 1000 years ago (or even 300 years ago) trying to devise the best social distribution of roles, privilege and money based on Rawls' scheme. All the options they would consider would involve some sort of slavery! It was impossible to conceive, back then, of a society that could function without slaves.

Does this mean that slavery was just? Of course not. What it means is that alternatives to the current social arrangements are created by historical change and cannot be anticipated in advance (with the exception of some wonderful minds who are usually dismissed, in their time, as deranged). Consequently, Rawls' scheme cannot generate *the* socially just outcome but only an outcome which is as good as the particular historical moment will allow people to conceive of.

Third, Rawls' scheme is susceptible to the criticism that Nozick would happily make; namely that it is a scheme which cannot handle change and time very well. Recall my metaphor in Section 9.3.2 with which I related Rawls' scheme: time freezes and we are asked to take a look at our society and rearrange it before starting the clock again. While the clock is stationary, while behind the *veil of ignorance* (to use Rawls' favourite term), we can decide who gets what – the distribution of income for example. However, once time is restarted, people will start doing things, they will use their resources to better themselves, to trade, etc. What if, in doing so, they mess up the income distribution decided upon behind the *veil?*

For example, some may take all the money that was allocated to them and gamble it at the nearest casino. Should society intervene and give them back what they lost? If it does not, then it will condone a violation of the income distribution which everyone agreed was best. If it does, it removes any sense of responsibility by those on the lower end of the income distribution who can gamble and take incredible risks safe in the knowledge that, if they win they will climb the social ladder, if not they cannot lose since the State will restore their income to the original level. Is this just? Rawls must claim that it is whereas his right-wing opponents treat such a claim with derision.

Turning to Nozick's internal contradictions, two will suffice for our discussion. Recall the first entitlement that, according to Nozick, we should all enjoy in the Just Society: the right to anything that we discovered or invented. At first it sounds fine. If I have invented a new time-travel machine, no one should have the right to snatch it from me. It is I who ought to have the right to exploit its commercial value by offering package tours to ancient Greece. But what if the situation is different? Imagine that a group of us are travelling by aeroplane when the damned thing crash-lands in the desert. After a while we find ourselves firmly in the clasp of thirst.

We disperse in search of water. One of us finds the only well in the area. Is this person entitled to exclusive use of the water? Is it legitimate, and in accordance to the rules of justice, to demand that we sign away all our earthly belongings for a few cupfuls of water?

Nozick shies away from admitting that this is what his first entitlement means. He invokes the English philosopher John Locke (1632–1704) who, when examining the same problem, declared that one is entitled to whatever one discovers (e.g. oil, water, metals, etc.) provided (1) one mixes what one finds with one's labour and (2) leaves sufficient quantities of this fruit of nature for others. Of course then the problem becomes one of interpretation: how much work does one need to put into excavation, or cultivation, to satisfy (1) above? And how much is enough – to satisfy (2) above? Who will judge?

Nozick's problem is compounded by some of his supporters who implore him to be less circumspect. For instance there have been calls to forget John Locke's two conditions in the last paragraph (commonly referred to as *Locke's Proviso*). Take another example: imagine that Jack finds out that Jill's farm is sitting on a glut of oil. Jill does not know this and agrees to sell that farm to Jack for a modest sum. Who has the right to the oil? Jack or Jill? Taking Nozick's first entitlement on face value, it is the discoverer who is entitled to the asset: Jack (since he found out about the oil first). In that case, the air-crash survivor who discovered the water spring should be equally entitled to exploit this discovery as he or she pleases.

Thus, Nozick's first entitlement will be espoused fully only by those who believe that Jill has no right to complain after she discovers the trick Jack pulled on her; and that the enterprising survivor's companions have no grounds for complaining about any attempts to charge them heftily for the water. Nozick's problem is that many will not agree and, therefore, will reject his Entitlement Theory of Justice.

Nozick's second major difficulty has to do with his third entitlement: the right to live in a society which protects its citizens from violations of their first two entitlements. If your car was stolen two years ago and you come across it today, are you entitled to police action that will return it to you? Of course you are. But how far back in time does this principle extend to?

For example, suppose that you come across documents which prove that a Mr Brown defrauded your great-grandparents to the tune of what was, back in 1921, a great deal of money. Spurred on by this discovery you pursue your research, only to find out that the Brown family, descendants of Mr Brown, have prospered enormously. The thief, long since dead, used your family's money to build a factory which turned out to be successful. Three generations later, it is a sprawling multinational netting multimillion profit for the Brown family. By contrast you have nothing to your name. Are you entitled to go to the courts and, wielding the documented evidence of the 1921 defrauding of your great-grandparents, claim ownership of the Brown assets?

It is not difficult to imagine the case that the Brown family's lawyers will put to the judge. 'It is the hard work, entrepreneurial talent and application, good fortune and wisdom of three generations of Browns that has produced this industrial miracle, m'lord,' they are likely to say. 'The initial sum, which was admittedly stolen, made a tiny contribution to the building of the Brown empire.' How can you prove otherwise? You cannot. But if the judge dismisses your case, then this means that the court will have ruled against Nozick's third entitlement. What is more likely is that the judge will order the Browns to pay you a sum in lieu of compensation for what happened back in 1921. But how will this sum be determined? A just decision must be made. And yet Nozick's principles of justice (his three entitlements) offer no guide. Thus a theory of just outcomes is necessary here; a theory which Nozick has vehemently argued against.

The Brown fraud case was meant as an introduction to a much more general problem with Nozick's theory. If we research the origin of any society we shall find, provided we look hard enough, that the distribution of wealth was determined by means which violate Nozick's entitlements. Wealth was distributed through stealth, banditry and conquest. Today's distribution of social roles and income mirrors to a significant effect the injustices of the past. How can we disentangle this mess and restore justice? How can Nozick's third entitlement become functional? The police and the courts will be inundated with cases if we seek to undo injustices lost in the historical archives.

One solution, favoured by those whose current wealth is due to the villainy of their ancestors, is to do nothing. But then how can we say that society is just and its citizens are entitled to a system which corrects violations of human rights? Do we really want to live in a society where such violations are white-washed provided the culprits escape retribution long enough? The other solution is to try to address past injustices. But as the Brown case demonstrated, this is not a simple matter. Indeed past injustices cannot be corrected by handing over to victims something that was taken from them. Time has changed both the value of the asset stolen and the identity of victim and culprit. It seems that the only way of undoing injustices is by re-distributing income in the direction of those who are currently under-privileged as a result of what was done to their ancestors. But how can we re-distribute income if Nozick has his way and the ability to redistribution income is taken out of the hands of the State?

Summarising this second contradiction in Nozick's theory, it seems his first two entitlements (i.e. that people are entitled to assets they discover or have acquired through trade) are in opposition to the third (i.e. the entitlement to a State that corrects injustices, past and present). The first two entitlements demand that the State should *never* forcibly remove from individuals assets that they created or acquired through trade, while the third entitlement requires that the State has the capacity to tax some and transfer income to others. The end result may be a schizophrenic State whose officials in the justice ministry, social services and tax office face an impossible dilemma: redistribute income in order to satisfy many under-privileged citizens' third entitlement only to be arrested by the police for having violated the privileged citizens' first or second entitlement.

Australian Aboriginals and Eastern Europe: two examples of Nozick's contradiction

Australian Aboriginals

When Europeans landed in Australia, they treated the native population as non-humans. Indeed Australian law, until recently, insisted that the Australian continent was uninhabited (*terra nulius*) by humans prior to the European invasion. After two centuries during which the Aboriginals' land was expropriated, farmed, mined and built on, while the Aboriginals were slaughtered, turned into slaves, infected with European diseases, etc., Australian society came to understand the injustices it had inflicted on the native population. According to Nozick's third entitlement, the Aboriginal population has a right to a 'correction' of this long sequence of injustices. How can they be compensated? Which part of Australia's gross domestic product are they entitled to? Which part of rural Australia, Sydney or Melbourne should they be given? Should land be forcibly taken away from descendants of Europeans and given to Aboriginals? The only viable solution is for some grand negotiation between Aboriginal and non-Aboriginal society to determine a redistribution of income, wealth and land along lines that all parties will agree to. Thus in order for Nozick's third entitlement to be activated on behalf of the Aboriginals, Nozick's worst nightmare must be realised: a State which actively re-distributes income along the lines of some principle of a socially just outcome.

Eastern Europe

A similar tale can be told about Eastern Europe. Since the collapse of the communist regimes it has become obvious that an elite has managed through totally illegitimate means (e.g. because of their position in the previous regime or because of Mafia links) to grab the most prized assets in those societies. As the dust settles and these societies will develop into law-abiding market societies, in the years to come the families of these elites will occupy the better social roles. How can these societies be rendered just? Unless there is some State intervention, redistributing wealth away from that elite, Nozick's third entitlement will have been violated. Thus once again we find that Nozick's entitlements contradict one another. The entitlement (of those who are well off) to be left alone by the State clashes violently with the entitlement (of those who have been cheated) to compensation.

9.6 Conclusion: economists and their textbooks at the deep end

Older economics textbooks did not acknowledge the problem. They carried on as if the public interest could be defined as easily in terms of a social utility (or welfare) function as the individual's preferences can be captured by a utility function. Most newer textbooks have retained this mythical notion of social utility (or welfare) although, increasingly, Kenneth Arrow's bombshell of a theorem (that is, the *third theorem* of welfare economics – see Section 8.1.6) is acknowledged. Arrow told us that no viable notion of social utility (or welfare) can be built out of individuals' utility functions. And yet textbooks refer often, and casually, to social utility (or welfare) when their authors want to support notions such as competition and innovation; e.g. 'Competition is good because it maximises social welfare,' they write. The result is that students are forced into confusion.

The worst culprit of such double-speak are chapters (or whole textbooks) on international trade in which a country is given indifference curves just like Jack's and Jill's in Chapter 2 – the diagrams used look something like that in Figure 8.2. Those indifference curves fly in the face of Kenneth Arrow's *third theorem* and are especially confusing when students who have been exposed to that theorem are asked to use them in models purporting to show that international trade boosts a country's collective utility (or social welfare). Why is this happening?

There are two explanations and the least flattering for economists is that they have not grasped the seriousness and potent message of the *third theorem*: that *it is impossible to justify social utility (or welfare) functions and social indifference curves*. Put bluntly, economists can still not wrap their minds around this devastating proposition. Thus when it comes to writing textbooks they still, out of inertia, refer to the notion of social utility (or welfare) even if in some (usually separate) chapter they do mention that some guy named Arrow proved the impossibility of such a notion. The second explanation is that it is just too inconvenient for neoclassical writers to be honest to students about the non-existence of social utility (or welfare) functions. For how else can they make claims in favour of the market, deregulation, privatisation, anti-monopoly legislation, etc. unless they can argue that all these things boost social utility and are therefore in the public interest.

The continuing presence of social utility (or welfare) functions in economics textbooks is testimony to a general problem with economics. It reveals how many economists, due to an imperfect grasp of their cherished discipline, rely on wishful thinking in order to force certain ideas and models down students' throats. Students may swallow but they are unlikely to digest. How can they? They get used to thinking of the good government policy as the one that maximises social utility (or welfare) only to discover in some later chapter that the very notion of social utility is ill defined. Is it surprising that they become sceptical about economics?

And it is not just the explicit references to social utility (or welfare) or the drawing of social indifference curves which confuse students and insult their intelligence. Textbooks have more subtle ways of confusing students. Often the benefits to society are measured by adding together the difference between the utility they derive from different commodities and the utility they lose when paying for them (the so-called *consumer surplus*). But is this not a case of summing utilities? And did neoclassical economics not explicitly ban such comparisons? (Recall how interpersonal utility comparisons were banished – see Sections 3.2).

So, what should you do? When you encounter in a textbook or course any notion of social utility (or welfare); when you see indifference curves which are supposed to portray the interests of a group, a country or a society, SMILE MOCKINGLY! Yes, I am perfectly serious. Immediately you should realise that either the author is confused or she/he is trying to confuse you – or perhaps both. And if a teacher insists that there is such a thing as a Public Interest which is derived exclusively from individuals' indifference curves and looks very much like a social utility function (complete with indifference curves like those in Chapter 2), then politely tell your teacher that this type of Public Interest is ill defined and cannot withstand serious scrutiny. If your teacher gets scornful, again with utmost courtesy, refer her or him to Kenneth Arrow's 1951 masterpiece *Social Choice and Individual Values* (Yale University Press).

With this out of the way, it is interesting to take a look at the better of the new crop of economics textbooks. They avoid references to the Public Interest as the maximisation of some social utility (or welfare) function and, instead, discuss what society would want in contractarian terms (see p. 268 for a definition of contractarianism). These better texts devote a few pages to Rawls and to Nozick and explain that, depending on which sets of rights you think are more important (the right to distributive justice or to property acquired by legitimate means), you will end up with different views as to what the State ought to be doing. Should it keep on the sidelines and let market transactions determine who ends up with what, or should it step in and play an active role in re-distributing wealth?

The problem these textbooks face is that it is virtually impossible not to take sides. For instance, when it comes to market failure due to the exploitation of public resources, or environmental pollution, the State must intervene in one way or another. The particular intervention it will choose will determine which group in society is favoured: producers or consumers, residents of the polluted areas or the rest who are unaffected by pollution and are unwilling to pay for the clean up; workers who may lose their jobs if the polluter is shut down or workers who live on the banks of the polluted river and whose children will suffer a higher incidence of disease?

If the economics textbook is to offer any guidance about how government can answer these questions, it can no longer dismiss the problem simply by saying: 'The government must choose the policy that maximises social utility (or welfare).' Since the latter means nothing (by itself), authors of economics textbooks have found themselves at the deep end of political controversy. If they are to say anything useful, they cannot avoid taking sides. They must tell us whether they favour a Rawls-like focus on outcomes or a Nozickian concern that no one's assets are touched by the State.

As this chapter draws to a close, we seem to have come full circle. In Chapter 1 we saw how economics turned to the neoclassical model in order to rid itself of political affiliations; to get out of the mud and stench of politics; to become the queen of social science, rising pristine and knowledgeable above the mire of small-minded, political skirmishes. By Chapter 8 the dream had vanished in a puff of smoke as it became obvious that, come what may, it is impossible to deliberate dispassionately as to what the Rational Society would look like.

After hovering in the ethereal world of mathematics and geometry, economics was forced to crash-land and take its place in the real world of political debate. Do economists wish to pursue the Good Society in the spirit of the social contract tradition which started some time in ancient Greece (see p. 268), reasserted itself in Europe with J.-J. Rousseau (see p. 264) and found its apotheosis in John Rawls (Section 9.3)? Or do they wish for a social contract which effectively rules the State out as anything other than a provider of order and security – a tradition which began with Thomas Hobbes (see p. 77) and culminated in Robert Nozick's theory (see Section 9.4)? Or, indeed can economists think of something in between?

Thus economics is back into the mire courtesy of Arrow's *third theorem*, which dispels any hopes of a Rational Society springing from some form of advanced utility maximisation. Economics can no longer escape the political, philosophical debates which resonate across the humanities – from literature to sociology and from politics to moral philosophy. This is a good thing. At last, economics can become interesting again after a century of continuous pedantry.

The problem is that economics textbooks are finding it hard to adapt to the new reality. As a result many of them continue to pretend that the dream goes on; that economics can debate the Good Society by some newer and cleverer disguise of the *Equi-Marginal Principle*. Token confessions (usually confined to small sections at the back of the textbook) to the contrary tend to confuse rather than to help students. But such is life: big deceptions lead to great confusion which cannot be corrected with footnotes.

Critique: can a capitalist society be good?

10.1 Economics at the mercy of ideology and history

10.1.1 Economics as ideology

Reasonable people try to adapt their ideas so as to make them conform with their world; to 'fit in'. The unreasonable struggle to change their world in accordance to their ideas. This is how George Bernard Shaw (the acerbic Irish socialist, intellectual, playwright, pamphleteer, etc.) used irony in order to give 'reasonableness' a bad name. Indeed it takes big ideas (or megalomania) to want to change the world. Perhaps Shaw is right: to think such ideas one must be unreasonable. But can people's ideas *really* change the world? John Maynard Keynes, perhaps the greatest twentieth-century economist, thought so (see next box). Others (like the revolutionary Friedrich Engels) put their hopes for a better world in the lap of history and its capacity for changing technological opportunities, social structure and, finally, men's and women's ideas about their world. Yet in the end, it matters little whether history is shaped by ideas or ideas by history. As the French postmodern philosopher Michel Foucault (1926–84) pointed out, even if ideas do not change the world, the fact that we have them thwarts 'madmen in authority' and hinders them from getting away with murder. Ideas are a crucial ingredient of what we call society (regardless of whether they are an *input* into or an *output* of the historical process). If economics courses and textbooks matter they do so because they wilfully toy with our ideas about the world we live in.

As we have been discovering in this book, neoclassical economists tried to create a theory of the social economy *independent of the ideas in people's heads*. Ingeniously they created a model of humans and then tried to show that the

---

Two views on history, ideology and economics

The ideas of economists and political philosophers both when they are right and when they are wrong, are more powerful than is commonly understood. Indeed the world is ruled by little else. Practical men, who believe themselves to be quite exempt from any intellectual influences, are usually the slaves of some defunct economist. Madmen in authority, who hear voices in the air, are distilling their frenzy from some academic scribbler of a few years back. I am sure that the power of vested interests is vastly exaggerated compared with the gradual encroachment of ideas.

> John Maynard Keynes, *General Theory of Employment, Interest and Money*, 1936

The ultimate cause of all social changes and political revolutions are to be sought, not in the minds of men, in their increasing insight into the eternal truth and justice, but in changes in the mode of production and exchange; they are to be sought not in the philosophy but in the economics of the epoch concerned.

> Friedrich Engels, *Socialism: Utopia– and Scientific* (in *Collected Works*), 1892

---

free-market (that is, capitalism) is the form of social organisation that serves their interests. However, at the end of Chapter 9 we saw how that long, gallant march came to a grinding halt: economics had crash-landed into the mire of political and philosophical debate from which neoclassical economists had tried to rescue it. In short, we found that it was impossible for neoclassical economics to tell us much about the Rational and Good Society without taking sides in the political and ideological debates of the past 300 years.

Thus we saw that if *anything at all* were to be said about what kind of society we want to live in, we have to look beyond neoclassical economics, e.g. to political philosophers such as John Rawls and Robert Nozick. It became a political question. Who should we turn to? The honest answer is: it depends on one's ideology. Those who have an inclination to social democracy (that is, societies in which the State plays an active role in providing for basic needs and redistributing income, wealth and social opportunities) will find a natural ally in Rawls and his followers. And those who despise a meddling State will side with Nozick. After all the technical economic analysis of Chapters 2, 5 and 8 we are back to square one: political prejudice and ideology.

10.1.2 Economics as history

Where have most practising economists turned to? This is where the other ruler of economics comes into the picture: history. The bulk of economists follow trends just like teenagers follow fashion. The economics' profession inclination regarding the role of the State oscillates with every change in the direction of the winds of history. Back in the 1960s and early 1970s, the tide was on Rawls' side. The western world had completed two decades of relative, uninterrupted prosperity and was beginning to prove to itself that it was possible to perform the great balancing act: to keep the market mechanism as the main means of coordinating economic activity while at the same time cordoning off a significant segment of the social economy which was preserved for the State – e.g. health, education, child benefits, natural monopolies such as electricity generation, railways, even so-called strategic sectors such as mining and steel. The so-called *mixed economy*.

This ideal of a mixed economy which would combine the best aspects of capitalism and socialism (while avoiding their worse traits) was still very much in vogue when I went to university in the late 1970s. However, it had already begun to fade. By the time I graduated in 1981 my teachers seemed to have changed their tune. As a whole the economics profession had become dominated, in a short space of time, by a new-found faith in the market and a pervasive suspicion of State intervention. What had happened? The simple answer is that the post-war economic miracle, whereby State interventions in the economy had kept unemployment and inequality low without jeopardising the price mechanism, had fizzled out.

Following the oil crises of the 1970s, the nightmare of simultaneously increasing prices and inequality/unemployment caught governments out. Until that point in time governments thought they could manage capitalism so as to attain social values (low unemployment, controllable poverty and inequality, etc.) *and* low inflation. At worst, they thought, they might have to sacrifice some of their social objectives in order to achieve more price stability and economic efficiency. Or vice versa. What they had not contemplated was the nightmare of observing, irrespectively of their actions, the *simultaneous* collapse of the market mechanism (i.e. spiralling price inflation) and of the social fabric (i.e. greatly increased unemployment, deteriorating income inequalities). For many, the State seemed to have lost the knack of managing the economy and society in tandem.

It was at that time that the voices of some hitherto unfashionable economists became, all of a sudden, flavour of the month. Writers like the American economist Milton Friedman (b. 1912) had, for years, been issuing polemical diatribes on the folly and hazards of government attempts to alter the quantity of a society's output and employment. By the late 1970s, Friedman and his followers made the transition from scorned eccentrics to opinion leaders within the profession and beyond. Economists groomed in

---

Milton Friedman and the limits of economic policy

Friedman's view that governments should not be attempting to 'manage' employment was founded on the simple neoclassical idea that if a commodity is not scarce, then it has no value; its price must be zero. If its price is not zero, it must be scarce and, therefore, in equilibrium there can be no unsold units of that commodity. Similarly, if the wage is non-zero all those who want to work for that wage will, in equilibrium, find a job. If the government tries to increase the number of those in employment further by borrowing and spending, all it will achieve is more inflation. In the long run employment levels will be the same.

Friedman's own university (the University of Chicago) had become the new prophets of untrammelled capitalism. By the mid-1980s, assisted by the establishment of radical conservative governments in the USA and the UK, the economic agenda, both in and out of universities, was (at least in theory) one in which the State played no role other than actively to divest itself of any economic role it had. If the State tried to intervene, the story went, even the best intentions would turn into economic catastrophe – runaway inflation and ultimately more (not less) unemployment.

It was of course not the first time that historical changes altered the dominant ideas within economics. In a sense the rise of pro-market economics, at the expense of Keynesian views of the State as manager of capitalism, was a revenge for the success of Keynesianism in the 1930 to 1970 period. When the Great Depression became a reality in the 1920s and 1930s, few people had any doubt that capitalism was unstable and unreliable. With the massive fall in production and the huge increase in unemployment, the claim that markets work well and coordinate economic activity efficiently had become laughable. No one could blame the trade unions for the mid-war crash nor could any one point an accusatory finger at the governments of the time. Indeed unions were rather weak before the crash while most governments believed strongly that they had no business meddling with the economy. So, how was it that the market system collapsed during a period of increasing liberalisation of international markets, negligible government intervention, and weak trade unions?

At that moment, and while the whole world was suffering under the unexpected depression of the 1930s, Keynes' message pierced the pro-market faith: markets cannot be trusted! To put it in economic terms, why should we assume habitually that in important markets (e.g. that for labour or capital) the price will *always* adjust so that supply equals demand and market equilibrium is restored? What if prices stop adjusting before this happens and the market gets stuck in a rut where large chunks of labour and capital remain unemployed? Keynes' great challenge to economic orthodoxy was this: he claimed that we should *expect* markets to 'get stuck' in this manner (see also Section 8.2.5). And that when they do, they are terrible at getting 'unstuck' by themselves. Unless the government rushes in with measures to shore up economic activity, markets will remain bogged down in a state of pathetic inactivity. Meanwhile millions of people will be suffering. Keynes' message had a remarkable resonance during the Great Depression. Young economists became enthralled with the prospect of participating in a major rejigging of society; of acting as the engineers to whom governments turn for advice on how the market mechanism ought to be assisted. Those were exciting times for economists. The Keynesian bandwagon was on its way.

Keynes' revolutionary idea

Of course if prices keep adjusting until scarce resources (including labour) are allocated according to how scarce (and valuable) they are, resources will be fully utilised (i.e. no unemployment: see previous box). But if prices do *not* adjust in this way, then prices cannot and will not reflect a commodity's relative scarcity. Why? Because resources will be under-utilised (or unemployed) and thus not scarce. If anything is scarce in such situations it is demand! Then the role of government should be to help the economy along by boosting demand.

An example of a 'stuck' price

In the Indian village of Palanpur, Jean Drèze observed an interesting 'market failure'. During a year of substantial unemployment among agricultural day labourers, a desperate worker offered his services for half the going wage. After he was hired, the wage of all workers was cut by half, at unchanged employment, and the under-cutter became the target of much animosity. The following year the wage was restored to its original level, unemployment remained more or less the same and no one tried again to get a job by offering to work for less than the going rate.

The Second World War gave Keynesians a major boost. The whole world saw how government intervention in the economy could eliminate unemployment, create new high technology sectors and lead to increased prosperity. Pity this was not a step towards the Good Society but a step towards mass carnage and destruction. The first government to put in effect (perhaps unwittingly) Keynes' recommendation was that of Nazi Germany in the 1930s. Huge government investment went into industry and road-building on the one hand and the armaments industry on the other. Hitler's popularity during the 1935–9 period has been widely attributed to the fact that his government's 'injection' of investment into the economy succeeded in giving markets the push that was necessary for demand to rise, income to grow and unemployment to be eliminated. Many years later, in the early 1980s in the United States, a similarly substantial increase in government expenditure on weapons (under the presidency of Ronald Reagan) again led to a sharp decline in unemployment. Fortunately for the world, given the infinite destructiveness of modern nuclear arsenals, Reagan's rearmament did not result in a war like Hitler's had done forty years earlier.

Once the Second World War was underway, other governments (in particular that of the USA and Britain) suspended any remaining doubts about the merits of intervention in the market-place and took over the reins of investment and economic decision making from the private sector. Large amounts were directed from savings and various economic activities (partly through rationing) to the weapons industry. The war period saw the emergence of an interesting hybrid: a State-controlled war capitalism in which entrepreneurs were directed in no uncertain terms to invest into particular economic activities by bureaucrats and politicians. American economic growth was startling and allowed the USA to become a dominant super-power soon after the war's end. After the dust had settled down, economists and politicians who had lived through that tumultuous period became convinced that if governments can alter for the better the course of economic history (by intervening, sponsoring new industries and thus eliminating unemployment) during war, surely they could do so also in peace.

Why should governments be able to intervene successfully in the economy only when it comes to increasing our efficiency at killing each other and not do so in order to create a better society? The post-war boom, which lasted two decades, confirmed these thoughts. Simultaneously it devastated traditional (neoclassical) free-market economic theories which, with the help of Keynes' (and his disciples') incisive writings, were increasingly ridiculed in the eyes of the world. Not only did economists and governments come to accept that a large dose of scepticism was called for concerning the markets' capacity to adjust prices so as to eliminate unemployment, but also they came to doubt an even more fundamental pillar of economic thinking since Adam Smith as well: the assumption that the capitalist, the entrepreneur, can always be trusted to invest his profits into more and better machines in order to become more competitive and maximise his long-term profit. Keynes shattered this idealist portrayal and warned governments that when the economy shows signs of stagnating, they should never rely on the rationality of capitalists for investing and therefore helping stave off a recession. In characteristic style he wrote:

> The modern capitalist is a fair weather sailor. As soon as a storm rises, he abandons the duties of navigation and even sinks the boat which might carry him to safety by his haste to push his neighbour off and himself in.
>
> (Keynes, *Essays in Persuasion*, 1931)

For at least two decades after the Second World War, the spirit of Keynes influenced the aims, methods and ideas of governments and mainstream economists alike. In the sphere of political philosophy John Rawls' 1971 book *A Theory of Justice* (which we examined in Section 9.3) is the culmination of the Keynesian, social-democratic, perspective. Written just before the fall of the Keynesian revolution, it captured the political philosophy of the whole project: yes, society can be good. What it needs is the *just* blend of efficiency and equity; a blend that requires an activist State which intervenes when it has to in pursuit of social objectives but knows when to get out of individuals' (and the market's) way too.

Rawls' contribution to the Keynesian side was to show that State intervention was not simply common sense (due to the frequent failures of markets in serving the public interest) but that it was a prerequisite for social justice and social rationality. And that letting the market do its job of coordinating economic activity, even if it created a certain degree of inequality, was not a concession to injustice but a promoter of fairness. Provided the State chose its policies sensitively and sensibly, the market in unison with the government's interventions could be pulling society towards its legitimate, just aim. In effect, Rawls' book marked the high tide of social democratic political economy. It positioned the latter in the middle ground of political and economic debate.

On the left of the Keynes–Rawls synthesis there was the Marxist left, suggesting that because capitalism is constitutionally inefficient and unjust the only solution was a radical transformation of society. On the right of Keynes–Rawls we had the scattered and isolated extreme free-marketeers. At a time when university campuses were seething with Marxist narratives, imagery and condemnations of capitalism, while the Soviet Union loomed as a major threat to capitalism (especially in the contest for souls in the emerging Third World countries), the Keynes–Rawls bandwagon dominated the pro-capitalist camp. Unlike the extreme free-marketeers, the Keynes–Rawls project had something for everyone; it posed as the golden compromise between the extremities; the titular occupier of the political, intellectual, economic middle ground. Free-marketeers had nowhere to go but straight into the margin.

Thus their rise from the dead in the 1970s and 1980s had many of the characteristics of a revenge match which the free-marketeers are enjoying to date. Not surprisingly the avalanche of free-market individualism ideas spread beyond economics. The new creed became endemic in most social sciences. We have already examined in some detail its greatest manifestation in political philosophy; namely Robert Nozick's theory of justice in Chapter 9 which was to free-marketeers what Rawls' theory of justice was to Keynesians: a philosophical justification, the icing on their cake. Now that the Keynesian revolution had been defeated in the battlefield of economic policy (i.e. now that unemployment and production could, for some reason which economists are still struggling to comprehend, no longer be controlled by government effectively) the road was clear for attacks on its political and philosophical foundation; that is, on the idea that government intervention could bring about the Good Society by blending the best aspects of markets with the advantages of State control of social policy.

It was Nozick's (see Section 9.4) book *Anarchy, State and Utopia* that twisted the knife in the injured body of Keynesianism. Published in 1974 it offered a great deal of ammunition to all wings of the libertarian right. Chicago economists like Milton Friedman and Gary Becker could now claim that not only is it economically wise that the State does not try to intervene (because if it does it will reap greater inflation and, in the long run, more unemployment) but also it is *fair* that the State refrains from such folly.

There is no such thing as society

Margaret Thatcher's infamous aphorism (November 1987)

A veneer of ethicality was thus added to the economic view that governments should not mess with the market mechanism. Further afield, politicians like Margaret Thatcher espoused Nozick's philosophy so whole-heartedly that in a famous interview with *Woman's Own* she drew the only honest conclusion from Nozick's treatise: the only just State is one that does not recognise social objectives but only the rights of individuals and families.

The revenge was complete: capitalism could now be celebrated without having to worry about proof that it can generate the Good Society. If no society exists (beyond the arrangements we make to safeguards the property rights of individuals: recall Section 9.4.2), then the idea of a Good Society is fraudulent; the sort of idea that woolly middle-class intellectuals and bureaucrats peddle in order to serve their own interests through spreading confusion.

The collapse of the Soviet Union and its satellites added further impetus to the free-marketeers. No longer could social democrats (the Keynes–Rawls brigade) claim to occupy the middle ground between Statism-gone-mad (e.g. the Communist East) and untrammelled market ideology.

Natural unemployment

This is defined by the pro-market economists who rose into prominence in the 1970s as the level of unemployment which prevails when price inflation remains constant. Even if 30 per cent of the population are without work, as long as inflation is not increasing, most economists would refer to that rate as *natural* unemployment. The only way of reducing such 'natural' unemployment sustainably, they argue, would be through reductions in the real wage or increases in productivity. (See also the box on the limits of economic policy on p. 282.)

Moreover the pro-marketeers succeeded in another, deeper, sense: in the space of merely one decade (approximately 1980–90) they eradicated the notion of full employment (i.e. the right to work) from popular culture. Unemployment levels of 8 per cent or more are now commonly being referred to by economists as *natural* unemployment. The very mention of the word 'natural' invokes images of inevitability and thus acceptability.

As I write these lines the domination in the economics profession of the pro-market views, which Keynes and the Keynesians had marginalised a few decades ago, is as strong as that of the Keynesian system of ideas and models previously. And just as the pro-market views were never eradicated during their lean years (1930s to 1970s), the Keynesian views have not died either. They live on in the minds of a number of economists who mostly keep a low profile, talk to each other in poorly attended conferences, publish in unfashionable journals, waiting for another wind of history to bring them back into fashion and give them a chance to exact revenge against today's economic mainstream.

A historian on economic amnesia

Those of us who lived through the years of the Great Slump still find it almost impossible to understand how the orthodoxies of the pure free market, then so obviously discredited, once again came to preside over a global period of depression in the late 1980s and 1990s, which, once again, they were equally unable to understand or to deal with. Still, this strange phenomenon should remind us of the major characteristic of history which it exemplifies: the incredible shortness of memory of both the theorists and the practitioners of economics.

Eric Hobsbawm, *The Age of Extremes*, 1994

10.1.3 Economics and change

Once upon a time, to be a free-marketeer was to be a revolutionary. Back in the dark days of feudalism, when the king and the bishop controlled people's lives, the suggestion that individuals should be allowed to do anything they wanted provided they did not harm others was utterly radical. Pitched battles were fought around this idea and countless men and women died at the barricades in its defence. Equally those who, back in the 1970s argued that the Soviet Union should become a market economy, were treated with similar disdain by the Soviet establishment. Thus a free-market ideology has a tradition of sponsoring change. However, once a market mechanism becomes established, the radicals of the past transform themselves into the new conservatives.

We saw in Section 9.4 how Nozick's individualist, pro-market, perspective on justice rules out any change which does not meet the agreement of every individual affected by it. This is a blueprint for the new, pro-market conservatives. The reason is simple: if everyone affected by a change must approve of that change before it is made, then very little change will ever take place. Nozick and the new right defend this conservatism by pointing out the impossibility of defining the public interest (see the discussion of Arrow's *third theorem* of welfare economics in Sections 8.1.6, 8.3.3, 9.1 and 9.2).

> **If democracy could change anything it would have been banned!**
>
> Anonymous

So the latest message is: as a community, do only those things that do not really change anything. Hold elections, form a government, set up ministries but please do nothing which will make even the worst bigot or sadist worse off – recall also Catherine Mackinnon's words in the extract on p. 93.

Returning to the first paragraph of this chapter (George Bernard Shaw's cheeky definition of the unreasonable as those people who want to change the world), effectively what the new dominant, pro-market theory of society is telling you is that you have one option: to adapt yourselves and your ideas to the world around you. Abandon all notions of altering society by bringing people together and asking them to campaign so that a collective agency, such as the State, can take steps to limit exploitation, oppressions, poverty, illness, etc. *unless no one is to lose any privileges in the process.* Collective action is out. The only option is private, individual, pursuits which recognise the right of the rich and powerful to remain so unless they *choose* not to.

With this prospect looking decidedly thin, and political change out of the frame, what is your best bet for acquiring the social power to effect the changes which your conscience prescribes? The answer is: increase your personal 'market-value' so that you can then cash it in at the market-place of life and use its proceeds in any which way you want. If such a prospect does not appeal (perhaps because the process of enriching one's self in the market also divests one of idealism), then perhaps the last remaining course of action is to change, not the world, but your ideas about what it should be like. At least, if you succeed, you will have avoided the disutility of unfulfilled dreams of a Good Society.

Many will find this message reasonable and eminently practical. Others will see this prospect as desperately bleak and, instead, follow Bernard Shaw's iconoclastic line: *be unreasonable and band together with other unreasonable people in a united effort to change the world according to your ideas about how it ought to be!* Assuming for a moment that you have an interest in pursuing this thought (just for the hell of it!), how does one prompt social change via collective action? What should the aim be? We have already seen one answer: John Rawls' thought process which led him to recommend a blend of the market and the State (Section 9.3). Well this is one alternative. In the remainder of this chapter I shall investigate a more radical alternative; one that is far more sceptical about the market.

The place of change and evolution in free-market ideology

Change is paramount in the pro-market theories of economists like Friedrich von Hayek and philosophers like Robert Nozick. Hayek (see Section 7.3.4) celebrates the market because of its capacity to generate innovation and introduce changes in the way we produce and consume commodities. It is for this reason that Hayek thinks that no attempt by governments to 'improve upon' the market can work. Similarly Nozick thinks that this process of evolution results in an income distribution which is in perpetual flux. As the market moves in mysterious and therefore unpredictable ways, people's fortunes change all the time. The change in their fortunes is followed by a change in their ideas about what is fair. But because these changes are anarchic, spontaneous and rapid, there is never any income distribution that (1) we can all agree is *fair* and (2) we shall continue thinking of as *fair* in the near future. Thus, Nozick concludes, there can be no single fair distribution that the State can legitimately aim at.

The notion of *evolutionary change* is the single most powerful idea underlying the new-right, ultra-libertarian, celebration of the market. However, economists like Hayek and political philosophers like Nozick espouse the concept of *change* provided it has resulted from individual action. Changes brought about by democratic means (e.g. a majority vote in favour of progressive taxation) or collective action (e.g. political movements to abolish sex or race discrimination) are treated with suspicion if not downright hostility. Consequently, although the notion of *change* plays a crucial role in pro-market narratives, political change through State institutions or democratic movements is ruled out.

10.2 Social justice and freedom FROM the market

10.2.1 Freedom from the labour market: Nozick's and Rawls' oversight

There is no doubt that for most people the vision of working for themselves (as opposed to working for somebody else) is a poignant vision of freedom. Why is that? Greengrocers and fishmongers do not, as a matter of course, dream of exiting the market for vegetables and fish. They dream only of more trade and higher prices. Why do workers dream of exiting the labour market? The answer has been foreshadowed in Chapter 7 (see Section 7.2 in particular): labour is not just any commodity. No contract can specify

---

Free-market ideologues and their worship of unpredictability

Free-market ideologues seem to base their whole theoretical apparatus on the idea that we are surrounded by a world which is certain to outsmart our collective efforts to control it. Why are our collective efforts to shape the world doomed? Because it is so chaotic and it evolves simultaneously in so many different places at once that it cannot be planned. They are convinced that, as in biological evolution, whatever we may think of it we cannot resist it successfully. However, here lies a contradiction: although they argue that nothing that we all (or most of us) want can be made to happen by government, almost anything can be accomplished through individualistic, decentralised, action. But if the social world is uncontrollable by humans, if it can be counted on to 'bite back' at our best efforts, how is it that they are convinced that free enterprise and the Invisible Hand will be exempt from the world's vengefulness?

---

how much labour effort is being exchanged and, therefore, this ambiguity means that the worker never knows when the employer's demands will be satisfied. Thus to put one's self in the position of employee is to step into the receiving end of a series of extractive efforts.

Of course employers are also in a bind. Not being in a position to know how much labour effort they are purchasing, they must compete with each other to extract as much of it from their employees as they can. The employer who hesitates before turning the screw on the worker is the one who will probably be the next to go out of business as the output per worker will fall below that of the competition. Thus it does not make sense to blame employers for the attempts to increase labour productivity by squeezing as much labour effort as they can from their workers. Exploitation is the name of the game played in all labour markets. Consequently one can understand why most people would like to work for themselves rather than for some boss: they just want to avoid putting themselves in the role of the 'squeezed'.

Is there a lesson here for Nozick and his theory of justice? Thinkers like Nozick ask how it is possible to speak of exploitation when workers *voluntarily* accept employment. If they sell their labour power voluntarily, then this transaction must be as just as any other. However, as I have argued previously (see Sections 4.3.3 and 7.2.4), desperate people do desperate things. That they choose to do them does not mean that it is fair that they should be doing them.

Labour markets make people accept conditions which they would have rejected if they had more than one alternative; namely, hunger and destitution in societies without a social security 'safety net', and the dole office queue in societies with a welfare state. As stated on p. 179 of Section 7.2.4 (see the box) the freedom behind a transaction cannot be ascertained by an observation that no one pointed a gun at the seller. If that were the case then the black workers in South Africa who worked and lived in gold and diamond mines, in circumstances that their bosses would not inflict on their pets, would not be able to describe their experience as one of unfreedom and exploitation. After all they chose to sell their 'labour units' to these mining companies, did they not?

Thus *a transaction is free and fair provided all parties had viable alternatives and yet decided to go ahead with it.* Labour markets, on the other hand, are founded on an extreme imbalance: workers who have no viable alternatives other than to supply labour to employers and employees with numerous viable alternatives to purchasing labour (e.g. live off their capital). That imbalance imbues employers with a power to exploit. If they do not use it, they are most likely to go bankrupt as there will always be competitors (perhaps in some other part of the globe) who reduce production cost by using their power to exploit. Labour markets are therefore a realm of un-freedom for those who *have to* act as sellers in them.

So unlike selling antiques, tomatoes or cars, selling one's labour is already a defeat; a failure; decisive evidence that one does not have alternative means of reproducing one's life. By contrast, buying labour is a sign of social power; of having the economic power to extract someone's sweat. In this context the urge of most labourers to set up their own firm, to become self-employed, is the manifestation of the longing for freedom from the labour market. If this is right, then labour market transactions may be criticised not only as unjust but also as inimical to basic freedom: the freedom to enjoy the fruits of one's endeavours. Then the assets gained by the buyers in labour markets (i.e. the employers) are the proceeds of exploitation; of the diminution of someone else's freedom. If Nozick's third principle is to be activated (the principle that the State ought to intervene whenever there is an injustice – see Section 9.4.2), then the police must move against all capitalist firms! In this sense, the State must outlaw the capitalist labour market.

The above point is not only a criticism of Nozick (and of the new right) but also a radical rejection of any attempt to reconcile justice with capitalism – i.e. with an economic system in which production relies on *purchased* labour. For labour to be purchased, there must be a purchaser belonging to the minority of owners of means of production (i.e. production lines, factories, farms, machines, etc.) whose income is not the result of their work but of their property rights. Property rights which place them in a position of social power *vis-à-vis* others who, because of an accident of history, do not own means of production and are, thus, forced to sell the only thing they have: their labour. But labour being what it is (i.e. not another commodity), its sale puts into motion a process of exploitation of non-owning workers by non-working owners.

Inevitably the distribution of income between the two groups (owners and non-owners) will reflect the fact that one group has the power to exploit the other because, as argued above, the sellers of labour are structurally in the disadvantageous position. Why is that? Because, as already argued, of the imbalanced distribution of options between the two groups. Looking at the wider picture, if all employers band together and fire all workers, workers will starve. By contrast, if all workers band together and withdraw their labour, employers can always liquidate their capital or, alternatively, work it themselves (e.g. landowners can farm the land and live off it, unlike farm workers who have no land to cultivate in case of a dispute with their landowner).

Although none of this is likely to happen, the distribution of income between the two groups reflects the balance of those options of the two sides. Moreover it reflects the fact that the owners' group comprises fewer and wealthier people than the non-owner's group, which means that the latter face greater obstacles (i.e. the *free-rider problem* – see Section 8.2.4) than the former in organising a collective stand. Not surprisingly, workers end up receiving not a just reward for their efforts but a fraction of it.

If this argument is sound, not only does it wreck Nozick's defence of untrammelled capitalism as a just society, but it demolishes Rawls' defence of a mixed economy (i.e. capitalism featuring an interventionist State) as well. Why? Because Rawls' injustice is blind to the *exploitation* rife in labour markets. Noting that labour markets are everywhere in capitalist societies and that most people make a living as sellers of labour, this is a pretty gigantic oversight on Rawls' behalf. But does Rawls not speak of *justice* in the distribution of income? Yes he does. However, he does not offer any analysis as to why the income distribution under capitalism tends to be unjust.

Rawls' view of the capitalist market seems like a mountaineering expedition where some succeed in reaching the peak while others inadvertedly fall into the crevice. In his Good Society everyone will agree rationally that those who prove fitter and stronger must slow down, pick up the injured and the weak, and carry them along. If they fail to reach the highest peak, they will have still managed to go as far up the mountain as possible without 'dumping' any of their colleagues. Indeed (recall Rawls' *Maximin Principle*) in this way the least accomplished climber is guaranteed to go furthest up the mountain. On the other hand, those who are slower and more inept at climbing must not expect that those who are faster and stronger should walk as slowly and unsteadily as them; they must agree to be carried. If the group's progress is to be made surer and safer by having the strong carry the weak, this is what should happen even if, in the end, 'mountaineering glory' is distributed unequally. Why *should* this happen? Because, Rawls claims, this is what rational climbers would agree to while at base camp, prior to finding out who is stronger and faster and who will be injured.

But what if this metaphor of the capitalist market is inappropriate? What if those who make it to the top, and get all the glory, are pseudo-mountaineers who reach the peak because they are carried all the way by local peasants who do all the legwork in exchange for some food? What would justice require then? Nothing short of ridicule for the 'masters' and the disbandment of their vile mountaineering club will do. And it would be not only justice that requires such drastic measures but also common sense: for it is clear that such an expedition would be less safe in treacherous weather conditions because those who get the glory cannot be of any help in case of an emergency and those who can will be too tired to act decisively. This last twist in the metaphor relays the left-wing (mainly Marxist) view of the impossibility of civilising capitalism *because of its inherent inefficiency and irrationality*.

In this left-wing light, the debate between Rawls (the social-democrat) and Nozick (the free-marketeer liberal) is ill conceived. If it were just a matter of some people being better climbers than others, perhaps Nozick might have a point when proclaiming: let the good climbers go to the top unencumbered; they are entitled to it (although most left-wingers would still support a publicly funded safety-net for those who 'fall' for reasons which cannot be blamed on anyone else). In the spirit of the previous paragraph, if the market operates according to the principles of Olympic competition, then perhaps right-wing liberals like Nozick are right: the rich are entitled to their wealth and the State has no business taxing them in order to assist the poor. But this is where left-wing thinkers put their foot down: capitalism is *not* problematic because some people are luckier, harder working, better planners or greater risk takers than others. Much more ominously capitalism is unacceptable because the success of the minority is built on exploiting the majority; on *causing* their 'failure' by exercising their power in the labour market. Moreover this is not just an ethical matter. The exercise and main-tenance of power by employers on workers in the labour market is, according to left-leaning thinkers, the cause of much inefficiency; in short, the labour market is a clumsy institution for organising and coordinating human effort. Witness, they would suggest, the production losses due to unemployment and industrial conflict (e.g. strikes).

So, if life under capitalism was like a 100 metre race or a genuine mountaineering expedition, then of course some would end up as winners while others would walk away losers. The Good Society, like all decent sporting officials, could ensure fairness and decency in the way proposed by Rawls or by Nozick. If we decided as a community to side with Rawls' concern for distributive justice, then we would all agree that the better athletes ought to slow down and pick up those who have collapsed during the race or the expedition. If, on the other hand, we agreed with Nozick, we would place more emphasis on the entitlement of the fast and furious to get to the top or the finishing line first without stopping on the way to help the casualties. However, the labour market is no Olympic Games. It is more like a Roman arena in which well-armed gladiators face unarmed victims. The latter end up in pools of blood not because they did not try hard enough, or because they are less talented, but because of the asym-metry in the initial distribution of armour (a primitive form of capital).

Similarly under capitalism, working people queue up outside the factory gates begging for the right to be exploited; that is, to sell their labour (images from a scene in Charlie Chaplin's movie *Modern Times*). As in the case of the Roman arena, in which decency demands that the whole sick-ening show is banned, so in our modern world the only way of bringing about social justice is to abolish this contemporary form of slavery; to free the majority from the fate of being sellers in the labour market. This is the crying call of left-wing social theory in general and left-wing economics in particular. Of course, it is not a modest call; it is an invitation to design an alternative economic system (see Section 10.4.5 for more on this) which, somehow, avoids the pitfalls of previous socialist systems (e.g. the Soviet Union).

10.2.2 Commodified information and the gift of knowledge

Imagine that you were the health minister in a Third World country. Countless children die every year of diseases that can be cured easily by drugs that are cheap to produce and which are already being made domestically by foreign-owned drug companies. The only problem is that the latter charge high prices which your ministry's budget cannot afford. What do you do? In the past Mexico tried to answer this problem by taking steps against the drug companies. It tried to force them to maintain production with reduced prices (and royalties). But the drug companies won the day by threatening to leave Mexico altogether.

Indira Gandhi, the assassinated Indian Prime Minister, said in 1982 when addressing the World Health Assembly: 'The idea of a better-ordered world is one in which medical discoveries will be free of patents and there will be no profiteering from life and death.' The neoclassical economist's rejection of her argument turns on the notion of efficiency: if cheaper and better drugs can be developed only through expensive research and development, corporations will take the risk of undertaking such large investment only if they can expect to make a profit out of these drugs. If Mexico, or anyone else who *needs* the drugs, is allowed to violate these property rights (or copyright) in order to cure those who are sick now then cheaper and better drugs will simply not be produced. So for the benefit of future generations of ill people, the economists conclude, we must be cruel to be kind.

Another way of putting the same argument is that information (or knowledge, knowhow, etc.) must be treated like a *commodity* and its provision must be left to the market. Why? Because, neoclassical economists believe, the market is the best organiser of the production of commodities. However, it is not obvious that information is a commodity like all others. Recall how we distinguished between a private commodity and a public good in Chapter 8: good X is private if it is scarce and if the consumption by a group of people of x per cent of the stock of X means that the stock has been depleted and only $(100 - x)$ per cent remains (e.g. consider a bunch of bananas; if half of them are eaten, the 'stock' has diminished by 50 per cent). If, on the other hand, a good can be consumed by everyone *at once* without any depletion of its 'stock' then it is a public good (e.g. a radio programme which can be listened to by 1 person or by 1 billion people). Thus information is a form of public good and the only thing that the law can do to protect its 'authors' is to restrict access to it. How does the law do this?

Looking at copyright law in Anglo-Saxon countries, we find that a 'work' (e.g. a book like this one, or the formula for some chemical) is divided in two: one part which can be held as private property and another which cannot belong to anyone. This division can be traced to the eighteenth century where literary works were seen as comprising (1) an 'idea' (i.e. the idea of a plot) which can be discussed over dinner by all, and therefore remains a public good, and (2) an 'expression' (i.e. the precise words used) which remains the author's property. However, it is not the usual kind of property. Unlike 'real' property (e.g. over land), copyright expires at some point and, once it has expired, no one can purchase it. Why this peculiarity? Because copyright law represents an attempt at negotiating the two 'natures' of information, knowledge or art: its private and its public nature. On the one hand, it attempts to provide a monetary incentive to 'creators' so that they will produce new information, knowledge, etc. while, on the other, it tries to protect public access to their creations (if only in order to allow future generations of 'creators' the opportunity to learn from previous knowledge before engendering further knowledge).

Since the eighteenth century society has experienced a tremendous transformation from a customs-driven system to a market society. As technology has improved and the market has invaded more realms of human activity, copyright law became relevant to areas that it was not initially designed for. To take an example, the capitalisation of farming (e.g. the use of tractors, combine harvesters and chemical pesticides) has led to the demise of the farmer who produced his own raw materials (e.g. feed, fuel and motive power). Now farmers even buy seeds (which used to be a byproduct of agricultural production) from large companies which, therefore, have every incentive to develop new types of genetically engineered seeds (e.g. frost resistant or hybrid species). An immediate result is that the nature of research and development on agriculture has changed profoundly. Gone are the public research laboratories as a major source of new knowledge on plants. Their place has been taken by conglomerates like Shell, ICI, BP and Ciba-Geigy who have also taken over traditional seed companies. These conglomerates invest a great sum of money into the development of new plants, new seeds, new biotechnology, hoping that they will cash in on them in the future. Naturally they are very possessive of their 'creations' and use every aspect of copyright legislation to protect them from 'unauthorised use'. A similar process can be observed in the area of pharmaceuticals.

An economist would argue that the above proves how effective the market is and how important it is to turn, through State (i.e. legal) intervention, knowledge into a private good (or at least restrict access to it). However, the copyright law's objective of striking the right balance between protection of the 'creator' and the protection of the public's right to knowledge and information, is being subverted by these new developments in biotechnology. For example, corporations seek out Third World plant varieties, perform some minor genetic modification to them and then cash them in. The West African cowpea, for instance, which African farmers developed to be resistant to pests over many centuries, was patented (again after slight genetic manipulation) thus making large profit for the wily corporation and nothing for the local community. Indeed, it is very likely that African communities themselves could be made to pay western companies

---

Twenty-first-century colonialism

The germplasm resources of the Third World have historically been considered a free good ... Germplasm ultimately contributing billions of dollars [to the First World companies] has been appropriated at little cost from – and with no direct remuneration to – the [Third World]. On the other hand, as the seed industry of the advanced industrial nations has matured, it has reached out for global markets. Plant varieties incorporating genetic material originally obtained from the Third World now appear there not as free goods but as commodities.

Jack Kloppenburg Jr, *First the Seed: The political economy of plant biotechnology 1492–2000*, 1988

Copyright law versus publicly produced knowledge

The chemical companies' scientists fit the paradigm of authorship. The [peasant] farmers are everything that authors should not be: their contribution comes from a community rather than an individual, tradition rather than an innovation, evolution rather than transformation. Guess who gets the intellectual rights?

James Boyle, *California Law Review*, 1992

---

for bio-products which they have been using in similar form for ages. Surely this was not what copyright law was meant to achieve. For what we have here is clear discrimination: 'peasant knowledge', which reflects the development of plants and animals through the centuries, is treated as value-less while 'expert knowledge', that of scientists working for corporations, is recognised as worthy.

The problem is not only one of injustice, of the imbalance of benefit between corporations and traditional communities. It is also a matter of efficiency. As research loses its public spirit and is increasingly driven by profit (i.e. as it leaves universities and government research organisations and is transferred to the laboratories of companies), less information is shared amongst scientists who work in the same field but for different companies. Open discussion of technical detail during the critical stage of research is discouraged by managers prior to the granting of patents. Thus the main reason for having patents and copyright law, that is efficiency, is undermined. The more the thin line dividing private and public knowledge is pushed by corporations to limit the latter, the greater these inefficiencies are likely to become. In 1980 copyright law was extended in the USA to genetically engineered animals. Even though nature (like language) could not be claimed by any individual (e.g. no one has the right to patent the cat, the lion or the English language), the court ruled that if scientists *altered* existing genes or DNA, they own them. Perhaps this makes sense in the context of similar provisions for plants. But where do we stop? In 1991 scientists began to patent human gene fragments. James Watson (formerly head of the *Human Genome Project*) was quoted in the *New York Times* as saying that such profit-driven attempts to restrict access to nature (even human nature) are likely to lead to worrying inefficiency: 'if someone has been working on a partic-ular gene for several years, but someone else has patented it before they even know what they have' [then] 'companies that uncovered the role of a particular gene could be forced to pay royalties to those that had merely isolated it.'

Information wants to be free!

(Anonymous computer hacker)

But is there an alternative to privatising information and letting the market drive its production and distribution? There is. Consider the well-known and loved (even if increasingly run-down) repository of shared information called the public library. What is a library? It is a publicly owned institution, housing material full of knowledge, whose purpose is to ration the information without treating it like a private good. Books, records and other material are lent to members of the public who use it, and share it, without acquiring property rights over it. And who pays for these materials (and, by extension, for the cost of producing them)? The public does through taxation. Of course to justify this system, and to extend it to public systems for research on human genes, pharmaceuticals, etc., one must first accept that there is a well-defined public interest which renders taxation legitimate; thus, we find ourselves back to the debates in Chapter 9. Nevertheless an important point has been made: information (like labour) is *not* a commodity; when it is treated like one the result may be not only inequitable but also inefficient.

In conclusion, the evolution of market societies is continuing. What started in the beginning as the commodification of human labour (see Chapter 1) evolved into the commodification of endeavours which, until recently, were considered to fall outside the reach of the market mechanism (e.g. athletics). Now we see that the market has penetrated the microcosm of genes (human and otherwise). And just as its triumph in the estates of Britain during the eighteenth century caused devastation amongst those forced to enter the market with the least economic power (i.e. the landless

---

The market's steady invasion into life

Life has been integrated into the market as easily as could be imagined because it has been a progressive process. It started with something that was symbolically far removed from mankind, the vegetable domain; from there it passed to the micro-organism, then to the most rudimentary forms of animal life like the oyster. The whole of the animal kingdom is now targeted and we are on the verge of the human, weighed down with precedents which ensure the closure of the system and make any resistance difficult. The work of man, which must be remunerated, claims repayment from the whole realm of nature which has traditionally been free of any property claims.

Bernard Edelman, *'Entre personne humaine et matériau humain: le sujet de droit'* [my translation], 1991

---

peasants), today's encroachments also benefit those with existing market power at the expense of the rest. The latter have therefore every incentive to demand 'freedom from the market' whereas the economists, whose primary assumption is that the market knows best, is to dismiss such cries as the mutterings of the irrational.

10.2.3 The profanity of putting the human condition on sale: blood, education and human remains

A famous British study by Richard Titmuss on the supply of blood surprised many economists. The major finding of *The Gift Relationship* (1970) was that the quantity of blood supplied was higher in countries, such as the UK, where no money was offered to those who gave blood. Why on earth are people more reluctant to give blood when they are offered money for it? It makes no sense to those thinking in terms of the neoclassical *Equi-marginal Principle*. For if there is an opportunity cost to giving blood (e.g. the inconvenience or the slight pain from the needle) surely people ought to be encouraged by payment. Even if there are many altruists who would give blood regardless of payment, there is no explanation as to why the offer of payment *discourages* them from giving blood. To the neoclassical economist this is a mystery.

However, the fact that people are put off from giving blood by payment ceases to be mysterious when we take a broader view of what human beings are about. In Chapter 4 (Section 4.2.5 and the whole of Section 4.3) I argued that as humans we are creative in the way we perceive experiences and that such creativity wrecks the simplistic attempts at social explanation based on the model of utility maximisation. In the case of blood-giving this argument takes the following form: people like to express themselves through various acts that are neither downright selfish nor particularly selfless. For instance we are courteous to strangers (e.g. opening doors for them) that we are unlikely to meet again. Why do we do it? Because we enjoy the way we look in other people's eyes when we do such decent things. It is part selfishness (caring about our image) and part selflessness (we might still do the right thing even if no one could see us).

In short, we indulge in acts of altruism which are so mild that we do not consider them as self-sacrifice. Imagine that, at this point, a market develops for these acts which rewards them with money. All of a sudden carrying out such acts acquires a money value. Will these acts become more frequent given that one gets paid to carry them out? Not necessarily because (1) the payment takes away the selfless element of the act (and with it a substantial part of the reason for doing it), and (2) carrying the act out anyway and refusing payment now feels like a significant sacrifice because it involves forgoing the offered payment.

To apply this exegesis to the blood-giving case in countries such as the UK where donating blood is a voluntary exercise, we need to imagine that walking into a Give-Blood-Save-Lives coach parked on the High Street is neither a sacrifice nor selfish. However if the coach were to become part of a commercial outfit, offering money for one's blood, walking into it takes a wholly different meaning. From an expressive move it becomes a *market transaction*. Many people are turned off by this transformation of an expressive act to a market transaction. To express the same thing differently, their decision to give blood loses its veneer of mild altruism if there is cash to be received as they exit. Why not give blood anyway and refuse to take money? Because that would be, not an act of unconscious mild altruism as before, but an act of conscious, almost militant, altruism as people scornfully ignore the hand that pushes a few banknotes their way. In short, taking blood-donations and turning them into a sale of blood removes the appeal of giving blood. The offered money is no compensation for that loss.

There are many similar examples where hitherto freely provided services are radically jeopardised and cheapened by the introduction of formal payment. Education is such an example. For committed teachers, teaching is more than a service provided in exchange for given payment; it is primarily a duty towards one's students, towards society. Of course teachers want to get paid; often they strike in order to prevent their standards of living from falling inexorably. Nevertheless they refuse to think of their efforts as a commodity and their employment contract as a pure exchange of those efforts for an agreed sum of money.

When I started teaching at university, I would often give extra seminars in the evening to students who had a special interest in the subject (or needed additional help). Of course there was never any question of being paid for this. Was this altruistic? Not really, since I relished the possibility of an interesting discussion and, in all honesty, I savoured the role of the conscientious teacher as reflected in my students' eyes. Was it utterly selfish? Again, not really, since I gave up my time and fell behind in my research on whose strength I would be able to secure my future employment. In summary, these classes fell in the grey area separating mild altruism from mild selfishness.

Then came the changes to the education system which pushed us all in the direction of commodification: departments were ranked according to how many hours of this and how many hours of that were performed; students were encouraged to think of themselves as clients to whom we, their teachers, were contracted to impart certain bits of knowledge; teachers were given merit points according to how many hours' contact we had with students, how much administration we carried out, how many articles we published, etc. Finally those merit points were cashed in during promotion rounds. In other words, our work as teachers began to get quantified and treated like some commodity. The market had penetrated academic life. Did this have desirable effects? Do teachers under this regime provide better education to students?

Whatever the merits of this new market-driven regime, one thing is clear: it is much rarer now for myself, as well as for other colleagues, to offer informal evening classes to interested students. Why? For the same reason that commodification of blood reduces its supply. With every aspect of my work now being seen as a commodity for which I am rewarded (or punished), giving an extra evening class is likely to be seen as an attempt to score merit points. Thus the appeal of offering them has waned since students and colleagues suspect that I would be doing this only to boost my promotion chances. On the other hand, the merit points I would get from offering the odd extra class are likely to be insufficient to justify the effort required (for example, I will most probably get more 'points' from working on a publishable paper). Thus I tend not to offer such classes.

In the end, the introduction of the market into university life has meant a diminution of those experiences that used to make it special. Have the gains outweighed this loss? Although university teachers run around a lot more than they used to (in search of the merit points that will lead them to the elusive promotion), I personally doubt it (though not everyone agrees). In my mind, the intrusion of the market has forced us to *seem* to do a lot more things that can be quantified at the expense of those other unquantifiable things that made universities exciting places (e.g. debating, thinking, reading outside one's immediate research area, arguing with students, etc.). Instead of taking ten years to write a substantial book (which people will still be reading in fifty years), we write many short articles. Instead of writing articles we compose applications, fill forms and rewrite our CV. Just as in the case of blood donation, also in education, converting hitherto communal activities into commodities to be exchanged in a market reduces the quality of the offered service.

One wonders what other realms of human endeavour the market may have jeopardised. In the previous sections I argued that commodifying knowledge is fraught with dangers. In the section before that I rehearsed the claim that men and women want to be free of the labour market. Here we saw that it may be for the best if the supply of blood and education is shielded from the market. Embarking from these examples it is easy to think of new ones. Most of us would express horror at the prospect of living in a society which allowed the free trade of human organs; we would fear of the prospect of living in a world in which the rich could purchase the organs of the desperately poor and where transplants were decided on the basis of bank balances rather than need. Rethinking this in the context of the discussion above, perhaps there is more to consider than an ethical objection to the market mechanism: there is also an economic argument against the market.

For if an organs' market ends up resembling the market for blood, it is plausible that a market for organs will *reduce*, rather than increase, the supply of kidneys, eyes, hearts, lungs and livers. I, for one, would like to put it on the public record that I would tear up my organ donor card if I suspected that they could be auctioned off to the highest bidder after my death. And I am convinced that the bereaved relatives of unfortunate victims of road accidents would be far more unlikely to authorise the taking of organs from their dead if they were offered money for them than if they were simply asked to do so without payment for the good of those most in need of transplantation. Thankfully as human beings we cannot all be bought – at least not yet.

In summary, this section weaves the critical musings of Chapter 4 into a wholesale attack on the blind faith that the spread of markets into new realms will, by definition, lead to improvements, efficiency and greater supply of valued services. By pointing to how the commodification of human endeavours can cheapen them, this line of thought castigates the profanity with which the market replaces human values with prices. How relevant is this argument? It depends on how strongly one feels in favour or against the market and capitalism. Recall that we all remain hostages to our twin masters: history and ideology.

10.3 Market failure or market nature?

10.3.1 Is market failure an exception or the rule?

Economics textbooks first offer their readers long passages on how wonderfully markets coordinate economic activity and only later discuss market

---

Machiavellian medicine

Niccolò Machiavelli, while defence secretary of Florence, was convinced that hiring professional soldiers at the market for mercenaries was a bad idea. Much better, he insisted, was to entrust the State's borders to a citizens' guard. For if the State employs mercenaries to fight wars on its behalf, then the wars will be never-ending since they would fight as little as possible in order to prolong the war and thus boost their income. The Medici, who ruled Florence, finally agreed with him when a mercenary captain was spotted beating back his own soldiers lest they succeed in taking a besieged city and render themselves unemployed.

Ed Nell, an American economist, draws an interesting parallel:

The parallel today might be the performing of unnecessary surgery, or dragging out a case at law. The orientation of medicine today, and its strategy of research, is to make war on disease, to concentrate on curing, which earns handsomely, and wins plaudits in the press. Yet the greatest successes by far have been due to public health and sanitation measures, simple prevention, carried out by public agencies, by which we have wholly eliminated formerly endemic plagues. However, the process has generated very few opportunities for private gain. And cutbacks on public health spending have allowed diseases that had been defeated, like TB, to rise again.

Ed Nell, *Making Sense of a Changing Economy*, 1996

---

failures (see Section 8.2). This leaves students, quite naturally, with an impression that markets all in all work well but that, occasionally, they fail. This belief is reinforced when students move from the core economics courses to more specialised ones such as International Trade in which markets are assumed to work efficiently all the time (e.g. perfect competition is assumed). By that stage the student has only distant memories, if any, of the chapter on market failures. The fact that most markets are uncompetitive and, even if they are competitive, make a mess of things when it comes to providing education, health, pollution control, natural resources (e.g. fisheries or the mining sector), law and order, national security, justice and equality of opportunity is all but forgotten.

So, who is right here? Should we focus on the market's (many) successes or its (also many) failures? Once more there is no unique answer. Those who are ideologically well disposed to free markets and capitalism will focus on the success stories; the rest will do a song and dance about the failures. Some will even go further by arguing that what is often portrayed as a market failure is a natural state of the market system. This being a critical chapter, I shall attempt to counterbalance the thousands of textbook pages which eulogise the market by airing the argument that what textbooks refer to as market failure is, in reality, a market's true nature. And there is no greater candidate for such a discussion than the labour market which has stubbornly failed to equalise the demand and the supply of labour – witness the countless decades of persistent unemployment all over the world.

10.3.2 Can the habitually failing labour market be corrected? Keynes' answer

The usual demand and supply story is as simple as it is powerful. If there are unwanted units of a certain commodity, then the price must be too high. Drop the price and there will remain no unsold units. Thus it is totally natural for economists who insist on seeing labour as a straightforward commodity to believe that, if only the price of labour (i.e. the wage) would fall, there would be no unwanted units of labour left (that is, there would be no unemployment). Taking this argument further, if there *is* unemployment it must be because, for some reason, the wage refuses stubbornly to fall. Then the search is on for the causes of this stubbornness (or wage rigidity as it is usually called).

Right-wing economists know exactly who to blame for wage rigidity: the trade unions (for using the threat of industrial action to push the wage up to some 'unnatural' level) and governments (for pushing the wage up either directly, by means of minimum wage legislation, or indirectly, by offering unemployment benefits which act as an effective minimum wage). Economists occupying the centre and centre-left (e.g. disciples of John Maynard Keynes, Nicholas Kaldor, Joan Robinson – all Cambridge economists spanning, roughly, the 1930–80 period) point out that unemployment was a problem long before trade unions were formed on a large scale or governments introduced unemployment benefits.

We already saw in Chapter 1 how, early on in the nineteenth century, David Ricardo, a strong believer in capitalism, feared that capitalism's engine could stall plunging the whole economy into a depression (see Section 1.2.3). Section 10.1.2 told a story about the historical ups and downs of economists' belief in the market system during the twentieth century. Central to this twentieth-century story was the figure of Keynes who, like Ricardo, was also a supporter of capitalism but not of the proposition that the markets can be trusted unconditionally. Keynes believed that, however wonderful capitalism might be, it was in its *nature* to falter and stall generating persistent unemployment and misery.

Free-marketeers have faith; they believe that a market is always self-correcting: whenever supply exceeds demand price falls until supply is reduced to the level of demand. Why does this not happen in the markets for capital and labour? Why is it that during recessions (or economic crises) when there is excess supply in the labour market, the wage does not fall until demand equals supply? And why does investment not rise in response to reductions of the interest rate (which is the price of borrowing money and therefore the price of investment)? If only these two markets were functioning as neoclassical economists expect, employment would never be scarce (at least for those willing to work for the going wage) and falls in the interest rate would avert a collapse of business investment. Thus if the markets are blameless, unemployment *must* be the fault of the unions and of governments.

Keynes had less faith in the free market and explained the stubbornness of unemployment and under-investment during recessions thus: suppose that, for some reason, demand for commodities were to diminish. Demand for capital by business falls as their sales, and confidence, decline. Soon after the 'price' of investment funds (that is, the interest rate) falls (as with any 'commodity' whose demand has suffered). Why is it that, following the reduction in the interest rate, investment does not pick up at all and, in spite of the falling interest rate, it continues to decline? Keynes' explanation is simple: capital is not some commodity whose demand fluctuates in direct proportion to its price. Business needs to be confident that the invested money will translate into future output that will find buyers. If there is doubt about the latter, business will not invest however low the interest rate (see also Section 8.2.5).

So, what is it that decides business confidence? The psychology of coordination, answers Keynes (see the box on p. 235–36). If each expects others to invest, *all* will invest due to the expectation of a healthy level of future sales (as the large volume of invested funds reaches the pockets of workers, suppliers and, sooner or later, metamorphoses into demand for commodities). If, on the other hand, each expects that others will not invest, then *no one* will invest, convinced that it will be money down the drain. Indeed a sequence of reductions in the rate of interest may, at least for a while, have the opposite effect as business sees in it further evidence that 'things are bad'.

Thus far Keynes has explained why, once the seed of fear has been planted, it might grow into an investment crisis. As the latter unfolds, workers will lose their jobs (because without investment employment suffers). Why does the wage not fall far enough to stop the decline in employment? For three reasons, according to Keynes and his neo-Keynesian successors:

1   First, because many employers prefer to sack workers than to reduce wages. Reducing wages creates more disaffection within the factory than a few sackings. Therefore employers assume that the disaffection

due to a pay cut may lead to major productivity losses which render the pay cut uneconomical. Keen to avoid jeopardising the productivity of those who remain employed, they seek cost cuts by sacking more workers; after all, the sacked carry their disaffection outside the factory gates.

2   Second, because workers often assess the level of their wage in relation to that of other workers in comparable jobs. For instance, steel workers may resist a pay cut, not just because they resent losing the money, but also because they do not want to see their wage fall below, say, that of miners. Therefore if the steel industry is in trouble but the mining industry is not, the wage of steelworkers will not be reduced to the extent that it would have to eliminate unemployment in that industry.

3   The third reason is that the labour and the capital markets fail in tandem and workers do not trust that if they accept lower wages their jobs will be saved. Recall Keynes' description of the captains of industry as 'fair-weather sailors' in a storm who are not only a danger to the economy but also a danger to themselves (see p. 285). Even if wages are reduced in response to an excess supply of labour (i.e. unemployment), this is not the end of the matter. Business may well interpret the fall in wages as a terrible omen for their future sales prospects; they see in it the terrible prospect of impending *under-consumption* (a fall in demand due to reduced wages). In that case, the fall in wages spearheads another drop in business confidence which leads to yet another reduction in investment. The outcome of all this is an ever-decreasing spiral from which no reduction of wages can save the economy. Government then becomes the only plausible white knight which can save capitalism from collapse.

Summing up so far, whereas the liberal (or libertarian) right thinks that there is nothing wrong with the labour market (provided the trade unions and government let it do its job properly), the centre and centre-left expect the labour market to fail. However, they then put forward suggestions on how it can be helped. Keynes made a name for himself, not only for diagnosing capitalism's endemic sickness (the tendency of capital and labour markets towards failure), but for proposing a cure as well. Whenever the market shows signs of backtracking, of being on the verge of a 'failure', the government ought to step in and spend money on public infrastructure. Thus it will steady the nerves of business-people who recognise in the extra government expenditure the prospect that there *will* be money in the pockets of common folk to buy their commodities. Keynes hoped that such measures would prevent (and even reverse) a collapse in business investment and, therefore, of the labour market. Capitalism could be salvaged provided the State kept a vigilant eye on it and stepped in to correct its failures.

A neo-Keynesian explanation of capital and labour market failures: uncertainty, coordination breakdown and free-riding

Capital markets do not bounce back following a fall in demand because uncertainty about future sales causes entrepreneurs to postpone investment. That uncertainty is made worse because of the nature of the game: each would invest if only he or she thought others will follow suit. Notice that this problem is identical to the *coordination problem* discussed in the box on p. 235. When firms fail to coordinate, investment falls and the pressure is on for labour costs to fall. Two problems emerge in the labour market: first, firms may prefer to reduce labour costs by sacking workers rather than by reducing wages. Second, as entrepreneurs observe their competitors reducing labour costs, they predict a further drop in demand for their output (since the workers' lost wages will translate into fewer purchases). Thus what is good for one firm (i.e. a reduction in money spent on wages) is seen as catastrophic for the economy as a whole (i.e. lower demand for all commodities and a recession). The result is that firms lose confidence further and cut, again, their level of investment. If they could band together and agree to stop cutting workers' income and, instead invest collectively, that would end the downward spiral and business would pick up again. However, they cannot reach such a sensible decision because they are involved in the type of *free-rider* problem we examined on p. 232. Their only chance is an interventionist government.

Keynes' neoclassical opponents were adamant that his recommendations would lead only to price increases and not much else. They argued that by borrowing and spending, the government would be 'injecting' more dollars, pounds or marks into the economy but that these coins and banknotes would correspond to the same commodities as before. So the result would be a higher ratio of money to commodities or, equivalently, higher prices but no more commodities. In summary they warned governments that if Keynes' advice were to be heeded, output and unemployment would be unchanged while inflation would go through the roof. Keynes' response was simple: if government pumps more money into a *stagnant* economy (i.e. one with substantial unemployment of labour, machinery, etc.) then this injection will stimulate it, factories would open again, the unemployed will be hired and, therefore, *more* commodities will be produced so, in the end, more money will chase more commodities. In this case, prices will not rise while employment and output will.

Keynes was proved right. Every time unemployment showed signs of rising, governments would boost spending and unemployment would ease off without a significant effect on prices. That is, until the early 1970s. Then, horror of horrors, unemployment would be rising, governments would be spending more but unemployment would fail to respond. Instead prices exploded and unemployment kept rising. Since then Keynes cuts a much less prominent figure in the imagination of economists.

10.3.3 Unemployment surges as capitalism's essential regulating device: Marx's view

In contradistinction to Keynes and the Keynesians, Karl Marx and his followers rejected the notion that unemployment is a kind of failure on the part of capitalism. Some of these Marxian ideas were rehearsed in Chapters 1, 6 and 7 (Sections 1.2.4, 6.1.1 and 7.3.3 respectively). On the question of the market's propensity to failure, they are unequivocal: periodic mass unemployment and recessions are to capitalism what hell is to Christianity: an unpleasant yet *essential* device without which the whole edifice would become highly unstable. To those who beat their chest about the fact that governments and elites do not do enough in order to battle unemployment and create jobs, Marxists say: 'The social and economic power of the ruling class is maintained by recessions and joblessness. Why should they want to eliminate unemployment; especially when those with jobs do not care much about the jobless and the jobless don't vote anyway?' In short, here we encounter the startling view that unemployment, rather than being an *accident* or some *failure* of capitalism, is actually a crucial aspect of free-market economies; one of capitalism's success stories!

Why is this view startling? Because, if correct, the fact that millions of jobless people suffer untold hardship on the margins of society is not some aberration brought about by mistake or by failure. And if it is not a failure, how could (or why should) a wise government (which by default represents those who benefit from unemployment directly or indirectly) try to undo it? Interestingly there seems to be some agreement here between free-market enthusiasts and Marxists: both accept that unemployment can be 'natural' (see the box on p. 287). Of course this agreement is only skin-deep in the sense that Marxists think of unemployment as a natural state of affairs *under capitalism* but do not for a moment accept capitalism as a natural state of affairs. Their point is that to rid society of the scourge of unemployment we need to rid it of capitalism.

Marxists approach the Keynesian analysis of Section 10.3.2 with a mixture of sympathy and disdain. They also think that it is in the nature of capitalist markets to stumble and fail. Indeed Marx had foretold Keynes' under-consumption argument; i.e. the *free-rider* problem amongst capitalists as explained in the box on p. 232 or, equivalently, point (3) on p. 306, whose gist was: *Each capitalist benefits from reducing the wage of her workers but, when they all do the same, then the working classes' income falls, demand by workers for the capitalists' wares declines and, as a result, entrepreneurs are left with masses of unwanted commodities.* On this count, many Marxists are in agreement with Keynes regarding the possibility that a clever government can prevent such a crisis by imposing effective minimum wages and expending much effort in boosting business confidence. However, for Marxists, the failure of capitalist markets is caused by an even more insidious process; one that goes beyond simply undermining business confidence and, thus, one that no government, however smart, can do anything about.

What is this insidious process that governments cannot undo? It is, Marx states, the tendency of capitalism to nurture the seeds of economic crises during the good times; a trend for things to get steadily worse for individual capitalists during periods of increasing prosperity. Even if firms do not realise it, periods of economic growth undermine the ground on which the growth of individual firms is founded. Thus there exists some limiting level of economic growth which, when reached, triggers a catastrophic domino-like sequence of collapsing firms. In a short space of time the whole economy plummets into a recession (i.e. falling output, increasing poverty and unemployment, etc.). In other words, things are bound to become much worse whenever it seems that they are getting better!

The source of profit according to Marx

As explained in Section 1.2.4, Marx sees profit springing out of the difference between

1   the value of a worker's labour as a commodity; that is, the *value of labour time* = *value of commodities necessary for the worker's reproduction* = *labour necessary to produce these commodities*

and

2   the value of the commodity produced for an employer and a worker which reflects the amount of labour the worker has 'invested' in the commodity.

Notice that labour-saving technology reduces the gap between the two and therefore reduces the profit margin.

But why does this happen? What is it that sustains this inverse relationship between the fortunes of individual capitalists and the state of capitalist economies? Recalling Marx's theory of value from Section 1.2.4 of Chapter 1, competition during a period of economic growth forces entrepreneurs to invest in labour-saving devices because this is the only way they can reduce cost and undermine their market rivals. However, as they do so, less human labour goes into commodities and firms' profit margin shrinks (see the previous box).

So, on the one hand, the economy seems to be flourishing. New orders for machines mean new production lines to produce them and more employment in the machine-producing sector. More employment means more money in the pockets of workers, who then spend it in supermarkets, cinemas, theatres and petrol stations. A phase of prosperity caused by investment on machines (or capital accumulation). However, the seeds of the impending crises have already grown roots under the surface of the happy times. What are these menacing roots of forthcoming doom? They are no other than the profit crisis (see the same box) which is about to start biting and culling the least profitable, and therefore most vulnerable, firms.

The moment the profit margin of some firms dips below zero a proportion of them will fold. Their employees, middle-managers, blue-collar workers, suppliers of raw materials and machines will all suffer a loss of income. In turn *they* will reduce their purchases of other commodities significantly. The firms which produce these other commodities will see their revenue decline. For many of them, already under the strain of decreasing profit rates, this latest setback will be the last straw. Bankruptcy! More workers and suppliers lose their income, less money is spent at the marketplace, there are more closures. An avalanche of misery will have started leading the whole economy into the doldrums.

Is there no end to this hideous cycle? Is there no salvation from the recessionary spiral? Yes, there is, writes Marx. There comes a time when the number of firms has shrunk so much that the surviving ones face much less competition. So, even though the size of the pie (i.e. total expenditure) to be distributed between all the firms will have decreased substantially, it is possible that the size of the slice for each of the surviving firms will be greater now than it was during the good times. Thus the financial health of surviving firms is better at the depth of the recession; which upholds Marx's point that the fortunes of capitalist firms are best when capitalism is doing badly and vice versa. It is in this sense that economic crises are good for capitalism: recessions help capitalists restore their profit rates after a period of incessant capital accumulation (that is, after a period of growth during which firms spent increasing amounts on new machines).

It is from this perspective that recessions are not an accident. Indeed they are crucial in helping capital overcome its inevitable profit crises which are brought about by increasing investment and competition. Without these recessions, capitalism would soon run out of steam. How do recessions prevent this? As we saw in the previous paragraph, once the economy reaches the depth of recession, surviving firms profit from their increasing market power (due to the 'death' of the competition). Moreover the desperation of unemployed workers is growing with every additional day of unemployment.

The higher the rate and duration of unemployment, the more willing are workers to work for a wage that is less than the value of their time. Immediately the profit margins for firms expand. But this is not all. Workers who never became unemployed are terrified by the prospect of joblessness (in view of the long dole queues) and work harder to avoid the sack, thus delivering more actual labour to employers in the context of the same labour time (which is all employers pay for anyway). So, firms end up paying less (courtesy of lower real wages) for more (greater labour productivity) and profit margins soar. Furthermore during recessions there is plenty of unused capital lying around (e.g. trucks, computers and boilers belonging to businesses that went bust) and on offer for a song.

The value of workers' time (i.e. the wage)

The value of a car equals, according to Marx, the total amount of labour necessary to produce it. But what of the value of workers' time? As explained in Section 1.2.4 (see also the previous box) workers' time is also a commodity which requires inputs in order to be maintained. Workers require a certain basket of *essential* commodities in order to be able to report for work every day (e.g. food, clothing, transport, basic entertainment, etc.). Well, the value of their labour time (i.e. the wage) equals the total value if these *essential* commodities (which, in turn, equals the total amount of labour effort other workers expended in order to create these *essential* commodities).

One objection to this model of wages is that it treats the time of men and women as another commodity (although it distinguishes it from *actual* labour which it sees as an activity that workers are coerced to perform during the time that they have sold to employers; i.e. labour as such – unlike labour time – is not a commodity). Feminists have pointed out that bringing children up so that they can then sell their 'labour' time to an employer is not a matter of blending some inputs together in order to 'produce' a person. Creating 'labour time' is different from building a car because this is a 'process of production' which takes place outside the market altogether. Thus the value of

312 MARKETS, THE STATE AND THE GOOD SOCIETY

grown-ups' labour time will depend not only on the value of the milk and cookies that they were fed, but also on the degree to which their mothers were exploited at home – e.g. all the hours the mother spent unacknowledged and unpaid nurturing the child. Similarly for maintaining adult workers (e.g. cleaning after them, feeding and support them, etc.). In short, the value of labour time (i.e. the wage) depends not only on the value of *essential* commodities that workers need but also on the degree to which those who count as workers in the public sphere benefited from the unpaid work of their mothers, sisters and wives who help 'create' and 'maintain' the labour time which they sell to employers.

Moreover whenever recessions force workers to work for wages below the value of their labour time, this means that those who care for them (traditionally their wives) have to produce more goods at home in order to replace the market goods that their husbands' wage can no longer purchase. Thus recessions intensify the exploitation not only of those who sell their labour in the labour market but also of those whose labour is not a commodity in the public sphere (e.g. the labour market) but is expended inside the isolation of the home.

In summary, firms which have survived the worst of the recession see the latter as a gift from heaven. Simultaneously they enjoy greater monopoly power (as their competitors go to the wall), lower wage costs (as unemployed workers are prepared, at least in the short run, to work for a wage less than the value of their time), greater productivity (as existing workers, fearing dismissal, work harder for no more pay), lower raw material prices and really cheap capital (i.e. machinery) prices. In this light, recessions are a magnificent device for regulating capitalism and not at all a fault or a failure. Of course they are still nasty, brutish and desperately long for those people who lose their incomes and peace of mind while they last, but such is the reality of the free market for workers: they set them free to lose.

Concluding Marx's argument, let me recall the essence of Section 7.3.3: *wasteful unemployment is an essential aspect of a successful capitalist economy (rather than a problem which can and should be addressed within such as economy).* Economic crises play an important role in reinvigorating capitalist firms which get increasingly sicker during periods of increasing prosperity. Mass unemployment during recessions is one of the important regulating devices of the system: by pushing wage costs down and, more importantly, by increasing the rate at which employers extract labour from workers (i.e. productivity), they reverse the trend of falling profit rates. Once this happens,

---

It was the recession we had to have

Thus Paul Keating, former Australian Labor Prime Minister, commented on the 1990–2 recession which his government oversaw. In a cartoon published in the *Sydney Morning Herald* a couple of years later Mr Keating is portrayed as decorating an unemployed family with 'the Distinguished Unemployment Cross for conspicuous poverty in the face of heavy profit making'.

---

a new period of growth looms. Nevertheless for exactly the same reasons as before, the new period of prosperity is pregnant with the next recession.

Marx would therefore agree, in part, with both Keynes and the libertarian free-marketeers. He would obviously agree with Keynes that capitalism has the tendency to falter and enter into periods of intense crisis. He would also agree that a clever government can lessen these crises (by employing some of the tricks that Keynes made famous) while a stupid government will prolong them. However, Marx would disagree that such crisis management can work in perpetuity. Capitalism would bite back those who tried to weed out its essential regulating mechanism (as it did in the 1970s). Underlying this thought we find Marx's assessment that periodic crises in business activity are the result of something more fundamental than the coordination problem highlighted by Keynes: a tension between technological progress and profitability which got worse as the economy expands. No government can do anything about that.

In this sense, Marx would agree with the free-marketeers on the impossibility of maintaining steady economic growth and minimal unemployment through government spending and other programs. He would even agree with the Austrian economists von Hayek and Schumpeter (see Section 7.3.4) that capitalism needs the law of the jungle, the rise and collapse of corporations, the oxygen of recession in order to maintain its vigour. However, he would laugh at the simplistic insistence that unemployment would never have occurred if only wages were flexible and low enough (and would agree with Keynes' rejection of this argument; see also the Indian village tale in the box on p. 283). Recall that, in Marx's theory, the reason for the recession has nothing to do with the level of the wage and everything with the way technological progress is antagonistic to profit rates. Indeed he argued that, however low the level of the wage (that is, however wretched and poor workers become) the capitalist system will always generate profit crises and therefore recessions.

Where Marx stands apart from both Keynesians and free-marketeers is in his insistence that crises and unemployment are inevitable. Free-marketeers think that a combination of low wages and untrammelled markets will avert any such problems. Keynes thought that with a helping hand from wise government there is no need for capitalism to hit the rocks of recession. Marx, by contrast, was convinced that, whatever the level of wages, however well markets may function, and independently of how wise and silly governments might be, capitalism will enter into recessions as surely as the ship will enter port. In effect, capitalism needs to sacrifice generations of workers and their families on the altar of those who happen to own the means of production and whose profit need to be replenished by frequent economic crises. Crises which produce higher profit margins for the minority in exchange for lower incomes, continuing misery and diminishing life prospects for the majority.

At the very least, Marx concludes, a capitalist market system fails because it does not meet the criteria that its champions (beginning with Adam Smith) set for it: it does a bad job at coordinating productive activities and human resources since it ensures the persistent and periodic condemnation of masses of willing and able workers to the scrap-heap of society. What is needed is neither a greater freedom for employers to exploit nor a wise government to regulate the degree of exploitation. We need to replace the current irrational system with one in which economic activities are rewarded in terms of their worth (rather than in terms of who has the social power to exploit whom) and surpluses not sustained by the further immiseration of the miserable and the exploitation of the many. In short, only social (or common) ownership of the means of production can lead to an economic system which stops technological change from being a cause of crises and which turns the gleaming new machinery into humanity's servant.

10.4 Conclusion: challenging the great liberal debate

10.4.1 No government intervention can civilise capitalism

Section 9.2 referred to the great debate which has been raging in political and economic circles for more than a hundred years: *to what extent should efficiency be compromised in the pursuit of equity?* Should the State help the poor? Even if this means that at least some of them will be quite happy to live off the State and make no effort to cure their own poverty? Or is it that a compassionate State must toughen its heart and deny assistance to many deserving poor in order to avoid creating a culture of dependency which traps them in a vicious circle of poverty and hand-outs? In Section 9.3, two answers to this question were borrowed from two of the most significant political philosophers of our time: Rawls and Nozick.

The two answers define the extremities of the liberal spectrum. For economic and political reasons Rawls and Nozick both value highly the freedom to transact, exchange and participate in markets. It is through participation in markets that individuals can better their lives. Thus for both

Rawls and Nozick, the market mechanism is unquestionably efficient in generating wealth. Where they take diametrically opposed views is on whether organised society (i.e. the State) should take an active interest not only in efficiency but also in equity. Rawls argues that it, in the name of (distributive) justice, it should while Nozick protests, in the name of individual entitlements, that the State cannot redistribute income legitimately.

What is interesting about the Marxist position we are investigating currently is that it bypasses that debate altogether. Marx would simply be bored and impatient with this disagreement. For a start, he would not accept for a moment that capitalism is efficient. As Section 10.3.3 reveals, Marx's own analysis of capitalist markets, and of their proclivity to engender crises, points to a structural irrationality built into any economy in which some people own means of production while the majority do not. His is not an ethical point as such (even though he never turned down an opportunity to invoke moral indignation amongst his readers) but an economic one: an economic system which relies for its survival on periodic but incredibly violent surges in unemployment, under-production and waste of resources (both human and non-human), cannot possibly be thought of as efficient. There must be a wiser system for organising economic and social life.

If Marx is right, Rawls' blueprint for civilising capitalism is in jeopardy. Recall (see Section 9.3) Rawls' idea on how a concern for efficiency can be blended with a concern for equity. To spare you the trouble of turning the page, on p. 262 I wrote: 'Rawls supports a degree of inequality which is in *everyone*'s benefit. If the introduction of some extra inequality increases the income of the worst off, then it is fair to introduce it. But, if inequality comes at the expense of lower living standards for those at the bottom end of the distribution, then it is deemed unjust ... The policy implication is clear: the State must intervene by taxing the rich, transferring income to the poor, creating a safety net with minimum health and education provision; in short, the rational State fosters social justice. But, there is a limit beyond which any further intervention is itself unjust. This limit is reached when any additional redistributive intervention reduces efficiency to such an extent that the people it is meant to assist are harmed. The State should leave alone any inequality which can be eliminated only if the income of the poorer members of society suffers.'

The above idea hinges on the *existence* of a limit to State interventions 'beyond which any further intervention is itself unjust'. Is there such a limit and if there is how can we know it? In practice we find that, in a capitalist society, the more the government re-distributes income from rich to poor the lower the level of inequality but also the lower the efficiency of the market (since redistribution means more taxes for business and the wealthy and thus an exodus of capital from the country, leading to reduction in investment and, ultimately, lower productivity and efficiency). So the limit to the State's intervention must be

1   high enough to undo the inequity which is incompatible with equal access to some basic goods (e.g. liberty)
2   low enough to ensure that no more efficiency is sacrificed than is necessary for social justice.

Marx's point would then be that, under capitalism, there is no degree of government intervention which can satisfy conditions (1) and (2) simultaneously. The social-justice-seeking State is doomed to fail because its intervention in favour of the poor will always be too little to undo the injustice suffered by the under-privileged in and around the labour market (see Section 10.3.3) while *simultaneously* being too high in the sense that *any* redistribution of wealth, in the long run, lessens the profit rates of business and bring us closer to the next economic crisis. When the latter hits us it is, once again, the weaker members of society who will pay back with interest whatever benefits or transfers they received from government earlier.

In short, Marx rejects Rawls' main argument, namely that there is a degree of State intervention which can temper the ruthlessness of the market and civilise capitalism. Attempts to do so, to use the State in order to combine labour markets and social justice, are utopian and destined to end in more misery for the exploited, the needy and the forgotten. Remarkably this radical left-wing repudiation of the social democratic agenda of Rawls (and the neo-Keynesians) seems akin to what Nozick had to say in Section 9.4. However the similarity conceals a tremendous disagreement with Nozick.

He too was convinced that the State can only make things worse when trying to infuse capitalism with more justice and equality. Better leave markets alone, was his conclusion. Why? Because, even if you do not fancy the income distribution that markets give rise to, at least at the end of trading at the market-place buyers and sellers will go home in the knowledge that no one got more or less than they bargained for, no one was forced to part with any commodity or asset, no one exploited anyone. In the end, Nozick concludes, let us all learn to respect each other's right to keep whatever asset one has acquired or created without violating the same right of others. 'Rubbish,' I can hear Marx shouting at Nozick from the grave. Transactions between employers and workers at the market for labour are a form of institutionalised theft; a prime example of how desperate people can consent to their own exploitation (see also Section 7.2.4).

As for capitalism as a whole, it is all about denying the majority of working people Nozick's cherished 'right to keep whatever asset one has acquired or created without violating the same right of others'. Moreover, to be able to sustain its momentum and prevent its collapse, capitalism needs to ensure that there are long periods during which a large proportion of workers are not allowed anywhere near the production process. So, workers either walk home at night with a fraction of the assets they created or wander aimlessly looking at jobs that do not exist because of the system's inability to regenerate itself without wasting resources, talents and lives.

In summary, Rawls' idea of how to civilise capitalism runs into Marxist opposition because of a belief that attempts to temper capitalism's hunger for inequality damage the machinery of capital accumulation which keeps it going. Thus they will never succeed in civilising the beast because the State's interventions will simultaneously be too feeble as a counterweight to the systematic exploitation which goes on *and* too much since they will be hindering the natural self-correcting mechanism of capitalism (i.e. the periodic surges in unemployment and the resulting inequity/poverty). There are, therefore, only two viable, consistent, honest routes one can take: either agree with Nozick that the best thing we can do collectively is to do nothing. Or change society; find an alternative way of organising economic activities. Marxists refer to the latter as socialism.

10.4.2 A public interest has no meaning in an exploitative, racist, sexist society

In this short section I invite you to revisit the debate at the centre of Chapters 8 and 9 regarding the existence or otherwise of such a thing as the Common Good or the Public Interest. You will recall, of course, that treacherous *third theorem* of welfare economics; the one that showed the impossibility of deducing what is in the Public Interest by inspection of individuals' utility orderings. The radical approach in the current chapter puts that problem in an interesting new light.

The new insight is the simple point that there can be no common interest in a deeply divided society; at least not one that its members can recognise and act upon. The economic approach to individuals' common objectives, as discussed in Chapter 8, neglects to look at the social context in which these individuals live. Such an abstraction is meaningless since people make their minds up about whether they share common aims or not depending on the type of social and economic relations that they have. Preferences are a product of those relations rather than vice versa. Thus neoclassical economists who try to infer a community's objectives by focusing on their preferences, while uninterested in the social links between them, should not be at all surprised if they end up discerning nothing.

Some communities develop such strong, cohesive common aspirations that individuals within them sacrifice their lives to turn them into reality. Other communities, e.g. Northern Ireland, are so deeply divided that to speak of the Public Interest is to miss the point of their reality. Between these two extremes there is the majority of communities which are characterised by a mixture of common objectives and significant divisions. Moreover there are divisions which have run their course and which could be overcome by some act of generosity and far-sightedness. For instance the French and the German governments set aside centuries of conflict and formed the strong Franco-German axis within the European Union from which both countries benefit.

However, there are other divisions which are more resilient because someone benefits continuously from them. For example, apartheid in South Africa was not just a matter of the whites being prejudiced against the blacks (although, of course, they were). It was fundamentally a matter of economic exploitation as the wealth of the white population was built on the backs of black workers in the mines, the farms, the factories, the whites' homes where they worked as servants; workers whose lack of constitutional rights translated into low wages for them and high profit for their white rulers. In that case, as in many others, institutionalised as well as informal discrimination is due to the existence of an effective mechanism of exploitation. Under such a social arrangement, it is futile to seek the Public Good. Unless the vile machinery of exploitation is uprooted altogether, the two sides cannot even *begin* to seek common ground.

One does not have to look at South African apartheid to find this type of social division which survives mainly because of the benefits it accrues to those with great social power. Women all over the world own 1 per cent of property, do more than 60 per cent of the work and are rewarded with no more than 20 per cent of the world's income (UN, *Social and Economics Statistics*, quartely). Societies, advanced as well as under-developed, are replete with institutional and informal mechanisms for discriminating against women; for restricting their access to the more powerful roles in society, for preventing them from claiming an income that is proportional to their efforts. When we speak of the Public Interest, how does the collective interest of women to end this pattern of exploitation and discrimination feature? Scanning Chapter 8 it soon becomes obvious that the economic debate on this matter makes no room for such a concern.

Another problem with patterns of exploitation is that they are usually woven into a tapestry of discrimination and injustice. Two examples: (1) The male worker goes home after a long day of working for a pittance under the watchful eye of a ruthless boss only to inflict another type of terror on his wife who was working all day, not even for a pittance, in order to keep the house and children going. (2) The woman who leaves the home as an escape into the public sphere (the sphere where all economic and social values are created and distributed) and employs a migrant woman whom she pays a pittance simply because she can get away with it. What both these examples depict is a situation where patterns of systematic exploitation emerge and are sustainable because they benefit those who have the power to keep them going (e.g. the ruthless boss who benefits from the systematic exploitation of labour, or the husband who profits from a sexist distribution of household labour, or the professional woman who profits from racism in the labour market).

Clearly in the presence of so many scrupulously preserved patterns of exploitation, the Public Interest is, at best, a mirage and, at worst, a sick joke. To create a widespread sense of a Common Good in a democratic, pluralist society we need to undo those patterns. Why do we not? Do we lack the necessary decency? No, I do not think so. The main reason is that these patterns are terribly intertwined. Particular individuals are affected badly by one while benefiting from others (think of the earlier example in which blue-collar workers are exploited in the capitalist labour market but, simultaneously, benefit from sexism; or white women suffer from sexism but often benefit from the cheap labour they can bring into their homes because of widespread racism). To terminate the whole network of exploitation and discrimination, and therefore to make a workable notion of a Public Interest possible, nothing short of a large coalition of citizens is needed. Bringing it together is a monumental task.

10.4.3 Brief glimpses of the Good Society

Right-wing social theorists, like Nozick, advise against dreaming of or planning for the Good Society. Only blood and anguish can result as these dreams have a tendency to turn into nightmares. Look at how the noble triptych of the French Revolution (equality, fraternity, liberty) was drowned in rivers of blood that flowed as the Revolution killed off its children one after the other. Take heed from the Russian Revolution, which started with great hopes for the workers and peasants of the world only to end in the industrial feudalism of the Soviet Union. According to this right-wing view, society changes best when it changes as a result of individual action whose only purpose is to enhance the interests of the individual. Grand projects which intend the improvement of society result in tyranny in the name of that society. Political activism to create the Good Society only brings into being Evil Empires.

Social-democrats (e.g. Keynesians, Rawlsians, etc.) believe that reform, not revolutionary changes, can do the trick. That through the civilising effects of public education, health and a constant, yet mild, redistribution of income from capital to labour and to the under-class (that is, to those who are neither owners of productive means nor workers but live in the margins of society), a Just Society can emerge.

Left-wingers, mining the rich vein that Karl Marx first struck in the nineteenth century, entertain no hope that capitalism can be reformed. From their perspective, capitalist societies can, at best, fake goodness but even then only for a while. After the Second World War, the threat of communism's appeal to the peoples of Europe and the Third World, in combination with the horrific memories from the previous capitalist crises in the 1930s, encouraged the State in Britain, France, Germany and elsewhere to redistribute income, to lessen exploitation and to try to suppress economic crises in a manner similar to that suggested by Keynes. Additionally the underprivileged were given access, for the first time, to universal education, health, social security. An illusion of social cohesion and of a Public Interest under capitalism was created. An illusion which, like all illusions, could not last.

By the late 1960s the signs of the next recession were becoming obvious. The gains of the underprivileged, as it always happens during recessions, were in danger. By the 1980s, a combination of another cruel crisis (the 1979–83 recession) and of the imminent collapse of any threat from the experiment with an alternative economic system (which went so badly wrong in the Soviet Union), caused the rapid erosion of those gains. As soon as the 1990s had arrived, capitalism had overcome its flirtation with social democracy and reversed fully towards the principles of the jungle that is the free market.

While the right celebrated its historic victory, the left also took heart: for its theory that capitalism cannot change its spots for long is evident today in the ruins of the British National Health Service or the French social security and higher education systems. The only side in the argument that remains baffled is the social-democratic corner which seems bereft of ideas as to how the dominant free-market ideologists can be persuaded about the need to pursue the Good Society now that the threat from the left (and the Soviets) has passed.

Meanwhile government policy (regardless of who is in power, right-wingers or social-democrats) pays occasional lip-service to the ideals of an inclusive society while increasingly dismantling any effective mechanism that it might have for effecting those ideals. Nozick and the new right have, undoubtedly, won this latest round. Their message to you can be heard loud and clear in all walks of life: the papers, television, the pop or fashion industry, school, university, and of course economics lectures and their off-shoot management courses: *adapt yourself to the world, rather than try to change it!*

Nevertheless in spite of this deafening message, you can still discern the faint ironic voice, which could even belong to George Bernard Shaw's ghost (recall the first paragraph of this chapter), telling you: 'Come on, have a go! Dream of a world that, unlike the mess that you encounter every time you turn the television on or walk the streets of your city, is consistent with *your* sense of what is decent. Be unreasonable, for goodness sake. At least avoid the sinking feeling when you are old and grey that you did not try.' What kind of world would you dream of? What would it look like?

Perhaps it would consist of individuals who are born into a society that has not already assigned to them particular odds for socio-economic success depending on whether their parents own shares in conglomerates, are unemployed or work nightshifts in factories. A world in which, to remember the US civil rights campaigner Martin Luther King Jr, social position is blind to the colour of one's skin but totally responsive to one's character. A society in which baby girls are born with the whole world to win ahead of them and without having to endure years of sadistic conditioning whose purpose is to box them into the lesser social roles in society. A community of persons who benefit according to personal effort and ingenuity from technological advances; not one where technology leads to crises and to the wholesale waste of chunks of humanity for the purpose of maintaining privilege and the right to exploit. In short, a social arrangement in which citizens can choose more of their partners in life and at work, can select from a wide variety of social roles, and have the opportunity to develop productive and creative powers for which they are rewarded in proportion to their efforts but also to their needs.

Does it all sound utopian? Of course it does. But not more so than the dream of a world without slavery sounded in centuries past. Is it not dangerous to dream? Of course it is. One can never be sure that the next dream will not turn out to be a nightmare. The conservative right-wing have a point: grand idealists either fail or, when they succeed, end up incarcerated in concentration camps whose guards claim to be inspired by them. And yet, where would we be without dreaming? Without the betrayed French revolutionaries of the 1770s the ideal of liberty, with which today's right is so enamoured, would not have taken the world by storm, reaching the shores of the Americas and inspiring the American Revolution (1775–83). And without another spurt of ideals, dreams and seemingly utopian efforts to change the world in our time, the future will remain a bleak recapitulation of the present. Who but a utility maximiser would want to inhabit such a future?

Conclusion to Book 1: Foundations and beyond

Compared to introductory textbooks, this book is tiny. Is its modest size a problem? Perhaps more worrying is the table of contents, which is bereft of the multitude of chapters that normally make up much of economics textbooks (that is, chapters on the components of national income, the determinants of aggregate consumption, investment, savings, taxation, the demand for money, etc.). Does this Lilliputian book have the right to masquerade as a general book on *Economics* when it has little or nothing at all to say on important topics such as inflation, exchange rates, international trade, aggregate investment and so on?

Surely the answer must be negative. None the less it does not pretend to be a book on general economics. Rather it is a book on the *foundations* of economic thinking. In its defence, to understand the structure of any edifice, be it the Eiffel Tower or economic theory, one has to descend to its basement; to enter through unremarkable side doors and go down steps that are not trod by the general public or the guests of honour. Although one will have missed the glamorous façade or the spectacular views, exploring the guts of the building furnishes a unique view of how the whole edifice hangs together. It may be the least dazzling yet the most insightful perspective.

I do hope that the preceding chapters offered you such a tour along the foundations of economic ideas. If they succeeded, ascending to the surface and mingling with the public once more you will find yourself equipped with more confidence and a keener eye for the glamour and complexity of the building. When for instance you encounter debates on the role of money, a government's fiscal policy, international trade or any of the topics missing from this book, you will be better able to classify the various views; ready to recognise which tradition they spring from; well placed to understand what the fuss is all about and what are the motives behind the musings of the different participants to these debates.

The structure of the three parts of Book 1 was devised to help the reader acquire these skills. The second ('history of textbook models') chapter of each part took us beyond the textbook to an enquiry of the source of the ideas in textbooks. It revealed, I hope, the philosophical and political roots of notions such as *consumption, commodity, preference, competition, efficiency, equity*, etc. Knowing these sources is a first step to learning to identify the political and philosophical bias of *any* idea that economists may put forward. The third ('critique') chapter of each part developed a radical critique of these ideas as they have evolved today. Even if you did not agree with the often polemical (and, some would argue, extreme) nature of those critiques, at least they offered a glimpse of how ideas that seem well established can be criticised. Knowing how to criticise is equivalent to knowing how to take ideas apart; how to *grasp* them.

Upon entering fields of study on topics not covered in this book, I hope that the combination of the history of models and of the critical chapters will prove handy. You will be surprised to see that most ideas and policy suggestions which make headlines today emanate from the three or four different theoretical perspectives that we have examined in some detail: the neoclassical free-marketeers who always model the world using some form of the *Equi-marginal Principle*; the libertarian (or new right) free-marketeers (e.g. von Hayek and Nozick) whose arguments in favour of the market and against State intervention are couched in evolutionary terms (see Sections 7.3.4 and 9.4), the Keynesian-Rawlsian Social Democrats who advocate a mix of State and Market (see Sections 9.3 and 10.3.2); and the Marxists who castigate capitalism for being unfair because it is inefficient (see Sections 1.2.4, 7.3.3, 10.2.1, 10.3.3, 10.4). Regardless of whose side you want to be on (or even if you want to propose your *own* worldly philosophy), when confronted by some economic argument it is terribly useful to know which of these broad traditions it came from. To demonstrate this, let us consider three examples.

Money and the State

You may be surprised to find out that in this book so far we have not had to deal with the concept of money. Yes, we did mention prices. Nevertheless we did not talk of actual money. When we discussed the price of bananas or labour or anything at all, prices in dollars and cents were used as numerical examples but, I must confess, those references were rather fraudulent! Why? Because there was no theory of money (e.g. of its origin, its value, etc.) behind any of it. Indeed all the prices we were looking at made sense only in relative terms. In Chapter 2 the price of one apple was always measured in terms of how many units of the other good, e.g. oranges, one can afford for the price of one apple (recall that the only price that mattered was the ratio of prices, that is the slope of the budget constraint). In this sense, we needed to speak only of *relative prices*, rather than actual prices. Similarly in Chapter 5 in which the price of labour was discussed relative to that of capital or land. Even the more radical theory of production in Section 7.4 only speaks of relative prices.

Two economists meet on the street. One enquires: 'How is your husband?' The other responds: 'Relative to what?'

So if all the economics we have covered hitherto are based on relative prices, then presumably our theories apply only to a barter economy; that is, an economy without money in which exchange values are expressed in relative terms: two oranges are worth one banana. The moment money is introduced, problems arise. What determines its value? To what extent does Jill's demand for money depend on the price of money (can you think what that might be?) or on her wealth? How should the government choose how *much* money should circulate in an economy? Should a government be authorised to make such decisions anyway? What is the link between the total quantity of money and prices (actual or relative)? As you can imagine these are crucial questions for economists. Even though this book has not entered into such debates, let me demonstrate how the foundations laid in previous chapters can help here.

A neoclassical free-marketeer thinks of the economy in terms of the first two fundamental theorems of welfare economics (see Chapter 8). What would she or he think of the effect of fluctuations in the quantity of money on the economy? Let us see. These theorems effectively assume that competitive markets in long-run equilibrium work beautifully in that they generate maximum output constantly. What does this output correspond to? Provided nothing stops markets from attaining their long-run equilibrium, output will be such that average cost of production is minimised. Well, why should the quantity of money make any difference with regard to this miracle of the market? It would not. Thus the quantity of money will not affect output. And since it will not affect the level or intensity of production it will not affect the quantities of labour, capital and other factors of production necessary to produce it.

However, if production and consumption are to remain constant, workers, producers, consumers must be unaffected by the quantity of money. How can that be? Easily, is the answer that the neoclassical economist will reply, if relative prices do not change (i.e. one banana is still worth two oranges and one tractor is twice as expensive to hire for a day as a farmhand). So, will nothing change if the government prints lots of extra banknotes and circulates them? Surely *something* will be affected. Since output will not change (i.e. the same number of commodities will be produced as before), but there will be *more* banknotes chasing these commodities around, the price of each commodity will rise. However, *relative* prices will not be affected. The greater the quantity of money in the economy, the larger the price tags on goods and services. However, neither the quantity of those commodities, nor employment or relative prices will change. And vice versa. If the government reduces the quantity of money in the economic system, the only thing that will change is absolute prices (they will fall). No one will be better or worse off; indeed no one will actually act (produce or consume) differently than before.

In conclusion, a belief that the first two theorems of welfare economics closely approximate the workings of capitalist markets, leads to the recommendation that the government should resist any temptation to change anything *real* (e.g. output, employment, quantity of machinery) by altering the amount of money in the economy. Neoclassical free-marketeers often concede that in the short run it *is* possible to cause short-term increases in production if suppliers mistake the increase in the money price of their commodity for an increase in its relative price. However, the moment they realise that relative prices are unaffected they will return to their previous production levels. In other words, the government can boost output and employment by increasing the supply of money only as long as it can fool people. The moment it is found out, output and employment will return to their 'natural' level. However, such deception ought to be avoided because they create uncertainty and diminish the trust that people have in the currency as well as in the government's credibility. Without such trust the long-term ill-effects of deceptive spendthrift policies may prove significant if capitalists stop investing or move abroad in search of greater price stability.

Of course had we started with one of the views of the market critical to the neoclassical one, the conclusions would have been quite different. Consider for instance the Keynesian standpoint. As we saw, Keynesians are convinced that capitalism periodically goes into sustainable recessions. When this happens, business and consumer confidence disappears and output falls catastrophically. If the government pumps some extra money into the economy at that point in time (e.g. puts it in the pockets of those who are desperate for commodities that could have been produced if only producers were confident enough to start up the production process thus employing them and providing them with the income necessary to purchase these commodities ...), that money can give the failed market a kick start. As production accelerates (in response to that injected money being spent on goods), new commodities will be produced and thus we will have avoided the situation where more money chase the same number of goods. Instead, the extra money will have bought goods that *would not have been produced otherwise*. Concluding this Keynesian view, governments *can* and *should* experiment with the supply of money (increasing it during the bad times and reining it in during the better ones) in order to manage the periodic crises of capitalism.

Wages and money illusion

Before money was introduced into the world, wages were paid in the form of commodities; e.g. workers would receive quantities of wheat for their labours. Discovering the value of the wage relative to wheat was therefore automatic. However, with wages being paid in banknotes, the size of the wage can be computed only after we calculate how much wheat this wage can buy. Thus the *real wage* is defined as the ratio of the money wage to the price of wheat (or more generally some average of the prices of all commodities workers purchase).

Neoclassical economists who think of labour as a commodity (not dissimilar to wheat) therefore define the price of labour that both employers and workers care for as the ratio of money wage and average prices, known as the *real wage*. In other words, workers are not interested in how much money they receive per hour of work but on how many commodities that money can buy them –the *real wage*. Makes sense, does it not? The interesting thing is that if workers and employers are solely interested in the real wage *and* labour is a commodity like all others (in the sense that its price will decline if supply exceeds demand), then there will never be any unemployment. Why?

Think about it. Suppose that demand of commodities, for some reason, falls. Firms will lower their demand for labour as they will wish to reduce output. Initially the fall in demand for labour will translate into a reduction in both the quantity and the remuneration of labour (i.e. employment and the money wage will fall). Some workers will quit not wanting to work for less. However, prices of commodities will also fall (recall that all this has been caused by the fall in the demand for commodities). Thus even though the money wage will come down, the *real wage* will remain (more or less) constant since the ratio of money wage to average prices will not have altered. In other words, workers will be paid less but the money they will now receive will buy them no fewer commodities than they could afford before the fall in money wage (because prices fell in tandem with their money wages).

Consequently workers will realise that their *real wage* has not fallen at all even though they take home less money every day. As a result they will supply the same labour as before. In the end the same number of workers will be producing the same commodities which will be sold at the market to the same consumers. The *only* thing that will have changed is that consumers will be paying less money for these commodities and workers will be receiving less money. Nevertheless nothing *real* will have changed: output and employment will remain unchanged in spite of the initial fall in demand for commodities (whose only effect will be that prices and wages will fall by the same proportion).

The above is another version of the neoclassical free-market point of view: the market knows best and can handle falls in demand without generating unemployment (at least in the long run). Keynes disagreed for a number of reasons (as we have seen). One of them is that, in his mind, people suffer from *money illusion*. That is, if prices *and* their income increase by 10 per cent they are happier than in a situation where their wage has fallen by 10 per cent in response to a 10 per cent reduction in prices. You can see why that might be true for purely psychological reasons. In *real terms* the two cases are identical: the amount of commodities that one's money wage can buy does not change in either case. Yet most people would feel more comfortable in the first case rather than in the second.

There are other reasons, however, beyond mere psychology as to why workers will resist a money wage cut during periods of falling prices. Income, and prices, almost always fall during periods of economic decline. What happens during such periods? Employers immediately abandon all investment projects – totally. Workers, who know this, expect a further fall in demand for commodities as a result of the collapse of investment expenditure. Thus they foresee that even if their wage goes down, their job security will not be affected as demand continues its downward spiral. They recognise, therefore, that all they will achieve by accepting lower wages is to boost their employers' profit without any guarantees that more jobs will result. Partly for this reason, and partly as a result of sociological effects, they determine their money (or nominal) wage targets not in proportion to the fluctuations of their real wage but in relation to the money wages of workers in other, comparable, industries. When this happens, the automatic servo-mechanism described on p. 326 will fail and a fall in demand will generate unemployment.

Again we see that the faith of neoclassical economists in the market leads them to the conclusion that horrors such as unemployment cannot be blamed on the market. Keynes, who had much less faith in people's capacity to see through the mist of uncertainty that covers the market-place, thought otherwise: he believed strongly that the market is fallible or, more likely, that humans unleashed in a free market are fallible and that their errors (e.g. their *money illusion*) snowball and may result in massive breakdown of the market mechanism.

Marxists, on the other hand, offer their own radical twist on this debate. They think that recessions (i.e. falling prices, real wages and unemployment) and inflation (i.e. rising prices) function as a means of returning to employers some of the value produced by workers which the workers have managed to claim for themselves (usually through trade union activity). Periods during which economic growth reduces unemployment are periods during which the unions' power to negotiate better deals for workers increases. In that case a price inflation exceeding wage inflation (i.e. prices rising faster than wages) is one way the unions' gains can be reversed. However, the greatest revenge must wait until the next recession (always around the corner) which deals a decisive blow against any union gains. In this light, the greater the degree of the workers' 'money illusion' during periods of growth (and rising prices) the more readily inflation can redistribute income in favour of the employers whereas, during recessions, the degree of workers' 'money illusion' will act as a (usually ineffective) break to the expansion of employers' profit margins.

International trade and the Third World

Remember (from Chapter 8) the neoclassical approach to social welfare? Neoclassical international trade theory is a mere extension of it. Recall how the first theorem of welfare economics (Section 8.1.2) states that a society comprising perfectly competitive markets in long-run equilibrium is efficient (in the sense that no individual could be made better off without someone having to suffer a drop in utility or well-being). The implication was that total output is greater the more competitive the different industries within an economy become. However, for this to be the case, government must place no restrictions on trade between the various individuals and industries who make it up. For if it does place such restrictions, gains from trade will be lost and the national economy will be less efficient. If society wants to redistribute income from rich to poor (or indeed vice versa) it must do so by one-off transfers of wealth but without affecting the quantities traded or the prices of commodities (that was the lesson from the second welfare theorem – see Section 8.1.4).

Now, instead of thinking in terms of a single country which consists of many industries, let us think big: think of the whole world as a collection of many countries which, in turn, consist of many industries. It only takes a small leap of the imagination to see how the first theorem of welfare economics can be extended: world output (and therefore income) is greater the more competitive the world economy is and the fewer restrictions there are for trade between the various countries (a simple extension of the first theorem of welfare economics) – a blueprint for free trade at the international level. And if the international community wants to redistribute world income from the rich to the poor countries, then they should not do so by altering the prices of traded commodities or the quantities traded, but instead they should directly transfer wealth to the poorer nations (again the second theorem of welfare economics).

In practice this means the following: do not allow countries (rich or poor) to introduce import-tariffs (i.e. taxes on imported commodities) or import-quotas (i.e. limits on the quantity of a commodity that is allowed to be imported) or subsidies (i.e. State payments to companies for producing certain amounts of commodities). Rather, keep the trade routes open and free and let free trade make the whole world richer. If the richer countries worry that the Third World is too wretched and poor, then they ought to give them more direct aid; especially the type of aid that helps them produce more goods which they can trade in the international market. For goodness sake, do not let them make the mistake of thinking that they can improve their situation by protecting their own industries through artificial barriers to external competition (e.g. tariffs, quotas or subsidies).

The above summarises the spirit of the 1995 GATT agreement (the 'general agreement on tariffs and trade') and of the World Trade Organization. A central pillar of this viewpoint is that developing and developed countries alike should not be allowed to protect their fledgling industries from the ruthless foreign competition. Why? We can see why by returning, again, to the model of welfare in Chapter 8: if one country protects its industry by raising a wall around it (either by introducing tariffs/quotas or subsidies), then others will follow suit. The result will be a world-wide loss of trade which will lead to less international competition and therefore lower world output and higher prices. *All* will then suffer, including the developing countries.

Observe that this is another rendition of the free-rider problem discussed in the box on p. 232. Each country would be better off in a world where no one imposes trade restrictions (than in a world were all did) but, none the less, each country has an incentive to impose restrictions regardless of what others do. Thus there is a strong temptation for a war on free trade to commence and that temptation must be resisted by means of some international agreement which forces all countries to keep trade routes free. The recent GATT is meant to serve this purpose.

Now that we have seen how the neoclassical theory of social welfare can be readily extended to engender a free-trade agenda for the world, we can examine what the critics of neoclassicism have to say on the matter. Those who doubt the capacity of market economies automatically to achieve optimal outcomes, would point out (as they did throughout Part 3 of Book 1) that it is one thing to show that competitive markets in long-run equilibrium are efficient and it is quite another to show that removing barriers to trade will boost competition and increase world output.

For instance, many will argue that world markets are dominated by relatively few, huge, multinational oligopolies. They dominate the markets in smaller countries in particular in which they dump cheap imports until they gain an unassailable monopoly. Then they restrict output (as all monopolies do – see Section 5.2.3), raise prices and achieve high profit rates. In such cases, if the government introduces a tariff on imports, the multinational firm may be encouraged to produce locally (to avoid the tariffs). In short, for those who do not believe that untrammelled markets are naturally competitive, carefully selected tariffs and subsidies can have positive effects for those countries who use them without posing a significant problem for world trade.

Finally those of a Marxist disposition understand international trade and the development of Third World countries in ways which reflect their fundamental model of capitalism. Briefly, they see capitalism as a system which is riddled with contradictions and inefficiencies. Generally speaking (and especially so during recessions) developed capitalism suffers from chronic tendencies towards over-capacity; that is, the economy, spurred on by rapid technological advances tends to produce more than it can absorb. As a result western firms are desperate for new markets both for their commodities but also for cheaper inputs (labour and raw materials). If they do not secure access to such markets, the impending domestic profit crisis will hit them hard (see Section 10.3.3). Consequently the Third World becomes the receptacle of unwanted western commodities which are dumped at prices low enough to ensure that no autonomous local capacity ever takes hold.

The excess capacity of the developed countries, in combination with free trade, acts as a continuous restraint on local development. The only economic activities encouraged by this combination are those involving the exploitation of raw materials and labour. Because of limited competition, rudimentary markets and the corruption of officials who are often on the payroll of the western multinationals, Third World resources are bought by multinationals for next to nothing. The result is the continuing dislocation of local communities as badly paid workers coalesce in the industrial areas (usually in slumps outside big cities). Because of the monopoly (and monopsony) power of the multinationals, growth in such countries does not mean the improvement of living standards, but the expansion of the slums around the cities. The development of underdevelopment, as some economists have labelled this type of growth. For them, free trade is the Third World's freedom to lose and to descend into greater misery.

Of course, there are other developing countries which contradict this picture (e.g. the countries of South East Asia). Marxists who do not espouse this view of the 'development of underdevelopment' point to the minority of developing countries which, for historical reasons, have recently experienced serious industrial development (often because they were selected for that purpose by multinational companies). Why have some Third World countries (e.g. the South East Asian economies) taken off? One possible reason is that, as new commodities are invented which require more high-tech production lines (e.g. super-computers), some of the older goods whose production has become straightforward (e.g. television sets) are no longer economical to produce in the West (or Japan). Thus the western (or, more likely, the Japanese) production lines concentrate on the newer, more complex to produce commodities with a higher market value, while whole production lines of the older products are shipped out to these developing countries (e.g. Malaysia, Korea).

Although such an export of older industrial sectors gives rise to significant growth in the host nations, only a relatively small number of countries have benefited in this way. Those which did went through a period (about twenty years long) of believing that growth had become a permanent feature of their society (e.g. South Korea). Soon however they realised what the developed world had been made to grasp, painfully, long before: The more a capitalist economy develops the more crisis-prone it becomes. Moreover the industrialisation of such countries was often accompanied by the deindustrialisation of certain regions within developed countries; mainly the older industrial areas in which the industrial revolution started one or two centuries ago (e.g. the Midlands and the North of England). It is as if bits of the Third World have been exported to the older industrial regions of the First World. In the end, a rich elite of capitalists grows richer by tapping into wealth created by workers in different parts of the world. However, their continuing capacity to extract these 'rents' depends on a patchwork of highly industrialising formerly underdeveloped countries which coexist with massive Third World immiseration as well as the deindustrialisation of the older industrial regions of the First World. Through this prism, international trade is *one* of the planks of an international capitalist system which thrives on exploitation and wastes monumental proportions of the world's human and natural resources.

In the final analysis, economics is like music. Once you have become familiar with a particular genre or composer, you can easily recognise a piece written in that style or by that person even if you have never heard it before. The purpose of this book was to give you enough of an insight into the foundations of the main schools of economic thought so that, when you hear some economist or politician tell you, using fancy terms, that *their* ideas are apolitical, objective, free of any bias, and true, you will know better. You will, I hope, see through their rhetoric and be able to pinpoint their underlying philosophy, recognise where they are coming from (are they neoclassical, new-right followers of von Hayek and Nozick, Keynesians or Marxists?) and unmask them. Of all the clichés, *Knowledge is Power* is the truest.

Book 2

Anxieties

Does economic theory matter?

11.1 Criticising assumptions: useful appraisal or romantic time-wasting?

From the very beginning, the Preface even, this book adopted a critical posture. Chapter 4 dedicated page upon page to attacking the economist's favourite assumption, namely that individuals are modelled best as utility maximisers. It traded on the thought that human beings are far more complex and rational creatures than the economics textbook would know. Chapter 7 took the fight to the realm of firms and markets by arguing that the neoclassical assumptions on what constitutes production, labour, capital and competition miss the mark. Chapters 9 and 10 completed the crusade by suggesting that societies inhabited by people whose behaviour and aspirations are compatible with the neoclassical assumptions cannot have a common purpose. Could all this criticism be a complete waste of time, even if not without a basis in truth?

Consider the following scene. A neoclassical economist enters the stage, having read all the criticisms in this book, and with an ironic grin tells me in front of all my readers:

> 'Well done, well done. Congratulations on a brilliant attack on what matters not one bit! Of course you are right. I would not want *my* children, or indeed those of anyone else, to be utility maximisers in the mould of those pathetic creatures in Chapter 2. And of course no real market resembles what we call perfect competition in Chapter 5. You are right about all these things. Unfortunately, my friend, you have missed the point of all this quite badly. We are not philosophers, psychologists or historians. Yes, philosophers have better ideas than

we economists about the human condition. So do psychologists. And future economic historians will give us, in good time, better accounts on how actual markets operate today than any economist's model.

What you seem to have forgotten however is that we economists are in business in order to create, not philosophy, history or anything else, but economics! Assumptions are just assumptions. Yes, I confess, usually these are pretty silly. Nevertheless an economic theory needs them in order to predict *something* tangible which can then be put to the test. At the end of the day, however, the theory is as good as its predictions – not its assumptions. It is, consequently, nonsensical to get all worked up about the character of the individual in Chapter 2 (as you do in Chapter 4) or the assumptions about the competitive market in Chapter 5 (as you do in Chapter 7). If these, admittedly stupid (or to be less emotive, these simplistic) assumptions produce a theory that predicts the price of lemons, cars and space rockets well, then this is all we need to know. Intellectual attacks against assumptions are meaningless since theories cannot be sustained by logical discourse: only facts and observation can give credence to, or alternatively damn, a theory.

Oops! This sounds like a devastating critique of all the criticisms that I have exposed you to in this book. Have I over-reacted wasting time and space with criticisms that, in the end, do not matter even if sound? Are assumptions just convenient building blocks whose truth-status does not matter much? Is my neoclassical colleague right in saying that an economic theory as such is irrelevant and the only thing that matters is its predictions? Before we try to answer these questions, let us look at the origins of the above argument.

My (hypothetical) neoclassical colleague's line of argument is consistent with what is known in philosophy as *Positivism*. Positivism itself is a branch of an older tradition called *Empiricism* and, for the purposes of our discussion, the two terms may be used interchangeably (see the next box). The dominant trait of both is a denial that anything can be known about the world a priori, that is without the benefit of experience.

Historically, Positivism must be seen as a healthy reaction to the dogmatism of the Church during the Middle-Ages. It countered the dictum *have faith and do not enquire into the eternal truths that the Church has exclusive access to* with another dictum, *question everything and accept no thought as a priori truth* (that is truth that is not underpinned by experimentation and observation).

Effectively, Galileo's defiance of the Church and his discovery that the earth revolves around its own axis is an early example of Positivism at work. A great deal of knowledge was made possible by the emergence of Positivism. Summing up, the history of the world appears to a positivist as a series of states in which there exist discernible patterns. The denial of a priori knowledge implies that no event is inevitable; everything *could* have been different. Logic and Reason on their own are incapable of disclosing which

---

Empiricism and posivitism defined

Empiricism

A family of theories to the effect that experience, mainly sensory, rather than reason or innate ideas, as claimed by rationalists (see the boxes on pp. 346–7), is the source of knowledge. Radical empiricism, which limits our knowledge strictly to the contents of our experience, is sceptical about even our most ordinary claims to knowledge.

Positivism

A philosophical offshoot of empiricism, traceable to Auguste Comte (1798–1857), that all genuine knowledge is based on sense experience and extended by means of systematic experimentation alone.

---

of all possible worlds we live in. Knowledge could be created a priori only if there was a single possible world.

Hence, since an infinity of possible worlds exists, we have to turn exclusively to observation if we are to discover the universe. Moreover, although we can observe that something is so, we can never claim that it *must* be so. For instance, the so-called Law of Diminishing Marginal Utility is not at all a law. It is just an observation of a relationship between consumption and marginal utility that often happens to be of the inverse kind, although it could have been a positive relation. The above can be summarised in two statements that define the Positivist method:

1   *Knowledge must be based on experience. Hence, a theory is to be judged only according to the accuracy of its predictions.*
2   *Whatever we observe could have been different.*

Therefore prediction is, according to Positivism, the only weapon we have in our struggle against ignorance: *To predict is to explain* or *Truth is what works!*

So far so good. The problems begin when Positivism is transplanted from early physics (i.e. classical mechanics) to modern physics (e.g. optics, quantum mechanics) and, more so, to the social sciences in general and economics in particular. The relevance of Positivism to economics is highlighted by the free-market enthusiast Milton Friedman (whose Nobel Prize-winning attacks on Keynesian ideas, as well as the setting up of a whole school of like-minded economists at the University of Chicago, have made him a guru of right-wing economics).

Friedman points out that: 'Positivism provides a system of generalisations that can be used to make correct predictions about the consequences

---

In favour of empiricism

As an empiricist I continue to think of the conceptual scheme of science as a tool, ultimately, for predicting future experience in the light of past experience.

Willard Quine, *From a Logical Point of View*, 1961

Indeed, such inadequacies as we have seemed to find in empiricism have been discovered by strict adherence to a doctrine by which empiricist philosophy has been inspired: that all human knowledge is uncertain, inexact and partial. To this doctrine we have not found any limitation whatever.

Bertrand Russell, *Human Knowledge: Its scope and limits*, 1948

---

of any change in circumstances.' In other words, a theory of consumer choice has only one intention: to predict how various changes will affect consumer demand. And how is it to be judged? Adopting an impeccable positivist line, Friedman adds that 'it is to be judged by its predictive power for the class of phenomena which it is intended to explain' (*Methodology of Positive Economics*, 1953).

On positivism

In favour

Each branch of our knowledge passes successively through three different theoretical states: the theological or fictitious, the metaphysical or abstract, and the scientific or positive . . . Since Bacon, all good intellects have agreed that there is no real knowledge save that which rests on observed facts.

Auguste Comte, *A General View of Positivism*, 1848

Against

Empiricism used to mean reliance on the past; now apparently all empirical truth regards only the future, since truth is said to arise by the verification of some presumption. Presumptions about the past can evidently never be verified; at best they may be corroborated by fresh presumptions about the past, equally dependent for their truth on a verification which in the nature of

---

> the case is impossible. Consistency is a jewel; and, as in the case of other jewels, we may marvel at the price some people will pay for it. In any case, we are led to this curious result: that radical empiricism ought to deny that any idea of the past can be true at all.
>
> George Santayana (1863-1952),
> *Character and Opinion in the United States*, 1921

In other words, forget about the implications of assumptions and ignore the despicable character of *Homo economicus*; neither the former nor the latter matter. What is important is the ability of the theory to predict prices and quantities correctly. If it does not, then Friedman would, presumably, agree that the model must go. But if it is accurate, then regardless of its assumptions, we must accept and use it. Unfortunately for positivists, things are not that straightforward.

11.2 The impossible task of separating the facts from the theory

Suppose we accept the positivist approach and set out to put a theory to the test. Surely, we must determine what the theory predicts, compare it with reality and come to a conclusion. Alas, this is not as good an idea as it sounds. For if we followed such a practice, many a good theory would have been unfairly discarded. Take the hypothesis that the demand curve for milk is downward sloping (i.e. the lower the price the greater the quantity sold). Now imagine that I gave you data from Europe in the mid-1980s showing that over a prolonged period of time, both prices and sales of milk were falling consistently. What conclusion do you draw? Do you surmise that the demand curve is upward sloping and thus reject the theory?

That would be unfair. If you had looked more closely at the time-frame of the data-set, you would have discovered that it was marked by the Chernobyl nuclear disaster in April 1986, which spread a radioactive cloud over Europe, causing anxiety about the quality of milk for years afterwards. Prices and quantities were falling because the demand curve began to shift down and to the left (and not because it was upward sloping). Clearly, a theory under test must be given a fair chance. But what is a fair test?

Positivists use the *ceteris paribus* (Latin for 'other things being equal') clause in order to deal with this problem. This means that we are not supposed to compare experience with what a theory predicts but, instead, with what the theory predicts if *ceteris* are *paribus*, that is, provided everything the theory assumes to be constant remains constant (e.g. that no nuclear contamination takes place between changes in the price of milk, that the supply of milk is constant, that people's taste for milk is unchanged, etc.).

But even this amendment to the positivist test is not enough. Consider the simple theory that a rational pedestrian who wishes to cross a road does not knowingly jump in front of a moving bus. If we happen to witness an incident where a person did exactly that under the influence of LSD, it would again be silly to reject the theory. So we must revise our testing ground further; we must compare experience not with what the theory predicts, nor with what it predicts if *everything else is constant* (the *ceteris paribus* clause), but with what it predicts if everything else is constant *and* the individual(s) concerned is (are) rational.

Heisenberg's principle of indeterminacy (1927)*

Modern physicists are sceptical about positivism. They have discovered that on many occasions 'objects' behave differently in the laboratory depending on the type of questions (or theories) that scientists ask (test). For example, in experiments designed to test the wave properties of light, light behaves like a wave. But in experiments designed to test its particle properties, it behaves as if it is made out of particles (instead of being a wave). Thus the theory's assumptions are not *independent* of the phenomenon observed and therefore it is not straightforward to test the theory by means of observation of how well it predicts behaviour.

(*Werner Karl Heisenberg (1901–76))

The above warns that positivism may be more problematic in the social sciences than in the natural sciences. In classical mechanics or chemistry (although not in quantum mechanics or optics: see box above), a theory's predictions on the properties or behaviour of some object (e.g. a pendulum or a chemical) can be compared fruitfully against the observed properties or behaviour of the object under study. If the two concur, the theory passes the test. Otherwise the theorist returns to the drawing board. Why is laboratory experimentation a legitimate means of getting to the truth about a theory's merits? The answer is because

1   the theory is not compatible with all possible experimental results (e.g. if no heat is produced, there is no way the chemist can claim that her theory predicted that outcome), and

2   the phenomenon under observation is *independent* of the theory's predictions. For example, when the chemist predicts that heat will be generated if substance X is mixed with substance Y, these substances

do not care! They will produce heat (when mixed together) only if this is what they always do (when mixed together) and totally independently of the chemist's theories.

So because of (1) and (2) the chemist's theory can be tested effectively (that is, deemed plausible, proved right or rejected) in the laboratory.

Can economists test their theories as effectively as our chemist above? It is unlikely that they can, for the simple reason that their theories are so structured that no observation can contradict them. To see this, consider again the simple theory: 'If rational, Jill will wait until the bus passes before crossing the road'. If Jill gets run over by the bus, the economist can retain the theory but blame its predictive failure on Jill's irrationality. Thus because the economist's definition of what a rational Jill will do is *assumed* (rather than tested), the observed facts cannot possibly pass straightforward judgment on the theory. In terms of the previous paragraph, economic theories respect neither of the two conditions (1) or (2) for fruitful empirical testing.

Social predictions and social reality: a science-fiction perspective

In his brilliant science-fiction novel *Foundation* (1951), Isaac Asimov told the story of a scientist who created a new discipline called *psychohistory*. His achievement was a capacity to predict human history with remarkable accuracy. However, he soon realised that the theory could *never* work if people had access to it. For if the rulers (or whoever) could use it in order to predict the future, they would act on these predictions and ensure that events would unfold in a manner that the theory had not predicted. So Asimov's hero, in order to guarantee that future generations of his disciples would have the advantage of accurate predictions, set them up on a planet in some isolated corner of the universe and prevented them from having more than minimal access to *psychohistory's* predictions. Their capacity to see the political and economic future depended on not being able to see too much of it.

Asimov's *psychohistory* offers us an excellent parable of the impossibility of modelling empirical testing in social science on the practices of natural scientists. In classical physics, meteorology and chemistry, the theory and the predictions of the scientists does not affect the phenomenon under observation. For instance, if the best meteorologist in the world predicts that there will be a hurricane in New York tomorrow, the probability of that event occurring will not be influenced by the fact that the meteorologist made this prediction. However, in social science, it may well do. If a celebrated stock exchange analyst predicts that the New York stock exchange will collapse tomorrow, it may very well collapse. However, this does not mean that the underlying theory was correct because the prediction was accurate; the analyst could have been joking!

In conclusion, in the social world, predictions are an integral part of the world (and the facts) we try to explain. Asimov's interesting story illustrates how an excellent social theory can become so intertwined with the social world that it fails to predict because it is so good. Thus a social theory is not necessarily as good as its predictions.

Looking at the same problem from another angle, the argument that assumptions do not matter (i.e. what *really* matters is how good the predictions are) is plainly false since, in economics, the assumptions are an integral part of the prediction (which is not the case in early nineteenth-century physics). We already saw how the prediction about Jill was conditional on her being something called 'rational': 'If Jill is rational, her preferences stable, and her purchasing power was maintained constant, she will choose more milk when its price declines.' Suppose now that the price declines and she buys more. Has the prediction been proved wrong? Not necessarily.

For instance it could be that, just before the price fell, she changed her mind about milk, deciding that she did not like it as much anymore. Thus the fact that she bought less does not contradict the prediction in the previous paragraph, which was conditional on Jill's preferences remaining unchanged. However, this means that such predictions can *never* be proved wrong since there is always some explanation of why the hypothesis could be valid but the subject failed to behave according to it (e.g. her preferences changed, or she experienced a momentary lapse of reason, etc.)

In conclusion, we have reason to fear that in economics it is difficult to take theories (e.g. the *Equi-marginal Principle*) and create predictions out of them which, when compared with the 'facts', will tell us whether the theory is good or false. The reason is that predictions in economics are impossible to separate from the assumptions that we want to assess. Whereas in physics a theory of electro-magnetic fields gives rise to predictions which can be tested in the laboratory in a manner that can verify or refute the theory, in economics no such tests exist. Why? Because if human beings do not behave according to the theory's predictions, economists are forced to do something that chemists cannot do: blame the humans, or their beliefs for the theory's predictive failure. Then they can modify predictors accordingly in order to accommodate the observed behaviour. By contrast, chemists and physicists cannot blame molecules and atoms for failing to behave according to the rules which ought to govern their behaviour. The downside for economists is that, even though no one can prove them wrong, they forfeit any claims to empirically verifiable positions.

11.3 Why economic theories cannot be judged by the facts

Consider the basic hypothesis of the neoclassical approach: 'All rational people are maximisers.' In this book I have spent many pages debating the merits of this theory as well as its political implications. Why do we not skip all this talk and find out whether this proposition is true or not? How do we do this? There are indeed many tests we can conduct in laboratories to find out if people behave in a manner consistent with the principles of utility maximisation. The problem is that such tests are not likely to settle the debate in favour or against the neoclassical hypothesis that people are maximisers. We have already had a glimpse of this problem in Section 11.2.

If people turn out not to maximise utility, neoclassical economists can modify their hypothesis subtly, for example they may put forward the amended hypothesis: 'There is *something* that people maximise.' Perhaps there is. The problem is that this hypothesis can *never* be refuted, nor can it be verified (see box below). If we establish that people do not maximise utility, the defender of neoclassical economics can always turn around and say: 'But how do you know that there is not *something* that they maximise?' The answer is: we cannot know. Thus the hypothesis that people maximise cannot be proved wrong (i.e. refuted) in which case we have a theory motivating all economic textbooks which is beyond the empiricists' and positivists' method of theory appraisal.

Verifiable and refutable theories

A theory is *verifiable* if it can be proved true when true. For example, the theory that 'there are some firms which have no capacity to alter prices' is verifiable. If we find one such firm, the theory has been confirmed.

A theory is *refutable* if it can be proved false when false. For example, 'all firms can substitute labour for machines without losing output'. If we find one firm for which this is not so, the theory has been refuted.

The theory 'all people maximise something' is neither verifiable nor refutable.

Actually it is no accident that the foundations of neoclassical economics cannot be tested. Shielding one's theory from empirical testing is one way of defending it, of making it immune to criticism. And it is not only neoclassical economics that has done this. Marxist economics is also founded on propositions which are untestable in the laboratory or statistically (e.g. the claim that the source of profit is the difference between the value of labour and the value of labour time). In general, the most important aspects of different schools of thought are assumptions which are deliberately put beyond empirical testing.

Let us examine three examples which illustrate the main point: *economic debates cannot be settled empirically*, that is by observing the facts through experimentation or statistical analysis. Consider the following three economic hypotheses, two neoclassical and one Marxist.

11.4 Three examples of untestable economic theories

11.4.1 Theory 1: the *Equi-marginal Principle* in consumption

Consider the case of optimal individual choices as modelled in Chapter 2. Jill is supposed to purchase more apples if their price drops and her income is adjusted in a way that her utility level has remained constant (that is, she remains on the same indifference curve). Neoclassical theory predicts unequivocally that, because her indifference curve between apples and all other goods is downward sloping, she should increase her consumption of apples. (This is also known as the *substitution effect*.)

What if Jill does not buy more apples under these circumstances? Do we reject the theory, or do we defend the theory by suggesting that her behaviour was due to the fact that either Jill actually dislikes apples (i.e. her indifference curves between apples and all other goods are not convex to the origin and downward sloping), or Jill has had a bad day at the office and did not really think about her purchase carefully (that is, she did not choose rationally)?

Our capacity to defend the theory even if it fails to predict Jill's behaviour makes the theory untestable: if it is proved correct then it is accepted, but if it proved wrong then it is the fault of the economic agent. Heads I win, tails you lose. The positivist approach leads to the recommendation of a test that is decisive only when sympathetic to the theory. It is like establishing a system of justice which would treat verdicts as just only when they are favourable to the defence!

11.4.2 Theory 2: the *Equi-marginal Principle* in production

Economics textbooks build their theory of the firm on a proposition which has proved rather contentious: firms maximise profit! Volumes upon volumes have been written as to whether this is a wise approach to what firms do. Is it all a waste of space and time? For instance, a positivist would argue that this is an empirical issue. Let us examine how we could put the neo-classical hypothesis to the test.

We need to test the hypothesis that *All firms tend to maximise profit* (statement 1). Neoclassical theory, as we saw in Chapter 5, derives from statement 1 a second analytical statement: *profit is at a maximum when marginal cost equal marginal revenue* (statement 2). The problem is that we cannot test both statements simultaneously. For example, if we assume that profit is maximised when marginal cost equals marginal revenue, we can test by means of careful measurement and observation the hypothesis that all firms maximise profit. Similarly, if we assume that firms tend to maximise profit, we can test the hypothesis that firms set marginal cost equal to marginal revenue.

Evidently, in order to test one of the statements we must assume the other. But that means that we either take for granted that firms maximise profit (in which case we do not put the maximisation hypothesis to the test), or we assume that marginal cost and marginal revenue are equal at the level of output that maximises profit (in which case we cannot test the *Equi-marginal Principle* in production).

The problem with the inability to test the two statements simultaneously is that when the facts do not fit one statement then we can blame that failure to predict on some problem with the second statement which is not being tested. For instance if firms assumed to set marginal cost equal to marginal revenue are shown to act in a manner that does not maximise profit, then the theorist can argue that the reason why this is so may have to do with uncertainty over (for example) marginal revenue which prevented the firm from setting marginal cost equal to marginal revenue.

In the final analysis, the thought that firms set marginal costs equal to marginal revenue, and by so doing maximise profits, is not testable.

11.4.3 Theory 3: Marx's theory of profit

As we saw in previous chapters, according to Marx, under capitalism all economic value springs from human labour and therefore *all* profit comes from the difference (retained by employers) between the value of workers' labour and the value of their time. Ostensibly this sounds like a hypothesis that can be put to the test. However this is not as straightforward as it seems. The reason is that Marx's theory comprises two (or more) hypotheses that cannot be tested simultaneously (just like we could not test the two statements together in the case of the *Equi-marginal Principle* in the theory of the firm above).

In the case of Marx's theory, the two statements are: *All economic value comes from human labour* (statement 1) and *All profit comes from the difference between the value of labour and the value of labour time* (statement 2). Again perhaps we can study the extent to which the second statement is true empirically by constructing measures of profit and observing how they fluctuate in time or from industry to industry.

Suppose however that the second statement is predicting badly, e.g. we find that profit increased when the difference between the value of labour and the value of labour time shrunk. Do we reject the theory? Its opponents would want us to. Its defenders, on the other hand, might blame the profit measures used for not having been constructed in accordance to the theory's assumptions (e.g. that profit reflects values determined in competitive capitalist markets). Again one cannot pin down the theory by testing one of its hypothesis if empirical failure (i.e. failure to predict) can be blamed on other hypotheses of the theory that are not, at that time, being tested.

In conclusion, we *cannot* test both statements simultaneously which means that Marx's vision of capitalism (just like the neoclassical views above) cannot be proved right or wrong by empirical means.

11.5 How do we find out the truth when the 'facts' are too compromised?

In Chapter 1 I drew a comparison between the research agenda of classical mechanics and neoclassical economics (see the boxes on p. 33). The last step in each (Step 4) was to discover the worth of the theory by putting it to the test. However, as we discovered in this chapter, this step cannot be taken in economics with the aplomb that physicists are used to.

On the one hand, we have no laboratory in which to control the conditions under which our economic data is usually derived. But even when, as economists, we do perform experiments in a laboratory (an increasingly fashionable pursuit) we are still stuck with human beings who bring all sorts of ideas with them in it; ideas that we cannot control in the same way that physicists do. Moreover, because economics deals with people, any test of economic theory must be based on the presumption that our subjects (i.e. the people whose behaviour we are observing) are rational. The problem is that we are not sure ourselves what that means (see the debate in Chapter 4). Even if some of us are confident that we know what rationality means (e.g. the neoclassical economists who are content with the idea of *instrumental rationality* in Chapter 2), we cannot put these ideas of ours to the test.

The reason is that the neoclassical view of rationality is too sketchy, based as it is on the assumption that objectives are fixed and that all that it takes to be rational is that one deploys one's means efficiently. Hence if the facts do not support the theory it is very easy to assume that subjects, after all, had different objectives. One can always concoct a set of objectives that will explain any observed behaviour. Moreover whereas a physicist cannot normally blame atoms for not behaving as they should, or for not obeying the rules governing their own behaviour, the economist can always salvage a theory by blaming its failure on irrationality.

Politically inspired facts

During the 1980s, the British Conservative government changed the definition of an 'unemployed person' dozens of times. With every redefinition, the rate of unemployment 'fell'.

In Australia in 1997, the newly elected conservative coalition government considered changing the official measurement of inflation by excluding interest payments and other prices 'not determined by consumer markets'. The reason was that doing so would reduce the reported inflation rate and the government would save about A$400 million as the inflation-linked benefits to unemployed, pensioners, mothers, etc. would not grow as fast. The moral of the story is that macro-economic variables are not only difficult to measure objectively; governments do not want them to be measured objectively either!

On the other hand, it is not just the problems that we encounter in an economic laboratory which stop us from assessing economic theories by looking at how well they predict. As economists we cannot even agree on the economic facts 'out there' (e.g. data on inflation, unemployment, etc.) because they are based on untested, controversial, and politically motivated economic theory. So, what do we do? How can we approach economic reality? If we cannot appeal to the 'facts' as the adjudicator between different economic theories, how can we decide which theory is right and which wrong?

Rationalist appraisal of economic theories

What assigns economics its peculiar and unique position . . . is the fact that its particular theorems are not open to verifications or falsification on the grounds of experience . . . The ultimate yardstick of an economic theorem's correctness is solely reason unaided by experience.

Ludwig von Mises, *Human Action: A treatise on economics*, 1949

The preliminary answer is that my neoclassical colleague who opened up this chapter by pouring scorn on this book's commitment to theoretical debate (e.g. discussing and scrutinising assumptions in order to assess different theories) must have been ill founded. If a theory cannot, after all, be judged according to how well it predicts the 'facts', then the *substance* of theory (that is, its logical structure, its assumptions, the realism of the picture of men and women that it is painting, etc.) must be important.

Indeed there is a long tradition in western social science and philosophy which argues exactly the opposite case from that of my neoclassical critic: different theories must be compared and judged according to how logically they are structured and how much sense they make when we study them (note the complete contrast between this approach and that of empiricism/positivism). The following boxes illustrate such a view for economics. Its roots can be found in the philosophy of Rationalism.

Rationalism defined

The view that reason rather than experience is the only or the main source of knowledge, and hence that we have innate ideas, that is concepts which pre-exist or shape our first encounters with the world.

René Descartes: I think therefore I am!

When we become aware that we are thinking things, this is a primary notion which is not derived by means of any syllogism. When someone says 'I am thinking therefore I am, I exist', he does not deduce existence from thought by means of a syllogism, but recognises it as something self-evident by a simple intuition of the mind.
René Descartes, *Second Set of Replies*, 1641.

Thus, Descartes suggests that the important truths are not a matter of observation (accumulation of facts) but of logic and intuition.

The view of Ludwig von Mises in the box on p. 347, namely that we must select between competing theories using judgment and reason alone, can be traced back to the ideas of the French rationalist philosopher René Descartes, who famously ended speculation as to whether we can *prove* that we exist by saying: 'I think therefore I am'. Descartes believed that a hypothesis or theory can be judged by the use of reason and logic (see above box). It can be refuted by showing that it was wrongly deduced or by refuting whatever it was deduced from.

In contrast to the positivist/empiricist who argues that when a hypothesis is opposed by the facts it is too bad for the hypothesis, the rationalist
would argue that when logic and mathematics contradict the facts then we
must rethink the way in which we compiled our 'facts'. Descartes believed
in the unity of knowledge. He saw knowledge as a tree; philosophy was its
roots, mathematics and physics its trunk and the social sciences its branches.

According to this account, a hypothesis (such as utility maximisation)
ought to be judged, not by its predictions, but by its logical coherence.
Descartes described a hypothesis as projectible (that is, convincing) if one
could show that it was formally deduced from a theory correctly lodged
further down the tree of knowledge. The first step would be to look at
the 'roots', that is the philosophy underpinning the theory. Is it appealing?
If it is, then go up the trunk of the knowledge-tree and examine its logical/
mathematical coherence. Finally end up at the tree's branches (the social
science descriptions and prescriptions that results from the theory): do they
contain wholesome suggestions about the world we live in? A theory that
passes these conceptual tests is accepted. Otherwise we are asked to return
to the drawing board.

In a sense this is the approach I followed in the critical chapters of
Book 1 (i.e. Chapters 4, 7 and 10). The first question asked was: what is
the philosophy of the economics textbook models of individuals, firms,
markets, etc. Are they appealing? Later on I looked at the logical coherence
of these models (e.g. does it make sense to assume that having many
competing firms will *necessarily* lead price to average cost? – see Chapter 7).
Finally I examined the social implications of the models (e.g. what will a
free-market society populated by utility maximisers be like? Will it constitute
the basis for the Good Society?).

So, have we discovered, at long last, a way for deciding unequivocally
which theory is worth our while and which deserves to be discarded? No
such luck I am afraid. First, we are likely to disagree as to what philosophical foundations (roots to the tree of knowledge) are desirable and sound.
Different views on human nature will spawn different social theories. Second,
many will insist that empiricism/positivism remains our best bet even if the
'facts' are contaminated or rely too heavily on theory. Just like rationalists
accuse them of being unable to construct meaningful tests in order to distinguish between good and bad theory, they will return the compliment by
accusing rationalists of being impervious to the actual reality surrounding
them, too caught up with their 'reasoning' to notice what is happening in
the world.

Of course the truth lies somewhere in the middle. It is just as silly to
argue, like committed positivists/empiricists do, that theory by itself does
not matter at all and human reason cannot arrive at the truth as it is ludi-
crous to argue, as fanatical rationalists would, that observation is unimpor-
tant. One way of blending the importance of reasoning and the pertinence

---

Is there anybody out there?

David Hume, the great empiricist philosopher who also had a hand in creating the model of men and women in economics texts (see Chapters 1 and 3), went as far as to argue against the existence of an external world; one that exists beyond our perception. With this grand claim he sought to impress upon us that our only chance of knowledge is by trial and error. Modern doubts about empirical (e.g. laboratory) tests give another spin to this claim. Consider the Heisenberg principle on p. 340. Physicists have concluded that in so far as a quantum entity behaves as either a wave or a particle, it does so in response to the kind of question we ask of it. In an experiment testing its wave properties, a quantum will behave as a wave. And in an experiment testing its particle properties it will act as a particle. But since everything in the cosmos consists of quantum entities, and since they cannot be proved to exist 'objectively', or to be 'real', then there is a temptation to conclude that the world exists *because* we are watching it. Against this dead-end of empiricist thinking, Descartes' contribution is a breath of fresh air: I think therefore I do not need to prove to myself or to anyone else that I exist. And if this is so, I can (through the power of my reasoning) understand the world and the fact that it exists *independently* of my senses.

The man who insists on proof is the man who never learns how wrong he is

Karl Popper, *Objective Knowledge*, 1972

---

of observation is to say that, although facts have to be discerned from the world around us, they can only be understood by means of judgment of the evidence in the context of a theory which is soundly placed on Descartes' tree of knowledge; not by means of mechanistic calculation or observation.

In any event, it is by now clear (I hope) that every debate in economics, even debates about how to settle debates, are highly political, philosophical and ideological contests which reflect ancient differences between humans on what social life is like and how it should be changed. It would be too presumptuous and downright boring to think that all this can be solved by some simple means (either by some empirical test or a pre-ordained rationalist thought process). The theoretical battles in the social sciences, and in economics, are old, fascinating and echo the skirmishes that have characterised philosophical and political thought for centuries. As long as there is more than one perception of human nature, they will continue. The question then remains: how do we pursue knowledge? The English philosopher Francis Bacon (1561–1626) answered this monumental question metaphorically. In his *First Book of Aphorisms* he wrote:

> those who have handled sciences have been either men of experiment [NB empiricist or positivist] or men of dogmas [NB rationalist]. The men of experiment are like ants, they only collect and use; the reasoners resemble spiders, who make cobwebs out of their own substance. But the bee takes a middle course: it gathers material from the flowers of the garden and of the field but transforms and digests it by a power of its own.

The trick is to know how to be a bee in social science.

11.6 So, do economic theories matter?

For positivists (or empiricists) especially those who like Milton Friedman take instrumental rationality to its logical extreme, theories are useful tools only to the extent that they generate predictions. Nevertheless the theory and its assumptions *as such* do not matter at all. It does not matter whether we think the assumptions are sound or realistic, whether the portrayal of human beings by the theory resembles angels or devils, whether the models of production offer an accurate picture of what happens in factories. All that matters is whether these theories help us predict prices, quantities produced and sold, wages, profit, and so on.

This positivist line is often used by neoclassical economists to scuttle criticism of the realism and substance of neoclassical economic theory like that in Chapters 4, 7 and 10. If it were correct, the life of economists (and of students of economics) would be made easier. We would all compile our theories, squeeze predictions out of them and then see which set of predictions did better in the laboratory of social life. The ones that performed better would be selected and the rest would be confined to the dustbin. Moreover as a profession we would be in a position to move in unison and present the world (and our students) a common position. Just like physicists, we would all agree on the basics of our discipline reserving disagreement for new hypotheses about esoteric matters (such as black holes on the other side of the universe) which we have not had a chance to put to the test as yet.

Unfortunately economics is condemned (or perhaps blessed) to be perpetually messier. As we saw in this chapter, there is no way we can conduct ourselves like physicists. Given that our object of study (the human being and human society) is not an object at all but the most subjective of subjects, our theory is part of the world we are trying to explain, our predictions cannot be tested and our data are heavily contaminated by our theories and ideas. This messiness ensures that the core of our competing theories is beyond testing. Thus no grand theoretical perspective (e.g. Keynesianism, neoclassicism, Marxism, etc.) can be *proved* either right or wrong.

The result is that almost no economic theory has been abandoned in the past 300 years. Unlike physicists who collectively laugh at some of the earlier attempts to understand nature, long lost economic ideas can make thoroughly legitimate comebacks. The popularity of economic theory (as argued elsewhere in this book) has little or nothing to do with a confirmation of its 'scientific' value and everything to do with the political and ideological twists and turns. Meanwhile theories which have gone out of fashion retain their following in economics departments and await for a comeback. For instance the current in-vogue perspective (a neo-liberal, neoclassical based, faith in free markets) used to be, in the 1950s, 1960s and up to the mid-1970s, a pariah supported by economists who were considered either extreme or eccentric. Today it is the turn for the more interventionist, Keynesian or socialist-leaning, theorists to lie low and be branded as the eccentrics of the profession.

So, does economic theory matter? Enormously, is my answer. The reason is, of course, political. Every prime minister, president, chancellor, treasurer, even education minister, who wants to change our lives in accordance with his or her political dogmas, utilises some economic theory in order to justify their intervention (or non-intervention) in our lives. In centuries past, rulers used religion in order to legitimise their deeds. Today they use economic theory. Once upon a time, the greatest enemy was sin. Today it is economic inefficiency. In the name of fighting against it, all sorts of policies are introduced to save us from it. Behind the talk of expunging inefficiency, however, lies a web of vested interests which we are never shown, blinded as we are by the complex language of economics which is used to dress up those interests and keep us in the dark. To recall Keynes' words from the box on p. 280, 'Practical men, who believe themselves to be quite exempt from any intellectual influences, are usually the slaves of some defunct economist. Madmen in authority, who hear voices in the air, are distilling their frenzy from some academic scribbler of a few years back'.

This is the reason why we need to understand, scrutinise and demystify economic theory: in order to prevent economists from confusing us and, in so doing, assisting 'madmen (and madwomen) in authority' from toying cruelly with our lives; from impeding our participation in the shaping of society. In short, economic theory matters because it is a huge political weapon if understood by the few and looked at with ignorant fascination by the many. In this sense, those who dislike economics (and economists) perhaps have greater cause than anyone else to study economic theory carefully; at least Voltaire would think so.

Voltaire and the Bible

Voltaire, the eighteenth-century atheist French writer, used to keep a copy of the Bible on his desk. Asked why an atheist would want to do that, Voltaire remarked that, being an atheist, he needed to understand the Bible better than the faithful.

There is one final reason why economic theory matters: because it meddles, quite violently, with our idea of ourselves and of the world around us. In short, after we have studied economics we are unlikely to be the same person. That is also true for physics or literature which have a profound civilising effect on those who make an effort to plough through novels, poetry and texts on quantum mechanics. The tragedy and travesty of economics is that exposure to it is often detrimental to the character of the student. The last chapter addresses this final anxiety.

Chapter 12

The curse of economics

12.1 Economics can seriously damage your character!

It used to be said that for every school that is built, society can afford to demolish one prison. The civilising influence of education is, happily, universally acclaimed. Not only does it reduce violence but also it is a well-tried antidote against deprivation and discontent. An educated society is better off even if (monetarily) poor. And yet there seems to be one type of education which has the opposite effect on those who receive it: a modern training in economics!

The experiment's structure

Two players are asked to choose between (1) acting 'aggressively' and (2) acting 'cooperatively'. They choose simultaneously and without knowing who they are playing against. They are told that their rewards will be determined as follows:

- If you play aggressively and your opponent cooperates you get $10
- If both of you cooperate your payoff is $5
- If both of you act aggressively you receive $2
- If you cooperate when your opponent acts aggressively you get nothing

Finally they are told that the same applies to their opponent.

Experiments have confirmed what some of us have suspected for a long time: the way in which undergraduate economics is being taught has ill-effects on the character of the students. Robert Frank, an American economist, conducted a series of experiments on the effect of an economics training on our students and published the bleak results in the *Journal of Economic Perspectives* (1993) (later reported in *The Economist*). The experiments involved interactions between students which had the structure of the free-rider problem (also known as the prisoner's dilemma) in the previous box.

In brief, each subject had a choice between two strategies: be cooperative or be aggressive. Both players would be better off financially if they cooperated (i.e. if each played cooperatively) than if they both acted aggressively. However, the best monetary payoff for each player was due if she played aggressively when her opposite number cooperated. Equally, the worst outcome for one occurred when she cooperated only to find out that her opposite number played aggressively. The box summarises the structure of this experiment.

Evidently both players would be better off if they cooperated than if they clashed (each would receive $5 rather than $2). And yet neoclassical economics' definition of *instrumental rationality* recommends that players play aggressively because one is better off doing so whatever one's opponent does. Does this mean that economists recommend to their students that, given a chance, they ought to cheat and be aggressive rather than take the risk of cooperating?

Neoclassical economists will protest that this is not what they recommend. As 'scientists' they simply point out that in games such as this, *if players care about money only*, they are better off *from an individual perspective* being aggressive. Of course, they would continue, it is better if people care about things other than money; e.g. if they derive 'utility' from the benefits reaped by others, from achieving cooperation, etc. Nevertheless, if people care only about the monetary payoffs, it is (instrumentally) rational to be aggressive even though the end result is bad for all.

Robert Frank and his collaborators invited students to play this type of game and observed their behaviour. They were seated in front of computer terminals which explained the game to them and, shielded behind the anonymity made possible by the computer, played these games against opponents whom they could not see. To cut the story short, the experimenters discovered that students of economics were significantly more aggressive (and less cooperative) than students of other disciplines. Moreover they were more pessimistic about the prospects of cooperation than all the rest and more prone to cheating.

The question then arose: is it that economics attracts the less cooperative, more ruthless young persons or is it that exposure to economics makes them relatively more ruthless, pessimistic and aggressive? To find out, the experiments were repeated as follows. First, they were conducted amongst first year undergraduate students at the beginning of their studies. The sample comprised students who had chosen to major in economics and students who had chosen some other field of study. The experiments showed that there was no difference between the two cohorts in terms of their propensity to cooperate. Therefore no evidence was found supporting the hypothesis that economics attracts misanthropes. Years later, when the same students were about to graduate, the experiments were repeated. It turns out that the economics students stood out from the rest: they were more pessimistic, less cooperative, more aggressive. The conclusion is inescapable: a training in economics significantly increases the probability that a person becomes less sociable, more aggressive, less cooperative – in short, miserable.

Should we worry about this? A neoclassical economist might defend economics by arguing that we ought not to blame economics for making students smarter in their pursuit of monetary gain. This is exactly what it means to be instrumentally rational: a capacity to get what you want by cleverly deploying the means at your disposal. What is wrong with that? A number of things, is the answer. First, economics students playing the above game against economics students will end up receiving much less money than a group of otherwise educated students (e.g. philosophers or engineers) who are more cooperative (notice that mutual defection, which is more likely amongst economists yields $2 for each player as opposed to the $5 from mutual cooperation). Thus if a training in instrumental rationality fails to maximise the group's payoffs, surely it must be registered as a failure according to its very own standards (which are all about getting more for less).

Second, it seems to me that as economists we have done a major disservice to our students by pretending that we have nothing to say about what people *ought* to want and that we concentrate only on how they will get whatever it is that they crave (recall that this was the main theme of Chapter 4). For instance in the context of the game above, we saw that neoclassical economists would wash their hands of any blame concerning the aggressiveness of players and claim that, though it is better if people care about things other than money, *if* it is money that they want, it is *instrumentally rational* to be aggressive. Where is the disservice? By labelling the strategy 'be aggressive' *instrumentally rational* (and hence the strategy 'cooperate' *instrumentally irrational*), we signal to students that being a miserable aggressor is somehow worthy while to be cooperative is to be a 'sucker' (after all who wants to be irrational?). As teachers we are guilty of a major assault on our students' character; of indirectly (and thus in a most cowardly way) influencing their motivation. We should be condemned by educational authorities the world over.

12.2 Economics courses as indoctrination

12.2.1 Example 1: the economists' narrative against cooperation

Consider again the game of the previous section. As we saw, students of economics are *trained* to see the aggressive strategy as the rational choice. Is it any wonder that they learn to cooperate less and become more suspicious of others? When we ask people to play this game once against anonymous opponents (whom they will never meet or be recognised by) neoclassical economists, as we have already seen, expect that people will learn to act aggressively (since this is the *instrumentally rational*) strategy.

Suppose however that we gave players a second chance. After having made their selection, and after having found out what their opponents have chosen, we give them a chance to change their minds. How should one play then? According to neoclassical economics, a player should do the following: initially one should select the cooperative strategy in the hope that, when one's opponents find out, they will switch to the cooperative strategy. But then, during the second round, one should switch to the aggressive strategy in order to receive the maximum payoff of $10. Under no circumstances, the theory continues, should the cooperative strategy be anyone's final choice (given that 'aggressive' remains the most profitable strategy regardless of what one's opponent selects).

Consider what we teach our students: we teach them that deceit, cheating and aggression are *instrumentally rational* while everything else is *irrational*. Is this not a course in how to become a sad person? In reality we find in the laboratory that people demonstrate a remarkable tendency to switch to the 'cooperative' strategy if they find out that their opponent chose 'cooperation' in the first instance. Not economics students though. How could they when their teachers judge them according to how well they understood that *not* cheating and cooperating is reserved for the unschooled and the irrational? Do we really want to claim as a profession that we are not messing with the character of our students?

12.2.2 Example 2: the economists' dilution of the concept of social responsibility

Imagine you are walking down the street when suddenly you spot an empty can of beer on the pavement. You have a choice: (1) Take the trouble to pick it up and carry it for about 500 metres until you come across a bin. Or (2) leave it there. How do you decide? As economists we tell our students that, in such cases, people rank (1) and (2) according to the net utility (i.e. utility minus dis-utility) these options offer them (see Chapter 2). Option (1) gives a person utility from knowing that she helped clean the city up, from doing the right thing, etc. while it takes utility away because of the effort she needs to expend to remove and dispose of the empty can. Option (2) does not provide her with utility from doing good but, on the other hand, it involves no effort (and thus dis-utility) on her part either. The decision between (1) and (2) will depend on which of the two options generates most net utility.

Put yourself in the shoes of that person. Remarkably, it makes no difference whether the can is there because you dropped it accidentally or you found it lying there. The calculation of the utility from (1) or (2) is not affected by the history of the can and your involvement in its current location; bygones are bygones when it comes to utility calculations (since it is only current utility that matters). You will choose (1) if you value a clean pavement and you derive net utility from putting an effort into keeping it clean. And you will choose (2) if moving on without delay or effort is a greater priority. Notice once more that the balance of utility from the two options is the same regardless of whether you dropped the can in the first place or someone else did. The reason is that utility maximisation is a member of a family of theories which philosophers refer to as *consequentialism*; that is, a theory of action and choice which is based on the consequences (as opposed to the history or character) of actions.

Briefly, the *consequentialism* of utility maximisation (and instrumental rationality) demands that decisions are based solely on the basis of the consequences of the various options under consideration. So, in this case, the only relevant information is how much utility you will get from a can-free pavement and how much effort (i.e. dis-utility) is involved in its disposal. Nothing else matters other than the utility consequences of your actions.

When we teach our students these ideas (especially when we do so uncritically), we cannot avoid telling them indirectly yet powerfully that there

---

From empty cans to exploitation

Extending the empty can example to more disturbing cases is straight-forward. Consider a person who is wretched and poor. Do we help him financially? Yes, is the neoclassical economist's answer, if we get utility from so doing which exceeds the utility lost when the money is handed over. However, in this utilitarian logic it does not matter whether this person is poor because of reasons external to us or whether he is in such a pathetic state because we exploited him, stole his assets and set him out on the street. In effect it recommends that the exploiters bear no responsibility for the hardship that they fashion.

is no such thing as *responsibility*. It matters not whether we have littered the street, or polluted the river, when it comes to doing something about it. What matters is solely how much utility our actions will entail. The notion that individuals must pick up their own rubbish because it is their *duty* to do so, is a notion totally alien to neoclassical economics. By distancing our students from such a notion, we do them another disservice.

12.2.3 Example 3: teaching that value exists only if it can be quantified

Economists pride themselves as practical people. They like to talk in facts and figures and leave fluffy notions for the philosophers, the psychologists and the political scientists. Theoretically speaking, economists accept that the value of things cannot be quantified fully since things have value to the extent that they give people utility but utility cannot be quantified. However, entranced by the idea of the market as the great mechanism which assigns things their correct value, they tend to assume that market prices are a faithful guide to the value society attaches to various things.

This is all understandable. How else can value be measured if one accepts the main premises of neoclassical theory? Understandable it might be yet it is also worrying from a pedagogical point of view. Consider a major bush-fire which destroys acres upon acres of an ecologically vital forest. Following such devastation, the country's national accounts will register an increase in national wealth: the reason is simple. The trees, as well as the fauna and flora, which were burnt to oblivion have no market price and thus their loss would not appear in the deficit column of the nation's accounts. On the other hand, the expenditure on petrol for the fire-fighting vehicles, the fire-fighters' overtime payments, etc. will be counted as additions to someone's income and will, thus, boost the nation's total income.

What are we saying to our students? Directly (and correctly) we tell them that ecological catastrophe cannot be evaluated since the ecosystem, however valuable to humanity, has no market price. Indirectly, we tell them that as economists we care more about the fluctuations in the price of oil than about an oil spill capable of destroying the marine life of a whole ocean. Of course economists should not be blamed for the way our society is structured. If it fails to assign economic value to valuable things, it is not the messenger's (i.e. the economist's) fault.

However, economists *are* to blame for not impressing sufficiently upon students the inadequacy and irrationality of a society which is too stupid to find a way of valuing things that are evidently of monumental value to humanity, until they become someone's private property. We are also guilty of idiocy of a grand scale when we pretend that these problems can be sold by privatising the environment (that is, distributing property rights to individuals or firms). In reality all we are doing is to concoct 'solutions' compatible with mainstream economic analysis not because of their merit but because of the fact that they are consistent with the way we have been trained to think.

More generally, economists have been responsible in recent years for promoting a free-market ethos in non-market institutions and areas of social policy (schools, public hospitals, universities, etc.) whose purpose, ostensibly, is to measure the value of hitherto non-quantifiable things (e.g. the performance of teachers) in a bid to enhance efficiency but its result, very often, is to devalue those practices. In Section 10.2.2 I gave an example of how attempts (inspired by neoclassical principles) of quantifying valuable contributions in education frequently end up demoralising teachers and cheapening the educational process. As some Greek politician said in the 1960s, the numbers prosper and the people suffer. Students of economics, raised in such an environment, are trained as the apostles of this crusade for quantifying the unquantifiable and devaluing the invaluable.

12.2.4 Example 4: the economists' apology for inexcusable social failures

In March 1995 the New York stock market suffered a sharp decline. Why? Economists blamed it on the fact that too many people had jobs! Disturbing figures from the US Commerce Department showed a fall in the rate of unemployment from 5.5 per cent to 5.3 per cent and, horror of horrors, an increase in the number of jobs by 705,000. 'Many economists believe that this is dangerously close to full employment,' wrote the *International Herald Tribune*.

We saw on p. 287 that neoclassical economists, having failed to articulate a believable theory of persistent involuntary unemployment, decided that whatever unemployment exists must be *natural*. By baptising an unemployment of 10 per cent *natural*, somehow it became acceptable. After all who are we to go against nature and the natural order? This mentality is not too dissimilar to that mocked by Voltaire in his *Candide*, which features a character named Pangloss who was a committed follower of the creed that the world we live in could not be better; that it is the best of all possible worlds and, therefore, that any attempt to improve upon it is doomed and likely to make things worse.

In pure Panglossian form, the economics profession seems to have concluded (by majority rule) that, as long as inflation is kept under control, the labour market cannot be improved without a fall in wages and/or an increase in the intensity with which workers labour for their employers' benefit; that the observed rate of unemployment is *natural* as long as the price system works decently (i.e. inflation is not accelerating) and that any government attempt to reduce it is doomed. As economists we can spend years debating these matters. However, as teachers, we must pause and think about the effect of such theories on our students. Should we not be telling them: 'Unemployment is a waste and a scourge which, as economists, we have failed to understand properly; it is your job, as the next generation of economists, to help crack it'? What are we telling them instead? We tell them: 'Unemployment is natural (provided inflation is kept on a leash).' Are they to blame if, by deduction, they conclude things could not be otherwise?

Selective sensitivity

In Chapter 3 we saw how economists, worried that interpersonal utility comparisons would, perhaps, license authoritarian interventions in people's lives (e.g. if it were possible to show that Jill would get more from an apple than Jack, the State could be excused grabbing Jack's apple in order to hand it over to Jill), took the step of abandoning cardinal utility and declaring that one person's utility gains should never be used as an *economic* excuse for another person's utility loss. Commendable sensitivity to liberal ideals, one may conclude. However, contrast this sensitivity to the ease with which the economics profession is happy to support the misery of countless people following 'down-sizing' drives by governments and big business alike in pursuit of 'efficiency'. What happened to their reluctance to sanction, through their economics, interventions in people's lives which cheat them of sizeable 'utility'?

12.3 The economics profession as a priesthood

Why do we teach economics the way we do? Why do we pollute the mind of the young with the indirect indoctrination sketched out in the previous section? To answer these questions it is important to understand how disciplines evolve. They progress and establish themselves in a manner reminiscent of ant colonies or human cults. Not just economics, but every discipline (physics, mathematics, medicine, etc.) develop their institutions in a manner which reflects only partly the quest for scientific truth. It is as if the profession develops a strong collective interest which it pursues just like bee or ant colonies pursue their species interest. Ironically, the idea of a common interest, which proved so elusive within neoclassical economics in Part 3 of Book 1, returns here to explain the evolution of the economics profession.

Every profession succeeds if it manages to convince society in general and university authorities in particular that it has valuable knowledge to contribute. More precisely, to succeed a profession must establish mechanisms which do three things:

1   fence out the charlatans who masquerade as 'experts' (that is, create some monopoly power)
2   evaluate and rank each contribution according to its value (that is, form a value-system)
3   convince society of its importance (that is, create a strong demand for its wares).

Traditionally scientific societies, such as the British Royal Society, put into place systems of peer review to ensure (1) and (2). Barriers to competition from non-scientists were erected by testing younger scientists' capacity to replicate the work of more established ones. Later they were assessed on their capacity to create new knowledge and different ranks were apportioned (e.g. assistant, research fellow, professor, Nobel Prize winner). Working their way through the hierarchy of their profession, eventually they were recognised as experts in particular fields and went on to scrutinise the next generation. Thus the professions evolved as social hierarchies with their internal codes of conduct and their overall objectives.

Of course the evolution of such hierarchies does not, by itself, guarantee the profession's success. Society must be convinced that there are gains to be had from subsidising a professional hierarchy. There must be a significant demand for the profession's ideas. Prior to the industrial revolution, scientific discoveries had little value. Indeed they were valued only by royalty as a provider of interesting topics for discussion around the dinner table. When social power shifted in the direction of manufacturers (and away from the aristocracy), the natural sciences became, for obvious reasons, all the rage. Once they established their systems of peer review for inventions and discoveries, they became their own advertisement and did not need to worry about marketing their wares (i.e. task (3) in the list).

The building of bridges, the invention of the steam engine and the telephone, all the magnificent developments made possible by the new scientific disciplines, ensured that society at large apportioned enormous value to those professions. Moreover their image was kept clean and glorious by the public understanding that all those slightly weird professors and engineers had the cruel laboratory to contend with. However, far-fetched or monumental their theories may have sounded in the lecture theatre (recall that back in the nineteenth century scientific lectures were attended not only by scientists but also by socialites), their legitimacy would be proved or disproved initially in the laboratory and later at the construction site.

Unfortunately economics, in spite of the hopes of neoclassical economists, could never emulate the social evolution of the natural sciences. The main reason is that neoclassical economics was, let's face it, merely a pretend natural science. We saw in Chapters 2, 5 and 8 how economists have been trying their damnedest since the end of the nineteenth century to turn economics into a kind of social physics; to share in the glory of the natural sciences. They ingenuously adopted *instrumental rationality* and *utility maximisation* in order to cleanse economics of as much philosophy, politics, psychology and sociology as they could and modelled its foundations along the lines of the queen of the natural sciences at the time: classical mechanics (see Section 1.3). Then they set up mechanisms, not dissimilar to those of the scientific societies, for peer review and assessment of the economists' work.

This is where the similarity with the splendour of physics, chemistry, engineering and biology ends. The way neoclassical economics was wrenched out of the rest of the social sciences and the political economy tradition of Smith, Ricardo and Marx (i.e. the purge of all politics, history, philosophy, psychology) meant that many highly intelligent students of a society's economy were not interested in becoming part of the new professional economics. Unlike physics where all physicists, regardless of whether they liked or agreed with each other, belonged to the same societies and argued in the same halls, professional economists were cut off from economists unwilling to follow them down the road of neoclassical economic theory. Moreover the new structures for peer review, set up as they were to pursue and promote the new social physics (i.e. neoclassical economics), erected a huge fence separating neoclassical economists from everyone else who had interesting ideas about how society works but disagreed with the neoclassical model of individuals and of society.

This gulf between neoclassical economists and all other social theorists with an interest in how economies work, could not be mediated in the way that disputes were mediated in the natural sciences. In physics or biology, experiments and the gathering of impartial data eventually settled even the hottest of disputes. In economics the facts could not adjudicate in the same way, for reasons amply discussed in Chapter 11. The result was that the gulf between neoclassical economists and other economists grew inexorably. It grew to the extent that the two camps did not even ask the same questions about how societies and economies function.

Cordoned off from anyone who did not take kindly to its assumptions and foundations, neoclassical economics faced the task (described as (3) on p. 362) of impressing the world with its discoveries and contribution to society. It lacked the persuasive power of the natural sciences; there were no bridges, cars, aeroplanes or cures to promote the economics profession. All they had was models of spiralling complexity which, at the end of the day, promoted, by increasingly clever means, the view that the market knows best. Especially in the mid-war period, when the public *knew* that there was

---

An economist's confession

The 1996 Nobel Prize winner in economics, William Vickrey, when asked by a *Times* reporter about his 1961 paper for which he was awarded the Prize, commented: 'At best, it is of minor importance in terms of human welfare'.

---

something wrong with the free-market economy, the economics profession was finding it hard to sell itself to lay-people.

Nevertheless that same period was one of political turbulence. Capitalism was in deep crisis, while the attempts at creating a socialist alternative in the Soviet Union, as well as the encroachment of fascism in Europe and elsewhere, gave economics a special place on the public stage. Neoclassical economics appeared as the defender of 'liberal' capitalism. Even if it could offer no cure to the gigantic problems of the times, its value as the 'scientific ideology' of capitalism was appreciated by universities and large parts of the social hierarchy. The economics profession survived those lean years. Moreover it prospered later when the iconoclastic Keynes imbued it with some of the forgotten political and philosophical ideas of the nineteenth century and, in so doing, raised hopes that economists could actually help society avoid many pitfalls.

And so the profession continued in the post-Second World War era (see also Section 10.1 for more on the historical path of economics since the war). The 1950s saw the development of the most important mathematical results of neoclassical economics (e.g. the complex theorems on which the welfare theorems discussed in Chapter 8 are founded). Their creators (economists like Kenneth Arrow, Gerard Debreu and later Frank Hahn) did not live under the illusion that their mathematics described the economy. They knew perfectly well that they were simply discovering the mathematical conditions under which certain theorems could be proved. Frank Hahn (b. 1925), to give one example, wrote:

> The great virtue of mathematical reasoning in economics is that by its precise account of assumptions it becomes crystal clear that application to the 'real world' could be at best provisional . . . the task we set ourselves after the last war, to deduce all that was required from a number of axioms, has almost been completed, and while not worthless has only made a small contribution to our understanding.
>
> (Hahn, 'Rerum cognescere causas', 1996)

No matter what the real creators of neoclassical economics thought, this brand of theory was unstoppable. By the time the heretical ideas of Keynes had been expunged from the profession (following the political and economic developments of the 1970s and 1980s), and the socialist alternative in Eastern Europe had collapsed (in the early 1990s), the neoclassical project had succeeded almost totally. Its mathematical theorems, which even its creators dismissed as inappropriate for assessing the economic reality of capitalism, were hailed as the biblical scrolls on which the free-market faith was founded. Taken totally out of their mathematical context, the first two theorems of welfare economics (see Chapter 8) have been underpinning every right-wing political turn. The neoclassical orthodoxy's opponents are marginalised, all textbooks are written in the spirit of neoclassicism, students are taught nothing else the world over and journalists interview neoclassically trained (yet not necessarily educated) economists (who lack the subtle understanding of neoclassical theory's limits of an Arrow, a Debreu or a Hahn) every time the stock exchange goes into a spin or inflation figures come in. Even though neither the journalist, nor our students, like the neoclassical economists (who have very little of interest to say about the real world journalists must report on or students are interested in), they are immersed in neoclassical rhetoric to the extent that they find it hard to think differently or to engage with ideas which do not simply reduce to 'more markets'. This political tide silenced the voices not only of the opponents of neoclassical models but also of their creators (see box below) whenever the latter cautioned that their economic theories could not be used to draw conclusions about the economy.

A creator ignored by the worshippers of his creation

Gerard Debreu (b. 1921) who, with Kenneth Arrow, proved some of the most significant welfare theorems of neoclassical economics says that 'the theory . . . is logically entirely disconnected from its interpretations.' Yet those practising neoclassical economics seem to forget this and issue all sorts of recommendations on economic policy (e.g. reduce wages, cut government expenditure, etc.) claiming that this is what Debreu's theory suggests!

The victory of capitalism over socialism during the 1980s and 1990s was echoed by another smaller victory in the corridors of social science faculties: the domination of (neoclassical) economics over the rest of the social sciences. Nowadays even sociologists, political scientists, anthropologists and historians learn the model of human behaviour in Chapter 2 and try to use it in their disciplines. Why? Neoclassical economists would argue that the reason is the superiority of their analysis. As my critical chapters suggest, I do not agree. More likely, the one feature of neoclassical economics which makes it successful in today's society is the fundamental claim to be offering an apolitical, totally objective and rational theory of society. Some of us may think that these are false claims but they are, none the less, significant ones. Indeed I am convinced that the popularity of neoclassical economics has nothing to do with its contribution in helping us understand or improve society (which I think to be non-existent) and everything to do with its *image* as a scientific, mathematised and therefore apolitical defender of the social status quo.

To illustrate this point, suppose that limited funds are to be distributed amongst sociologists, philosophers or economists. The sociologists, in their application, promise to use the money to investigate the evolution of different layers within the middle classes with a particular focus on the effect of internal migration. The philosophers propose to organise an international conference, with taxpayers' money, to debate the concept of the Good Society. Finally the economists outline their plan to measure the effect of a change in local government taxation schemes on the productivity of exporting industries.

Which application is most likely to succeed? The economists seem to have the best chance. Notice however that their success has nothing to do with the value of the research itself. Instead it is determined by two things: first, their application seems comfortably apolitical (and thus uncontroversial from the point of view of the ministry). Second, the capacity of economists to *market* their wares as scientific and practical. Even if totally useless to all intents and purposes, the report on the effect of the structure of local taxes on export performance *sounds* valuable in terms of dollars and cents in a manner that the sociologists and the philosophers cannot compete against. What gives economists an even sharper edge is the fact that all their theory is based on a scientific-looking, yet simplistic, theory of individual behaviour. By comparison the views of philosophers and historians seem (to governments and grant councils) too muddled for words. In the end, the government officials responsible for allocating taxpayers' money think that they will find it easier to explain why they gave the money to the economists if they are ever asked to explain their decision. This is *all* that matters!

To recap, the success of neoclassical economics has been based on two achievements: first, it erected a fence which kept out of economics departments social scientists who doubted its foundations (e.g. *utility maximisation* as a basis for building a theory of society). Second, it built a narrative which appealed to governments, to business and, generally, to the strong and powerful in society. Based on that narrative, it marginalised the rest of the social sciences and became their undisputed queen. The result was that most of the funds for the social sciences were being appropriated by economics departments. To give you a tangible example, in my university economists until recently received a salary bonus (unlike philosophers, sociologists and other social scientists) as recognition of our 'market value'. Effectively, the economics profession has succeeded, on the back of the neoclassical approach to social theory, to convince the powers that be that we are the only 'real scientists' amongst the social sciences.

Indeed the more neoclassically inclined a department, the greater the funds that it attracts from other sources (e.g. ministries, business, research councils). In a never-ending circle, the greater the success at attracting funds, the more likely that aspiring economists will want to join them. Predictably, ambitious young economists would be mad to do anything other than acquire a solid training in neoclassical economics and attempt to become successful neoclassical practitioners. The icing on the neoclassical cake came when sociologists and other non-economists paid neoclassical economists the highest complement by borrowing their models (mainly those of Chapter 2) in order to share a piece of the action (and the funding). Thus economics became the grand imperialist within social science faculties.

What I find fascinating is that this momentous success is so disproportional to the 'scientific' contribution of the economics discipline. In the natural sciences, the output of research can be judged simply: did the aeroplane you promised to design fly or did it hit the ground at enormous speed? In economics, however, there is no such simple test. Indeed, throughout this book we have encountered weakness after weakness and (conceptual) problem after problem. As we saw in Chapters 4, 7 and 10, economists' views on the individual, the firm, markets and the State are rudimentary and full of contradictions. Moreover Chapter 11 explained that, unlike engineering or chemistry, the theories cannot be discarded or celebrated on the basis of their performance (the reason being that their performance cannot be assessed independently of the theory). So, how come economists' views have been so successful?

The answer is that the profession has managed to weave a web of interlocking explanations of all sorts of phenomena and to market that web effectively. After a while, professional economists have stopped caring altogether about the truth-status of their theories. What they do care about is that their theories are *seen* by others (e.g. the government, the public, business, etc.) to hold water. In the words of economist Alan Kirman (1987), economists do not care enough about the seaworthiness of their vessel (i.e. of their theory). As I mentioned in passing earlier, economists care about success and their

---

Much ado about nothing

There is something scandalous in the spectacle of so many people refining the analysis of economic states which they have no reason to suppose will ever . . . come about . . . It is an unsatisfactory and slightly dishonest state of affairs.

Frank Hahn, addressing the *Econometric Society*, 1968

success is best understood in sociological, or perhaps anthropological, terms. The English social anthropologist E. E. Evans-Pritchard (1902–73) analysed the social success of the priesthood within the Azande society, as well as their continuing dominance, in spite of the fact that the priests and the oracles failed to predict or avert disasters. His explanation of the Azande's unshakeable belief in witchcraft, oracles and magic goes like this:

> Azande see as well as we that the failure of their oracle to prophesy truly calls for explanation, but so entangled are they in mystical notions that they must make use of them to account for failure. The contradiction between experience and one mystical notion is explained by reference to other mystical notions.
> Evans-Pritchard, *Witchcraft, Oracles and Magic among the Azande*, 1937

Economics is not much different. Whenever it fails to predict properly some economic phenomenon (which is more often than not), that failure is accounted for by appealing to the same mystical economic notions which failed in the first place. Occasionally new notions are created in order to account for the failure of the earlier ones. For instance, the notion of *natural* unemployment was created in order to explain the failure of the market to engender full employment and of economics to explain that failure. More generally, unemployment and excess demand (or supply) is 'proof' of insufficient competition which is to be fought by the magic of deregulation. If deregulation does not work, more privatisation will do the trick. If this fails, it must have been the fault of the labour market which is not sufficiently liberated from the spell of unions and government social security benefits. And so on.

In conclusion, the success of neoclassical economics, just like the success of the Azande's priesthood, is due to the fact that it offers full explanations of its failures. It is also due to the capacity of its priesthood to maintain its position of monopoly on economic witchcraft by ensuring that only neoclassical economists are listened to. All that it takes for this to be so is

---

The rituals of economics

Every cult has its rituals. This is how Ronald Coase, a Nobel Prize winner in economics, describes those that economists subject their students to: 'The new theoretical apparatus had the advantage that one could cover the blackboard with diagrams and fill the hour in one's lectures without the need to find out anything about what happened in the real world.'

Ronald Coase, *The nature of the firm*, 1978

that those who want to become economists feel the need to become part of the priesthood.

Another fascinating aspect of the profession is that, unlike the Azande, in the economics profession there are no head-priests with the capacity to silence the infidels. Anyone can write a book which criticises neoclassical economics. Indeed, many do. However, as I claimed earlier, in an academic environment in which financial success (and by extension fame and power) comes to the departments of economics which are more central to the neoclassical project, economists have a strong vested interest to publish in journals and book series which specialise in neoclassical economics. Even economists who disagree strongly with the neoclassical approach are under enormous (often self-imposed) pressure to publish articles which are acceptable to the neoclassicists because, otherwise, they will not be helping their department in the quest for funding (and by extension they will be undermining themselves).

In the end, the non-neoclassical (or anti-neoclassical) books and articles either will not get published (since publishers find that the market value of their products is positively linked to their neoclassical content) or will be assigned a lowly notional value by the profession. Why? Because if, as an economist, you are agonising about how you will manage to write and publish in the neoclassical genre, reading an anti-mainstream piece does not help. What you need is some neoclassical text which will give you ideas about how to alter *your* neoclassical model so as to make it more marketable. Thus the demand for non-neoclassical work is low. There is nothing like low demand to reduce quantity and economic value. In the end the non-neoclassical voices are silenced without ever being persecuted.

Turning to students of economics, if one wants to become an academic, one is likely to want to be considered a successful economist. Given the dominance of neoclassical economics, this means that the aspiring student will have to go through rigorous induction into neoclassical techniques; through many years of positing utility and cost functions, maximising or minimising them and then inspecting the various equilibrium solutions given different assumptions about information, preferences and the like. On graduation, one's chances of getting a job will depend on one's ability to

---

Truth in teaching

It seems paradoxical beyond endurance to rule that a manufacturer of shampoos may not endanger a student's scalp but a premier education institution is free to stuff his skull with nonsense.
Judge Howlson, quoted by Robert Clower, 'Economics as an inductive science', 1994

add a small patch to the neoclassical web of explanations. Approximately ten years after the first fledgling steps as an economist, he or she will have become part of the priesthood.

By contrast if a bright student decides that the neoclassical way of thinking has little merit, it takes a heroic disposition to decide to submit oneself to many years of neoclassical training in the hope of becoming established professionally and only then articulating one's objections. Such intelligent students will either abort their anti-neoclassical sentiments or move to another department, e.g. history, mathematics, sociology or anthropology. Either way, the norms of the economics profession will have been perpetuated even though no individual or group of individuals has conspired to perpetuate them (i.e. a version of Adam Smith's invisible hand – see p. 17 – determining the character of economics).

12.4 Payback time: economics departments in crisis

Despite its decisive victory over the rest of the social sciences, economics is gradually becoming the victim of its own success. In most universities, student numbers have fallen drastically and, as a result, economics departments are facing significant cuts in their funding. Management, accounting, marketing, advertising and public relations are emerging as competing 'disciplines' and find it extremely easy to persuade students to abandon economics. Between 1992 and 1994 the number of undergraduates majoring in economics fell by 15 per cent in the USA. At elite liberal arts colleges the drop was more than 30 per cent. Whereas until recently social science students had a basic choice between political science, philosophy, sociology or economics, now that free-market ideology has prevailed, those who want to succeed in the free-market find courses in economics rather unhelpful (compared to marketing or accounting courses). It is as if neoclassical economics fought the intellectual and ideological war on behalf of markets and, now that it has been declared the victor, it is being discarded.

The major threat to the economics profession is the mushrooming of these new 'disciplines'. Nevertheless this development is not independent

---

Drifting

Two balloonists, after drifting for days in stormy weather, see a house. They descend over it and ask a man who came out to see what they wanted: 'Where are we?' they ask. 'In a balloon', the man replies: 'He must be an economist' remarks one of the balloonists. 'Totally rigorous and utterly useless.'

of the evolution of economics. Back in the 1920s and 1930s, the great question was: should a society rely on the market for coordinating economic activities or should we plan them centrally? In other words, the debates were heated, interesting, politically crucial. Neoclassical economists fought the pro-market corner fiercely. Later on, in the 1960s and 1970s, the focus shifted somewhat but the essence remained: should governments try to strike some balance between inflation and unemployment or should they combat inflation at all cost? Again, the debate was highly charged and the battles central to political life.

With these debates raging, and before they were won conclusively by neoclassical economics, the latter was recognised as essential. Once, however, it won these debates hands down (that is, by the late 1980s), the lack of serious opposition to the ideology of the market meant that the neoclassical defence of that ideology also lost a great part of its importance. Government departments and employer organisations no longer needed to recruit (as they did in the past) graduates with a rigorous training in theoretical defences of the market mechanism. Instead they turned to those with practical skills. Most companies demanded that their recruits know about advertising, marketing and accounting rather than about the mathematics behind neoclassical theory's welfare theorems. Add to that the fact that these disciplines (e.g. marketing) are far less demanding on students' brain cells, and you will see why the demand for economics courses dropped spectacularly.

As for large banks and government departments which *need* economists for forecasting purposes, they are disenchanted by academic economists and econometricians. Why? Because the latter are highly rigid, indeed almost fanatical, in their assumptions about how well markets behave, how instrumentally rational people are, how incompetent governments must always be, etc. Students who are trained to think in this manner are simply not very good at predicting real events brought about by the actions of real people. A past chairman of one of the largest commercial banks (Morgan Stanley in Wall Street) recently explained that when they look for new staff 'we insist on at least three to four years' cleansing experience to neutralise the brainwashing that takes place in these graduate programmes'. In short, neoclassical economics is on the decline not only in terms of student demand but also in terms of respectability. An article in the *New Yorker* magazine (December 1996), entitled 'The decline of economics', proposed that the Nobel Prize be scrapped. Its opening line read: 'John Maynard Keynes was one of the most revered men of his time. Fifty years later, where are his successors?'

12.5 In defence of economics

The British author Iris Murdoch once wrote (in her excellent Gothic novel *The Unicorn*, 1963) that 'it is the punishment of a false God to become

---

From students of rational allocations under scarcity to *idiots savants*

In 1991 the United States' Commission of Graduate Education in Economics, a group of twelve eminent (mostly neoclassical) economists, issues a report expressing the fear that the universities were churning out a generation of *'idiots savants*, skilled in technique but innocent of real economic issues'. Anne Krueger, Economics Professor at Stanford University, who headed the Commission, later wrote: 'That report took a lot of time and energy on the part of everyone involved. Yet, basically, if only the report and a pin had dropped at the same time, the pin would have sounded noisy.'

---

unreal'. This seems to be the unfolding fate of economics. Yes, it succeeded in becoming the queen of the social sciences, but it ended up holding a poisoned sceptre. With its success founded not on undisputed scientific truth but, instead, on the late-twentieth-century historical and political victory of the ideology of the market, its students are now abandoning it and its dominance is becoming increasingly irrelevant.

Economists all over the world are wondering why students are leaving our courses in droves. Why it is that we are becoming 'service' teachers for other courses (that is, we increasingly teach compulsory introductory economics courses to unwilling accounting and marketing students, rather than courses in advanced economic theory to students who make it their choice to study economics) and have a thousand students in our first year but only twenty in our final year. The answer is to be found in the intellectual aridity of economics textbooks. Reread Section 12.2 and ask the question: do intelligent students not feel short-changed by such a callous approach to social life? Of course they do and this, together with the ill-explained emphasis on highly complex techniques, is why they abandon economics. In my experience (and that of most of my colleagues), the vast majority of our students have a particularly low opinion of economics. Indeed there is no other discipline I know (save perhaps accounting) which is so despised by its students. How can they think otherwise when we peddle ideas such as those in Section 12.2 incessantly?

Some may ask: but why did hordes of students take economics in the early 1980s? Were we not teaching the same things? The answer is that, although our textbooks are more or less the same, back then economics was still a contested terrain. There was still a socialist Eastern Europe to pose as an alternative (however miserable) economic system. Non-neoclassicists and market-sceptics still had a discernible voice within economics departments and prompted interesting debate. Thus economics was an extension of crucial political disagreements and there was a demand for neoclassical defences of free-markets. In a sense, economics was the highest form of political debate. The complete domination of neoclassical economics ended all this. Economics became a set of techniques that students were asked to emulate mechanistically. Why should they bother, especially when other simpler and practical techniques were on offer (e.g. marketing)?

In summary, economics built its success on the claim that it had expunged politics, philosophy, sociology, psychology and history from a theory of society. This was, as we have seen in this book, a clever political strategy. However, once it succeeded, what was left was a colourless and complicated economic theory, foundationally disconnected from economic reality, which could neither address the big issues (e.g. which ecological strategy is in the public interest) nor stir the passions amongst the young. The moment 'practical' competitors (e.g. marketing) with greater market value (fewer demands on one's brain) appeared in universities and colleges, the game was lost.

A forgotten prescription for an education in economics

The study of economics does not seem to require any specialised gifts of an unusually high order. Is it not, intellectually regarded, a very easy subject compared with the higher branches of philosophy and pure science? Yet good, or even competent, economists are the rarest of birds. An easy subject at which very few excel! The paradox finds its explanation perhaps, in that the master-economist must possess a rare combination of gifts. He must reach a high standard in several different directions and must combine talents not often found together. He must be mathematician, historian, statesman, philosopher – in some degree. He must understand symbols and speak in words. He must contemplate the particular in terms of the general, and touch abstract and concrete in the same flight of thought. He must study the present in the light of the past for the purposes of the future. No part of man's nature or his institutions must lie entirely outside his regard. He must be purposeful and disinterested in a simultaneous mood; as aloof and incorruptible as an artist, yet sometimes as near the earth as a politician.

John Maynard Keynes, quoted in Robert Heilbroner,
The Wordly Philosophers, 1953

What should happen now? I have already expressed my view on this in the book's preface: we should give the passions another stir; rediscover the politics and the philosophy which are already lurking in between the lines of economics textbooks. Only if we do this will we revitalise economics and attract students to our ever so complex and dull discipline.

Should we bother? Has the time not come to admit that economics over-reached itself? That, following the wonders of the industrial revolution and the elevation of the economy to a privileged position in our collective psyche, society no longer needs grand stories like those of Adam Smith or Karl Marx or even of the neoclassical economists? Perhaps what societies now need is technicians (e.g. experts in marketing, finance, accounting, etc.) rather than story-tellers.

The above would be the right conclusion if we have, as claimed by some, arrived at the end of history; at a historical juncture where all the great conflicts are settled and all the great questions answered, leaving behind a series of smaller problems which can be resolved by technical means.

This view of humanity at the end of history gained credence after the collapse of the Soviet Union and its allies. If correct, it would mean that everyone has become part of the same world-system and ruled by the laws of the market, concerned only with how to increase their efficiency and market value. Under such circumstances, with societies totally embedded in markets, and with each one of us featuring solely as buyers and sellers in a homogeneous international market, there would be no need for grand stories (save perhaps the occasional reciting of Adam Smith's *invisible hand*) to help us conceive of our world. Economics, as imagined by the great economists, would give its place to localised specialists in finance, insurance, taxation, marketing, and so on.

But have we 'arrived'? Or is it that we live in a new 'Middle Ages', a period devoid of clarity but pregnant with new tectonic shifts of economic and social relations which will lead to new heated debates (note how stagnant the Middle Ages were before the eighteenth-century revolutions)? Only history will tell. For my part, I know two things.

First, a false feeling of having 'arrived' at our destiny threatens to lead us to the most idiotic of servitudes. To a life of constant recapitulation of textbooks, to a slavish acceptance of whatever *is* as the best of all possible realities, and to the demise of the natural human curiosity about how the world *really* works.

Second, if the current state of things is our destiny, it is a pretty miserable one. We live in a world capable of feeding itself many times over and yet this increasing capacity goes hand in hand with accelerating misery for the many and spiralling opulence for the few. This contradictory coexistence of (1) an ever-developing technical capacity to make everyone better off and (2) a constant worsening of the living conditions of the majority, signals a fundamental irrationality in the way society is structured.

These two points combine in the following simple conclusion: economics must become once again a vibrant terrain on which armies of different ideas about how social and economic relations, the State, markets, institutions, etc. clash. Without such a debate about the big issues the totalitarianism of privilege and idiocy beckons.

The only antidote to such totalitarianism is to delve into time-honoured economic, political and philosophical debates. This book was based on this philosophy. The gallant reader who has reached thus far will have gathered that I am not one of neoclassical economics' greatest fans. Nevertheless I wish to urge you to study neoclassical economics carefully and enthusiastically. It is a magnificent edifice, beautifully constructed and full of well-hidden politics and philosophy. By approaching it critically, the student will gain an unmissable glimpse of the highest form of defence of the capitalist society we live in. Does it tell the truth?

I do not think so. Personally I think it offers a wonderfully spurious apology for an irrational system based on an inadequate model of human nature and on a misleading analysis of the manner in which we produce and reproduce our material existence. Of course I am in the minority and you should not pay much attention to *my* conclusions. Draw your own. But why do I, a declared enemy of neoclassicism, urge you to study it?

For the same reason I would urge you to study in detail the myths and magic of the Azande if you wanted to understand their society. Also because the difference between a decent society and a despicable one is that

---

Why read dead economists?

Because of a peculiar feature of social theory: it is possible to lose sight of what was once more clearly seen, and it is possible to discard truth together with the mistakes with which it became entangled.

Lifting the curse!

Approaching economic ideas critically, and philosophically, is the best antidote to the ill-effects (discussed in Section 12.1) of a mechanistic, pseudo-technocratic, neoclassical training. Regardless of whether students agree or disagree with criticisms such as those in Chapter 4, the experience of such debate shields them from the odious character-altering effects of contemporary economics. Additionally it might encourage the excellent students which are now lost to the other humanities to stick to economics and help humanise it.

the former is populated by curious people who constantly try to work out how things are, and how others believe them to be, in order to envision how they *ought* to be. And to work out one's ideal society, the first thing one should study is that society's dominant ideology.

In societies past, the dominant ideology was religion, mythology, witchcraft. These were the ideas forming the web of beliefs which acted as the glue holding together society's institutions, gave priests and leaders power over their subjects and determined the capacity of society to hang together.

In today's society, religion has been substituted by neoclassical economics. It is the ideas, the diagrams and the far-fetched assumptions in economic textbooks which underpin contemporary society's web of beliefs about the inevitability of markets, the joys of competition, the merits of privatisation, the sinfulness of Pareto inefficiency and the blessed powerlessness of government.

Think big!

Great ideas share skulls with foolish thoughts. Nonsense runs with greatness, like vermin in a zoo, and no intellectual pesticide can guarantee to kill it and leave truth alive. Common sense has a particularly bad track record as a check on what is possible.

P. Cambell, reviewing *Great Mambo Chicken and the Transhuman Condition* by Ed Regis, in the *London Review of Books*, 1993

Neoclassical economics is therefore the source of *today's* legends, rituals, spells and sermons. To understand how current social arrangements and political structures are maintained despite the contradictions and centrifugal forces that threaten to tear them apart, there is no better place to start looking than an economics textbook. Approach it critically and you will be rewarded.

The most crucial point in all this is that one does not need to entertain expectations of learning the 'truth' from such study to make it exciting and worthwhile. An anthropologist studying some tribe learns much about its social reality by examining their creation myths. Yet these myths do not contain much truth about how the world was created. None the less they contain masses of information about that tribe's history as well as its social and economic reality.

Similarly with neoclassical economics. Even if I am right that it contains very little actual truth about economics, what makes it a fascinating source of insights is the fact that it is the dominant ideology (or mythology) of our era. And if you find, as some of us did, that after years of travelling the highways and narrow alleys of neoclassical theory you have returned to the beginning without much knowledge about the actual economy, the journey will not have been in vain. You will have returned wiser and immune to the lies of economists and the deceptions of politicians who employ economists to weave their poisonous webs.

Further reading

The main reason for writing this book was a lack of sources to which I could refer my students for a more wholesome diet than that offered by conventional textbooks. The problem with books and articles which treat their reader to the fascinating debates is that they are too hard for beginners; especially for today's university environment which is more demanding on first year undergraduates' time than once was the case. Thus in order to achieve maximum emphasis I will confine myself to a small number of suggestions for further reading.

The one book you must read

First, I must recommend Robert Heilbroner's bewitching introduction to the evolution of economic ideas entitled *The Wordly Philosophers* (1953). If you are to read one book beyond the standard economics textbook (and perhaps the one you are holding), attempt this one; you will not regret it.

Textbooks

The first economics textbook which set the scene for today's multi-colour glossy door-stops was written by Paul Samuelson (first published in 1948). It is entitled *Economics* and is published by McGraw-Hill (I have lost count of which edition it is currently in). It is the most famous text since the Second World War and, still, the most interesting (notwithstanding my overall displeasure with economics textbooks). All the textbooks have since attempted to emulate Samuelson and, as is always the case with imitators, they succeeded only partially. Those of you with a sense of textbook history will benefit from reading Samuelson's mega-hit.

An economist's ambition

I don't care who writes a nation's laws – or crafts its advanced treatises – as long as I can write its textbooks.

Paul Samuelson

If you want something more contemporary, helpful on a day-to-day basis (especially for first year economics students) and with an appreciation of the limitations of economics and the importance of history and political debate, try the large (though not expensive) volume which was put together by the economists at the Open University. Being part of a distance-learning institution, the Open University team (comprising M. Mackintosh, V. Brown, N. Costello, G. Dawson, G. Thompson and A. Trigg) edited a book that students can read independently as opposed to a reference manual to be consulted after a lecture. Its title is *Economics and Changing Economies* (published by the Open University in association with Thomson Business Press in 1996). It contains chapters on everything that you are likely to encounter in your first (perhaps even your second) year as an undergraduate and each topic is treated sensitively and with a humility that is uncommon (unfortunately) amongst economics texts. If you want to improve your essay skills and dazzle your tutor with your command of particular topics, don't miss this book.

If you wish for something smaller and somewhat simpler (e.g. if you are an interested general reader rather than a student worried about particular assignments), I suggest Robert Heilbroner and Lester Thurrow's *Economics Explained* (Simon and Schuster, 1994). On the other hand, if you want a 'cutting-edge' neoclassical textbook, I find Robert Frank's *Microeconomics and Behavior* (McGraw-Hill, 1993) to be the most (although still insufficiently) open-minded of the introductions to neoclassical thinking.

Unconventional textbooks

I will mention only two. For a holistic, open-minded and rather comprehensive approach to economics, I suggest Vicky Allsopp's *Understanding Economics* (Routledge, 1995). Allsopp manages to remain well within the mainstream while reorganising the various topics in such a way as to make it easier for the beginner to see economic thinking as more than technical gymnastics. For instance, she offers her readers a chapter on 'Law, custom and money' which is a far better introduction to the concept of money (not an easy one!) than the standard chapters on money demand, money supply, assets, etc. which pollute most textbooks. Additionally Allsopp offers a comprehensive chapter on 'Investment', a much neglected yet crucial topic.

The second suggestion here is one for those of you whose appetite was whetted by the glimpses of non-neoclassical economic theory in this book. If you wish to explore those ideas further, a good place to start is Malcolm Sawyer's *Introduction to Radical Economics* (Macmillan, 1989). There you will find simple introductions to the Ricardian, Marxist, Neo-Keynesian and Neo-Austrian ideas mentioned in this book's more critical chapters (primarily Chapters 6 and 7).

The road to paradise

Let's face it: economics is boring most of the time. Economists' best efforts (of course I include myself in this sad category) are unlikely to offer excitement and reading pleasure for more than a few moments. To punctuate the boredom, I suggest that you move to the borderline between economics and the other social sciences. That is the way, if not to heaven, to less arid fields of thought.

Looking at books I enjoyed as a student, one book whose effects I have tried to emulate here is *Economics: An anti-text*, edited by Francis Green and Peter Nore (Macmillan, 1977), a book devoted to countering the brainwashing of economics textbooks. I also recall fondly another book whose influence stays with me today: Ed Nell and Martin Hollis's *Rational Economic Man* (Cambridge University Press, 1976). I remember it was hard-going in parts but lucid and simple, as well as very exciting, in other parts. Much of my Chapters 4 and 11 have been inspired by that book. Unfortunately time has left its mark on it and it will perhaps seem somewhat dated to a fresh pair of eyes. None the less it may still be a good idea to borrow a well-thumbed copy from a library for perusal. Since then Nell and Hollis have published other books which are more up to date. Nell's *Making Sense of a Changing Economy: Technology, markets and morals* is an interesting read (Routledge, 1996). However, again with a view to narrowing down your 'shopping list', I want to urge you to read some of Hollis' work. (If you could see and hear me I would be gesticulating very energetically in support of this recommendation!)

Although not an economist (Hollis is a philosopher), his writings pack great insight and inspiration for students of the economy. Have a look at his enticing (and easy-going) *The Philosophy of Social Science: An introduction* (Cambridge University Press, 1994). And if you feel more adventurous and altruistic to your future self, tackle two more of his books: *Reason in Action* (1996) is a collection of articles on many philosophical issues central to economics (e.g. the free-rider problem) whereas *The Cunning of Reason* (1987) is a wonderful investigation on what it means for a social animal to be rational. Be warned: these two books (both published by Cambridge University Press) are hard work for first year students and you are unlikely to plough through their entirety. Nevertheless even reading bits of them, and making a point of returning to them in the years to come, will fill you with joy and pride.

Dead economists and their legacy

Having read Robert Heibroner's *Wordly Philosophers* (which you will do if you want me to speak to you again!), you may crave more material on the ideas of the dead economists who are responsible for the debates and concepts squirming in our heads today. In *Worldly Philosophers'* last edition, the author makes a number of useful suggestions on what to read on Smith, Ricardo, Marx, Veblen, and others. Consult it carefully and choose according to whatever it is that has tickled your imagination. Finally let me suggest a couple of books by non-economists that tackle brilliantly parts of the legacy left behind by the dead economists: Karl Polanyi's *The Great Transformation* (a beautiful book, published in 1944 by Farrar and Rinehart, on how silly it is for modern economists to try to assume that their understanding of values and motives are timeless and apply in all societies) and C. B. Macpherson's *The Political Theory of Possessive Individualism* (published by Oxford University Press, in 1962 a masterful critique of the philosophy of neoclassical economics).

Enjoy your freedom from the textbook!

References

Aesop (1975) *Fables*, ed. S. Richardson, New York: Garland Press.

Allsopp, V. (1995) *Understanding Economics*, London: Routledge.

Aristotle (1995) *Politics, Books I and II*, transl. T. J. Saunders, Oxford: Clarendon.

Arrow, K. ([1951] 1963) *Social Choice and Individual Values*, 2nd edn, New Haven, CT: Yale University Press.

Asimov, I. (1951) *Foundation*, New York: Doubleday.

Bacon, F. (1996) *Selections*, ed. G. Rees, Oxford: Oxford University Press.

Becker, G. (1976) *The Economic Approach to Human Behavior*, Chicago: Chicago University Press.

Bentham, J. ([1789] 1970) *An Introduction to the Principles of Morals and Legislation*, eds J. Burns and L. Hart, London: Athlone Press.

Berlin, I. ([1958] 1969) *Two Concepts of Liberty*, reprinted in *Four Essays on Liberty*, London: Oxford University Press.

Bowles, S. (1985) 'The production process in a competitive economy: Walrasian, neo-Hobbesian, and Marxian models', *American Economic Review*, 75, 16–36.

Boyle, J. (1992) 'A theory of law and information: copyright, spleens, blackmail and insider trading', *California Law Review*, 80, 1529–30.

Caldwell, B. (1984) *Beyond Positivism: Economic methodology in the 20th century*, London: Allen and Unwin.

Cassidy, J. (1996) 'The decline of economics', *The New Yorker*, 2 Dec.

Clower, R. (1994) 'Economics as an inductive science' *Southern Economic Journal*, 60, 805–14.

Coase, R. (1978) 'The nature of the firm', *Economica*, 4, 386–405.

Comte, A. ([1848] 1957) *A General View of Positivism*, transl. J. H. Bridges, New York: Speller.

Descartes, R. ([1637] 1912) *A Discourse on Method*, transl. J. Veitch, London: Dent.

Descartes, R. ([1641] 1954) *Second Set of Replies*, in *Philosophical Writings of Descartes*, transl. and ed. E. Anscombe and P. Geach, London: Nelson.

Edelman, B. (1979) *Ownership of the Image: Elements for a Marxist theory of law*, transl. E. Kingdom, London: Routledge and Kegan Paul.

Edelman, B. (1991) Entre personne humaine et natériau humain: le sujet de droit', eds B. Edelman and M. Hermitte, *L'Homme, la nature et le droit* [*Man, Nature and the Law*], Paris.

Ellsberg, D. (1961) 'Risk, ambiguity, and the savage axioms', *Quarterly Journal of Economics*, 75, 643–69.

Elster, J. (1979) *Ulysses and the Sirens*, Cambridge: Cambridge University Press.

Engels, F. ([1878] 1975) *Anti-Dühring: Herr Eugen Dühring's revolution in science*, London: Lawrence and Wishart.

Epicurus (1974) *Letter to Menoeceus on Joy*, in *Hellenistic Philosophy: Stoics, Epicureans, Sceptics*, ed. A. A. Long, London: Duckworth.

Evans-Pritchard, E. ([1937] 1976) *Witchcraft, Oracles and Magic among the Azande*, Oxford; Clarendon.

Frank, R. (1993) *Microeconomics and Behavior*, New York: McGraw-Hill.

Frank, R., T. Gilovich and D. Regan (1993) 'Does studying economics inhibit cooperation?' *Journal of Economic Perspectives*, Spring, 159–71.

Friedman, M. (1953) *The Methodology of Positive Economics*, Chicago: Chicago University Press.

Friedman, M. and R. Friedman (1962) *Free to Choose*, Melbourne: Macmillan.

Gordon, S. (1991) *The History and Philosophy of Social Science*, London: Routledge.

Green, F. and P. Nore (eds) (1977) *Economics: An anti-text*, London: Macmillan.

Hahn, F. (1973) *On the Notion of Equilibrium in Economics: An inaugural lecture*, London: Cambridge University Press.

Hahn, F. (1980) *Money and Inflation*, Oxford: Blackwell.

Hahn, F. (1996) 'Rerum cognescere causas', *Economics and Philosophy*, 12.

Hanson, N. (1958) *Patterns of Discovery*, San Francisco, CA: Freeman and Cooper.

Hargreaves Heap, S. (1989) *Rationality in Economics*, Oxford: Blackwell.

Hayek, F. von (1937) 'Economics and knowledge', *Economica*, 4, 33–54.

Hegel, G. W. F. ([1837] 1953) *Reasons in History*, transl. R. Hartman, New York: Library of Liberal Arts/Macmillan.

Heilbroner, R. (1953) *The Worldly Philosophers: The lives, times, and ideas of the great economic thinkers* (various editions), New York: Simon and Schuster.

Heilbroner, R. and L. Thurrow (1994) *Economics Explained*, New York: Simon and Schuster.

Himmelweit, S. (1995) 'The discovery of unpaid work: the social consequences and the expansion of work', *Feminist Economics*, 1, 1–19.

Hobbes, T. ([1642] 1983) *De Cive (Philosophical Rudiments concerning Government and Society)*, ed. H. Warrender, Oxford: Clarendon.

Hobbes, T. ([1651] 1991) *Leviathan*, ed. R. Tuck, Cambridge: Cambridge University Press.

Hobsbawm, E. (1994) *The Age of Extremes: The short twentieth century 1914–1991*, London: Michael Joseph.

Hollis, M. (1987) *The Cunning of Reason*, Cambridge: Cambridge University Press.

Hollis, M. (1994) *The Philosophy of Social Science: An introduction*, Cambridge: Cambridge University Press.

Hollis, M. (1996) *Reason in Action*, Cambridge: Cambridge University Press.

Hume, D. ([1739] 1888) *A Treatise of Human Nature*, ed. L. A. Selby-Bigge, Oxford: Oxford University Press.

Kagel, J., R. Battalio, H. Rachlin and L. Green (1981) 'Demand curves for animal consumers', *Quarterly Journal of Economics*, 96, 1–15.

Kaldor, N. (1939) 'Welfare propositions of economics and inter-personal comparisons of utility', *Economic Journal*, 47, 263–91.

Kant, I. ([1788] 1949) *Critique of Practical Reason*, transl. and ed. L. W. Beck, in *Critique of Practical Reason and Other Writings*, Cambridge: Cambridge University Press.

Keynes, J. M. (1921) *A Treatise on Probability*, London: Macmillan.

Keynes, J. M. (1931) *Essays in Persuasion*, London: Macmillan.

Keynes, J. M. (1935) 'A self-adjusting economic system', *The New Republic*, 20 Feb., 35–7.

Keynes, J. M. (1936) *The General Theory of Employment, Interest and Money*, London: Macmillan.

Kirman, A. (1987) *The Intrinsic Limits of Modern Economic Theory*, Working Paper 87/323, Florence, Italy: European University Institute.

Kloppenburg, J. (1988) *First the Seed: The political economy of plant biotechnology 1492–2000*, Cambridge: Cambridge University Press.

Lipsey, R. (1963) *An Introduction to Positive Economics*, London: Weidenfeld and Nicolson.

Machiavelli, N. ([1513] 1985) *The Prince*, transl. H. Mansfield, Chicago: Chicago University Press.

Mackinnon, C. (1989) *Towards a Feminist Theory of the State*, Cambridge, MA: Harvard University Press.

Mackintosh, M., V. Brown, N. Costello, G. Dawson, G. Thompson and A. Trigg (1996) *Economics and Changing Economies*, Milton Keynes: Open University with Thomson Business Press.

McNeil, B., S. Pauker, H. Sox and A. Tversky (1982) 'On the elicitation of therapies for alternative therapies', *New England Journal of Medicine*, 306, 1259–62.

Macpherson, C. B. (1962) *The Political Theory of Possessive Individualism*, Oxford: Oxford University Press.

Marshall, A. (1891) *Principles of Economics*, London: Macmillan.

Marx, K. ([1847] 1963) *The Poverty of Philosophy*, New York: International Publishers.

Marx, K. ([1867–95] 1967) *Capital Volumes 1 and 2*, New York: International Publishers.

Marx, K. and F. Engels (1979) *Collected Works Volumes 1 and 2*, London: Lawrence and Wishart.

Mill, J. S. ([1843] 1973–4) *A System of Logic*, London: Routledge & Kegan Paul.

Mill, J. S. ([1859] 1962) *On Liberty*, ed. M. Warnock, London: Fontana.

Mill, J. S. ([1861] 1972) *Representative Government*, ed. H. B. Acton, London: Dent.

Mill, J. S. ([1863] 1962) *Utilitarianism*, ed. M. Warnock, London: Fontana.

Mises, L. von (1949) *Human Action: A treatise on economics*, London: Hodge.

Murdoch, I. (1963) *The Unicorn*, London: Chatto and Windus.

Nell, E. (1996) *Making Sense of a Changing Economy: Technology, markets and morals*, New York: Routledge.

Nell, E. and M. Hollis (1976) *Rational Economic Man*, Cambridge: Cambridge University Press.

Nozick, R. (1974) *Anarchy, State and Utopia*, Oxford: Basil Blackwell.

Pareto, V. ([1909] 1972) *Manual of Political Economy*, transl. A. Schwier and A. Page, London: Macmillan.

Pateman, C. (1988) *The Sexual Contract*, Oxford: Polity.

Pericles, *Epitaph*, in Thucydides' *The History of the Peloponnesian War*. See the translation by Dr Smith (1759) *Two Orations in Praise of Athenians Slain in Battle*, Oxford: J. Fletcher and J. Rivington.

Pigou, A. C. (1920) *The Economics of Welfare*, London: Macmillan.

Polanyi, K. (1944) *The Great Transformation*, New York: Farrar and Rinehart.

Popper, K. (1972) *Objective Knowledge: An Evolutionary Approach*, Oxford: Oxford University Press.

Quine, W. (1961) 'Two dogmas of empiricism', in *From a Logical Point of View*, Cambridge, MA: Harvard University Press.

Radford, R. (1945) 'The economic organisation of a P.O.W. camp', *Economica*, 189–201.

Rawls, J. (1971) *A Theory of Justice*, Cambridge, MA: Belknap Press of Harvard University Press.

Ricardo, D. (1817) *On the Principles of Political Economy and Taxation*, London: J. Murray.

Robinson, J. ([1969] 1973) 'Economics Today', Basel Lecture, reprinted in *Collected Works Volume 4*, Oxford: Blackwell.

Rousseau, J-J. ([1754] 1973) *Discourses on the Origins of Inequality*, ed. G. Cole, London: Dent.

Rousseau, J-J. ([1762] 1973) *The Social Contract*, ed. G. Cole, London: Dent.

Russell, B. (1916) *Principles of Social Reconstruction*, London: Allen and Unwin.

Russell, B. (1921) *The Analysis of Mind*, London: Allen and Unwin.

Russell, B. (1948) *Human Knowledge: Its scope and limits*, London: Simon and Schuster.

Samuelson, P. ([1948] 1994) *Economics*, 15th edn, New York: McGraw-Hill.

Santayana, G. (1921) *Character and Opinion in the United States*, New York: Scribner.

Santayana, G. (1944) *Persons and Places: The background of my life*, New York: Scribner.

Sartre, J-P. (1957) (L'Etre et le néant), (*Being and Nothingness*) transl. H. E. Barnes, London: Methuen.

Sawyer, M. (1989) *An Introduction to Radical Economics*, London: Macmillan.

Schumpeter, J. ([1942] 1976) *Capitalism Socialism and Democracy*, London: Allen and Unwin.

Scitovsky, T. (1976) *The Joyless Economy*, Oxford: Oxford University Press.

Sen, A. (1970) 'Rational fools', *Philosophy and Public Affairs*, 6, 317–44.

Shackle, G. L. S. (1955) *Uncertainty in Economics*, Cambridge: Cambridge University Press.

Shackle, G. L. S. (1966) *The Nature of Economic Thought*, Cambridge: Cambridge University Press.

Shaw, G. B. ([1894] 1955) *Arms and the Man: An anti-romantic comedy and in three parts*, London: Longman.

Shaw, G. B. ([1905] 1958) Preface to *Major Barbara*, London: Longman.

Smith, A. ([1776] 1976) *An Inquiry into the Nature and Causes of the Wealth of Nations*, Oxford: Clarendon.

Sraffa, P. (1975) *The Production of Commodities by Means of Commodities: Prelude to a critique of political economy*, Cambridge: Cambridge University Press.

Sweezy, P. (1972) *Modern Capitalism and Other Essays*, New York: Monthly Review Press.

Titmuss, R. M. (1970) *The Gift Relationship*, London: Allen and Unwin.

Walras, L. ([1874] 1954 *Elements of Economics*, transl. W. Jaffe, London: Allen and Unwin.

Wood, E. M. (1994) 'From opportunity to imperative: the history of the market', *Monthly Review*, 46, 14–40.

Name Index

Subject Index

money illusion 326–8
money wage 326, 327
monopoly 137–8, 144, 163–5, 209;
  power 189, 190, 210, 237, 312, 330,
  362; profit 240, 241; as social failure
  237, 239–40
monopsony 146–8, 330
moral philosophy (of Smith) 16–21
morality 79, 80, 151

Napoleonic Wars 22, 25, 30
natural law philosophy 31, 46, 158–60
natural resources, exploitation of 228–9
natural societies 31, 34, 362–3
Nature of Economic Thought, The (Shackle) 3
Nature of the Firm (Coase) 368
negative consequences (unintended) 16
neo-classical economics: defence of
  capitalism 187–90; distributive justice
  and 247, 254–65; domination of
  (critical analysis) 371–7; entitlement
  theory of justice 265–8; market failures
  226–46; production models 149–50,
  155–8; professional economists in (role)
  361–71; on rational societies 244–6;
  theory of choice 76–93; transition
  to/rise of 30–40; utility and 82–4;
  utility maximisation (critique) 94–117;
  welfare economics 205–26, 247–9
neo-Keynesianism 305, 307, 316
net utility 49, 51, 53, 357
New England Journal of Medicine 55
non-dictatorship (welfare economics) 224
normative economics 29, 175

Objective Knowledge (Popper) 350
oil crisis (1970s) 281
oligopoly power 210, 329
oligopsony 147
On Liberty (Mill) 114, 115
opportunity cost 59, 70, 123, 132, 151,
  167, 180, 299
ordinal utility 84–90, 219, 223, 248
organisations (as systems) 112
outputs 6, 121–2, 131–3, 134–40
over-production 226–8

pain 80, 82, 107–8, 115–16
Panglossianism 360
Pareto efficiency 129–30, 207, 216, 241,
  376
Pareto improvement 243
Pareto optimality 130

passions 79–80, 81, 84–5, 87, 90, 92
patents 297
'peasant knowledge' 297
peasants 7–8, 10, 11, 12, 13, 14, 15
peer review 362, 363
perfect competition 141–6, 189, 190; as
  ideal market 162–5; textbook models
  (history of) 149–65
Philosophical Rudiments (Hobbes) 78
Philosophy of Social Science, The (Hollis) 380
physics method 31–3, 36
planned economy 189
plant biotechnology 296–7
pleasure 80, 81–2; calculus of 47–9
political dimension of profit 180–1
political equilibrium 245–6
political power 13, 14–15, 16–17, 77,
  250
*Political Theory of Possessive Individualism,
  The* (Macpherson) 381
politics: of isoquants 177–8; of labour
  theory 175–8; of market society 13; of
  pure production model 199–200; of
  utility maximisation 83, 90–3
pollution 237–9, 241, 277
positive consequences (unintended) 16
positive economics 29, 175
positivism 336–40, 344, 348–9, 351
poverty 247, 251–2, 314, 315–16
power: economic 14–17, 21, 292, 298–9,
  308; industrial society 13–15; market
  237, 240, 299; oligopoly 210, 329;
  political 13, 14–15, 16–17, 77, 250;
  social 184, 200, 288, 292, 308, 362;
  struggles 180
pre-industrial societies 4–9, 10, 38, 149
prediction 337–8, 340–2, 344, 351–2
preferences 44–5, 65, 98–9; aggregate
  (impossibility theorem) 222–6;
  consistent (as rationality) 53–7, 58;
  satisfaction 46–7, 57, 68–71, 77, 84 5,
  112, trade-offs 56, 125; transitivity 54,
  224–5; utility maximisation and 77,
  84–7, 90, 92–3, 106–10, 114–16
price discrimination 210,
price mechanism 217, 281
price stickiness 283
prices 20, 160, 195–8, 234, 307–8; ratio
  of 58–62, 63, 70, 117, 126, 128, 194,
  324–5
Principal–Agent Problem 172
Principles of Economics (Marshall) 32
Principles of Political Economy (Ricardo) 22